CW00504613

Unconscious Thought in Philosophy and Psychoanalysis

Also by John Shannon Hendrix

AESTHETICS AND THE PHILOSOPHY OF SPIRIT: From Plotinus to Schelling and Hegel

ARCHITECTURAL FORMS AND PHILOSOPHICAL STRUCTURES

ARCHITECTURE AS COSMOLOGY: Lincoln Cathedral and English Gothic Architecture

ARCHITECTURE AND PSYCHOANALYSIS: Peter Eisenman and Jacques Lacan

BISHOP ROBERT GROSSETESTE AND LINCOLN CATHEDRAL: Tracing Relationships between Medieval Concepts of Order and Built Form (*co-edited with Christian Frost and Nicholas Temple*)

THE CONTRADICTION BETWEEN FORM AND FUNCTION IN ARCHITECTURE

THE CULTURAL ROLE OF ARCHITECTURE: Contemporary and Historical Perspectives (*co-edited with Paul Emmons and Jane Lomholt*)

HISTORY AND CULTURE IN ITALY

NEOPLATONIC AESTHETICS: Music, Literature, and the Visual Arts (*co-edited with Liana Cheney*)

NEOPLATONISM AND THE ARTS (*co-edited with Liana Cheney*)

PLATONIC ARCHITECTONICS: Platonic Philosophies and the Visual Arts

THE RELATION BETWEEN ARCHITECTURAL FORMS AND PHILOSOPHICAL STRUCTURES IN THE WORK OF FRANCESCO BORROMINI IN SEVENTEENTH-CENTURY ROME

RENAISSANCE THEORIES OF VISION (*co-edited with Charles H. Carman*)

ROBERT GROSSETESTE: Philosophy of Intellect and Vision

Unconscious Thought in Philosophy and Psychoanalysis

John Shannon Hendrix
University of Lincoln, UK and Roger Williams University, US

First published 2015 by
PALGRAVE MACMILLAN

Palgrave Macmillan in the UK is an imprint of Macmillan Publishers Limited, registered in England, company number 785998, of Houndmills, Basingstoke, Hampshire RG21 6XS.

Palgrave Macmillan in the US is a division of St Martin's Press LLC, 175 Fifth Avenue, New York, NY 10010.

Palgrave Macmillan is the global academic imprint of the above companies and has companies and representatives throughout the world.

Palgrave® and Macmillan® are registered trademarks in the United States, the United Kingdom, Europe and other countries.

ISBN: 978–1–137–53812–3

This book is printed on paper suitable for recycling and made from fully managed and sustained forest sources. Logging, pulping and manufacturing processes are expected to conform to the environmental regulations of the country of origin.

A catalogue record for this book is available from the British Library.

Library of Congress Cataloging-in-Publication Data

Hendrix, John Shannon.
    Unconscious thought in philosophy and psychoanalysis / John Shannon Hendrix, University of Lincoln, UK and Roger Williams University, US.
        pages cm
    Includes bibliographical references.
    ISBN 978–1–137–53812–3 (hardback)
        1. Consciousness – Philosophy. 2. Subconsciousness – Philosophy.
    3. Psychoanalysis – Philosophy. I. Title.

B105.C477.H46 2015
127—dc23   2015012998

Contents

Acknowledgments

I would like to acknowledge the Society for Ancient Greek Philosophy and the International Society for Neoplatonic Studies for providing forums and discussions over many years. Many individuals provided inspiration and contributed to the development of ideas, especially Liana Cheney, Aphrodite Alexandrakis, Panayiota Vassilopoulou, Jean-Marc Narbonne, Michael Wagner, Stephen Gersh, Jay Bregman, Bruce MacLennan, Marilynn Lawrence, Emilie Kutash, Robert Wallace, and Eric Perl. Current collaborators on the subject of unconscious thought include Lorens Holm, Thomas Mical, Gordana Korolija Fontana-Giusti, Christina Malathouni, Alla Vronskaya, Francesco Proto, Hugh Campbell, Jane Rendell, Spyros Papapetros, Nikos Sideris, Stephen Kite, Andrew Ballantyne, Kati Blom, Emma Cheatle, and Tim Martin. The research and writing have been possible with the support of Lincoln University, UK, and Roger Williams University, US. Valuable colleagues at Lincoln have included Nicholas Temple, Nader El-Bizri, Renée Tobe, Jane Lomholt, Francesco Proto, Kathleen Watt, Behzad Sodagar, and Amira Elnokaly. Valuable colleagues at Roger Williams have included Dean Stephen White, Andrew Thurlow, Edgar Adams, Andrea Adams, Hasan-Uddin Khan, Mete Turan, Sara Butler, Nermin Kura, and Philip Marshall. I would like to express my gratitude and admiration for my editors at Palgrave Macmillan, Brendan George and Esme Chapman. I had the opportunity to meet with them in London, which made an otherwise anonymous process much more enjoyable.

Introduction

What is unconscious thought? Does it exist? How does it work? What is its relation to conscious thought? How does it contribute to human identity? This book attempts to answer these questions, in philosophical and psychoanalytic terms. There are many books with "the unconscious" in the title, but no other book attempts to answer these questions, focusing on the mechanisms of unconscious thought, or thought of which we are not aware. In order to answer these questions, this book undertakes a thorough analysis of works throughout the history of philosophy and psychoanalysis that lay a groundwork for understanding the concept, organization, structure, mechanisms, contradictions, effects and consequences of unconscious thought. The analysis is undertaken in chronological order from the classical to the present in order to understand how the concept of unconscious thought has evolved and developed in relation to changing philosophical and epistemological frameworks. Classical, medieval, and modern conceptions of unconscious thought laid the groundwork for concepts of unconscious thought in psychoanalytic theory. It is necessary to explore and understand the philosophical concepts in order to understand modern concepts of the unconscious.

How is conscious thought influenced by unconscious thought? What role does unconscious thought play in sense experience, perception, vision, intellection, the formation of ideas, abstract thought, language, creativity, judgment, imagination, dreams, artistic production, and relationships with other people? It becomes clear that unconscious thought plays an important role in all of these intellective activities; it is therefore important to understand how unconscious thought works. There is currently much interest in unconscious thought in cognitive science. For example, Unconscious Thought Theory examines the role that unconscious thought plays in everyday thought activities and events.

It is necessary to look to philosophy and psychoanalysis to understand the possible roles that unconscious thought plays in more advanced intellective activities. How is unconscious thought known, conceived, and apprehended by conscious thought? Is conscious thought possible without unconscious thought? In order to answer these questions, it is necessary to consider, not just pathologies, as introduced by Freud, but the history of philosophy, and the ways in which an unconscious element of thought has been conceived, prior to the coining of the term "unconscious," and after.

In relation to books that might be seen as complementary works, the goal of this book is to explore concepts throughout the history of philosophy, in the Classical, Scholastic, Idealist and Romantic traditions, and to illustrate the extent to which philosophical concepts of unconscious thought, as part of the workings of conscious thought in philosophy of intellect, which plays a role in psychoanalytic theory, are rooted in the philosophical tradition. This book focuses on a unique philosophical tradition: the classical tradition, from Plato and Aristotle, Plotinus, the Peripatetics, and Robert Grosseteste, and the modern tradition from Leibniz and Kant to Schelling, and Hegel, as philosophical forerunners to the understanding of the workings of unconscious thought in psychoanalytic theory. Rather than focus on the empirical phenomenon of the unconscious as established by Freud, this book focuses specifically on the functions of unconscious thought in relation to conscious thought in philosophical and metaphysical terms. This is the reason for the focus on these particular philosophers. There is no book that investigates the development of theories of unconscious thought from Plotinus to contemporary psychoanalytic theory. The interest of this book is in the psychological mechanisms of thought in philosophy and psychoanalysis, rather than defining the unconscious as an empirical phenomenon. This is a book about the philosophy of intellect, how thoughts are formed, the relation between thinking and perceiving, how self-consciousness and self-identity are manifested.

The book contributes to the project of exploring the roots of contemporary theory in the history of philosophy, bridging the gap between ancient and modern understanding, and establishing a continuity through the different traditions. The book should be of interest to academics, and undergraduate and graduate students in philosophy, intellectual history, history of psychology and psychoanalysis, and the medical humanities. The subject is of increasing interest in academic discourses in Western intellectual history, especially in Europe and the United States. The book should also be of interest to people working within psychoanalysis or psychology, such as therapists or historians, as the study of psychoanalysis is turning more and more to philosophical roots, suggesting new alternatives. The focus of the philosophical roots of psychoanalytic theory is the concept of the unconscious.

Important secondary sources for this study include *Das Unbewusste*, edited by Günter Gödde and Michael Buchholz; *The Discovery of the Unconscious* by Henri F. Ellenberger; *The Foundation of the Unconscious: Schelling, Freud and the Birth of the Modern Psyche* by Matt Ffytche; *Thinking the Unconscious: Nineteenth-Century German Thought*, edited by Angus Nicholls and Martin Liebscher; and *The Unconscious Before Freud* by Lancelot Law Whyte.

Various modern thinkers have been given credit for inventing the unconscious. Leibniz, Kant, Platner, Schelling, Hegel, Carus, Hartmann, and Freud have all been given credit. The truth is that the concept of the unconscious, that part of our mind that functions without our awareness in conscious thought, although the word "unconscious" was not used, has been around since the beginning of philosophy. Classical and medieval conceptions of the unconscious were very different from Enlightenment and psychoanalytic conceptions, which is not surprising given the different epistemological frameworks. The classical and medieval conceptions in philosophy and metaphysics focused on a higher form of thinking in our minds that comes from an external source, of which we are not aware, an immaterial agent or divine intellect that deals in intelligibles not connected to sense perception or sensory awareness. This concept persisted through the writings of Kant and Hartmann, but with Schelling and Hegel the source of unconscious thought is located in the organic real, the noumenal being of the material world. Elements of metaphysical philosophies persist in psychoanalysis, but the focus of psychoanalysis is empirical and materialist, grounding conceptions of the unconscious in experience, in particular dreams and language.

The book considers the philosophical, metaphysical concept of unconscious thought, as thought of which we are not aware, which plays a role in our conscious thought processes. The concept of unconscious thought is distinguished from the concept of "the unconscious," which is seen as an empirical or scientific phenomenon, as an entity in the human mind defined by observation of behavior or personality, and as an actual objective thing in the world in Freudian terms. The unconscious is only seen here to exist to the extent that unconscious thought plays a role in conscious thought, in opposition to it but not exterior to it, in cognition, intellection, language, perception, and imagination.

Unconscious thought is understood as being other to conscious thought but within conscious thought, not external to it.

The book explores a variety of philosophical, conceptual, and metaphysical theories of unconscious thought as they are developed throughout the history of Western philosophy, and the role that they play in the development of psychoanalysis. The writers whose work is explored are those writers who specifically developed theories involving what can be called "unconscious thought." Those theories include the anamnesis of Plato (429–347 BC), the active intellect of Aristotle (384–322 BC), a kind of universal intellect, and the classical concept of *nous poietikos* or noetic thought, intellectual activity not connected to sense perception. In the thought of Plotinus (204–70), seen as the first philosopher to develop a systematic conception of the presence of unconscious thought in conscious thought, concepts that contribute to a theory of unconscious thought include the *nous poietikos* (what Plotinus calls Intellect), the intelligible (what can be understood but not experienced by the senses), *phantasia* (imagination), and the *logos endia-thetos* (the unuttered word through which the intelligible is translated into the presentation to discursive reason or conscious thought; similar to what Hegel would call the *Vorstellung*).

There is much Neoplatonic content in the writings of the Peripatetics, the commentators on Aristotle, who made much use of the *De anima* of Aristotle and the *Enneads* of Plotinus through various manifestations such as the *Theology of Aristotle*. The *Enneads* were also influenced by the earliest of the Peripatetics, Alexander of Aphrodisias (fl. c. 198–209). Alexander saw the active intellect (unconscious thought) as the cause of the material intellect (*nous hylikos*, *nous pathetikos*, conscious thought). According to Themistius (317–c. 387), imagination requires something other than conscious thought. According to Abu Nasr Alfarabi (c. 872–951), the objects of thought of discursive reason or conscious thought are provided by the intelligibles of actual intellect: what can be seen as unconscious thought. According to Avicenna (Ibn Sīnā, c. 980–1037), material intellect or conscious thought is a passive substratum of ideas in which the intelligible ideas of active intellect or unconscious thought are perishable in their connection to sense perceptions. According to Averroes (Ibn Rushd, 1126–98), the first principles of thought are given without conscious act of will. Active intellect makes images intelligible in a kind of unconscious thought. Forms of objects are conceived unconsciously.

In the conclusion of the classical tradition, the Scholastic philosopher Robert Grosseteste (c. 1175–1253) can be seen as a Peripatetic (he wrote the first commentary on Aristotle in Latin), and his writings are similarly infused with Neoplatonic influence. In the thought of Grosseteste, the sensible form in conscious thought and perception is a product of the intelligible form in *intelligentia*, comparable to the active intellect of Aristotle, what can be seen as unconscious thought. Objects of perception correspond to a *visus mentalis* or image in the mind made possible by an *irradiatio spiritualis*, an incorporeal light in the imagination, as in the thought of Plotinus.

At the beginning of modern philosophy, Gottfried Wilhelm Leibniz (1646–1716) and Immanuel Kant (1724–1804) laid the groundwork for concepts of unconscious thought that would be developed in psychoanalysis. According to Leibniz, most of our perceptions and representations are inaccessible to conscious thought. In the thought of Kant, many of our ideas and representations are too obscure for us to be aware of them. The higher levels of imagination are not connected to sense perception or empirical experience; as in classical and medieval philosophy, the forms of sense perception are determined by intelligibles, called categories of a priori intuition. Conscious thought depends on the transcendental synthesis of the imagination, which is inaccessible to conscious thought.

A number of philosophers in the eighteenth and nineteenth centuries made important contributions to the modern philosophical foundations for unconscious thought in psychoanalytic theory. The book provides brief summaries of the contributions, as none of the concepts are extensively developed in philosophical terms in the writings of the various philosophers, but they are nevertheless important collectively as a link between classical and modern philosophy, and between classical philosophy and psychoanalysis. The emphasis in the treatment of these philosophers, as it will be in the treatment of Sigmund Freud and Jacques Lacan, is on the influence of the classical and medieval philosophical conceptions.

According to Christian Wolff (1679–1754), conscious thought is the ability to differentiate particulars (as in discursive reason), and there are many thoughts and perceptions of which we are not aware. For Alexander Gottlieb Baumgarten (1714–62), clear thoughts are connected to a higher form of intellection (as in *nous poietikos*), while obscure thoughts are connected to the particulars of sensual cognition (as in *nous pathetikos*). In the thought of Johann Georg Sulzer (1720–79), conscious ideas are caused by unconscious ideas, which are indecipherable. Ernst Platner (1744–1818) first used the term "unconscious" (*Unbewusstsein*) to distinguish between sense perception and higher forms of intellection in apperception (a concept going back to both Leibniz and Plotinus). He reversed the classical model and connected unconscious thought with sense perception, and conscious thought with apperception.

Friedrich Wilhelm Joseph von Schelling (1775–1854) saw unconscious thought as operating in opposition to conscious thought in a dialectic with conscious thought. Conscious thought is an organic product of unconscious thought, but unconscious thought is inaccessible to conscious thought. The ground of both conscious and unconscious thought is the imagination. Unconscious thought is also inaccessible to conscious thought in the philosophy of Georg Wilhelm Friedrich Hegel (1770–1831). The universals or intelligibles of unconscious thought are transformed into the particulars of conscious thought or discursive reason through the *Vorstellung* or representation, as in classical philosophy. Conscious and unconscious thought are united in the appearances of sense perception, which are ephemeral and perishable, as in classical philosophy.

Johann Friedrich Herbart (1776–1841) followed Platner in associating conscious thought with apperception and unconscious thought with sense perception, and also developed a more dynamic model for the relation between unconscious and conscious thought, the "law of the threshold." According to Carl Gustav Carus (1789–1869), thoughts travel between conscious and unconscious realms in a dynamic cycle or an organic system, on a biological model. Unconscious thought is the basis of conscious thought, and it is actually possible to be aware of unconscious thought in conscious thought. Carus further developed the dynamic model of the law of the threshold, as did Gustav Fechner (1801–87), who saw unconscious thought as a dynamic force within conscious thought. Karl Robert Eduard von Hartmann (1842–1906) further blurred the distinction between conscious and unconscious thought, but referred to the classical formula in distinguishing the conscious perception from the unconscious representation. Sense perception conforms to unconscious representation in the imagination, as intelligible forms are produced by intellectual intuition. The unconscious is a metaphysical principle, as what lies beyond empirical experience in thought. Theodor Lipps (1851–1914) claimed that all psychical phenomena exist unconsciously, and conscious thought is seen as being a part of unconscious thought, as the equivalent of a sense organ.

The culmination of the development of the philosophical concept of unconscious thought is found in the psychoanalytic theory of Sigmund Freud (1856–1939) and Jacques Lacan (1901–81). For Sigmund Freud, unconscious thought can be revealed through the analysis of the dream.

The thought process in the dream is a *Vorstellungsrepräsentanz*, the *eidos* as a representation in *phantasia*, as in classical philosophy. Freud concluded that unconscious thought is necessary for conscious thought. In the concepts of the ego and the id (*das ich* and *das es*, literally the I and the It), the psyche is divided into conscious and unconscious thought. There is a dynamic transformation of unconscious thoughts to conscious thoughts, through the word-presentation (*Vorstellung, logos endiathetos*), and unconscious dream thoughts are transformed into dream images, the residues of which become the subject of conscious thought, through the imagination (*phantasia*). Unconscious thought is seen as the basis of the psyche.

For Jacques Lacan, the unconscious is language, the Other, so unconscious thought can only be conceived with the same linguistic structure as conscious thought. Unconscious thought is present in conscious thought as an absence. The mechanisms of the transition from the unconscious thought to the dream image, condensation and displacement, in Freudian dream work, are the linguistic mechanisms of metaphor and metonymy. The Imaginary order of Lacan involves the role of the image or *imago* in imagination and sense perception. The Symbolic order is the matrix of language into which the *imago* is inserted, in both conscious and unconscious thought. The Real is that which is inaccessible to both the Imaginary and Symbolic, and can be compared to the One of Plotinus, that which is inaccessible to *nous poietikos* or *nous pathetikos*, unconscious thought or conscious thought. For Lacan, unconscious and conscious thought are interwoven, along with the Imaginary and Symbolic, in a Borromean knot. Because conscious thought cannot know itself as based in unconscious thought, it cannot know itself. It can only experience *méconnaissance*, misknowing. The resistance to unconscious thought is the same as the resistance of the signifier to the signified in language. The signifier represents the subject, and the subject becomes an absence to itself in unconscious thought. Absence and presence oscillate in language, as do unconscious and conscious thought. The absence in conscious thought, the "gaze," is the source of desire, desire for the Other as a substitute for the missing subject or object (*objet a*), in the impossibility of fulfillment caused by the inaccessibility of unconscious thought.

The theories of Carl Jung (1875–1961) are not included in this study because they are a product of neither analytical philosophy nor scientific analysis. Jung did not define the unconscious and did not construct a model of the psychic apparatus. The present treatise is a treatise on philosophy of intellect; it attempts to better understand how thought

and intellect work, along with language, memory, perception and imagination. Jung's theories focus on phenomena such as magic, alchemy,
divination, theurgy, gnosis, mythology, mandalas and other mystical
practices and symbols.

In Jung's theories, the soul is the inner personality, a mirror of the
exterior personality. Spirit (insight) is intellect combined with soul.
Intellect is conscious thought, the rational side of the individual; it does
not involve unconscious thought. Sensation and intuition are irrational
functions. The unconscious consists of emotions and impulses which
are irrational; the unconscious encompasses all irrational phenomena.
Introversion and extraversion are attitude types; anima and animus are
personality types, images of the soul. Creativity is the process of activating
eternal symbols of mankind which lie dormant in the unconscious. The
persona is the attitude toward the world. The collective unconscious
is the spiritual heritage of mankind, its mythologies and symbols. The
unconscious is the impersonal objectivity of nature. Psychotherapy is
a spiritual guidance and seeks a higher state of consciousness, through
meditation, in order to give symbolic form to experience. Symbols in
mythology and mandalas transcend consciousness and possess magic
power. Individuation, the discovery of the self, is an alchemical process.
In gnosis, man is redeemed from matter in unity with the divine. The
soul corresponds to God, and the relation of the soul to God is the archetype of the God image. Jung describes the unconscious as a religious
phenomenon. Completeness results from a devotion to a transcendent
power. Jung's symbolic language of dreams is the same as that employed
in religion and mythology.

Also not included in this analysis are the theories of Arthur
Schopenhauer (1788–1860) and Friedrich Nietzsche (1844–1900) on
biological drive and will, or the theories of Melanie Klein (1882–1960),
Anna Freud (1895–1982), and Donald Winnicott (1896–1971) on depth
psychology, object relations theory, transitional object theory, empathy
theory, defense mechanisms, clinical practice or therapy, neuroses or
psychoses. As important as these ideas are, they do not help in this particular project of defining the functions of unconscious thought in relation
to conscious thought, as a form of analytical philosophy or philosophy
of intellect, and they do not help in understanding how thought, intellect, perception, language, memory, or imagination work in relation to
the mechanisms of unconscious thought. This is the goal of this project,
to contribute to some understanding of these processes, by exploring
specific analytical or metaphysical philosophical traditions, and seeing
how they apply to psychoanalytic theory. What follows is an outline of

the contents of the book, a chronological survey through the history of philosophy and psychoanalysis, addressing the concept of unconscious thought and its ramifications. The issues summarized in the outline are unfolded and examined in detail in the chapters.

In Chapter One, "Plotinus: The First Philosopher of the Unconscious," Plotinus is seen as the first to develop a systematic philosophy of intellect involving unconscious thought. In the *Enneads*, we do not always apprehend our intellectual activity, although, according to Aristotle in the *De anima*, mind is always active. Intelligibles in *nous poietikos*, higher intellect, can be seen as a form of unconscious thought, in opposition to the sense-based thinking of *nous hylikos*, material intellect, or discursive reason. Activity of intellect goes unnoticed when it is not connected to objects of sense. There must be an activity prior to awareness of perceptions. Perceptions are based on images formed in the imagination (*phantasia*) from intelligibles, given form through language, or *logos endiathetos* (the unuttered word). We are not aware of the inner functions of intellect that make perception and discursive reason possible. Discursive reason (conscious thought) is given in the multiplicity of particulars, while Intellect (unconscious thought) involves abstractions and universals, the creation of a manifold or totality of experience that would be described by Immanuel Kant. The ability of forming abstractions and universals is seen as a kind of internal light, that allows us to see the conceptual structure of a perceived object beyond its material form. While Intellect (*nous poietikos*) is always active, we are not always aware of its activity, because we are distracted by sense perceptions causing *pathos* in *nous pathetikos*, material intellect connected to the passions. Discursive reason or conscious thought is not always active.

There are two levels of imagination, the *noetic* of intelligibles, and the *dianoetic* of sense perception. The two levels are connected by the logos, the principle of knowledge in language, or the product of a "rational forming principle": much like the categories of intuition of Kant. Through the logos, thoughts are unfolded and presented as images in imagination, and the apprehension of the thought by imagination is the basis for conscious thought. "An image accompanies every intellectual act," according to Plotinus. The intellectual act has not "come out into the open, but remains unobserved within," as unconscious thought, as it were. Since they are connected to sense perceptions, conscious thoughts appear to operate only at that level. Conscious thoughts are reflections of intelligibles, which are ideas not connected to sense perception, and the *logos prophorikos*, the spoken word, is a reflection of the *logos endiathetos*. So it can be concluded that conscious thought is a reflection of unconscious thought, in modern terminology. Although the term "unconscious" was not in use until the eighteenth century, like the term "aesthetics," these terms can easily be applied to classical and medieval concepts. Plotinus saw art as being a product of intelligibles in Intellect, thus being a product of unconscious thought, as are judgments of beauty, anticipating Kant's *Critique of Judgment*. The philosophy of Plotinus is rich in concepts that suggest unconscious thought, as has been noted by a number of scholars. Plotinian philosophy laid an important groundwork for the philosophy of intellect of the Peripatetics, and many of its tenets continued in modern philosophy and psychoanalytic theory.

In Chapter Two, "The Peripatetics and Unconscious Thought," the Peripatetics are the commentators on Aristotle. In the *De anima* of Aristotle, the intellect thinks the *eidos* or form connected to the sense object, and the sensible form is related to the intelligible form. The relation between intellect and object is not accessible to discursive reason or conscious thought. The active intellect is opposed to the material intellect as being immutable, unaffected by sense experience. Alexander of Aphrodisias, in his commentary on the *De anima* of Aristotle, saw the active intellect as the cause of the material intellect, allowing the material intellect to develop in its ability to apprehend universals in abstraction. The sense object is seen as the intelligible, as two sides of the same coin. While the material intellect is corporeal and perishable, the active intellect is incorporeal. There is a third, productive intellect, that leads material intellect to active intellect. The productive intellect is the "intelligible in act."

Enmattered form is seen in contrast to immaterial form. The imagination is composed of traces of actual sensations. Imagination illuminates intelligible forms, and facilitates the material intellect toward active intellect. In the *De intellectu* of Alexander, productive intellect is the intellect of Aristotle "which makes all things." Enmattered forms become objects of thought through intellect, thus intelligibles. The sensible object only exists insofar as an idea of it exists, in a process of productive intellect inaccessible to discursive reason or sense perception. "What it is to be intellect does not lie in its being thought by us," according to Alexander; it is unconscious. Alexander had an important influence on Plotinus, and on the subsequent Peripatetics, in the development of the Aristotelian theories of perception, imagination, and active intellect, and in the synthesis of Platonic and Aristotelian doctrine, establishing important precedents for modern philosophy.

Themistius, in his commentary on the *De anima* of Aristotle, saw imagination as requiring something other than discursive reason and sense perception, something not available to conscious thought. The process of imagination involves the entelechy of material intellect to active intellect. As the intelligible form corresponds to the sensible form, "thinking is analogous to perceiving," though material intellect cannot be identical to the object it thinks. Actual intellect, which is a product of active intellect, is not subject to material conditions, while discursive reason is. Active intellect illuminates, from an unknowable source, the contents of potential intellect. This will be seen to be very similar to the way in which the categories of a priori intuition of Immanuel Kant illuminate sense perception. The category of space, for example, illuminates the experience of space when space is seen as an abstract concept or intuition, a universal condition that makes possible the particular experiences of space. The conceptualization of active intellect as "unconscious thought" would be continued by the Arabic commentators on Aristotle – Alfarabi, Avicenna, and Averroes – and would lead to ideas in later writers such as Robert Grosseteste, Kant and Freud.

In the *Risala* (*De intellectu*) of Alfarabi, a potential intelligible is distinguished from an actual intelligible, and intellect is divided into potential, actual, acquired, and agent. Potential intellect is material intellect and agent intellect is active intellect. Actual intellect knows actual intelligibles, and acquired intellect is aware of its knowledge of intelligibles. Actual intelligibles are forms abstracted from matter, not subject to material intellect. Actual intelligibles become objects of thought in discursive reason. When intellect thinks the actual intelligible, "it does not think an existing thing outside of itself but it only thinks itself." Thus, the objects of conscious thought are the products of unconscious thought. Forms in agent intellect are indivisible, while forms in material intellect are divisible. The forms of agent intellect are received as divided and corrupted; intellect is perfected when it is independent of sense perception. In his advocacy of an ascent to that which is unknown in conscious thought, as in the ascent of Plato or Plotinus to noetic thought, Alfarabi made an important contribution to the development of the concept of unconscious thought.

In the *Liber Naturalis* of Avicenna, sensory thought, *nous hylikos*, is illuminated by active intellect, *intelligentia agens*. Material intellect is a passive substratum of ideas, a potency in relation to the act of apprehending intelligibles, which is incorporeal. The active intellect is the giver and illuminator of forms, which when received by material intellect is particular and differentiated in sequential arrangements. *Intellectus in habitu* leads from material intellect to active intellect. Sensible forms are distractions in the intellective process. While intelligible forms are permanent in active intellect, they are not always accessible to material intellect, conscious thought, and in material intellect they are perishable. Material intellect is not capable of retaining concepts and abstractions. Sense perceptions have no permanence until they have been transformed into intelligibles, through higher intellection, involving the influence of unconscious thought. Full access to intelligibles in unconscious thought is only possible when intellection is detached from sense perception, and ultimately when the soul is released from the body in a state of beatitude. In the *Shifā: De anima* (*Metaphysica*) of Avicenna, intelligibles are differentiated in the imagination. The *eidos* is formed in the *sensus communis* and then received by *phantasia*, which combines images according to discursive reason. The *sensus communis* is sensory representation in the common sense, coordinating the external senses. The healthy intellect is able to perceive the intelligible form, the product of unconscious thought, in the sensible form.

In Chapter Three, "The Active Intellect of Averroes," the active intellect can be seen as a form of unconscious thought. In Averroes' *Long Commentary on the De anima*, the soul consists of three intelligences: active intellect, material intellect, and acquired intellect, based on his interpretation of the *De anima* of Aristotle. Thought requires both material and active intellect, both the objects of sense perception and intelligibles. The first principles of thought are given without an act of will, thus unconsciously. The *forma imaginativa* in the *imaginatio* is a *species apprehensibilis*, an intelligible form, but it is both corporeal and incorporeal, bridging material and active intellects. Union with active intellect, unconscious thought, is the goal of philosophy and the highest bliss in life. Acquired intellect is *intellectus speculativus*, making it possible for material intellect to be united with active intellect. Intellect distinguishes the *formae imaginativae* or *phantasmata* in *imaginatio* and organizes them into totalities, in the most rudimentary forms of abstraction, as in the thought of Plotinus and Kant. According to Franz Brentano, Averroes' active intellect makes "images intelligible in unconscious thought," and the material intellect "receives from the images the concepts of sensible things." Perhaps Brentano's attribution of unconscious thought to Averroes was discussed in his philosophy seminars at the University of Vienna, attended by Sigmund Freud.

According to Averroes, the *formae imaginativae* act on material intellect after they have been illuminated by active intellect, which also illuminates material intellect. The intelligible is formed through the combination of material and active intellect. While the material intellect, tied to the particulars of sense perception, cannot produce meaning or communication, active intellect can create meaning and communication through the universals of intelligibles, in what is called "monopsychism," a kind of collective unconscious. As material intellect is actualized by active intellect through the *formae imaginativae*, the form of the object is conceived unconsciously, as in Plotinus. Incoherent forms are gathered together in a process of apperception, the combining of perceptions into an intelligible totality. Perception results from the combination of unconscious and conscious thought. The intellectual act behind the intelligible form remains unobserved, in unconscious thought. The Peripatetic concept of unconscious thought, in the synthesis of Plato, Aristotle, Neoplatonism, and Neoaristotelianism, would influence Robert Grosseteste and ultimately Hegel, Kant, Freud and Lacan.

Robert Grosseteste can be seen as a culmination of the Peripatetic tradition in his synthesis of Plato, Aristotle, Neoplatonism and Neoaristotelianism. He is also seen as a Scholastic who anticipated the Great Synthesis of Albertus Magnus and Thomas Aquinas, by combining Aristotle with Catholic theology, resulting in a unique conception of "unconscious thought." In Chapter Four, "Robert Grosseteste: Imagination and Unconscious Thought," Averroes may have influenced Robert Grosseteste, who in his *Hexaëmeron*, described the sensible form, *species sensibilis*, as a product of the intelligible form, *species apprehensibilis*, which is formed in the imagination and presented to discursive reason in the process of perception. The intelligible form is illuminated by active intellect.

In Grosseteste's *Commentary on the Posterior Analytics*, active intellect is compared to *intelligentia* or divine intellect. *Intelligentia* is a faculty of contemplation, with no connection to imagination or discursive reason. Universals or *principia* exist in intellect potentially or unconsciously, and are activated to actuality. While discursive reason apprehends intelligible form as a particular, active intellect apprehends the intelligible as a universal. The illumination of active intellect is a *lux spiritualis*, spiritual light, that produces a *lumen spiritualis*, reflected spiritual light, that allows the *visus mentalis*, mental sight, to apprehend the intelligible in the *oculus mentis*. The power of the mind, *acies mentis*, is a spiritual light, *irradiatio spiritualis*. In the *Hexaëmeron*, sense perception is the "power of receiving and grasping sensible likenesses without matter," but involves turbulences of the body, and clouding of the *oculus mentis*, that must be overcome through *solertia*, the will to higher intellection. Sense perception cannot apprehend universals. Scientific knowledge must be based on *principia essendi ante rem*, universals, rather than the corruptible and variable knowledge of particulars given by sense perception. The goal of intellection is to uncloud the *oculus mentis* so that the *principia essendi* are seen as clearly as possible, in *solertia*.

In the *Commentary*, corporeal things are understood to the extent that they correspond to the *visus mentalis*, the mental vision of them, made possible by the *irradiatio spiritualis*. The goal of intellection is *sapientia*, knowledge of intelligibles. Sense perception is not a cause of knowledge, but a condition by which knowledge is possible. *Intelligentia*, as unconscious thought, is not accessible to material intellect. The singularity of the sensible form in sense perception and discursive reason is determined by the preconditions of space and time in *intelligentia*, of which the perceiving subject is unaware. Space and time are the principal categories in the a priori intuition of Immanuel Kant, also unavailable to discursive reason in sense perception. As perception is determined by the unconscious intelligibles of space and time, there is no possibility of immediate sense experience. Grosseteste's theories predicted elements of the philosophies of Kant and Hegel, in turn influencing the thought of Freud and Lacan.

In Chapter Five, "Unconscious Thought in the Philosophy of Immanuel Kant," the modern concept of unconscious thought, though the term "unconscious" was still not in use, began in many ways with Immanuel Kant. In an early treatise, *Attempt to Introduce the Concept of Negative Magnitudes into Philosophy*, Kant developed a theory about thoughts that are negated or canceled, obscured or darkened. While certain thoughts become clearer, other thoughts become more obscure. Thoughts come to be and pass away. Influenced by the concept of *petites perceptions* in the *New Essays on Human Understanding* of Gottfried Wilhelm Leibniz, only a small portion of perceptions and representations are made accessible to conscious thought. According to Leibniz, most perceptions are of too little intensity to effect conscious thought. Traces of previous perceptions contribute to conscious thought, which is determined by unconscious thought. Intellectual ideas do not come from conscious thought, as in the classical tradition. We are unconscious of how individual sense perceptions are received, as in *An Essay Towards a New Theory of Vision* of George Berkeley, spatial relations are learned judgments rather than immediate perceptions. What we perceive are not the immediate objects of sight. Judgment is learned through an accumulation of sense perceptions, and involves memory and imagination. In the *Alciphron* of Berkeley, distance is perceived by mediation of a sign, which is the proper object of sight, rather than objects themselves. A sign signifies an object in perception, and it is easy to confuse the two.

In the Kant's *Critique of Pure Reason*, it is impossible to know an object outside its conception as an intelligible. The whole of appearances, the manifold of the sensible world, can only be an idea: "Reason is never in immediate relation to an object, but only to the understanding." In Kant's *Anthropology from a Pragmatic Point of View*, there is an immeasurable field of sense perceptions and obscure ideas of which we are not aware. Clear ideas are only a minute portion of all ideas. Obscure representations are the product of a mediated consciousness as opposed to an unmediated consciousness. Kant sees obscure ideas and perceptions as a function of natural processes, in what he calls physiological anthropology, as opposed to pragmatic anthropology, which is concerned with free will. Kant sees the human being as free from mechanical causality. Apperception is in contrast to perception; it involves the apprehension of the manifold of perception. Time is the category of a priori intuition that makes possible inner experience and sense perception in discursive reason. The perceiving subject is not conscious of the role of time in intuition.

In the *Reflections on Anthropology* of Kant, there are higher productive levels of imagination not connected to sense perception or empirical experience, but solely the product of intellectual cognition or unconscious thought. Images are formed by the schemata from the categories of a priori intuition. Conscious functions of the lower reproductive imagination were elaborated upon in the *Lectures on Metaphysics*, leading to further discussions in the *Critique of Pure Reason* and the *Critique of Judgment*. In the *Critique of Pure Reason*, the transcendental aesthetic is the science of the principles of a priori sensibility. Space and time are categories applied to sense experience; they do not exist in empirical reality. Space is the condition of the possibility of appearance; it is a manifold, an unconscious intuition. Space and time underlie the possibility of all sense experience and discursive reason. Space is the form of outer sense and time is the form of inner sense. Divisions of space and time are functions of discursive reason. Appearances in perception are not things in themselves but rather plays of representation, phenomena rather than noumena. The transcendental synthesis of the imagination, in unconscious thought, is the condition for the possibility of all experience. The unity of the manifold can only be given as a representation in conscious thought. Conscious thought is not possible without unconscious thought. A priori intuition, pure synthesis of the imagination, the manifold, and apperception can all be seen as unconscious thought.

The a priori synthesis of the sensible manifold of intuition as represented to discursive reason is labeled the figurative synthesis, while the synthesis of the manifold in the categories of intuition in understanding or apprehension is labeled the intellectual synthesis. Self-consciousness is given by the transcendental synthesis of the manifold and the synthetic unity of apperception, although self-consciousness is "very far from being knowledge of the self." The schematism of understanding as it is applied to appearances and representations "is an art concealed in the depths of the human soul, whose real modes of activity nature is hardly ever likely to allow us to discover...."

Productive imagination and intellectual synthesis are unconscious processes, while reproductive imagination and figurative synthesis are conscious processes. As Theodor Lipps observed in *Psychological Studies*, "the pure concepts of the understanding (categories) seem to belong to the unconscious ideas...." In the *Critique of Judgment*, all sense perception is dependent on the synthesis of apprehension. Sensations are synthesized in the imagination to create a form or appearance. Judgments of beauty are judgments of the conformity of a sensible object to the cognitive faculties, thus they are the product of unconscious processes. In order to be judged beautiful and give pleasure, a sense object must conform to an intelligible appearance (representation) in the imagination. Pleasure and aesthetic judgment are products of the manifold. No creative artist can be conscious of his or her process of creation. The sublime is that which exceeds conscious thought and perception. Kant laid the groundwork in many ways for concepts of unconscious thought in psychoanalytic theory.

In Chapter Six, "Unconscious Thought in Eighteenth- and Nineteenth-Century Philosophies," several other thinkers contributed to the development of the modern concept of the unconscious and unconscious thought. While only brief summaries are presented in chronological order, the concepts developed, though only adumbrated and not elaborately explained in philosophical terms by the writers, are essential in linking classical and medieval, Neoplatonic and Peripatetic, concepts of unconscious thought, with the Kantian development of those concepts (after Sulzer), and the psychoanalytic theories of Freud and Lacan. The writers are Christian Wolff, Alexander Gottlieb Baumgarten, Johann Georg Sulzer, Ernst Platner, Friedrich Wilhelm Joseph von Schelling, Georg Wilhelm Friedrich Hegel, Johann Friedrich Herbart, Carl Gustav Carus, Gustav Fechner, Karl Robert Eduard von Hartmann, and Theodor Lipps.

Christian Wolff, in *Rational Thoughts on God, the Soul of Man, and also All things in General*, defined conscious thought as the representation of external objects of thought and sense perception. Conscious thought is the ability to differentiate particulars, and to differentiate external objects from the self. There are many objects that we are capable of perceiving but do not. Awareness is the basis of conscious thought, and it is possible to infer unconscious thought through conscious thought, to identify ideas in conscious thought that are caused by unconscious thought. Alexander Gottlieb Baumgarten, in *Metaphysica*, saw obscure perceptions as being the foundation for the soul. In the *Aesthetica*, obscure thoughts and perceptions are connected to the particulars of sensuous cognition, while distinct thoughts are connected to higher forms of intellect. Johann Georg Sulzer, in the *Brief Definition of All Sciences and Other Parts of Learning*, saw unconscious ideas as underlying and causing conscious ideas. Unconscious ideas are dark and unclear, but have considerable effect. Dreams prove the existence of unconscious thought. Conscious thought is connected to apperception, and the differentiation between self and the perceived world. Abstract thoughts have no connection to the perceived world. Conscious thought is dependent on representation (*Vorstellung*) in the imagination. Conscious thought is itself a representation. The most fundamental activity of the mind is seen as the production of representations. Ernst Platner, in *Philosophical Aphorisms*, is credited with being the first to use the term "unconscious" (*Unbewusstsein*). Unconscious ideas play a role in conscious ideas. Conscious ideas are connected to apperception, while unconscious ideas are connected to perception. Unconscious ideas are obscure images or representations. Conscious and unconscious, apperception and perception, are in constant oscillation.

Friedrich Wilhelm Joseph von Schelling has been called the first to offer a coherent and systematic theory of the unconscious, laying the groundwork for the thought of Sigmund Freud, Carl Jung, and Jacques Lacan. The term "unconscious" was by then in circulation. In the *System of Transcendental Idealism*, conscious thought is composed of both conscious and unconscious thought, operating in opposition to each other in a dialectic. Unconscious thought is a product of nature, as in the physiological anthropology of Kant. The combination of conscious and unconscious thought in intuition is seen in relation to the combination of the ideal (the world as it is thought) and real (the world as it is perceived, the objective world of nature) in the absolute, which is the synthesis of the two, and of the subjective (ideal) and objective (real). The objective world is the unconscious poetry of the spirit, the basis of all philosophy, which is revealed in the aesthetic. The organic is the making conscious of unconscious activity; conscious thought is the product of unconscious thought. The work of art displays the synthesis of conscious and unconscious thought. Unconscious thought is inaccessible to conscious thought, but it is the necessary ground of being.

Primordial and productive intuitions are brought together in the imagination, providing the ground for both unconscious and conscious thought. Aesthetic intuition is the transcendental intuition that has become objective, toward the original unity of unconscious and conscious thought, which is inaccessible. The unity of the absolute is the equivalent of unconscious thought. Unconscious thought and conscious thought are originally intertwined as if in a Borromean knot, as in the thought of Lacan. In Schelling's *Bruno, or On the Natural and the Divine Principle of Things*, sensible beauty is a representation of absolute beauty in the sensible world, a projection of the inner self into the world. The sensible and intelligible are combined in the absolute, which is manifested in the particulars of sensible experience. The goal of art is the union of the real and ideal, the union of sensible beauty and absolute beauty.

In *Philosophy of Mind*, Georg Wilhelm Friedrich Hegel described unconscious thought as an intelligence inaccessible to conscious thought. The unconscious is found in nature or the real, as the origin of the universal as a representation. Images of unconscious thought are presented to conscious intelligence through intuition, as objective representations of universals (intelligibles) transformed into the particulars of discursive reason. The objective images in the *Vorstellung*, picture-thinking, are representations of the content of unconscious thought. Conscious thought is dependent upon images in the reproductive imagination, following Kant. The reproductive imagination is an imitation of the productive imagination. Intuition is unfolded as image in imagination through the production of symbols and signs in the productive or creative imagination. Through the imagination, the particular is subsumed in the universal, conscious in unconscious.

In the *Phenomenology of Spirit*, unconscious thought is the basis of conscious thought, but inaccessible to it. Appearance unites conscious and unconscious thought, understanding and essence, but it is a vanishing "surface show." Unconscious thought is the supersensible world that becomes the object of understanding above the sensible world, a being-in-self as opposed to a being-for-self. Supersensible being comes about through appearance, which is a representation of intuition. The universal in inner being is an outcome of the flux of appearance. Spirit or unconscious thought unfolds in conscious thought, being-in-self to being-for-self, in ephemeral representations, as in the classical tradition. Spirit becomes self-conscious through perception and the *Vorstellung* in imagination, which mediates between the absolute and existence, unconscious and conscious thought. The absolute unfolds toward existence through essence, being-for-self as the other of essence, and being-for-self as self-consciousness in the other. Being-for-self, as the other of essence, is the logos, signification in language, the externalization of essence. The *Vorstellung* enacts the otherness of the absolute in differentiation, in conscious thought.

Johann Friedrich Herbart wrote textbooks on psychology: *Textbook in Psychology*, and *Psychology as a Science Newly Founded on Experience, Metaphysics and Mathematics*. He developed theories on apperception, representation, and conscious and unconscious thought. Apperception, the cognitive combining of perceptions into totalities, is associated with conscious thought. Ideas are products of representations, as for Sulzer, which are seen as dynamic forces, both conscious and unconscious. Obscure ideas are unconscious and distinct ideas are conscious. Unconscious ideas may become conscious ideas as they pass a threshold or limen in the "law of the threshold" (*Schwellengesetz*).

Carl Gustav Carus, with the publication of *Psyche: On the Developmental History of the Soul*, is considered to be the first to develop a systematic theory of the unconscious, with the unconscious as the focus of a theory of mind. *Psyche* begins: "The key to an understanding of the nature of the conscious life of the soul lies in the sphere of the unconscious." Conscious thought can only be understood through unconscious thought. It is actually possible to be aware of unconscious thought in conscious thought; it is the task of science to discover how unconscious thought can be accessed. The majority of the psyche is unknown to us in a present moment, lying in "the night of the unconscious." If the evolution of an idea is traced, its unconscious components can be discovered. Thoughts travel between conscious and unconscious realms in a dynamic cycle. The external world cannot be the source of conscious thought, necessitating the existence of unconscious thought. Conscious thoughts are based on images that have been formed in the imagination, but have then sunk into unconscious thought. Ideas that have traveled from conscious to unconscious thought continue to develop in unconscious thought. We do not stop thinking while we are sleeping, for example. Unconscious thought is instinctual, the necessary organic real of nature, following Schelling. The oscillations between conscious and unconscious thought are seen as a dynamic flux in an organic system. The passage from conscious to unconscious thought is the highest form of human fulfillment, and is connected to pleasure and desire.

In *Lectures on Psychology*, Carus outlined the development of unconscious thought on a biological model. The development of the psyche, the ontogeny, is a microcosm of the evolutionary development of a species, the phylogeny. This theory would influence both Freud and Jung. The conscious psyche is divided into consciousness of the world and consciousness of the self. The unconscious psyche is divided into the relative unconscious, predicting the preconscious of Freud, and the absolute unconscious. The absolute unconscious is the most basic biological aspect of mind, and can involve both sentient and non-sentient activity. The absolute unconscious is the basis of organic growth, and is in constant activity. The sentient absolute unconscious is created by the nervous system of the biological organism. Mental activity takes place in the relative unconscious, which is connected to conscious thought. The relative unconscious is the permanent repository for conscious ideas, the storehouse for memories. There is both conscious and unconscious memory, and conscious and unconscious imagination, reproductive and productive, following Kant.

The relative unconscious is also where dreams are produced. Dreams are combinations of biological forces from the absolute unconscious and traces or residues of images that are formed in the imagination and that enter the relative unconscious from conscious thought. The relative unconscious is a threshold, as in the *Schwellengesetz* of Herbart, between the absolute unconscious and conscious thought, what can be revealed to conscious thought of the unconscious. Ideas flow back and forth as dynamic forces, as in the psychophysiological energy of Fechner. The psychophysiological energy of the nervous system causes unconscious sensations and causes them to emerge in conscious thought. In conscious thought, consciousness of world is given by the faculties of sense, connected to the dynamic energy of the nervous system, and continuously affected by the relative unconscious. Consciousness of world depends on "the condition of one's own organization," and is also dependent on memory and representations (*Vorstellungen*) in imagination. While unconscious mind is an undifferentiated universal shared by all organisms, the individual is differentiated and made particular in conscious thought.

Herbart's law of the threshold was developed by Gustav Theodor Fechner in his *Elements of Psychophysics*. For Fechner, unconscious ideas are dynamic forces that are lost in conscious thought. The psychological threshold is an important basis of the concept of the unconscious in psychoanalysis. Fechner's adherence to empirical science had an influence on Freud. He was a pioneer in experimental psychology and the founder of psychophysics, the study of the relation between physical stimuli and sensations and perceptions. Freud followed Fechner in differentiating dream processes from conscious thought.

Karl Robert Eduard von Hartmann is known as the "philosopher of the unconscious" because of his most influential work, *Philosophy of the Unconscious*. Hartmann saw Kant as the inventor of the unconscious. In contrast to Kant, for Hartmann not every conscious idea is a clear idea, and not every obscure idea is an unconscious idea. A conscious idea is only clear when it can be distinguished from other ideas, in a "consciousness of the discrimination." The unconscious idea is distinguished from the conscious idea in the form of representation, the *repraesentatio* that is the genus of the idea, which is differentiated from the *perceptio* in the conscious idea. In *The Interpretation of Dreams* of Sigmund Freud, Hartmann was quoted as asserting that the unconscious underlies combinations of sensuous representations in the imagination, and that all unconscious ideas are purposive. Hartmann, in the classical tradition, saw intellectual intuition as "divine understanding" that produces intelligible objects and creates the "world of noumena," while conscious thought is a "derived and dependent human understanding," as in material intellect. Hartmann saw the unconscious as a metaphysical principle in a system of "transcendental realism," involving the induction of what lies beyond experience by first considering all possible experience. The unconscious is pure potentiality, the noumenal or thing-in-itself. It is the ground of existence, combining reason and will. The redemption of the human condition is a return to the unconscious, as it is seen as the absolute in transcendental idealist terms.

Theodor Lipps was a leading figure in academic psychology and an influence on Sigmund Freud. In *The Interpretation of Dreams*, Freud cited Lipps as establishing the unconscious as the key issue of psychology, and establishing the study of the unconscious as a science. It was thus Lipps who began the focus on unconscious thought in psychoanalysis, broadening psychological studies from studies of sensations and empirical experience. Despite Freud's claim that his goal was to move beyond the "metaphysical" conception of the unconscious, the classical metaphysical conceptions of unconscious thought play a core role in Freud's definition of the psyche. According to Lipps, from a lecture on "The Concept of the Unconscious in Psychology," delivered at the Third International Congress for Psychology, all psychical phenomena exist unconsciously; "the unconscious must be assumed to be the general basis of psychical life." Freud also cited Lipps from Lipps' most influential work, *Fundamental Facts of the Inner Life*, as refuting the theory of somatic stimulation, arguing that dreams are not determined by external stimuli. Lipps is also well known for his aesthetic theory, in particular his theory of empathy (*Einfühlung*), the act of projecting oneself into the object of a perception.

In Chapter Seven, "Unconscious Thought in Freud," Sigmund Freud is seen as the founder of the science of psychoanalysis. The purpose of this chapter is to examine the role of unconscious thought in the formation of dream images, and in the distinction between the ego and the id (*das Ich* and *das es*, literally the I and the It). In *The Interpretation of Dreams*, dreams are the "royal road to a knowledge of the unconscious activities of the mind." The dream is not unconscious thought, although it reveals the structures of unconscious thought, and only the memory of the dream can be analyzed. Unconscious thoughts are revealed as images in the dream. The content of the memory of the dream is the manifest content, and the object of the conceptual analysis of the dream is the latent content, or dream thought, unconscious thought. The conceptual analysis itself is a product of conscious thought. Dream work transforms the latent content of the dream into the manifest content, the dream images, in the process by which the dream is generated from unconscious thought.

The mechanisms of representation in the dream, as they are developed between the dream thought and the dream image, are different from conscious mechanisms of representation, although conscious and unconscious thought share particular linguistic constructions. Unconscious mechanisms are seen as a variation of conscious mechanisms not under the control of conscious thought. The ego – conscious thought and perception – is always present in the dream. The mechanism of the transposition from dream thoughts to dream images is labeled imagination, which is liberated from the control of reason. The linguistic structure of the dream image is missing the organization of conscious thought, while its forms are mimetic of it. Dreams have no ability to represent logical relations between dream thoughts or conscious thoughts. Dreams have no intention of communicating anything.

Unconscious thoughts are brought into the dream as fragmented and recombined, in displacement (*Verschiebung*) and condensation (*Verdichtung*). Dream interpretation involves the restoration of the connections between dream thoughts that the dream work has destroyed. Thinking does not occur in dreams themselves. A thought process in a dream is a representation of a thought process in the dream thought, which is a representation of a conscious thought process. The thought process in the dream is thus a *Vorstellungsrepräsentanz*, a representation of a representation. This theory can be traced to the classical definition of *eidos* and the formation of images in *phantasia* or imagination. The logic of the dream is independent of conscious logic. The network of logical relations between dream images is too complex to be unraveled in dream analysis. "The most complicated achievements of thought are possible without the assistance of consciousness," according to Freud. Traces of perception (*Wahrnehmungszeichen*) become mnemic residues, memory images, between perception and consciousness, the representations of which are the dream images. Unconscious thought can also be made known in conscious thought as the absence in the gaps in conscious thought. As for Lacan, the goal of psychoanalysis is to fill in those gaps in order to have access to unconscious processes: it is impossible for conscious thought to fully understand itself or unconscious thought.

In other writings (*Beyond the Pleasure Principle*, *The Ego and the Id*, *An Outline of Psycho-Analysis*), Freud expanded his concept of the unconscious to include the elements of *eros* and *thanatos*, life and death instincts (the death drive), and dynamic relationships between the ego, id and superego, the divisions of the psyche. In *An Outline of Psycho-Analysis*, the dream consists of visual residue (*Sachvorstellung*) and auditory residue (*Wortvorstellung*), combining into a "double inscription" (*Niederschrift*) involving displacement and condensation, as described in the analysis of Jacques Lacan. Freud sees unconscious thought as repressed in relation to conscious thought, and can be revealed in the dream. The id (*das es*, the It) is located in unconscious thought and is the source of libidinal and destructive impulses. The "it" suggests an other to the "I" (*das Ich*, the ego), as unconscious thought is an other to conscious thought. The ego is a modification of the id in the development of the subject. The ego involves both conscious and unconscious thought. The superego projects the ego into the macrocosm of culture and universal ideas, what Lacan would call the Other.

In *The Ego and the Id*, the premise of psychoanalysis is the division of the psychical into the conscious and unconscious. The essence of the psychical cannot be found in conscious thought. The inaccessible unconscious, "cut off from the external world," is dynamically repressed; though there is also a preconscious (*Vorbewusste*), which is that which is accessible to conscious thought in the unconscious, and that which is capable of becoming conscious. The theory of the preconscious can be related to the productive intellect of the Peripatetics (*intellectus in habitu* or *intellectus speculativus*), connecting material intellect to active intellect or conscious thought to unconscious thought. It can also be related to the *Schwellengesetz* of Herbart. What passes from preconscious to conscious thought is not sustained in consciousness. The ego is defined as the organization of mental processes, and is the ground for conscious thought. The preconscious thought becomes a conscious thought when it is connected with word presentations or language.

Freud's goal was to replace the philosophical, metaphysical concept of unconscious thought with an empirical, experiential explanation for "the unconscious" as an objective phenomenon. Nevertheless, the metaphysical concept, and classical, medieval, and modern philosophical influences still played an important role in his theories of language, perception, imagination, dream images, and the divisions of the psyche. Jacques Lacan, like Freud, distinguished between psychoanalysis and philosophy, but again philosophical and metaphysical concepts continued to play a role in Lacan's psychoanalytic theory, interwoven with the Freudian theories of the unconscious and the influence of structural linguistics.

In Chapter Eight, "Unconscious Thought in Lacan," Jacques Lacan is considered to be the most important post-Freudian writer on the science of psychoanalysis, or the science of the letter as Lacan calls it. The purpose of this chapter is to examine the role of unconscious thought in Lacan's linguistic structuring of unconscious processes, and in the definitions of the Imaginary and Symbolic orders of the psyche, and the Real. Lacan's concept of unconscious thought combines an analysis of Freudian dream work with an analysis of the structural linguistics of Ferdinand de Saussure. In this way Lacan was able to make a substantial development of Freudian psychoanalysis. In the structural linguistics of Saussure, the word is divided into the signifier, the phonetic sound, and the signified, the idea to which the phonetic sound corresponds. Saussure, in the *Course in General Linguistics*, suggested that any relationship between the two is arbitrary. In Lacan's *Écrits*, a bar between the two suggests the inaccessibility of the signifier to the signified, or the inaccessibility of conscious thought to unconscious thought. The signifier, according to Lacan, represents the speaking subject to another signifier; it represents the insertion of the speaking subject into language. The sliding (*glissement*) of the signifier across the bar constitutes a system of relations between signifiers, and a deferral of meaning, as in the *différance* of Jacques Derrida. Meaning can only be present as an absence, as unconscious thought can only be present as an absence in conscious thought.

Metaphor and metonymy are the principal operational rules that determine language. A metaphor is a condensation and a metonym is a displacement, in the terms of Freudian dream work. The bar between signifier and signified is maintained in the metonym, but it is crossed in the metaphor, in the elision of a second signified, which creates an absence in the signifying chain. The bar is only crossed because one signifier is substituted for another. The absence in the signifying chain is what constitutes the speaking subject, which is other to itself, as conscious thought is other to unconscious thought. Signification only occurs retroactively (in retroactive anticipation) in the play of signifiers, at the "anchoring point" (*point de capiton*), which is the point at which the subject inserts itself into language as absence. I can only communicate an idea to someone when they anticipate what I am going to say, which cancels me as a communicator of an idea. Language is a self-enclosed system with gaps or absences that reveal a connection to what is other to its enunciation – unconscious thought. In structural linguistics, language is divided into *parole* and *langue*. While *parole* is individual enunciation, *langue* is the collective system of relationships. *Parole* is the conscious use in speech of unconsciously determined structures, or *langue*.

Lacan divided the Freudian psyche into the Imaginary, Symbolic, and Real. The Real is that which is inaccessible to the Imaginary or Symbolic orders. The Imaginary, the identity of the perceiving subject in image, precedes the Symbolic, the speaking subject in language. The Imaginary ego is formed at the "mirror stage," when the infant first identifies itself as an image in a mirror. The Imaginary other is then interwoven into the Symbolic order, in the matrix of language which is the Other, and which Lacan defined as the unconscious. The Imaginary and Symbolic are interwoven in conscious and unconscious thought, as in a Borromean knot. The Imaginary is primarily the conscious ego in image identification, while the Symbolic is primarily the unconscious in language, as the matrix of language is the unconscious. The subject becomes divided between the Imaginary and the Symbolic, causing a gap in the subject between image and word. This is the fundamental problem for Lacanian psychoanalysis. The Other is the network of relations that determines the subject, and constitutes unconscious thought.

Perception is a dialectic of the Imaginary and Symbolic; as the Imaginary is absorbed into the Symbolic, immediate perception of sense objects is impossible. As in classical philosophy, perceived objects are given by intelligible concepts in unconscious thought. As in Kantian philosophy, experience is determined by the categories of a priori intuition in unconscious thought. The thinking subject is formed when it enters into a symbolic relationship in language. When the subject enters into language, it is represented by a signifier – a pronoun, and the subject is excluded from the signifying chain (becomes an absence) at the point that it is represented in it. Language defines the subject and at the same time assures its non-being. The ego is formed as a replacement for the elided subject in language.

The subject is composed of the ego, the unconscious, the Other and the other (perceived object identification). Conscious thought in the ego is determined by unconscious thought as the Other. The resistance of the conscious ego to the unconscious is the resistance of the signifier to the signified, the inaccessible source of conscious ideas. The subject speaks through unconscious thought, but conscious thought cannot know unconscious thought, or itself. Conscious thought is constituted by *méconnaissance* – misknowing or misrecognition. The reality beyond language of unconscious thought is revealed in the absences in language, the gaps and scotomata. Freud drew attention to these gaps (jokes, puns, slips of the tongue, etc.) but he failed to recognize their significance, according to Lacan. The unconscious is found in the gaps between signifiers, where the ego is revealed as representation. Absence and presence oscillate in the *glissement* of signifiers.

In Lacan's *The Four Fundamental Concepts of Psycho-Analysis*, unconscious thought is "manifested as that which vacillates in a split in the subject," between the Imaginary and Symbolic. The unconscious is a primordial cut in thought, manifested in a temporal pulsation in language, as the subject is elided and then re-emerges. The oscillation is also present in the dream, which contains the dialectic of the Imaginary and Symbolic. Unconscious thought perpetually opens and closes with conscious thought. It is only present as an absence in the gap between the Imaginary and the Symbolic, in which the subject is "born divided." The subject becomes the network of signifiers in language, and in the layers of images in dreams.

That which passes in the gap between perception and consciousness, Imaginary and Symbolic, other and Other, and in the *glissement* in the signifying chain in language, is what Lacan calls the "Gaze." The Gaze is the absence in conscious thought. The result of the split between Imaginary and Symbolic in the subject is desire, caused by the impossibility of fulfillment, and the absence in conscious thought, the inability to know unconscious thought. The object of desire is the Other, which is a substitute for the absence of the subject (the *objet a*). *Llanguage*, in *Seminar XX*, is the language of the unconscious that exceeds conscious thought but incorporates it. *Llanguage* cannot be enunciated by the speaking subject; it is what is articulated by the subject beyond language. The speaking subject is an instrument of *llanguage* in the discourse of the Other. The being of the subject is elsewhere than language. Language is a metaphor for lack of being, the absence that it replaces as supplement.

The Real of Lacan can be compared to the One of Plotinus, a subject that Lacan addresses in his writings. Approach toward both the Real and the One entails the realization of the absence of the subject. Intellect for both Plotinus and Lacan can be seen to operate in part without connection to sense perception. Elements of the Imaginary order of Lacan can be found in the *phantasia* of Plotinus, and the *Vorstellung* of Hegel. Elements of the role of language in the unconscious of Lacan can be found in the Intellect of Plotinus, in the revealing of the intelligible by the logos.

The theories summarized in the preceding outline are explored in detail in the chapters in the book, in order to answer some of the questions as to what is unconscious thought, whether it exists, how it works, and how it relates to conscious thought; the role it plays in perception, imagination, and intellection; and the role it plays in human identity, in conceptions of unconscious thought throughout the history of philosophy and psychoanalysis. The book attempts to answer the ultimate question as to why unconscious thought is vital to all of our intellective activities. The theme of the role of unconscious thought and conscious thought has been present in several books that I have written previously, going back ten years: *The Contradiction Between Form and Function in Architecture*; *Robert Grosseteste: Philosophy of Intellect and Vision*; *Architecture and Psychoanalysis: Peter Eisenman and Jacques Lacan*; *Aesthetics and the Philosophy of Spirit: From Plotinus to Schelling and Hegel*; *Architectural Forms and Philosophical Structures*. I found it necessary in this book to address the theme of unconscious thought that has been developing and which is integral to the issues that have been addressed in the previous books, in the fields of aesthetics, creativity, perception, imagination, and artistic composition. Pieces of some of the essays in this book have been developed from essays in the previous books, rewritten for the purpose of addressing the subject of unconscious thought. References to the previous essays can be found throughout the text.

There is a continuity of thought throughout Western history that is often neglected. Despite advances in scientific knowledge and technology, there is still to date a continuity throughout history in the definition of what it is to be human, and there is much to learn from the history of thought. Analytical philosophy has been neglected in favor of science, but analytical philosophy, including metaphysics, offers a foundational concept of unconscious thought as it participates in conscious thought, a concept that has a great deal to offer psychoanalytic theories of the unconscious based on empirical observations. This book examines the development of concepts of unconscious thought throughout the history of Western philosophy, concepts that are metaphysical, addressing what is beyond empirical experience in intellect, contrasting the empirical or scientific phenomena of "the unconscious" in psychoanalysis. A variety of concepts in philosophy throughout history suggest what we now call unconscious thought, before the use of the term. These include: active intellect, productive intellect, *noesis, nous poietikos*, intelligible, apperception, *virtus intellectiva, petites perceptions*, intuition, a priori intuition, subjectivity, inner experience, apprehension, noumenal, real, absolute, and being-in-self. The book examines the role that the philosophical or metaphysical concept of unconscious thought plays in psychoanalysis, and the contribution that it can make to psychoanalytic theory. In the text, all uncited quotations are continuations of the most recent citations.

1
Plotinus: The First Philosopher of the Unconscious

In the thought of Plotinus (204–70), seen as the first philosopher to develop a systematic conception of the presence of unconscious thought in conscious thought, or a systematic philosophy of intellect involving unconscious thought, concepts that contribute to a theory of unconscious thought include the *nous poietikos* (noetic thought, Intellect), the intelligible, *phantasia* (imagination), and the *logos endiathetos* (unuttered word) which aids in translating the intelligible into the presentation of it available to discursive reason or conscious thought.

Plotinus is sometimes referred to as "the first philosopher of the unconscious." In his 1960 essay "Consciousness and Unconsciousness in Plotinus," Hans Rudolph Schwyzer called Plotinus the discoverer of the unconscious. In the same year, Eric Robertson Dodds wrote that in the thought of Plotinus "there are sensations which do not reach consciousness," and there are desires that are "unknown to us" (Dodds, 1960, pp. 1–7). In 1965 Dodds wrote: "Plotinus was the first writer to recognize that the psyche includes sensations, desires and dispositions of which the ego is normally unconscious..." (Dodds, 1990, p. 88, n. 4). In the *Meno* (80d, 81b–c) and *Phaedo* (68b–d, 74b), Plato (429–347 BC) suggested that we have knowledge of which we are not aware at the moment, in anamnesis. But Plotinus was the first writer to address the thought of which we are not aware, and incorporate it into a philosophy of intellect. What exactly was Plotinus' unconscious? In the *Enneads*, Plotinus asked about soul and intellect: "Why then...do we not consciously grasp them...? For not everything which is in the soul is immediately perceptible" (V.1.12.1–15) (Plotinus, 1966). In the *De anima* of Aristotle (384–322 BC), "Mind does not think intermittently" (430a10–25) (Aristotle, 1964). We cannot remember eternal mind in us, because passive mind is perishable. Is the productive intelligence in our mind that of which we are not conscious? Can productive intelligence be compared to unconscious thought?

Plotinus suggested that we do not notice the activity of intellect because it is not engaged with objects of sense perception. The intellect must involve an activity prior to awareness. Awareness of intellectual activity only occurs when thinking is reflected as in a mirror, but knowledge in discursive reason, reason transitioning from one object to the next in a temporal sequence, is not self-knowledge. Only in the activity of intellect inaccessible to discursive reason is thinking as the equivalent of being. The intellectual act in mind is only apprehended when it is brought into the image-making power of mind through the logos or linguistic articulation; "we are always intellectually active but do not always apprehend our activity" (IV.3.30.1–17) (Plotinus, 1966). If the Intellectual is the unconscious, then unconscious reason is superior to conscious reason. The inability of conscious reason to know itself is the premise of psychoanalysis in the twentieth century.

In *Enneads* V.1.11.1–15, the human mind or soul "sometimes reasons about the right and good and sometimes does not...." If this is the case, then there must be an element of thought which knows what the right and good are, not intermittently and indecisively, but permanently and without question. This must be intellect, which rather than reason discursively about the right and the good, *possesses* the right and the good, based on the principle and cause of Intellect. The principle and cause of Intellect is undivided in discursive reason, and abides in mind but not in place. As such, the principle and cause can remain undivided, just as the center of a circle remains undivided by the individual radii connected to it.

"Why then," Plotinus asked, "when we have such great possessions, do we not consciously grasp them, but are mostly inactive in these ways, and some of us are never active at all?" (V.1.12.1–15). Intellect, what comes before Intellect (the first cause), and what results from Intellect (soul, which is itself "ever-moving"), are all "always occupied in their own activities," but those activities are not always perceptible; they are only perceptible when they somehow enter into perception, when their activity is shared. Since we are mostly preoccupied with our activities of perception, it is difficult to be aware of when the activities of Intellect are shared. Nevertheless, when the activities are shared with perception, then "conscious awareness takes place." Otherwise we are unconscious of the activities of Intellect in discursive or conscious reason; we are not aware of the role that unconscious thought plays in the activities of our conscious thought and perception. In order to become aware of the activities of unconscious thought or Intellect, "we must turn our power of apprehension inwards, and make it attend to what is there."

First it is necessary to examine one's soul. The powers of perception in soul are only capable of perceiving external objects. Discursive reason in soul makes judgments based on the mental images which come from sense perception. The mental images come from sensible objects and are organized by reason, in combinations and divisions. It should be kept in mind that the mental images themselves are not entirely dependent on the sensible forms, though, because the mental images play a role in the determination of the sensible forms to begin with, and the result is not just the sensible form imprinted in the mind's eye, but a combination of the sensible form and the intelligible form. As Plotinus said, "as for the things which come to it from Intellect," the intelligible forms, "it observes what one might call their imprints, and has the same power also in dealing with these ... " (V.3.2.1–26). Understanding in perception on the part of reason is the result of a dialectical process of combinations of sensible and intelligible forms in the mind, which is an unconscious process.

Any knowledge or awareness of this process can only come from Intellect, and not discursive reason in soul. But a part of Intellect has to be in soul, just as a part of the Aristotelian active intellect has to be in potential intellect. The part of Intellect which is in soul, though, does not have the capacity of pure Intellect to be aware of itself – self-awareness in soul can only come from Intellect higher than soul, intellect not connected to the body or sense perception. In other words, conscious reason cannot know itself. This is in contradiction of the Cartesian premise of modern philosophy, a premise that was refuted by Kant, Schelling, and Hegel. Discursive reason in soul cannot know itself or have self-awareness, but it can know where it is: somewhere between Intellect and sense perception. Discursive or conscious reason "has understanding of the impressions which it receives from both sides," from Intellect and sense perception. It can be aware of what it receives from perception, and it can be aware of what it receives from Intellect, the higher forms to which it has access. How does conscious reason have such understanding?

In *Enneads* V.3.3, impressions are received by discursive reason from sense perception, but discursive reason can only respond to them with the help of memory. With the help of memory, discursive reason then performs analytical operations on the impressions from sense perception, "taking to pieces what the image-making power gave it...." Any judgments that discursive reason makes about what it receives from sense perception can only be the result of what is already in discursive reason. In order for discursive reason to make any particular judgment about something perceived, discursive reason has to contain the quality that it judges. The only way that discursive reason can contain a quality is if it is illuminated by Intellect, as the sun would illuminate an object in vision. Discursive reason is not conscious of the illumination of Intellect, of the reception of the reflection of Intellect, as in a mirror, because again it is too engaged in perceiving and judging external objects. Only Intellect is capable of observing and knowing itself, which is a kind of reason inaccessible to discursive or conscious reason. Discursive reason makes use of Intellect, unknowingly, in perception and logical thought, when discursive reason is in accord with Intellect, and can be affected by it. Discursive reason is only in accord with Intellect to the extent that discursive reason has knowledge of such accord; in other words, unconscious thought can only be known in conscious thought.

While impressions are received through sense perception, "it is not we ourselves who are the perceivers...," because the mechanisms that allow perception to take place, from Intellect, are not accessible by conscious thought. We can define ourselves and have self-identity only in our conscious, discursive reason, not in the unconscious mechanisms behind perception, and not in the unconscious mechanisms of Intellect. Thus "we are this, the principal part of soul, in the middle between two powers...," neither of which is accessible to our knowledge or awareness. Thus our self-knowledge and identity can be described as being caught between two mirrors; we can perceive the reflections of sense perception and Intellect, but we cannot see beyond the source of the reflections.

We do not notice the activity of Intellect because "it is not concerned with any object of sense," as Plotinus said in *Enneads* I.4.10. We are generally only aware of our mind's activity when it is connected to sense perception and thinking about the objects of sense, the *nous hylikos*. If Intellect, and soul, are understood to come before sense perception and discursive reason, as necessary ground for those activities, then it must be considered that the activities of Intellect and soul are continually active, in making sense perception and discursive reason possible, although we do not have immediate awareness of or access to those activities. "There must be an activity prior to awareness," said Plotinus, if "thinking and being are the same"; that is, if being is given by thought. When awareness of the activity of Intellect exists, or is produced, intellectual activity is reflected back to conscious thought as in a mirror reflection, perhaps at an angle, since the activity of Intellect itself is not present to the dianoetic self: in front of the mirror as it were. Or the activity of Intellect is reflected back to dianoetic thought as logos, since the lower soul can only perceive it as such. In order for that to happen, the surface of the mirror has to be clear, or, in other words, the power of soul has to be clear of disturbances or distractions from sense perceptions. It is necessary for the individual to not be distracted by or focused on the objects of sense perception, in order to disconnect the mind's activities from them, and concentrated on the premises for the possibilities of those sense perceptions. It is in self-consciousness that the mind is able to perceive the unconscious activity which makes conscious activity possible.

What is reflected as a mirror image, which is a function of the image-making power or imagination (*phantasia*) in soul, is the activity of Intellect, which must always be there, whether the mirror reflects it or not. The reflective power of the mirror needs to be turned on, through the will of thinking, and the mirror needs to function correctly. It is not possible to have direct access to the activities of Intellect or unconscious thought, but only to their reflections in soul or conscious thought. In the same way, it is not possible to have direct access to dreams, but only to their images as preserved by memory in waking, conscious life. Memory serves the image-making power to preserve images and translate them into words, so that the images which are the product of sense perception can play a role as the vocabulary elements of thinking activity in discursive reason.

When the mirror imaging power of imagination is functioning correctly, the activity and images of Intellect, what is prior to sense perception, can be perceived by soul in the same way that objects of sense perception are perceived by sight, although the light by which they are illuminated is not the light of the sun, but rather an inner light, the light of Intellect itself. In order for the activities and images of Intellect to be perceived in the same way as sense objects, they have to mimic or take the form of sense objects and activities. Unconscious thought can only be known by conscious thought to the extent that it mimics conscious thought, and conforms to its boundaries and limitations. The full extent of unconscious thought cannot be known by conscious thought because of the limitations of conscious thought, just as the full extent of the sensible world cannot be known by sense perception, because of the limitations of sense perception. On this premise alone the existence of the metaphysical is necessary.

The operation of the mirror of self-reflection, or self-consciousness of intellectual activity, depends on the smooth functioning, harmony and balance of the body in relation to the sensible world. The mirror is a property of *nous hylikos*, the physical functioning of mind in relation to body. If the body does not function properly, the self-reflexive powers of mind cannot function properly. This is in contradiction to the thought of Plato. If the mirror is broken because the body is not functioning properly, there is no image for thought and intellect to operate with; the image-making power or imagination is a also a property of *nous hylikos* and bodily function in the sensible, although, as will be seen, it is also a property of Intellect, and in fact was seen by Plotinus as occupying the midpoint between Intellect and sense perception. But for these purposes, the mirror in the mind, as a property of the body, is necessary for the mind to perceive the activities of Intellect in connection with images, the images reflected in the well-functioning mirror of the soul. The activity of Intellect itself does not necessarily involve a connection with images, but its connection with images is necessary in order to be perceived.

According to Plotinus, there are "a great many valuable activities, theoretical and practical, which we carry on both in our contemplative and active life even when we are fully conscious, which do not make us aware of them" (I.4.10.20–34). This is an explicit recognition of the existence of the modern concept of the unconscious. It is possible to be involved in an activity or an act of contemplation, virtuous action or reading, for example, without being aware of such activity or thought. In fact, conscious awareness, according to Plotinus, "is likely to enfeeble the very activities of which there is consciousness...." Plotinus seemed to be suggesting that there is something stronger and superior in mind to conscious thought, which is Intellect. Conscious thought and activity, and consciousness itself, are weak forms of thought and activity. Nowhere in the *Enneads* did Plotinus suggest the possibility or concept of a "higher consciousness," contrary to the opinion of some commentators. Instead, Plotinus said that "only when they are alone," referring to the activities of thought of which there is consciousness, "are they pure and more genuinely active and living." Thoughts are stronger and purer when they are "alone," when they are unperceived by conscious thought and perception, when they are what we call "unconscious."

Thoughts are purer before they have been connected to the images which allow them to be perceptible to consciousness; they are closer to their source, the One, in Intellect. They are purer as the prior ground for consciousness and experience in sense perception. The unconscious is the pure ground for conscious thought and activity, and unconscious thoughts are necessarily corrupted when they become conscious thoughts, if just in their connection to the image in imagination. The power of imagination is the great facilitator for Plotinus, but also the great corruptor. The value of life is increased, and the quality of the soul is increased, when mind is less fragmented and dispersed in the acts of sense perception and discursive reason, but rather "gathered together in one in itself."

Conscious thought and sense perception involve a fragmentation, dispersal, and diminution of the powers of thought. In order to avoid this fragmentation and diminution of thought, it is necessary to will oneself into self-reflection, and to will one's intellect away from the objects of sense perception toward the images of Intellect reflected in soul, then away from those images to the prior source of the images in Intellect. It is necessary to will oneself towards one's unconscious; the more access there is to the unconscious activities of one's mind, the stronger and purer are the conscious activities. As John Gale recently wrote, "According to Neo-Platonism the analytic withdrawal into the psyche demanded an examination of unconscious desire, which amounted to a therapeutic process" (Gale, 2014, p. 157). For Plotinus this withdrawal was "a kind of catharsis – a breaking through the ego to get in touch with excluded, disassociated parts of the self."

Plotinus also called the reflections of the images of Intellect "imprints" or "impressions," so they are seen as the *eidos* or form which is not connected to a material form or *morphe*, in the same way that the images of sense perception themselves are the *eidos* and not the *morphe*, imprints or impressions of forms that are received in connection to the material objects, as if there are two lights, or a double light, shining on the material object: the light of the intelligible, which illuminates the *eidos*, and the light of the sensible (the sun), which illuminates matter. Judgment in discursive reason is based on the perception of the *eidos* of the sensible object, as it is subjected to the mechanisms of combination and division in apperception, which are the same mechanisms which Sigmund Freud attributed to the image-making power of unconscious thought in the formation of dream images from dream thoughts, what he called condensation and displacement. The judgment in discursive reason is also based on the perception of the image connected to thoughts from Intellect, as the objects of sense perception are processed through the unconscious mechanisms of imagination and memory which make the sense perception possible in the first place, then translate the objects of sense perception into a totality (what Immanuel Kant would call the "manifold"), even through the combinations and divisions, which makes being possible, and which makes thinking equivalent to being.

Thinking for Plotinus is a dialectical process which is facilitated by imagination, which is suspended between Intellect, the source of thinking, and sense perception, the object of thinking. The dialectical process involves the imprint of the sense object or sensible form in perception, the imprint of the idea of the object or intelligible form in the imagination or image-making power, the memory or recollection of past thoughts and perceptions in relation to the present thought, the "recollections" of the soul, the transformation of the image – both sensible and intelligible – into the word in language, both the spoken word and the word prior to speech in Intellect, and the fitting together of sensible image, intelligible image, recollected sensible image, recollected intelligible image, sensible word, and intelligible word, in a process which requires the anticipation of the perception of the image or word in relation to the recollection of the intelligible image or word in Intellect, as it is perceived as a reflection or imprint in mind. When the soul is "in the intelligible world it has itself too the characteristic of unchangeability" (IV.4.2) (Plotinus, 1966), but "if it comes out of the intelligible world, and cannot endure unity, but embraces its own individuality and wants to be different" (IV.4.3) it then acquires memory, in discursive reason and temporal succession. Memory helps keep the soul partly in the intelligible world, the rational soul, but it also brings soul down to the sensible world, the irrational soul (Nyvlt, 2012, p. 169).

As Jacques Lacan would say, meaning and communication are only possible in the anticipation of a signifier in language and perception, in relation to both the recollection of the signifier from prior perception, and the intelligible or signified (the idea) in relation the signifier (the word). Lacan called this the *point de capiton*, the "button hole" which connects the floating kingdoms of signifiers, or words in language, to the signifieds, or intelligible ideas with which they are connected, as described by Ferdinand de Saussure. Clearly the concepts of the signifier and signified in modern linguistics are derivations of the concepts of the sensible and intelligible, and the functions of perception and Intellect.

As the perception of a sensible object entails both the *eidos* of the object and the *eidos* of the intelligible idea of the object in unconscious thought, "actual seeing is double" (*Enneads* V.5.7). The eye "has one object of sight which is the form of the object perceived by the sense, and one which is the medium through which the form of its object is perceived...." The medium, the intelligible idea of the object, which comes from Intellect and is connected to the imprint that is reflected in the mirror of the mind's eye, precedes the perception of the sensible form, and is the cause of the perception of the sensible form. In normal conscious thought and perception, the form and the medium cannot be separated, and the form of the sensible object is unknowingly perceived as a sensible object, without its sensible or intelligible form. While vision in sense perception is distracted in the act of perception of an object, it is not capable of self-reflection in its outer act.

Mind must be made aware of the medium without the object in order to understand how the object is perceived. Plotinus gave as an example the sun's light, which is perceived without the body of the sun which is the source of its light. Although only the sun's light is perceived, it would not exist without the mass of the body which lies behind it. Saying that the sun is all light is the equivalent of saying that sensible objects are only the forms that they are perceived as. So, seeing the Intellect is to see objects by another light than that which illuminates the perceptible form; the seeing of the intellect can detach itself from the illuminated perceptible form and see the source of the light as well as the light itself. In that way mind can perceive the source of its perception or thought, and not just the object perceived or the act of perception.

The eye then, through the knowledge of Intellect, is able to perceive not just the external light which illuminates the form of the sensible object, but an internal light as well, which illuminates the intelligible idea of the form as an intelligible light, or a priori intuitive light, or unconscious light. Evidence of the internal light can be seen when the eyelids are closed, or in the dark, when light appears in the eyes. Plotinus was following Plato in suggesting that vision itself depends on the external light entering the eye (intromission) as well as internal light from the eye illuminating the object (extramission). If the eye abandons the external light and external form, it can concentrate on the internal light and internal form, just as mind can concentrate on the intelligible idea, and "then in not seeing it sees, and sees then most of all..." (*Enneads* V.5.7) (Plotinus, 1966).

The external world of sense objects needs to be renounced in order to understand its existence in relation to the perception of it, in the equivalence of thinking and being, and conscious thought and perception have to be renounced in order to understand their existence in relation to human thought and identity, which can be found suspended somewhere between Intellect and sense perception. The renunciation of conscious thought is necessary in order to access unconscious thought, the prior ground of all thought and perception. In not seeing, the eye "sees light; but the other things which it saw had the form of light but were not the light," not the original light. The intelligible light which Intellect sees when "veiling itself from other things and drawing itself inward," is a light "alone by itself in independent purity," its source inaccessible and unknown even to Intellect, being that of the One, which is not being or thought. The intelligible light can be reflected, through the medium of unconscious thought, and known to conscious thought.

In V.3.8, Plotinus explained that intelligibles exist prior to bodies, and cannot be thought of in terms of color or form (until they are connected to such in imagination). Intelligibles themselves are "naturally invisible," invisible even to the soul which possesses them. In the physical world, an object can be seen when it is illuminated by enough light. In the intelligible world, something can only be seen by itself, because seeing is only through itself, and not through a medium. Seeing something through itself in the intelligible is like light seeing itself, seeing itself as the source of itself, which is inaccessible even to Intellect. Once the intelligible light is seen, sensible light in perception is no longer necessary for understanding. Soul is an image, a reflection or likeness of Intellect; conscious thought is an image, a reflection or likeness of unconscious thought. The illumination of a sensible object by light is a reflection or likeness of the illumination of Intellect by intelligible light. Knowledge of Intellect depends on the separation of the soul from the body, as in the *Phaedo* of Plato and the *De anima* of Aristotle.

In the *Phaedo*, Plato "separates the soul from communion with the body" (64e3–10) (Plato, 1982). Mind thinks best when it is untroubled by sense perceptions and affections, and "avoiding, so far as it can, all association or contact with the body, reaches out toward the reality" (65c3–8), the archetypal reality or intelligible reality of Intellect for Aristotle and Plotinus. Mind is only deceived when it "tries to consider anything in company with the body" (65b9–12), in relation to sense perception and imagination. According to Aristotle in the *De anima*, it is necessary that mind, "since it thinks all things, should be uncontaminated" (429a10–30) (Aristotle, 1964), because "the intrusion of anything foreign hinders and obstructs it." Mind cannot be seen to be mixed with body, because then it would be qualitative; mind can only be receptive – it can have "no actual existence until it thinks."

In *Enneads* V.8.9, Plotinus asked us to apprehend in our thought, or form a mental picture of, the visible universe with all its parts – the sun, heavenly bodies, earth and its creatures – organized in a sphere. In the soul then is a "shining imagination of a sphere" informed by an image connected to the intelligible understanding of the universe as reflected as if in a mirror into the image-making power. Then Plotinus asked us to subtract the mass, spatial relations and matter, and apprehend the universe without the "petty power of body." In that way the universe can be apprehended more clearly, in its conceptual organization not dependent upon its physical appearance to the senses. The same exercise might be applied to the apprehension of a house, for example. If one forms a mental picture of the house in the imagination, derived from the picture of the house as given by perception, and then subtracts the physical properties of the house, one would have a true understanding of the house, as an entity given in the beginning by the intelligible idea, or concept, of "house," prior to the sensible perception of the house. The house would be understood as a set of spatial relationships and preconceptions about form and function, all of which are present in unconscious thought during the act of conscious perception.

In VI.4.7, Plotinus asked us to perform the same exercise with a hand holding a piece of wood. Imagine the "corporeal bulk of the hand to be taken away," so that only the power to hold the wood would remain, in the same way that light, or the power of light, would remain if the bulk of a material body were removed: for example, the bulk of a body at the center of a sphere and illuminating the sphere from the inside. Physical light itself is illuminated by intelligible light, which is a reflection of the originary inaccessible source of light itself. The visible universe is illuminated by conscious thought and perception; conscious thought and perception are illuminated by intelligible or unconscious thought and imagination; and unconscious thought is illuminated by a mystical light from an unknowable source beyond being. In modern psychoanalysis there is no mystical unknowable source beyond being, although there was in modern philosophical concepts of the unconscious (Schelling, for example). There is also no ultimate explanation for the source of unconscious thought in modern psychoanalysis.

Intellect is "that which is actually and always intellect" (V.9.5); it "thinks from itself and derives the content of its thought from itself, it is itself what it thinks." This defines its actuality, as opposed to its potentiality. In Aristotle's *De anima*, mind is "separable, impassive and unmixed" (430a10–25), an originating cause, identical to its object of knowledge. In isolation, mind, or Intellect, "is its true self and nothing more, and this alone is immortal and everlasting…and without this nothing thinks." For Plotinus, Intellect both thinks the "real beings," intelligible forms, and is the real beings. It is necessary that "primary reality is not what is perceived by the senses" (*Enneads* V.9.5), as in the Allegory of the Cave in Plato's *Republic*, because "the form of the matter in the things of sense is an image of the real form," the archetypal or intelligible form known to conscious reason as a reflection, and a likeness of the intelligible form with which it is connected. Intellect is composed of "rational forming principles" which precede not only visible forms but also the mechanisms of soul, which can only be potential; as in

Aristotle's *De anima*, two distinct elements must be present in soul, like everything in nature.

There is, on the one hand, "something which is their matter, i.e., which is potentially all the individuals," and on the other hand "something else which is their cause or agent in that it makes them all ... " (*Enneads* V.9.5). For Aristotle, it is the sensible object which "makes the sense faculty actually operative from being only potential ... " (*De anima* 431a1–10) (Aristotle, 1964). But it is not the object itself that actualizes the sense faculty, but rather the *eidos* or form of the object, pre-given in intellection, as "sense is that which is receptive of the form of sensible objects without the matter ... " (424a17–26). Imagination is a "movement produced by sensation actively operating" (429a1–7), but it is not produced by sense objects themselves, or anything in matter.

Imagination facilitates the translation of sensible objects in perception to intellection. Following Aristotle, the intellectual act is not possible without an accompanying mental image, according to Plotinus. The power (*virtus*) to form the image in the mind's eye is conversely always accompanied by the "verbal expression" (*Enneads* IV.3.30) (Plotinus, 1966); or, more accurately, the *logos endiathetos*, the word in thought, as Plotinus intended it. The intelligible image, and thus the sensible image, is not possible without its linguistic expression, and linguistic expression is not possible without the intelligible image. Perception of sensible objects is only possible after the idea of the sensible object is articulated in language in intellection. While the "intellectual act is without parts," as it has not been differentiated in discursive reason, and thus in perception, it "has not, so to speak, come out into the open, but remains unobserved within," as unconscious thought.

But "the verbal expression unfolds its content," as a signifier would unfold the signified, "and brings it out of the intellectual act into the image-making power," allowing imagination to form the intelligible image which corresponds to the sensible image in memory. In doing so, the linguistic articulation "shows the intellectual act as if in a mirror," as a mirror reflection might represent a sensible object, but the linguistic articulation in discursive reason does not contain the intellectual act; the intellectual act remains separated from sense perception and sensible reality. The intellectual act itself is inaccessible, as the unconscious. In the same way, it might be said that conscious thought contains a reflection or representation of unconscious thought, but conscious thought does not contain unconscious thought; unconscious thought is inaccessible to conscious thought.

The reflection of the intellectual act in the imagination – in the image-making power in language and discursive reason, conscious thought – might be described as Plotinus' "royal road to the unconscious," as dream images – which are also translations of unconscious intellectual acts into images in the imagination, through the medium of articulated thoughts in language – were Sigmund Freud's "royal road to the unconscious." Freud described the "dream image" as derived, unconsciously, from the "dream thought," which is a product of the unarticulated intellectual act during sleep. The dream image is transformed in "dream work" from an unarticulated idea in unconscious thought, through words in thought which mimic words in conscious thought, and finally the logos is then translated into dream images, exactly as for Plotinus. The transformation of thought into image depends on the mechanisms of condensation and displacement, according to Freud, so that dream images do not have the same rational organization as sensible images in perception. This, according to Freud, is because dreams do not have any intention of communicating anything, although the mechanisms of their formation mimic the mechanisms of the formation of the intelligible form – through perception and language, or, as Plotinus says, the formation of the *eidos* of the sensible object as it is subjected to the mechanisms of combination and division in apperception.

The intellectual act, the intelligent activity of the soul, is only apprehended through a reflection or representation, "when it comes to be in the image-making power" (*Enneads* IV.3.30) (Plotinus, 1966), as an intelligible form in the imagination produced through perception, language and memory, or as a dream image. Freud called the dream image formed in imagination a *Vortellungsrepräsentanz*, a representation of a representation, as it was for Plotinus. For Plotinus, "the intellectual act is one thing," inaccessible in the unconscious, but "the apprehension of it another," through the representation in the mirror reflection of the representation in the logos or word in thought. Thus, while we are always intellectually active, including while we are sleeping, we "do not always apprehend our activity" because we are distracted by our conscious thought and sense perceptions. That which apprehends acts of intelligence – the imagination – also apprehends perceptions, which are necessary for the apprehension of intellectual acts in imagination; both word and image together are necessary for comprehension. Conscious thought prevents the apprehension of unconscious thought, as discursive reason prevents apprehension of the Intellectual. The imaginative faculty is a unitary activity which unites the sensible in perception and the intelligible in intellection, but it seems to be fragmented because of the lack of conscious apprehension of all of its activities (Blumenthal, 1971, p. 88).

Plotinus asserted that there are two souls, or two parts of soul: that which is connected to material reality in sense perception and *nous hylikos*, and that of the pure Intellectual, not connected to material reality. The mechanisms of perception, imagination, language and memory are active in both souls, but function differently and distinctly in each one. There are thus "two image-making powers" in *Enneads* IV.3.31, but in life in the sensible world, the two powers act in unison; thus, images in perception and imagination, both sensible and intelligible, are double images. Sensible images are not possible without intelligible images, and intelligible images are not possible without sensible images. Conscious thought is not possible without unconscious thought and vice versa. We cannot recognize the difference between the sensible image and the intelligible image in conscious thought.

In *Enneads* IV.3.31 Plotinus asked, "when the souls are separate we can grant that each of them will have an imaging power, but when they are together, in our earthly life, how are there two powers, and in which of them does memory reside?" Clearly the soul has two imaginative faculties, one concerned with the intelligible and the other with the sensible, although the intelligible imaginative faculty does not depend in any way on the sensible imaginative faculty. According to H. J. Blumenthal, Plotinus "wishes to preserve the impassibility of the higher soul, and so tries to detach it as far as possible from the lower, and thus from a faculty of imagination which is closely connected with the body's needs and activities" (Blumenthal, 1977, p. 169). The activities and images of imagination in the lower soul are duplications of the activities and images in the higher soul, and contribute nothing to them. The higher imagination is a condition of the functioning of the lower imagination; the lower imagination receives the intelligible image as a shadow or copy, which is subsumed in the light of the higher intelligible image. The only connection between the two faculties is one of dependence, which is inapprehensible in conscious, discursive reason and sense perception, waking experience.

If we are able to apprehend the intellectual act as a reflection in a clean mirror, if we are pure and healthy of body and mind, then we are able to apprehend that the intelligible image is more powerful and important than the sensible image, because the intelligible image precedes the sensible image, which is dependent upon it. It is as if every image has two lights shining on it, or is illuminated from two different sources: intellection and perception. When we apprehend the intellectual act it is clear to see that the intelligible light is stronger than the sensible light, that the sensible light is just a shadow of the intelligible light, as in the shadows reflected on the wall of Plato's cave in *The Republic*. If the representation of the Intellectual in imagination is not apprehended clearly, if the body is impure or unhealthy or distracted by sensible objects in perception, then there is disharmony between the two images and only the sensible image can be apprehended. Dominated by the stronger light of the intelligible, the inferior light of the sensible is apprehended as if alone: only a shadow of reality can be comprehended, which is that portion of reality limited to sense perception, discursive reason, and conscious thought. For Plotinus, unconscious thought, as the Intellectual, is necessary for a full understanding of reality and human identity.

Thus, in the soul, "if the part which is in the world of sense perception gets control, or rather if it is itself brought under control, and thrown into confusion, it prevents us from perceiving the things which the upper part of the soul contemplates" (*Enneads* IV.8.8) (Plotinus, 1966), which are the intelligible forms in Intellect, inaccessible to conscious thought. We can only apprehend Intellect when it is reflected and perceived in imagination, descending into the material world. It is not possible to "know everything which happens in any part of the soul before it reaches the whole soul," as representation, *Vortellungsrepräsentanz*. Consciousness of Intellect itself is not possible. All elements of Intellect, including desire, are only known in their manifestations in material soul. Desire is not instinctual; it is a sensible manifestation of an intellectual quality, manifested in the combination of idea, perception, and language. As psychoanalysts would say, desire is the impetus which circulates around the void of being: it is propelled by that which cannot be known, which prevents fulfillment, which is the unconscious.

As every soul, according to Plotinus, "has something of what is below, in the direction of the body, and of what is above, in the direction of Intellect," the soul which is whole and functioning correctly maintains the balance and coexistence of its parts. But this cannot be accomplished by material soul or discursive reason, but only by Intellect: by the healthy functioning of unconscious thought, as psychoanalysis would propose. To quote Aristotle (*Physics* B 199b28–9), only Intellect can maintain the "beauty and order of the whole in effortless transcendence…as art does not deliberate." Art is seen as a product of Intellect, not discursive reason or sense perception. Art is not empirical: all art is metaphysical, an expression of intelligible form in imagination, of an intellectual idea that can be differentiated from sensible form in intellectual apprehension. Discursive reason and sense perception, conscious thought, are considered by Plotinus to be defective on their own, and can be hazardous to the Intellectual. They can introduce impurities and malfunctions, and can prevent the individual from an understanding of reality and human identity, and access to Intellect, or unconscious thought.

In *Enneads* VI.4.4, the wholeness of the soul is always present, as is intellectual activity, though it is not always discernible. The whole soul is present along with the divisions of soul, and the multiplicity of being in sense perception and discursive reason. The unity of the whole soul pervades all divisions and multiplicities, like the One pervades all being in Plotinus' cosmological scheme. In the same way, unconscious thought pervades all conscious thought. Multiplicity in soul precedes multiplicity in material reality, as intelligible form precedes sensible form in imagination. The whole contains the multiplicity a priori, as apperception precedes perception. The multiplicity in material reality does not mean that the parts are separated and inaccessible to each other: all of the parts participate in the whole, as all of the sensible forms in perception participate in the intelligible forms in apperception, forming the totality or manifold of experience and existence. Sensible objects are separated from each other by physical limits, but those physical limits do not exist in the Intellectual, in apperception and imagination. Division and multiplicity are qualities of the physical world in sense perception, in conscious thought and discursive reason, but they are not qualities of intelligible forms in Intellect or unconscious thought.

Imagination and unconscious thought

Plato defined imagination (*phantasia*) as the ability of mind to make images or likenesses, although images played little role in apprehension. Imagination was much more important for Aristotle, as thinking should be regarded as a "form of perceiving" (*De anima* 427a22) (Aristotle, 1964). Images are transmitted through sensory perception as phantasms, which are necessary for thought. The ability to understand is connected to the ability to perceive, but perception does not guarantee speculative thinking and judgment, or perception with imagination. Sensation, imagination, and speculative thinking should be seen as distinct faculties. Imagination is the product of a movement caused by sensation in perception. Light is the most important of the sensations; thus, the name for imagination is derived from the name for light (429a5). So vision is the most important form of perception. While the perception of sensible objects is necessary for thought, mind cannot be affected by those sensible objects in order to think.

In order to be in control of them, mind must be "uncontaminated" (429a20), as "the intrusion of anything foreign hinders and obstructs it." Mind must thus control sensory perceptions without letting them disturb it. Mind can thus not be connected to body, as "soul is the place of forms." Mind only exists when it is thinking, and when it is possessed of forms. Mind has a passive quality in its potentiality to think, and an active quality in its ability to create, which results from the combination of the possession of the forms and the imagination through perception. Mind "does not think intermittently" (430a23), isolated as it is from the affects of sense perception. Like mind, sense perception only exists when it is acted upon by a sensible object; then "the sensible object makes the sense-faculty actually operative from being only potential ... "(431a5).

The soul "never thinks without a mental image" (431a17), but "for the thinking soul images take the place of direct perceptions," as mind must be separated from body in order to function properly. Perceptions of objects can only help the mind think when the images of the perceptions are disassociated from the objects, when the *eidos* is disassociated from the *morphe* or *hyle*. Mind can only think sensible objects as images, and it can only think the forms as images, therefore the power of making images, the imagination, is essential for thought from both the sensible and the intelligible. As for Plotinus, imagination mediates between lower and higher soul, bringing them together in thought: without imagination, both lower and higher soul would only be potential, and not creative or productive. Without perception, there could be no imagination: "no one could ever learn or understand anything without the exercise of perception ... " (432a8). Even in speculative thinking, which necessitates a separation from sense perception, "we must have some mental picture of which to think....." These mental images resemble perceived objects, but they are "without matter." Like sense perception, practical mind (discursive reason) – as opposed to speculative mind (intellect) – causes movement and disturbance in soul, and thus causes appetite (*pathos*). Movement and appetite are also always present in imagination, and appetite is always present in movement.

Plotinus followed Aristotle in asserting that it is not sensible objects themselves that are perceived, but rather their images or impressions: "soul's power of sense-perception need not be perception of sense-objects, but rather it must be receptive of the impressions produced by sensation on the living being; these are already intelligible entities" (*Enneads* I.1.7) (Plotinus, 1966). Direct, unmediated sense perception of the sensible world is not possible, because perceived forms result from the combination of the sensible perception or sensible forms, and the conceptual formation of the forms in intellect, or intelligible forms, and in perception the intelligible form must precede the sensible form in order for there to be a relation between the objects of perception and reason. This most certainly makes Plotinus an "Idealist." The perceived form, the external sensation, is thus "the image of this perception of the soul," which is "a contemplation of forms alone without being affected." In order for perception of the sensible world to occur, soul must be able to operate without being affected by the sensible world. Soul then has "lordship over the living being": it controls all human experience, and from its forms come all "reasonings, and opinions and acts of intuitive intelligence...."

The undescended soul, or pure intellect, is the highest level of consciousness in mind for Plotinus, according to D. M. Hutchinson in "Apprehension of Thought in *Ennead* 4.3.30" – the *"noetic* self" (Hutchinson, 2011, p. 264). It is clear, though, that Plotinus does not see this as a level of complete consciousness, given all his references to its unconscious nature in relation to rational soul. The lowest level of consciousness involves an awareness of the body and its sensations in the physical world, though again it is clear that Plotinus would not regard this as "consciousness" either, because it is impossible to have direct knowledge of the material world. The middle level of consciousness is the *"dianoetic* self," the self-identity that derives from the imagination, which is the only actual source of consciousness or self-consciousness in thought. It is in fact the *illusion* of consciousness, as in the Cartesian "I think therefore I am," and thus a major tenet in philosophy, that Plotinus reveals.

Nature is an "image of intelligence" (*Enneads* IV.4.13) which itself has "no power of imaging" and "no grasp or consciousness of anything." The imaging faculty is solely in the province of the dianoetic self or the imagination, which "gives to the one who has the image the power to know what he has experienced": that is, consciousness. Both the image and the consciousness which reside in the imagination originate from Intellect. The soul receives what the Intellect possesses: the reception of the images and the knowledge of the images through time – unfolded and divided in a temporal duration – is what creates consciousness. The images from Intellect are coupled with the images from the sensible world in temporal duration, but neither of them on their own are sources of conscious thought. They are brought together as a totality or manifold in soul which is the source of their apprehension (*antilêpsis*) and the soul's conscious activities. According to Plotinus, "what is grasped by the intellect reaches us when it arrives at perception in its descent, for we do not know everything which happens in any part of the soul before it reaches the whole soul ..." (IV.8.8). Thus "every soul has some-thing of what is below, in the direction of the body, and what is above, in the direction of Intellect." This would be the basis of Humanism in the Renaissance, as described by Giovanni Pico della Mirandola in the *Oration on the Dignity of Man*: it is what makes the human being the most important cog in the cosmos, the ability to connect the material world of sense perception with the spiritual world of Intellect.

While the apprehension of the images that come from Intellect, or the linguistic articulation which represents them, is a type of conscious-ness, the source of the images remains unconscious to apprehension. Consciousness results from the confluence of the sensible form, the intelligible form, and the logos or linguistic articulation, what was trans-lated by A. H. Armstrong as "verbal expression," though the logos is not articulated verbally. The intelligible form is attained by imagination through the mechanisms of desire, as "when the desiring part of the soul is moved, the mental image of its object comes like a perception," reflected as if in a mirror, as it were, and "announcing and informing us of the experience, and demanding that we should follow along with it and obtain the desired object for it" (*Enneads* IV.4.17), the sensible form. Desire, or *pathos*, is responsible for making the mind subject to the conditions of the sensible world, as explained by Sara Rappe in *Reading Neoplatonism* (Rappe, 2000).

The conditions of the external world, as they affect the mind, erode the autonomy of the higher soul, compromising it as intellect descends into perception. The original condition of mind is a state of *apatheia*, which is intellect unaffected or unchanged by experience. It is neces-sary for reason to eliminate the *pathos* caused by a representation from the sensible world, as well as the representation itself, in reason's ascent to Intellect and its original state of *apatheia*. As the representation is the cause of the *pathos*, the representation must be eliminated from the apprehension of experience. An example would be Plotinus' exercise in *Enneads* V.8.9, where we are asked to form a mental picture of the visible universe and then subtract the mass, spatial relations and matter, so that the visible universe can be apprehended more clearly. In III.6.5, "the mental image (so to call it) which penetrates it," the soul, "at the part which is said to be subject to affections," the lower soul in sense percep-tion (*sunaisthêsis*), "produces the consequent affection, disturbance, and the likeness of the expected evil is coupled with the disturbance ...." Matter without form is evil; it has no connection to the good, the source of which is Intellect. As an affection caused by the mental image, "reason thought it right to do away with it altogether and not to allow it to occur in the soul," so that the soul might remain free from affections. Such purification, of the part of the soul subject to affections, is "the waking up from inappropriate images," including dream images, which create *pathos* and disturb the soul, and "not inclining much downwards and not having a mental picture of the things below."

Plotinus differentiated the role of memory in intellect from the role of memory in sense perception. In the Divided Line in the *Republic* of Plato, the sensible or visible realm (*to horāton*) consists of the sensible objects and their images. Thinking that is solely connected to the sensible realm can only consist of belief (*pistis*) and illusion (*eikasia*), which form opinion (*doxa*). The intelligible realm (*to noēton*) consists of the forms, which include the *eidos*, geometry and mathematics, and are detached from the sensible realm. Thinking in the intelligible realm can be either mathematical or discursive reasoning (*dianoia, nous logizomenos, logistikon*: to do with reason) or intelligence or dialectical reasoning (*noēsis*), which form knowledge (*epistēmē*). The images in the sensible world begin with shadows and reflections in water. Thinking in intellect based on the forms alone is based on a first principle that requires no assumption. The objects of investigation in the sensible world, which are represented as images in sense perception, are in reality "invisible except to the eye of reason" (*Republic* 510d–511a) (Plato, 1955): that is, they exist only as intelligibles.

Plato, like Plotinus, can be called an "Idealist," in that perceived forms of sensible objects are not possible except as a consequence of the corresponding intelligible forms which precede them in the process of perception. This is a function of the process of intellection. Dialectic or *noesis*, the Intellect of Plotinus, descends from the apprehension of a principle to a conclusion, basing its activity completely on the forms – the archetypal principles – in a procedure which "involves nothing in the sensible world" (511b) and is completely detached from sensible reality, as in Plotinus. *Dianoia* deals with objects in succession and division, while *noesis* involves a simultaneous cognition that is without division of objects and not subject to time.

According to Aristotle in *De memoria*, memory, like thought, requires an image. While the image, both sensible and intelligible, is not possible without the form received in perception, memory must be a function of perception: "…while memory, even memory of intelligible things, is not without an image, and the image is an attribute of the common receiving power" (450a13) (Aristotle, 2001). Consequently, memory is the possession of intellect, "but in its own right it belongs to the perceptive potency." The perceiving power (*hē koinē aesthēsis*) is seen as the power to perceive both sensible and intelligible objects. Because memory belongs to sensible perception, imagination must also belong to sensible perception. Nevertheless, the more disturbance there is in the soul from the sensible world, the less memory is able to function, suggesting that memory must be a function of higher soul or Intellect. Memory functions well when Intellect is in control of sense perceptions, so that the sense perceptions do not cause disturbances. Intellect is in control of sense perceptions when it is not affected by them, in a state of *apatheia*. Memory is not of sensible objects themselves, but of their images: memory is "an active holding of an image as a likeness of that of which it is an image..." (451a18).

While imagination is seen to belong to sense perception in *De memoria*, in the *De anima* of Aristotle imagination is clearly distinguished from sense perception. Because imagination involves judgment, "imagination is not sensation" (*De anima* 428a5) (Aristotle, 1964), and "sensation is always present but imagination is not." While "imagination seems to be some kind of movement, and not to occur apart from sensation" (428b12), "imagination cannot be either opinion in conjunction with sensation, or opinion based on sensation, or a blend of opinion and sensation" (428a26). Imagination is both connected to sense perception and disconnected from sense perception. The content of imagination, the objects of thought – "both the so-called abstractions of mathematics and all states and affections of sensible things – reside in the sensible forms" (432a6). This marks a clear distinction among Aristotle, Plato and Plotinus. For Plotinus the imagination is not dependent on sense perception and the objects of thought are not to be found in sensible things. In *Enneads* IV.7.8, "thinking cannot be comprehension through the body, or it will be the same as sense-perception."

Aristotle made it clear that imagination is a bodily function. In the *De anima*, "if this too is a kind of imagination, or at least is dependent upon imagination, even this cannot exist apart from the body" (403a8), referring to affections such as desire and sensation. For Plotinus, "it is clear that sense-perception belongs to the soul in the body and working through the body," but "it belongs to another discussion to determine whether what is to be judged must be immediately linked to the organ..." (*Enneads* IV.4.23). Sense perception and memory must be seen as two distinct entities, and "thinking cannot be comprehension through the body, or it will be the same as sense-perception" (IV.7.8). Thus "this reasoning part of the soul, which needs no bodily instrument for its reasoning... preserves its activity in purity in order that it may be able to engage in pure reasoning..." (V.1.10). It is as in Plato's

Republic – "relying on reason without any aid from the senses" (*Republic* 532a) (Plato, 1955) in the exercise of dialectic. As described by Plotinus, "we and what is ours go back to real being and ascend to that and to the first which comes from it, and we think the intelligibles..." (*Enneads* VI.5.7) (Plotinus, 1966).

According to Plotinus, memory of thoughts occurs when the contents of the thoughts are unfolded or articulated (but not verbally) and are presented to the imagination as images, as if they are reflected in a mirror in the mind's eye. The medium of the unfolding of the thoughts is the logos. The thoughts as they are prior to being unfolded are properties of Intellect and thus not accessible to conscious thought. Consciousness in thought comes about when the logos articulates the thought as an image in imagination. The logos is produced in discursive thinking and the image is produced in imagination in its connection to sense perception, so the embodied soul is instrumental in the perception and apprehension of the forms, the unitary thoughts in Intellect. The logos is usually defined as the principle of knowledge, from Heraclitus, or reasoned discourse, from Aristotle. Philo distinguished between *logos prophorikos*, the uttered word or verbal expression, and *logos endiathetos*, the word remaining within. Although Armstrong translated Plotinus' logos as *logos prophorikos*, it is clear that Plotinus meant the *logos endiathetos*, as pointed out by Hutchinson.

The *logos endiathetos* is the source of the structure of the sensible world as it is perceived, reproduced in imagination, and organized according to archetypal principles. The logos is thus the connector of the hypostases of being, at both the cosmic or world soul level and the level of the individual soul. The *logos endiathetos*, the unarticulated word, is perhaps Plotinus' "silent rational form" (III.8.6) and the "rational principle" which "must not be outside but must be united with the soul of the learner, until it finds that it is its own." Once the soul has "become akin to and disposed according to the rational principle," the logos, it "utters and propounds it," expresses it verbally. It is driven to utter the rational principle from Intellect by its *pathos* and desire, stirred by sense perception and imagination, because soul is incomplete. Soul is missing something: "it is not full, but has something wanting in relation to what comes before it"; that is, Intellect. Verbal expression in language is driven by the void at the center of being, as for Freud and Lacan, and verbal expression in language contributes to the inaccessibility of the void, the inaccessibility of Intellect to soul, or unconscious thought to conscious thought. Linguistic expression is a compensation for a lack: "but what it utters, it utters because of its deficiency...."

In Plato's *Theaetetus* (189c7–190a7), thinking is seen as an internal dialogue in the soul (Hutchinson, 2011, p. 269). This is repeated in the *Sophist* (263e) where thought (*dianoia*) and speech (*logos*) are the same except that thought is "the silent, inner dialogue that the soul has with itself..." (Plato, 1990). *Dianoia* is an inner logos, *logos endiathetos*. Discursive thought has the same predicative structure as speech, the same propositional logic. The dianoetic is the noetic descended into the material world of speech acts and sense perception, dependent upon the senses and sense objects, able to apprehend discursively in divisions and successions. In order to signify dianoetically it is necessary to "use the forms of letters which follow the order of words and propositions and imitate sounds and the enunciations of philosophical statements..." (*Enneads* V.8.6) (Plotinus, 1966). *Dianoia* is a "dividing intellect" which places objects of thought in temporal succession; the objects of thought are brought out from undivided Intellect, the intelligible universe, where they are "in repose" (V.9.9), not available to conscious thought, as if in the unconscious. Dianoetic thought has access to the reflections of the intelligibles, as "this world should in its imitation of the eternal nature resemble as closely as possible the perfect intelligible Living Creature" (*Timaeus* 39e) (Plato, 1965), in the words of Plato. Conscious thought has access to reflections of unconscious thought. According to Plotinus, while there exists "the rational forming principle of a living creature," the unconscious intelligible, there also exists "matter which receives the seminal forming principle," and "the living creature must necessarily come into being..." (*Enneads* V.9.9).

The objects of dianoetic thought and discursive reason are the *logoi*, the product of divided intellect, in the same way that the objects of noetic thought in Intellect are the archetypal forms. "As the spoken word is an imitation of that in the soul, so the word in the soul is an imitation of that in something else..." (I.2.3); the *logos prophorikos* is an imitation of the *logos endiathetos*. In modern terms, structural linguistics, the signifier would be an imitation of the signified. The spoken word, then, "is broken up into parts as compared with that in the soul, so is that in the soul as compared with that before it, which it interprets," which is Intellect. In *Enneads* V.5.1, the objects of sense perception should not be taken in their self-evidence; their existence depends on the way the sense faculties are affected, and on the judgments made about them by discursive reason. The underlying realities of that which is grasped by sense perception are not accessible to sense perception; the underlying realities are only known by Intellect, unconscious thought. The *logoi* are the products of the "rational formative principle" (III.2.2) flowing from Intellect. When the rational principles are diffuse, they occupy the soul (III.5.9). The rational principles occupy soul as foreign bodies: they are not intrinsically part of soul as they are of Intellect; therefore, they cannot be possessed by soul, or at one with soul, as they are with Intellect. The rational principles *are* Intellect, while they are mere adornments in soul.

In *Enneads* V.1.3 (Plotinus, 1966), "just as a thought in its utterance is an image of the thought in soul," the *logos prophorikos* and the *logos endiathetos*, "so soul itself is the expressed thought of Intellect, and its whole activity, and the life which it sends out to establish another reality...." But the activity which flows from Intellect into soul is something distinct from the activity of Intellect itself. Soul depends on Intellect but does not have access to its internal activity, as conscious thought does not have access to unconscious thought, only its manifestations. The *logos endiathetos* cannot be a copy of the unrevealed, enfolded and unitary Forms or rational principles in Intellect in the same way that the *logos prophorikos* is a copy of the *logos endiathetos*.

The logos represent a thought and unfolds it and makes it visible to imagination, accompanied by an image. The apprehension of the thought by the imagination is responsible for conscious thought, connected with the consciousness of sense perception, although that consciousness is deceptive, as sense perception is made possible by the underlying realities or intelligibles that form the sensible world. Conscious thoughts, "by means of sense-perception – which is a kind of intermediary when dealing with sensible things – do appear to work on the level of sense and think about sense objects" (I.4.10). Conscious thought in discursive reason depends on representations of thought in Intellect rather than the copies of the logos in the verbal expression; the relation is less direct, but also less deceptive.

Awareness, or conscious thought, "exists and is produced when intellectual activity is reflexive and when that in the life of the soul which is active in thinking is in a way projected back," as a representation formed by logos, "as happens with a mirror-reflection when there is a smooth, bright, untroubled surface," though the content of Intellect is not present in front of a mirror in lower soul to be directly reflected. Perhaps the logos is the mirror reflection of the intellectual act. If the logos forms the reflection, the reflection must occur at an angle, with the content that is reflected not visible to the reflection. The reflection is achieved when the disturbances of the physical world are overcome and *apatheia* is achieved, through the will of the subject to access the realm of the unconscious.

According to Plato in *Timaeus* 70–71 (Plato, 1965), the digestive functions of the body are purposely located at a distance from the soul (in the head) so that they would cause the least disturbance to the deliberations of the soul. Knowing that the appetites of the body, the functions of the body and sense perception governed by *pathos*, "would not understand reason or be capable of paying attention to rational argument even if it became aware of it," and "would easily fall under the spell of images and phantoms," it was necessary to put the liver far away from the head. Having a surface smooth in texture and thus reflective like a mirror, the liver could receive thoughts from the mind and reflect them "in the form of visible images, like a mirror." As in Plotinus, the mirror is a function of the body and *nous hylikos*, receiving representations from Intellect as provided by the logos. In *Republic* 510a (Plato, 1955), the images in the visible realm of the Divided Line are described as "shadows, then reflections in water and other close-grained, polished surfaces," as in a liver or a mirror; thus, Plato likened the images of sense perception to the images of imagination.

In the same way that the *logos prophorikos* is a copy of the *logos endiathetos*, expressed speech in the sensible world is a copy of dianoetic thought, which is a representation of noetic thought, so the perceived image in the sensible world as given by sense perception is a copy of the image of dianoetic thought formed in the imagination, the representation created by logos which is, as it were, reflected in a mirror. In *Enneads* IV.3.31 (Plotinus, 1966), "the images will always be double," the intelligible image of the higher soul and the perceptible image of the lower soul. The image appears as if it is a singular image because "that of the better soul is dominant," and "the image becomes one, as if a shadow followed the other and as if a little light slipped in under the greater one…." It is only possible to apprehend the presence of the more dominant intelligible form when the two parts of the soul are in harmony, body and mind; when disturbances of the body distract from the harmony of mind, the sensible image can only be apprehended on its own. But the sensible image has no possible existence independent of the intelligible image. In I.4.10, when the "mirror" which represents the content of Intellect in dianoetic thought is "broken" because of physical disturbances, then "thought and intellect operate without an image, and then intellectual activity takes place without a mind-picture." This leads to the conclusion that "intellectual activity is [normally] accompanied by a mind-picture but is not a mind-picture," and that there are many activities of which we are not conscious. Conscious thought is given by the formation of the image in dianoetic thought through the logos by the imagination. The content and activities of Intellect are always present, but it is necessary for them to be unfolded by logos and reflected by imagination in order for them to come into consciousness from unconscious thought.

It is conceivable that dianoetic thoughts can occur independently of images (Nyvlt, 2012, p. 173), but no consciousness of them would be possible, as no consciousness of objects in themselves (*principia essendi*, noumena) is possible in sense perception. Equally, no consciousness is possible of the "activity prior to awareness" in Intellect, prior to the activity of the intelligible imagination, discursive reason, and sense perception. Sense perception is always only a derivative of imagination and intelligible thinking, *nous poietikos*. The true self in intellect, the true identity of the subject, is in unconscious thought, which underlies all conscious thought. Only the function of imagination, the power to form images, which is irrational and defective, provides conscious thought with a glimpse of the presence and activities of unconscious thought. Without the images provided by imagination, the human subject would remain unconscious of itself.

As long as there is harmony between the intelligible and sensible souls, the duality of images in perception and imagination, illuminated by both the intelligible and sensible, will go unnoticed, will remain inaccessible to conscious thought. While such unconsciousness might be considered a virtue (Nyvlt, 2012, p. 171) – as it is conditioned by rational soul – the harmony also prevents intellect from knowing itself. Intellectual development requires access to Intellect, to unconscious thought, beyond imagination, which allows for conscious thought. While imagination is responsible for the consciousness of reason, as connected to sense perception, the operations of Intellect are independent of the images of *phantasia* and are thus not accessible to conscious thought. However, their presence can be known, just as the presence of the unconscious can be known, through traces in discursive reason and imagination, and gaps and scotomata therein as well. Imagination, occupying the gap between intelligible and sensible thought, belongs to neither but adapts to both – as a passive *intellectus materialis*, in the words of the Peripatetics.

Imagination can perhaps be seen as a form of *nous pathetikos*, connected to *pathos*, affections and emotions, as movement and appetite are present in imagination, and appetite is present in movement. In *Enneads* III.6.5, the mental image that penetrates the soul produces affections and disturbances. *Nous pathetikos* is a perishable, passive intellect (Aristotle, *De anima* 430a: *ho de pathêtikos nous phthartos*), subject to disintegration in time, which may be nevertheless more advanced than *dianoia*, as the term was first used by Alexander of Aphrodisias, a writer known to Plotinus (Blumenthal, 1996, p. 153). *Nous pathetikos* implies the impassioned and irrational, in contrast to *nous poietikos*, the active and creative intellect associated with noetic thought. *Nous pathetikos* is also seen in contrast to *apatheia*, the original condition of mind unaffected by the sensible world, the body and the objects of sense perception. Imagination is *pathetikos* in that it has the ability to assimilate to its objects, whether they are sensible or intelligible, between discursive reason and Intellect. *Pathê*, affections and emotions, do not occur in the soul itself, or in sense perception. In *Enneads* III.6.1 (Plotinus, 1966), "sense-perceptions are not affections but activities and judgements concerned with affections....." While the judgment belongs to the soul, affections "belong to something else," which must be the imagination, which is not a function of intelligible soul or sensible soul, but mediates between them.

In *Enneads* I.8.15, "Imagination is a stroke from something irrational from outside; and the soul is accessible to the stroke because of that in it which is not undivided." Imagination, because it is connected to the sensible forms of perception, is susceptible to the multiplicity and contradictions of matter outside the intelligible conception of it, outside of archetypal reason originating in Intellect. Sigmund Freud showed that the irrational images and sequences in dreams are derived from rational unconscious thoughts during sleep, but are transposed and rendered irrational through the mechanisms of condensation and displacement, in a process which has no intention of communicating anything, of being articulated by logos in dianoetic thought. Jacques Lacan identified the mechanisms of condensation and displacement as forms of metaphor and metonymy in tropic or rhetorical language. Rhetorical language plays a role in unconscious processes to disguise rational thoughts in the unconscious and render them irrational to the imagination; in the same way, the rational content of Intellect may be rendered irrational as it is unfolded in imagination and then perception, through the formation by the logos (which incorporates rhetorical language) of the images accompanying the rational content in the imagination.

For Plotinus, wisdom for the wise person does not require "awareness and consciousness of its presence" (I.4.9), because wisdom as the substance of Intellect "does not cease to exist in someone who is asleep or what is called unconscious," just as the thinking activity of Intellect does not cease when there is no image in the imagination to accompany it. While the substance of Intellect is active and the activities of the individual are active, in *dianoia*, imagination and sense perception, the individual can only be partially conscious of the thought in Intellect: the unconscious thought, to the extent that the individual is able to achieve *apatheia*. We are distracted by sense perception, and the irrationality of imagination, but the activities of logos in the reflection of the content of Intellect create awareness, or conscious thought through the images accompanying the noetic activity. Ascent from sense perception to Intellect is a process of purification involving the imagination. As "not everything which is in the soul is immediately perceptible, but it reaches us when it enters into perception" (V.1.12), perception involves both sensible perception and the perception of images by imagination. Conscious awareness of the activity of Intellect begins with sensible perception and develops when we "turn our power of apprehension inwards, and make it attend to what is there," as if attempting to hear a distant voice over other distracting sounds. Access to unconscious thought requires that the individual "keep the soul's power of apprehension pure and ready to hear the voices from on high."

Philip Merlan, in *Monopsychism Mysticism Metaconsciousness*, asserted that the source of Plotinus' theory of the unconscious, Aristotle's proposition in the *De anima* that mind "does not think intermittently" (430a10–25) (Aristotle, 1964), is not a reference to human thinking, but rather divine thinking – completely separate from the human mind – and thus should not be taken as a source for Plotinus' theories. This proposition appears to be contradicted in the text of the *De anima*: when mind is isolated, "it is its true self and nothing more, and this alone is immortal and everlasting." This suggests the human mind, which when isolated from the body, does not think intermittently. Merlan himself said that "productive intelligence as treated in *De anima* is supposed to be human intelligence exclusively..." (p. 49) (Merlan, 1963), and it is the productive intelligence that thinks incessantly according to Aristotle. The author nevertheless recognized that it is possible to interpret in Plotinus that "the productive intelligence indeed operates in every man incessantly" (p. 50), and the author recognized the importance of unconscious thought in Plotinus: "it is obvious how important the concept of the unconscious is within the framework of the system of Plotinus" (p. 53).

But then the author asserted that the intelligence which does not think intermittently in Plotinus, the intelligence of Intellect, "cannot be described as an unconscious, because it is eminently *rational*" (p. 83), given that Freud and Jung understood the unconscious as the repository of *irrational* forces. But this is also incorrect: for Freud, in *The Interpretation of Dreams*, it is not the unconscious which is irrational, but rather the mechanisms of "dream work" which transpose dream thoughts into dream images. These irrational mechanisms are the image-making power or the imagination, exactly as in Plotinus. The operative logos for Freud in the formation of dream images is tropic language, condensation and displacement as metaphor and metonymy, which results in irrational sequences that must be deciphered in order to discover the rational unconscious that is behind the images. Dreams, like natural forms, may appear to be irrational to conscious thought as a result of the mechanisms of condensation and displacement, because of the underlying intelligible reality that is not accessible to discursive reason and sense perception. The presence of the irrational within rational thought might suggest the unconscious, but it is not the unconscious itself.

The content of the memory of the dream was labeled by Freud the *manifest content* of the dream – the dream's images, and the product of the conceptual analysis of the dream is labeled the *latent content* – the dream's thoughts. Freud saw unconscious thought as a mimesis of rational, conscious thought. As Freud described in *The Interpretation of Dreams* (p. 116), the mechanism of the transposition from dream thoughts to dream images is labeled imagination, and the "mental activity which may be described as 'imagination'" is "liberated from the domination of reason," as in Plotinus, "and from any moderating control" (Freud, 1965). Dream imagination "makes use of recent waking memories for its building material," in mimesis and repetition, and "it erects them into structures bearing not the remotest resemblance to those of waking life." Dream imagination is "without the power of conceptual speech" and has "no concepts to exercise an attenuating influence," thus being "obliged to paint what it has to say pictorially."

Dreams have "no means at their disposal for representing these logical relations between the dream-thoughts" (p. 347), rational unconscious thought, or for representing logical relations between conscious thoughts, the relations created by syntactical rules. It is the function of the imagination, the formation of dream images, that is irrational. Thinking does not occur in the dreams themselves. Diachronic sequences, as they are understood in conscious reason, may be compressed into synchronic events or images, or they may be fragmented, or reversed, in condensation and displacement. Condensation and displacement, the mechanisms of imagination, are responsible for the fact that dream images do not correspond to conscious reason, and cause the dream to be seen as a distortion of reason, while the dream has no intention of communicating anything.

Merlan acceded to the presence of an intelligence which does not think intermittently within the human mind, and thus can be interpreted as unconscious thought: the "higher intelligence, though it transcends our intelligence is in some way present and (incessantly) active in us, though we are not conscious of its presence or activity" (Merlan, 1963, p. 84). Merlan suggested the term "metaconscious," a collective higher consciousness, as a substitute for "unconscious" in that we become united with Intellect, but the fact is that we do not become united with Intellect in the thought of Plotinus: we can only apprehend Intellect indirectly, through the imagination, the unfolding of *noesis* by logos into intelligible images, according to Plotinus. Merlan stated that a union with Intellect takes place in an ecstatic, irrational experience, a concept which does not exist in Plotinus; for Plotinus, the irrational is a quality of everything *but* Intellect, everything that is connected to the sensible world and corrupted by it.

In Plotinus the mental images are the affections which cause disturbances in the soul. A purification of the soul would involve a scenario where "if someone who wanted to take away the mental pictures seen in dreams were to bring the soul which was picturing them to wakefulness" (*Enneads* III.6.5), disconnecting it from physical sensations, the mechanisms of imagination (Hendrix, 2004). Intelligible reality must be free from the affections that manifest it in the sensible world. It must be "eternal and always the same, and unreceptive of anything, and nothing must come into it…" (*Enneads*, III.6.6). It is possible to apprehend intelligible reality as the product of an intellectual exercise. For example, Plotinus said "Often I have woken up out of the body to my self and have entered into myself, going out from all other things…setting myself above all else in the realm of Intellect" (IV.8.1). The image of Intellect in soul preserves "something of its light" (V.3.9), by which the soul "and any other soul of the same kind can see it by itself": that is, Intellect. Seeing in the intelligible world is not through an external medium of light, because Intellect is light itself, illuminating the realities of the sensible world.

The light in the soul, a trace of the light above, is united with the light of Intellect and allows soul to see Intellect within itself. Again, the illumination of the soul is the product of an intellectual exercise, and the will of the individual. Soul (discursive reason) is led to Intellect (unconscious thought), and seeks "a trace of the life of Intellect" (V.3.8), because soul sees itself as an image of Intellect, but Intellect itself is "the first light shining primarily for itself and an outshining upon itself, at once illuminating and illuminated," not particularly concerned with the soul or the sensible world below.

Art and unconscious thought

According to Plotinus, the imagination is responsible for the apprehension of the activity of Intellect, unconscious thought. If creativity in the arts involves an exercise of the imagination, the image-making power that links sense perception to noetic thought and the *nous poietikos*, the poetic or creative intellect, then the arts exercise the apprehension of intellectual activity and unconscious thought. Creative expression in art is a "royal road" to the unconscious, to use Freud's phrase. According to John Dillon in "Plotinus and the Transcendental Imagination" (Dillon, 1986), Plotinus' conception of the imagination led to the formulation of the imagination as a basis of artistic creativity.

Imagination operates on several different levels: it produces images in sense perception, it synthesizes images in dianoetic thought, and it produces images in correspondence with the articulation through logos of noetic thought. In *Enneads* III.6.4 (Plotinus, 1966), "the mental picture is in the soul, both the first one, which we call opinion," the intelligible form in *nous hylikos*, "and that which derives from it, which is no longer opinion, but an obscure quasi-opinion and an uncriticised mental picture," the sensible form in perception, "like the activity inherent in what is called nature in so far as it produces individual things ... without a mental image," unintelligible matter and the particulars thereof prior to the apperception of it. The spiritual exercises described in *Enneads* V.8.9 or VI.4.7 are types of intellection rooted in the creative use of the imagination. The "shining imagination of a sphere" of the visible universe in the soul can be stripped of its body and mass; the corporeal bulk of a hand can be taken away while its power can remain.

The ascent from the apprehension of physical beauty to the comprehension of the idea of beauty in Plato's *Symposium* is another example of such a spiritual exercise (Hendrix, 2005). As Diotima says, a person, like "someone using a staircase" (*Symposium* 211c) (Plato, 1999), should ascend "from one to two and from two to all beautiful bodies," then "from beautiful bodies to beautiful practices, and from practices to beautiful forms of learning" and knowledge. The knowledge of beauty is beauty itself, as knowledge in Intellect is equivalent to its object of knowledge. Beauty in Intellect is "absolute, pure, unmixed," uncontaminated by imagination, *dianoia* or sense perception. Such apprehension would allow the individual to "give birth not just to images of virtue ... but to true virtue" (212a). In the *Enneads*, in such apprehension "the soul by a kind of delight and intense concentration on the vision and by the passion of its gazing generates something from itself which is worthy of itself and of the vision" (*Enneads* III.5.3) (Plotinus, 1966), with the help of imagination.

In *Enneads* V.8.1, "the arts do not simply imitate what they see, but they run back up to the forming principles from which nature derives ...." The forming principles of nature are the intelligible forms perceived by the imagination, as derived from Intellect. It is impossible to apprehend the forming principles in conscious perception or *dianoia*; it is necessary to apprehend the unconscious thoughts which are the forming principles of noetic thought in Intellect, through the execution of the spiritual or intellectual exercises as described above. Plotinus imagined an art which is a product of noetic thought as made possible by the imagination, in contrast to an art which is a product of sense perception and discursive reason. The forming principles possess true beauty, as described by Diotima, and thus "they make up what is defective in things," which includes the imagination itself. The "forming principle which is not in matter but in the maker, the first immaterial one" (V.8.2), is the true beauty. The mass is beautiful because it follows the beauty in Intellect, as the light of the sensible form follows the light of the intelligible form. Beauty is in the eye of the beholder: the beauty of the perceived object is a shadow of the beauty in the soul of the individual.

There is thus "in nature a rational forming principle which is the archetype of the beauty in body" (V.8.3), and "the rational principle in soul is more beautiful than that in nature and is also the source of that in nature." The primary principle of beauty is Intellect, from which all images should be taken, as facilitated by imagination. Forms of art, like the forms of nature, are the product of Intellect. Producing a work of art, in the exercise of the intellect and the imagination, reproduces the formation of forms in nature as they are perceived and understood. The production of a work of art is an intellectual or spiritual exercise of the imagination which allows apprehension of Intellect and *noesis* in *nous poietikos*, unconscious thought. A work of art is "in the intelligible world" (V.9.10) if it "starts from the proportions of [individual] living things and goes on from there to consider the proportions of living things in general ... " (V.9.11), as in the ascent in the *Symposium*. A work of art cannot be traced back to the intelligible world if it is merely composed of elements of the sensible world and is modeled on sense perception. The work of art in the intelligible world would be considered *natura naturans*, "nurturing nature," while a work of art copying the forms of nature would be considered *natura naturata*. A work of art that considers the idea of proportion takes part in the power of the higher world. Architecture, since it makes use of proportions, takes its principles from the intelligible, such as geometry, but cannot be completely in the intelligible since it is engaged in "what is perceived by the senses" in physical and functional requirements.

Beauty is the product of the soul which "when it is purified becomes form and formative power, altogether bodiless and intellectual ... " (I.6.6):

the beauty which is a product of the purified soul informs the beauty of the sensible world. Intellect is the beauty of soul, defining soul in its reality. Originary beauty, like the forming principles, is unconscious, inaccessible to discursive reason and sense perception in their conscious apprehension. The beautiful soul makes bodies beautiful, and every other kind of entity "as far as they are capable of participation." In *Enneads* I.6.8, another intellectual exercise is proposed, modeled on the *Symposium*. We must not pursue beauty in bodies or bodily splendors; "we must know that they are images, traces, shadows," the shadows on the wall in the Allegory of the Cave, "and hurry away to that which they image," the forming principles in the intelligible. To cling to the beauty of bodies would be to "sink down into the dark depths where intellect has no delight...." The soul must thus be trained, as in the *Symposium*, "to look at beautiful ways of life: then at beautiful works" (*Enneads* I.6.9), not works of art but rather works of virtue, although the work of virtue may be in the work of art, "then look at the souls of the people who produce the beautiful works." Only beauty in soul can perceive beauty in soul, as an intelligible forming principle; thus, it is necessary to look inward and treat your soul as a work of art, sculpting it according to the rational forming principles of the intelligible in Intellect, until "the divine glory of virtue shines out on you...." When this is accomplished, the soul is purified, "not measured by dimensions, or bounded by shape... but everywhere unmeasured...." The object of vision becomes vision itself, intelligible vision; the object of judgment becomes judgment itself, the archetypal idea in Intellect; the object of the beautiful form is beauty itself.

Apprehension of intelligible beauty in Intellect or unconscious thought, and the ascension to Intellect from sense perception and *dianoia*, leads to apprehension of true beauty in the sensible world: "How could there be anyone skilled in geometry and numbers who will not be pleased when he sees right relation, proportion and order with his eyes?" (II.9.16). Perception of the representation of beauty in the sensible world facilitates apprehension of Intellect in imagination, through the *pathos* or disturbance, from which love arises. Sense perception perceives forms in bodies organizing the shapeless matter of which bodies are composed; sense perception, or apperception, then "gathers into one that which appears dispersed and brings it back and takes it in, now without parts, to the soul's interior" (I.6.3), representing in imagination that which is in tune with soul, the forming principle.

The image formed by imagination based on sense perception is accorded to the image formed in imagination by logos from the forming principle. An architect, for example, can "declare the house beautiful by fitting it to the form of house within him," the intelligible form of the house based on the geometry, mathematics and proportions of the forming principle in noetic thought. An intellectual exercise is necessary to overcome the hindrance of the body in sense perception of the apprehension of the higher soul: "they should have stripped off this bodily nature in their thought and seen what remained" (II.9.17), which was "an intelligible sphere embracing the form imposed upon the universe," souls without bodies which organize the intelligible pattern in the sensible world which is equal to the "partlessness of its archetype." The beauty of the forming principle in soul, in unconscious thought, is the source and archetype of beauty in nature, and is necessarily a higher form of beauty (V.8.3).

The philosophy of Plotinus is rich in concepts that suggest unconscious thought, as has been noted by a number of scholars. Plotinian philosophy laid an important groundwork for the philosophy of intellect of the Peripatetics, in a combination of Plato and Aristotle. This philosophical position persisted as a dominant way of thinking until the Renaissance, although the last philosopher to elaborate a system suggestive of unconscious thought in the peripatetic tradition was Robert Grosseteste, a Scholastic who anticipated the Great Synthesis of Albertus Magnus and Thomas Aquinas by synthesizing Aristotelian ideas with Catholic theology, producing a unique alternative way of conceiving unconscious thought. As the classical tradition ceased to be dominant, modern philosophy began with figures such as Leibniz and Kant, who developed a different epistemological framework that led directly to the psychoanalytic concepts of unconscious thought. Many of the tenets of the modern tradition can nevertheless be found in the classical tradition.

Plotinus' interest in the unconscious, as we call it, was for the benefit of the growth and development of the individual. With the Freudian science of psychoanalysis in the twentieth century, the concept of the unconscious has taken on different meanings, as the source of conflict and discord in conscious thought and activity, and as the source of cures and solutions for that conflict and discord. Psychoanalysts have turned the unconscious into a storehouse of memories and experiences, and the unconscious is no longer seen as a purer form of thought that can be accessed by each individual in order to grow and develop in thought and action, as Plotinus clearly intended it to be. Perhaps a return to the concept of the unconscious in Plotinus could add a great deal to the practice of psychoanalysis.

2
The Peripatetics and Unconscious Thought

There is much Neoplatonic content in the writings of the Peripatetics, the commentators on Aristotle. As in Aristotle's *De anima* and the *Enneads* of Plotinus, a concept of what we would call unconscious thought played a role in the philosophy of intellect. Through the writings of Alexander of Aphrodisias, Themistius, Abu Nasr Alfarabi, and Avicenna (Ibn Sīnā), this concept developed from the classical to the medieval traditions and laid the groundwork for developments in modern philosophy and psychoanalysis. Subsequent chapters also analyze the thought of Averroes (Ibn Rushd) and Robert Grosseteste.

Alexander of Aphrodisias

Alexander of Aphrodisias (fl. c. 198–209) was born somewhere around 150, in Aphrodisia on the Aegean Sea. He began his career in Alexandria during the reign of Septimius Severus, was appointed to the peripatetic chair at the Lyceum in Athens in 198, a post established by Marcus Aurelius, wrote a commentary on Aristotle's *De anima*, and died in 211. According to Porphyry, Alexander was an authority read in the seminars of Plotinus in Rome. He was the earliest philosopher who saw the active intellect implied in Book III of Aristotle's *De anima* as transcendent in relation to the material intellect. He connected the active intellect with the incorporeal and eternal cause of the universe described by Aristotle in Book XII of the *Metaphysics*. Plotinus would make a similar connection, between the One as First Cause and Intellect, in which it participates (Hendrix, 2010).

In Aristotle's *De anima* 3.7, the human intellect thinks the form or *eidos*, and processes it conceptually, as an image which must be imprinted in the imaginative faculty. In 3.4, the sensible object is related to sense perception as the form of the object is related to intellect: the intelligible form, which is related to the sensible form, is imprinted in the imagination through sense perception. Thus the intellect is to what is intelligible as sense perception is to what is perceptible. The intellect is receptive of the form as intelligible: it must think the form in order to perceive it. As sensible form, the objects of the senses are only fragmented and disconnected: they make no sense in relation to each other, or to the perceiving subject. It is only when the form is perceived as an intelligible, or as thought by intellect, that the form in the sensible world might be understandable or participate in a congruent whole of experience.

In Aristotle's *De anima* 3.5, knowledge is identical with its object: the object only exists because it is known, or thought, to be intelligible. Intellect is identical with the thought it thinks, and the thought it thinks is identical with the object that it perceives. The relation between intellect and thought and thought and object is not accessible to discursive thought, or *dianoia*; an understanding of the relation requires *nous*, intuitive or "unconscious" thought. In *De anima* 3.4, although the intellect receives a form as an imprint in sensation and becomes identical in thought with the form, the intellect is not affected or altered in any way by the form or the sense object connected with it. Sense perception is also not affected or altered by the sense objects which it perceives, but intellect is free of the affection and alteration to a higher degree than sense perception. Sense perception is more subject to variation, alteration, and deception, or misconstruction, or fragmentation and disconnection, because it is connected to the corporeal. As discursive reason or *dianoia* is connected to sense perception and the corporeal, it is also more subject to those shortcomings, while intellect or *nous* is not connected to sense perception or the corporeal, and is free from the limitations and affectations.

In *De anima* 3.5, Aristotle compared the "active" intellect to light, because light makes potential colors actual. Likewise, the active intellect might lead the potential, material intellect to actuality, or the sensible form to the intelligible form, in the images presented by the imaginative faculty. The active intellect would thus lead *dianoia* to *nous*, the corporeal intellect to the incorporeal intellect. The potential, material intellect becomes actual when it can see the intelligible, because it is illuminated by the active intellect, in the same way that light illuminates colors. This is suggested in Plato's *Republic*, wherein "philosophers have the capacity to grasp the eternal and immutable," and those without such a capacity "are lost in multiplicity and change" (484b) (Plato, 1955). The active intellect is seen as eternal and immutable, and is accessible to discursive reason only sporadically and ephemerally, depending on the extent to which the capacities of intellect are developed.

In his commentary on Aristotle's *De anima*, Alexander of Aphrodisias described matter as a potential receptor of things which are generated in it by an agent. Intellect is capable of distinguishing between matter and agent, between matter as potential and matter as actual in intellection. Thus, intellect must be seen as consisting of both a material and active element. The active intellect is seen as the cause of the *"habitus"* of the material intellect (Alexander, *De anima* 88) (Alexander of Aphrodisias, 1979), its habit or appearance, form or perfection (85) (Davidson, 1992, p. 20). Through the cause of active intellect, the material intellect develops from the potential intellect "through instruction and habituation," to varying degrees, depending on the individual. The *habitus* develops in the material intellect "from its activity in apprehending the universal and in separating forms from their matter" (*De anima* 85), in other words, from its dianoetic process of the exercising of abstraction and conceptualization, in combination with the extent to which it is illuminated by active intellect in order to see itself from outside itself in its mechanisms: that is, to have consciousness, and to understand the extent to which its mechanisms are manipulated and determined by the processes of perception in relation to intellect, and the unconscious processes of active intellect. The development of the *habitus* in material intellect requires the element of self-consciousness in thought.

A third intellect, productive intellect, operates through material intellect in order to make material or potential intellect actual by "producing a state where thought is possessed," as Alexander explained in his *De intellectu* (1990, 107), which was written between 198 and 209 and translated into Latin by Gerard of Cremona. The productive intellect corresponds to that which Aristotle described as "the cause or agent which makes all things" (Aristotle, *De anima* 3.5.430a12, 1952a). According to Aristotle, the intellect is passive in that it becomes all things, and active in that it makes all things. In that thought is possessed, for Alexander productive intellect "is that which is in its own nature an object of thought and is such in actuality ... " (*De intellectu* 107). In order to be in actuality, thought must have itself as an object of its own activity, that is, be self-conscious.

The thought which is an object of thought is immaterial, or unconscious, while the thought of which immaterial thought is an object is material. In the same way, in the *De intellectu*, the "enmattered forms that are potentially objects of thought" become objects of thought – immaterial, through intellect, as intellect separates them from their matter just as it separates itself from its matter, and in this way the enmattered forms become actual just as thought becomes actual because the enmattered form, as an object of thought, is identical to thought itself: "intellect in actuality is nothing other than the form that is thought of" (108), the intelligible form of the object, which is the object as the immaterial object of thought. Knowledge, then, "in actuality is identical with the actual object of knowledge."

Thus "perception in actuality is identical with the actual object of perception," because the act of perception requires the identification of the sensible form of the object with the intelligible form of the object: the sensible object or enmattered form is actualized by intellect. The sensible object only exists insofar as an idea of it exists, which is the result of the influence of active intellect on material intellect, through productive intellect. Thus intellect is "in actuality identical with the actual object of thought and the actual object of thought identical with the actual intellect." Active intellect, as both intellect in actuality and object of thought, is "the cause of the material intellect's separating, imitating and thinking with reference to such a form," the enmattered form made actual as object of thought in discursive, conscious reason. Active intellect is the cause of the mechanisms of discursive and dialectical reasoning on the part of material intellect as productive intellect. The functions of discursive reason are subject to active intellect as they are subject to the formation of the intelligible.

The productive intellect is "called from without," and "comes to exist in us from outside," because it is immaterial, and because it is itself an object of thought, as thinking "occurs through the reception of form," intelligible form, in perception. Actualized thought is able to separate the sensible object as enmattered form and the idea of the object as intelligible form, as it separates the mechanisms of discursive reason in material intellect from the role of the intelligible in perception. Because of this, there must be something at work in thought, in the activity of intellect, for which "what it is to be intellect does not lie in its being thought by us," that is, unconscious thought.

Material intellect, in discursive reason, does not think objects of thought; rather, it thinks objects of perception, which are only potentially objects of thought. The object of perception, the sensible form, becomes an object of thought, the intelligible form, "by the agency of the intellect" (110), productive intellect as an agency of active intellect. The activity of intellect is to "separate and abstract by its own power objects of perception that are such in actuality" from the sensible object which accompanies the object of perception, and to define the object of perception as such. The activity of intellect is caused by productive intellect, which makes potential intellect capable of being active, capable of thinking, capable of understanding forms in perception. Active intellect does not produce intellect of itself, but completes intellect which already exists. It enables potential intellect to develop and come to completion, without being affected, or "coming into existence through something else" (111). When potential intellect is developed and completed, it is capable of independently thinking objects of thought.

In the *De anima* of Alexander, the *habitus* in material intellect develops according to the ability to apprehend the universal in abstraction and to separate forms from matter, to know the sensible form for what it is. The apprehension of the universal requires the ability to separate form from matter. The acquiring of the *habitus* begins with the perception of sensible objects, which develops into an intellectual perception or vision in the form of a "concept"; thus, the concept is a product of the experience of mind in relation to the sensible world. Universals are first intuited by material intellect in relation to the sensible objects which are perceived; then, as the *habitus* of the material intellect develops it is able to intuit universals without any connection to sensible objects, and at that point it becomes pure intellect. While material intellect is passive in relation to the sensible objects in perception, intellect in *habitus* is active in relation to the concepts which it forms. This can be seen in the fact that different sensible objects are perceived in different levels of clarity and intensity, while intelligible concepts have no variation in relation to clarity or intensity.

Because the intellect in *habitus* can apprehend the intelligible form in independent intellectual activity, and the intelligible form is identical to the act of the intellect in *habitus*, the intellect in *habitus* has the ability to "know itself" (Alexander, *De anima* 86), to be self-conscious. The intellect in *habitus* has the ability to know itself habitually in the same way that it can know the intelligible form habitually. The intellect becomes the object in its act of knowing. The apprehension of the intelligible form is the product of a cognitive act on the part of the material intellect in *habitus*, and the apprehension is a result of the identity between the intellect itself and the object which it knows, the self-consciousness, and not knowledge of the actual object, which is only *"per accidens."* Following Aristotle, the intelligible is a product of sense knowledge, and not something given to intellect from without as an archetype.

Prior to the act of knowing on the part of the material intellect in *habitus*, "the knowing faculty and the thing known stand apart," separate and unconnected. The individual is not conscious of the relationship between intellect and sensible objects as they are perceived; reality is structured in unconscious thought. When the *habitus* is actualized, the distinction between sensible object and the thought of it dissolves. The sensible object no longer has a relation to the intelligible thought, because they can be seen to be identical, as in a double lighting. The sensible object is no longer seen as matter, but as *eidos*, incorporeal and intelligible. Sensation is only capable of perceiving objects as matter, as particular existents; thus, sensation is not capable of sensing itself in the way that intellect is capable of knowing itself. The perception of the sensible object and the sensible object itself remain separate in sensation, because sensation on its own cannot discern the relation between matter and form. This is because the sense faculty cannot receive a form in the way that matter receives a form. The sense faculty is only capable of perceiving a form as it has already been received by matter, as indistinguishable from matter. The composite of form and matter can only be perceived in sensation as a particular existent, not as a universal quiddity or intelligible.

Intellect, material intellect in *habitus*, receives the form of the thing, both sensible and intelligible, as if imprinted on a writing tablet, and is able to see the sensible object as matter in relation to *eidos*, particularly in relation to the universal. In intellection, or the development of concept, intellect is able to see the relation between the particulars themselves, in discursive reason, and is able to distinguish the particulars in their interrelationships from what it is that they have in common, their quiddity or essence, which allows them to be seen to participate in a universal. Then, when intellect is able to see the form or *eidos*, which is a universal, in relation to the matter, as a particular itself in relation to other forms, then the form can be understood as distinct from the matter, as incorporeal.

The active intellect is the productive intellect, according to Alexander, in contrast to the material intellect – or the material intellect in *habitus*, in a developmental state. In the *De anima* (3.5.430a14–15) (Aristotle, 1952a), Aristotle distinguished between the quality of mind which is "what it is by virtue of becoming all things," and the quality "which is what it is by virtue of making all things," the making of the actual from the potential. The productive intellect is independent from matter, and is the cause of the existence of the sensible object as form or *eidos*. That which is most purely intelligible is the cause or producer of all objects of knowledge. The production of an intelligible from a sensible object requires an unconscious, intelligible cause, which is prior to the sensible object. The productive intellect is impassible and unmixed: it has none of the qualities of material existence, of the relations between particulars; the passive recipient of its action is substrate matter, that which is subject to change and affect. The productive intellect is thus incorruptible, not subject to the change and affect of which it is the cause. Singular sensible objects are cognized by productive intellect in singular acts, not because of the relation between particulars in productive intellect, but because of the role of discursive reason in material intellect, before the intelligible form has been separated from the material substrate in intellect in *habitus*.

In Plotinus' *Enneads*, when the fragmented and variable objects of perception "reach the ruling principle they will become like partless thoughts..." (IV.7.6) (Plotinus, 1966). They are organized in a conceptual process in material intellect in *habitus* by productive intellect, in Alexander's terms. The perception of forms in matter is determined by the self-consciousness of reason. In *Enneads* I.1.7, "soul's power of sense perception need not be perception of sense-objects, but rather it must be receptive of the impressions produced by sensation on the living being," which are "already intelligible entities," produced in unconscious thought. The discerning of the impression printed upon the intellect by sensation is then the function of discursive reason: Alexander's material intellect in *habitus*. Since the sensual impressions, or mnemic residues, in perception are copies and derivatives of intelligible forms, perception itself is a copy and derivative of reason. Thought in Plotinus is composed of mnemic residues of perceived objects, what Plotinus calls "imprints" in "recollections" in *Enneads* V.3.2. Our thoughts in discursive reason are composed of the relations between the particulars of the multiple and fragmented images of perception reconstructed as mnemic residues in memory: "the reasoning power in soul makes its judgment, derived from the mental images present to it which come from sense perception, but combining and dividing them...."

In *Enneads* IV.7.6, sense perceptions merge together in the subject like "lines coming together from the circumference of the circle," from multiplicity to unity, subject to the ruling principle: that is, Alexander's productive intellect. In reality, sense objects are variable and differentiated in terms of size and location as particulars; they are multiple and fragmented, and it is only the reason of the subject, the material intellect in *habitus* as developed by active intellect as productive intellect, which allows them to be apprehended as whole and congruent as intelligibles. In Plotinus, once the diverse and multiple sense objects have been transformed into a whole by apprehension in sense perception, through the self-consciousness of reason, they cannot return to their original state. Apprehension caused by active intellect permanently transforms sensual reality in conformance with the principles of material intellect in *habitus*.

Similarly, according to Alexander, "at the moment when [material] intellect comprehends this supreme [active] intellect in its act of intellective vision – when, I mean, it is actually knowing it – it becomes in some way that supreme intellect" (Alexander, *De anima* 89), and it would be impossible for objects to return to their original state in sense perception, where the object and the form, the sensible and the intelligible forms, are undifferentiated, only perceived as multiple particulars, and only cognized as such in material intellect. In the same way, once material intellect knows that it knows the perceived sensible objects as multiple particulars, it can apprehend them as intelligibles taking part in universals, and cannot return to the limited form of knowledge according to which it operated previously. At that point it is apparent to material intellect that "there exists no intellect at all with respect to material forms unless they are being actually cognized," unconsciously, "because their entire reality as intelligible objects consists in their being the objects of a present cognitive act," in contrast to their previous identity as singular sensible objects, as multiple and fragmented particulars.

As with Aristotle, the universal and intelligible are potentially present in the sensible particular, but they are only actual when they are known and apprehended by material intellect in *habitus*. At the same time, material intellect in *habitus* is only actual when it apprehends the intelligible in relation to the sense object. If the material intellect in *habitus* did not apprehend the intelligible in relation to the sense object, the sense object would not exist, and material intellect would not know itself. For Alexander "the objects of mathematical thinking," and forms that result from abstraction in general in discursive thought, are subject to the same conditions as material forms in sense perception: corruption, inconsistency, lack of clarity, fragmentation.

Thus, for Alexander material intellect is corruptible, while intelligibles continue to exist whether or not they are presently cognized. The material intellect perishes as the soul perishes in its attachment to the corporeal. If the soul goes out of existence, then the capacity for discursive reason is exhausted, as is the *habitus* for material intellect, and the sensible object, if apprehended in complicity with matter, is destructible. The imperishable intellect – active intellect – comes from outside, but the intelligibles which the active intellect allows the material intellect in *habitus* to understand, are only the products of cognition. The intelligible is thus not fully corporeal and not fully incorporeal, but requires the participation of both sensible perception and active intellect. The material intellect apprehends the intelligible by conforming itself to the intelligible, and it is through the apprehension of the intelligible that potential, material intellect becomes actual intellect. The soul has the potential to be both corporeal and incorporeal.

There are thus three intellects: material, in *habitus*, and productive. Matter is defined as the substrate which can become a particular being through the presence of a form, as potential intellect can become actual intellect through the presence of an intelligible. According to Aristotle in the *Metaphysica*, the substratum of matter "is that of which everything else is predicated, while it is itself not predicated of anything else" (7.3.1028b36) (Aristotle, 1952b), meaning that matter can be seen as participating in anything which can be affirmed as a quality, but matter itself cannot be affirmed as a quality. Matter can be seen as neither a quality nor a particular (7.3.1029a20–21); it is a vocabulary element of neither the apprehension of the intelligible nor discursive thought. Matter can only be seen as a potentiality, and anything which can be described as material is so only as potentiality. Material intellect is thus potential intellect, and not an actual intellect. The material intellect has the potential to become actual intellect to the extent to which "existents are possible objects of knowledge" (Alexander, *De anima* 106) (Alexander of Aphrodisias, 1979). The faculty in material intellect which can apprehend an intelligible cannot be an intelligible itself, because then its own intelligible form would appear and interfere with the grasping of the intelligible. The faculty of intellect to know intelligibles can only be a potentiality, able to conform to the intelligible from without, in the same way that matter can only be a potentiality able to conform to the form of an object as it is perceived.

Alexander compared the second intellect, the material intellect in *habitus*, which is capable of apprehending intelligibles, to artisans who can perform a task from their own resources through an acquired mastery of the craft. Intellect in *habitus* is acquired through practice and experience, in discursive reason and intellection, to the point that the reason is not entirely conscious or deliberate, but at times intuitive or automatic, unconscious, as it participates in intellect; it is also able to see itself in practice, become self-conscious, as the artisans are advanced enough to be able to observe themselves as they work. They are able to recognize the framework within which their developed skills are operating, as material intellect is able to see from outside the relation between form and matter in a sensible object, the framework within which sense perception operates. Material intellect is compared to the apprentice who, as yet, only has the aptitude for acquiring the skill necessary to perform a task.

The third intellect, the productive intellect, leads the material intellect to actual intellect as intellect in *habitus*, in the same way that light makes potentially visible colors actually visible. The productive intellect is "the intelligible in act" (Alexander, *De anima* 107), which produces the "activity of knowing" in material intellect, the self-consciousness on the part of reason. The productive intellect is not the intelligible itself, but actualizes the intelligible, by developing the *habitus* of the material intellect. The intelligible, in turn, is an intellect, because it is incorporeal. The intelligible is the form which has been separated from matter in the imprint of the sensible object in sense perception, so the intelligible can also be called "intellect in act," and is itself intellect. The form of the sensible object can only become an intelligible and an intellect "when it is actually being cognized," by material intellect in *habitus*; otherwise, it is only potentially intelligible. The intelligible is thus the product of material intellect in sense perception, and at the same time of something from without, which is the active intellect.

In Alexander's *De anima*, "there must necessarily exist an intellect that, because it is in act, can function as active agent to make intellect, heretofore only potential, capable of acting – that is, of thinking. But such precisely is the intellect that enters…from outside" (110). Though Alexander does not elaborate on how that might occur, except to say that it is the result of prior activity, unconscious as it were, of an essential property. The metaphor of fire is invoked to suggest that active intellect is some kind of natural force that is capable of transforming while it is being acted upon. The active intellect transforms sensible objects into intelligible objects by a quality that only exists in active intellect itself, the intelligible, in the same way that fire can ignite and burn a material object by a quality that only exists in fire, but transforms the material object into fire. The active intellect "makes intelligible things that, as they exist, are not actually intelligible. There does not in fact exist any intelligible other than the subsistent intellect that is in act" (Alexander, *De anima* 111). The intelligible only exists because of intellect, and only exists at the moment of intellection, "when the cognitive activity is going on."

In the *De intellectu* of Alexander, the active intellect produces intellectual thinking and leads the material intellect to actuality. The active intellect, in contrast to the material intellect, is intelligible, as it is incorporeal. Alexander follows Aristotle's suggestion in describing active intellect as analogous to light (*De intellectu* 107), as light makes potentially visible colors actual. The active intellect therefore illuminates potential objects of intellect, the sensible forms, and transforms them to actual objects of intellect, the intelligible forms. Again, the active intellect illuminates the potential intellect by creating a *habitus* for intellective thought, by putting material intellect in the particular state in which it can see the intelligibles of the active intellect, which are eternal and immutable.

The active intellect allows the material intellect to abstract and conceive material form, and it is an acquired intellect from without, from outside the material intellect; it is not an inherent part of material intellect, the capacity of intellect on its own (*De intellectu* 108). In that active intellect is to material intellect as sense perception is to the material form, each productive relation must contain three elements: that which is affected, the activity of being affected, and something generated from the affection. Material intellect is affected, as is the sense faculty, and both are tied to corporeal matter. The active intellect from without acts on material intellect, bringing it to actuality, making it capable of thinking, in the same way that a form is made perceptible in sense perception as intelligible. Intellection is generated from the interaction of active and material intellect in the same way that perception is generated from the senses.

The human material intellect, according to Alexander in *De intellectu* 110, is both passive and active, in the same way that fire is both passive and active. As active, fire destroys matter, and as passive fire feeds on matter, and is passively affected. The material intellect is active when it separates forms, when it exercises its discursive and dialectical functions, and it is passive when it takes hold of the form, when the form is given to it as the intelligible by active intellect. The material intellect acts both independently of its own corporeal functions, and as assisted by the active intellect. The active intellect assists the material intellect as light assists the process of vision, perfecting the object of thought and establishing the *habitus* for material intellect to operate. As the object of thought is perfected in material intellect as the intelligible, the active intellect becomes identical to the object of thought in material intellect, in the same way that light becomes identical to the object of sight in sense perception. The object of sight in vision is not distinguished from the sensible form or the intelligible form by material intellect; material intellect is not conscious of the existence of the perceived form as an intelligible, as active intellect is a form of unconscious thinking.

Alexander described the material intellect as a "tablet on which nothing has been written" in *De anima* 84, as it is a "kind of propensity

suitable for the reception of intelligible forms." According to Aristotle in
De anima 3.4.429b30–430a10, what mind thinks "must be in it just as
characters may be said to be on a writing-tablet on which as yet nothing
actually stands written ...." The suggestion is that all intelligible thoughts
are eternally present, that the intellectual development or creativity of
mind is defined by the extent to which the material intellect can acquire
knowledge and understanding of the intelligibles of active intellect.
Human thinking participates in a cosmic intellect which is infinite in
scope in relation to it and which contains all possibilities of thought, as
a "collective unconscious."

Alexander preferred to compare the material intellect not to the writing
tablet itself, but to the blank surface of the tablet. The tablet is mind, the
surface of the tablet is the soul or individual mind, and the material intellect is the propensity of the blank surface to receive intelligible forms. If
intelligible forms are inscribed on the surface of the tablet, the soul as the
surface would be changed and affected, but the disposition or propensity
of the surface to receive the inscriptions, the material intellect, would not
be changed or affected. The material intellect does not experience any
change or affect in the inscription of intelligible forms because it does
not actually exist, or cannot be seen as any of the "things which actually
exist." The "things which actually exist" can only be seen as identical to
objects of thought, which are the product of active intellect, in the same
way that sensible objects cannot be seen to exist in their material consti-
tuency, which is only a potential substratum, but as intelligible forms as
they are thought. The inscription or imprint of the sensible form in the
imagination or *phantasia* likewise cannot be seen to exist unless in relation to the inscription of the intelligible form.

In *De anima* 3.4.429a27–28, Aristotle called the soul the "place of
forms," what Alexander called the "depository of form." According to
Aristotle, this only applies to the "intellective soul." The forms in the
soul can only be potential, not actual; and the forms are only in the soul
figuratively, as representations, and only in the highest part of the soul,
the highest capacity of intellection. Thus, for Alexander, the material
intellect cannot be a "locus of actual forms," because it cannot possess
them, although it is capable of apprehending them, through the influence of the active intellect on the material intellect. The soul can thus
be called a "potential seat of forms," in its attachment to the body, just
as sensible objects in their material substrate are potential forms that
can be apprehended in sense perception. In the same way, conscious
thought cannot be seen as a locus of unconscious thought, but unconscious thought can be apprehended by conscious thought.

In the *De anima* of Alexander, the enmattered form (*noêta ta enula*; Alexander, *De anima* 87) or sensible form is contrasted to the immaterial or transcendent form (*aülon eidos*; Alexander, *De anima* 88) or intelligible form (Alexander of Aphrodisias, 1979). The immaterial form is eternal, as an archetype or intelligible, and is identical with the act of thinking – thus, inaccessible to material intellect, or the consciousness of the subject in discursive reason – but is the cause of all enmattered form in conscious thought and sensation. The enmattered form does not exist in intellection until it is abstracted: until it is subjected to the processes of discursive and dialectical reasoning, as illuminated by active intellect. Human intelligence is the locus of the juxtaposition or dialectic of the immanent and transcendent, the corporeal and incorporeal, sensible and intelligible, conscious and unconscious thought.

Alexander described the content of imagination or *phantasia* as "traces that perdure as a result of actual sensation" (Alexander, *De anima* 68–9), as the mnemic residue of sense perception, the sensible form which becomes the intelligible form through the interaction of intellect, and "representations which are perceptible to it even when the real sensibles have disappeared." In that the real sensible is a representation to begin with, the trace in *phantasia* is a representation of a representation, what Sigmund Freud would call a *Vorstellungsrepräsentanz*. The trace should only be called an impression in the metaphysical sense, according to Alexander, because the sensible object does not make an imprint in vision like the traces in wax of a signet ring, for example. The initial apprehension of the sensible form does not involve an imprint of a form, nor does the mnemic residue of the sensible form in the *phantasia*, as Alexander said "even the initial apprehension of sensibles does not involve any kind of shape or figure" (72), as for example color or odor. The word "impression" is used to describe the residual trace remaining in the *oculus mentis* only in a metaphorical sense, and for lack of a better term.

The shape or figure of a perceived object, the sensible as an imprint or form, requires the participation of intellectual activity to give it shape or form. Otherwise, as Plotinus would have it in *Enneads* IV.7.6, perceived objects are unconnected and incomprehensible, and only recognizable as formed in reason, which combines the varied sensations, the "imprints" and "recollections" (V.3.2), which are already functions of intellection in a process inaccessible to conscious reason, until they have "become like partless thoughts" and have reached the "ruling principle." The intelligible form is a partless thought, as discernible by discursive reason through the formation in *phantasia* through the logos; though it is in fact composed of the object as given to sensation, the form of the object as given to it by intellection, and the form of the object as understood in reason which is based on the form of the object as given to it by intellection.

In Alexander's *De anima* 72 (Alexander of Aphrodisias, 1979), imagination is "accompanied by an assent," and therefore "desire usually results from imagination," as in Plotinus. Desire is in part a product of the assent, the acceptance or concurrence on the part of reason of the sensible form in relation to the perceived object, as given by intellection in imagination, and the intelligible in relation to the sensible in intellection. Plotinus described perception itself as a function of desire, as a mechanism of the conceptual process, and memory in particular. In *Enneads* IV.3.28 (Plotinus, 1966), desire accompanies memory, or retention of the mnemic residues, the traces of perception: "the desiring power is moved by what it enjoyed when it sees the desired object again, obviously by means of the memory."

In *Enneads* V.3.2, imagination is a process which engenders desire in the process which Alexander called assent. According to Plotinus, "as for the things which came to it from Intellect," the soul "observes what one might call their imprints," and "it continues to acquire understanding as if by recognizing the new and recently arrived impressions and fitting them to those which have long been within it…." These are the "recollections" of the soul. The assent is the agreement reached in reason between the sensible which is the product of sense perception (and intellection, though unconscious), and the intelligible which is given to reason by Intellect, in the process of organizing sensible experience. Desire is the product of the relation between the multiple and fragmented objects of sense perception and their organization in reason, a gap which needs to be filled, and the relation between the objects as understood in reason and the objects as defined in intellection, another gap which needs to be filled. Desire is the product of the impossibility of filling those gaps in human thought, as for Freud and Lacan, but it is that impossibility which propels the function of the imagination and defines the human condition. It is the gap between conscious and unconscious thought.

In *De anima* 73, Alexander identified sight or vision as the most important power of the senses, because sight depends on light, and "the name 'imagination' is therefore derived from the name for 'light'," referring to Aristotle in *De anima* 3.3.429a2–3, where the word *phantasia* comes from the word for light, *phôs*. The light of the imagination is a metaphorical light, the internal light of Intellect as described by Plotinus. Imagination (*phantasia*) was seen by Alexander as a light, which operates in the productive intellect, *nous poietikos*, to illuminate the intelligible form, and the *virtus* or power is strongest when the object is the least material and conforms most easily to the immaterial *eidos*.

When Plotinus, in *Enneads* V.5.7, distinguished between "the form of the object perceived by the sense," the sensible form, and "the medium through which the form of its object is perceived," he distinguished between the sensible and intelligible, between the object as it exists in the corporeal realm, and the object as it is conceived in the imagination, as given by light in vision. The light of the sun is perceptible to the eye, and is distinct from the *eidos*, the form which it makes possible, thus the light is the cause of the seeing, as the imagination is the cause of the seeing. The light of the sun is within the eye as well as without. The eye "will itself sometimes know a light which is not the external," but it "momentarily sees before the external light a light of its own, a brighter one," which illuminates the imagination, or is equivalent to it in the case of Alexander. The inner light of the eye for Plotinus is the equivalent of Intellect. In *Enneads* V.5.7, Intellect "will see a light, not a distinct light in something different from itself," but "alone by itself in independent purity...."

For Alexander in the *De anima*, imagination is not the impression itself, but the "vital activity of the imaginative power," as the activity of the imagination is separate from the activity of the senses. The trace in sensation, which is a product of imagination, is an internal sensible object, as opposed to the sensation itself, which is an external sensible object. According to Alexander, it is impossible to receive external sensible objects alone in sensation without the activity of the imagination, without the presence of the traces or mnemic residues of sensible objects already processed in productive intellect, in an interaction between sense and intellect. "For to be actually sensing means, in effect, that the agent possesses within himself these impressions of sensible objects that lie outside him" (Alexander, *De anima* 68). Theoretically, a newborn baby can have no sense impressions until it has memories of sense impressions.

The imaginative power is nothing other than the sensory power in the act of reason. The traces of sensations are no different from the sensations themselves, except that they are permanent or archetypal as opposed to fleeting and ephemeral: "imagination will contain truth and falsity in the same measure as do the sensations on which it depends" (70). Imagination is reliable to the extent that sense perception is reliable, but if the senses are deceived by "residual impressions which derive from common sensibles" or "objects that are only incidentally perceptible," which contain falsity, then imagination can be prone to error as well, and unreliable, as for Plotinus. Thus "imaginative representations are very unreliable when they are based on residual impressions which have been only imperfectly preserved, and which have been partly formed by the activity of imagination itself."

The imaginative faculty is seen here by Alexander as a cognitive faculty, a function of the soul, which, because of its attachment to the corporeal in sense perception, is limited in its ability to see the intelligibles as distinct from the sensory traces in the *oculus mentis* in the process of imagination. While the newborn baby can have no sense impressions until it has memories of sense impressions, the human being is born with the powers of sense perception, in Alexander's *De anima* 83, and as the senses are used, sense perception and the imagination develop. As each individual sense experience leaves an impression on the individual, the memory of sense experience develops, and the individual builds a catalogue of the sensibles experienced, and intelligibles thought, forming a vocabulary for the imagination. The discursive functions in the soul of abstraction and conceptualization result from sense perception and memory, forming a cumulative process in imagination, so that individual particulars are incorporated into collective universals. The individual "takes a kind of step upward from the 'this particular something' to the 'something of this general kind'," as in the ascent in Plato's *Symposium*. The result is a "comprehensive perception," which develops the universal from the particular, and which is equated with an "intellective act."

The comprehensive perception of Alexander, which is an intellective act, "lays hold of the universal by means of the likeness that exists among particular sensible objects" (Alexander, *De anima* 83), bringing them together in unity, as in Plotinus a comprehensive perception forms a congruent unity of experience out of multiple particulars, in the dialectic of the sensible and intelligible. "Actual sensation" is that which "takes place by means of the apprehension of the forms of sensible objects without their matter," which "must be conceived of as taking place in the way in which a piece of wax takes on the impress of a signet ring...." The material substance of the signet ring is irrelevant to how it is apprehended, except insofar as its quality can be understood conceptually, "i.e. in what ratio its constituents are combined," in intellectual activity. Objects of sense are only understood in relation to the unconscious concept of form which is projected onto them, onto the underlying substratum of matter, by intellect. Intellect is capable of both understanding the form of a sensible object as it is related to but separate from matter, according to Alexander, and of understanding the form of a sensible object as it is not related to matter in any way: intellect "not only grasps its forms in a different way than matter, but has for its object forms that do not exist in matter nor under any material conditions." It is only within the framework of the immaterial forms that the forms can be grasped in relation to matter.

In Aristotle's *De anima* 3.4.429b30–430a10 (1952a), mind is "thinkable in exactly the same way as its objects are," either "in the case of objects which involve no matter," or "in the case of those which contain matter." Mind is identical to the objects of thought in thought because objects of thought are products of thought. The object of thought is only potentially present in relation to the object which contains matter, because discursive reason cannot see the material object as an object of thought, because it does not have immediate access to the unconscious construct of the intelligible in productive intellect in relation to the sensible in discursive reason, which is necessary for the perception of the material object. The potentiality of thought in the material object is made possible by the active intellect, which can reveal the hidden mechanisms of unconscious thought to discursive reason.

In Aristotle's *De anima* (3.8.432a1–10), there is nothing outside and separate in existence from sensible spatial magnitudes, as the objects of thought are in the sensible forms, both the abstract objects and all the states and affections of sensible things. Everything that can be known as a product of sense experience can only be known within the framework of the objects of thought. According to Alexander, "intellect separates its forms from any possible material circumstance, and thus, apprehending them as they are in themselves, it beholds them in their complete isolation" (Alexander, *De anima* 84) (Alexander of Aphrodisias, 1979). In Aristotle's *De anima*, it is held that concepts can only be formed through the perception of sensible objects, through sense perception, but at the same time it is suggested by Aristotle that the perception of sensible objects is determined by the conceptualization of them, in the form of intelligibles, which are products of thought. Alexander explained that "intellect makes no use of any bodily organ in its apprehension of its intelligible objects, since it is totally self-sufficient for the act of knowing the intelligible" (Alexander, *De anima* 84).

As in Plotinus, the shape of an object as perceived corresponds to a predetermined form as its imprint, the intelligible form as the sensible form, which makes the object possible to exist in relation to human thought. According to Alexander, "everything that exists is a possible object of the intellect, since existents are divided into intelligible and sensible objects; and intellect makes even sensibles into objects suitable for its own cognition by separating them from matter and considering them in their essence." Therefore the material intellect, corresponding to the material substrate of sensible forms, "is not actually any existing thing, but is potentially all existents," as if to say that material reality is only a potential reality, and becomes a reality when it is perceived, or conceived, by intellect.

For Aristotle, in *De anima* 3.5.430a10–12, sensible objects can be divided into potential matter, as defined by their particulars, and a productive cause, which makes them reality, in the same way that art can be seen in relation to its material. The productive cause of sensible objects must be human intellect, by which the objects exist. The same division can be found, according to Aristotle, in the soul, as potential and productive intellects. At the instant that the material intellect knows a sensible object, according to Alexander, "it becomes the object that is known – for its act of knowing consists in its possessing the form that is cognized" (Alexander, *De anima* 84), following Aristotle in *De anima* 3.5. An object can only be known if it exists as a thought, and is identical to that thought.

Alexander of Aphrodisias, the first of the Peripatetics discussed here, had an important influence on Plotinus in his development of the Aristotelian theories of perception, imagination, and active intellect: all involving a suggestion of unconscious thought. The remainder of the Peripatetics in this discussion display the influence of Plotinus, and the synthesis of Platonic and Aristotelian doctrine, in their commentaries on Aristotle.

Themistius

Themistius (317–c. 387) was born into an aristocratic family and ran a peripatetic school of philosophy in Constantinople in the mid-fourth century – between 345 and 355. He made use of Alexander's *De anima* in his commentary on Aristotle's *De anima*. Themistius may also have been influenced by Plotinus, and Porphyry (232–309), whom he criticized. Themistius referred to Plato's works, especially the *Timaeus*, and attempted a synthesis of Aristotle and Plato, a synthesis which was continued in the Neoplatonic tradition. In the thought of Alexander, thought and perception are intimately connected, almost identical, but Themistius went to greater lengths to differentiate the two. Sense perception must be distinguished from reasoning, because all animals are capable of sense perception, while only humans are capable of reasoning; while there are only five kinds of sense perception, there are many varieties of the capacity for reasoning; and the functions of sense perception and reasoning can be differentiated.

In contrasting sense perception and reason, Themistius did not distinguish between the types of reason as established in the Aristotelian tradition: intellect (*nous*), thinking (*noêsis*), capacity for reasoning (*logikê dunamis*), and discursive thinking (*dianoia*). Thinking is divided into the capacity for imagination and the capacity for judgment, and the two are clearly distinguished, as belief and assent play no role in imagination. Imagination (*phantasia*) is that part of thinking which is most closely related to sense perception, because imagination depends on the reception of the sensible image, and the retention of the image in thought, the mnemic residue. Imagination is a necessary precondition for intellect, but the two must still be distinguished. Imagination is the process in which an image or *phantasma* "comes to exist in us" (Themistius, *De anima* 89) (Themistius, 1996) as an imprint or *tupos* and "form of the sense-impression" or *aisthêma* in the soul. It is concluded from this that imagination is a capacity or *hexeis* of the soul for discernment, excluding the faculties of belief or assent. Imagination must be a faculty for discernment for Themistius because the *phantasma* must be in part a product of thought and not just a pure imprint of the sensible object; it must be an intelligible, not just a sensible.

According to Themistius, sense perception must be distinguished from imagination because imagination occurs in sleep while sense perception does not. Imagination thus requires an unconscious thought activity, something other than discursive reason, but not self-conscious, an element of *noesis* as a product of active intellect, intellect from without. While sense perception is both potential and actual, like material intellect, both tied to the sensible object and incorporeal, potential sense perception, the engagement with the sensible, corporeal object, does not occur in dreams. Dreams only consist of the residues of sense perception, the mnemic residues of the traces of the imprints, or *enkataleimmata*, involving the intelligible as a product of active intellect. Themistius pointed out that it is difficult to distinguish between the activity of perception and the activity of imagination in relation to the sense object as it is perceived: that is, between the sensible and intelligible form, and the activities of discursive reason and *nous*.

Such a distinction would require a consciousness of the influence of active intellect, and a self-consciousness of reason in perception. Imagination is active while sense perception focuses on the object: sense perception acts on the sensible object as imagination acts on sense perception. The imprint is formed as sensible and intelligible simultaneously, but the intelligible endures in *memoria* while the sensible does not. As in Plato's *Republic*: when "the mind's eye is fixed on objects illuminated by truth and reality, it understands and knows them," and is in possession of intelligence; "but when it is fixed on the twilight world of change and decay, it can only form opinions, its vision is confused and its opinions shifting, and it seems to lack intelligence" (508d5) (Plato, 1955).

In Themistius' *De anima*, the relation between the object of sense perception and sense perception is the same as the relation between sense perception and imagination, in part because both require the imprinting of the *eidos*: the former being the sensible, the latter the intelligible. Themistius compared the intelligible form to the print of a wax block on air, the wax block being the *phantasia*, "just as though the wax received the imprint of the seal right through itself, and after receiving the imprint and being enfolded in it had gone on to stamp the same imprint on the air" (Themistius, *De anima* 92), the result being that "even though the wax and ring had gone away, the surrounding air had acquired a structure," the intelligible structure. The enfolding of the *phantasia* in material intellect constitutes the process of actualization or entelechy of the material intellect to active intellect, in the perfection of the imagination through sense perception: imagination is "perfected by progressing to actuality through the agency of sense perception, just as sense perception is through the agency of the objects of perception." Alexander of Aphrodisias described sensation, or sense perception, as that which "takes place by means of the apprehension of the forms of sensible objects without their matter," which "must be conceived of as taking place in the way in which a piece of wax takes on the impress of a signet ring..." (Alexander, *De anima* 83). In Plotinus' *Enneads*, "since the object being perceived is a body, perception could not occur in any other way than that in which seal-impressions are imprinted in wax from seal-rings..." (IV.7.6) (Plotinus, 1966).

In Themistius' *De anima*, to the extent that *phantasia* is composed in part of material intellect, the material intellect can be seen as the wax block, or piece of wax, which receives the imprint or *tupos* of the *phantasma* of the sensible object. The material or potential intellect "must therefore be, while impassible," that is, unmoved by belief or assent, "capable of receiving the form of an object" (Themistius, *De anima* 94). In order to receive the form of an object, the material intellect in sense perception "must be potentially identical in character with its object." The material intellect must potentially perceive the intelligible form in order to perceive the sensible form; it must potentially have an idea of the object in order to receive the form of the object in perception. In this way "thinking is analogous to perceiving" and intellect is affected by its object, the intelligible form, just as perception is affected by the object of perception, the sensible form. In this way intellect is perfected, by "being advanced from potentiality to actuality," through the mechanisms of sense perception.

In that material intellect is impassible or unchangeable, but experiences affection at the same time, it must "not have a structure of its own but be capable of receiving every form," like the blank writing tablet described by Alexander of Aphrodisias in his *De anima* 84, with a propensity to receive intelligible forms, or by Aristotle in his *De anima* 3.4.429b30–430a10, with no characters written on it. Themistius distinguished between the affection of the material intellect and the perfection of it. The material intellect is perfected as if it were letters "written on a tablet that has nothing actually written on it" (Themistius, *De anima* 97) (Themistius, 1996). The potential intellect, as the tablet, is perfected without being affected, "since it has received that for which it came into existence," but remains unchanged, because it is impassible, but must be capable of receiving the form of the object in sense perception. The potential intellect is perfected as actual intellect when it is "active towards the intelligible objects," and as such it must be "unmixed and uncompounded," incorporeal. While the thought of the potential intellect cannot be identical to the object of the thought, because potential intellect "is actually none of the things that exist," actual intellect comes into existence simultaneously with the thoughts which come into existence for potential intellect, like the letters written on the tablet with nothing written on it; thus, actual intellect is identical with the object of thought. The potential intellect is not affected by the objects of thought, but rather becomes them; or, identical to them as actual intellect.

Material intellect, for Themistius, cannot be identical to the objects that it thinks; it must remain potentially all things, which differentiates it from actual intellect, through the influence of productive intellect, which becomes identical to the objects that it thinks. The material intellect is "none of the objects that exist prior to its thinking" (Themistius, *De anima* 94), and is thus not real or actual, but potential. Intellect, as both material and actual, can be compared to a line which is both bent and straight – one line in two different states. The actual intellect is like the straight line – uncompounded, while the material intellect is like the bent line – compounded and doubled, since it must contend with both matter and form. Aristotle compared the activities of the intellect to a straight line and a bent line, according to Themistius. Plato, in the

Timaeus, compared the activities of the intellect to circular motion and rectilinear motion – a contrast between the celestial spheres and the sublunary spheres, and between the intelligibles and discursive reason. For Aristotle, the bent line corresponds to intellect when it becomes engaged in matter and becomes doubled, or embodied. When the intellect thinks about a compound, a material object, it becomes compounded, as a bent line, and when it thinks about a form, it becomes uncompounded, as a straight line, in actual intellect.

The active intellect perfects the material intellect in the same way that a craft perfects matter in architecture or sculpture, according to Themistius. All things in nature consist of "a matter which is potentially all the particulars included" (Themistius, *De anima* 98), the material substrate, including potential intellect, and "a cause which is productive in the sense that it makes them all," the active intellect. The potential house and potential sculpture as material substrate receive their structure through the craft of architecture or sculpture, through the application of the *virtus* of the craft, and the imposition of the form of the craft on the material; equally, active intellect imposes the intelligible form on the sensible object, through the corporeal form, in the activation of potential intellect. In that way the house and sculpture are brought to completion as compounds, just as potential intellect is brought to completion. The craft is in a state of perfection, like active intellect, and the house or sculpture are brought to a state of perfection through it. Active intellect "moves the potential intellect analogously to the craft...." The craft is separate and unaffected, like active intellect. The matter of the house or sculpture is unaffected and impassible, but is brought to perfection, like material intellect, through the craft.

In the *Enneads*, Plotinus asked, "How does the architect declare the house outside beautiful by fitting it to the form of house within him?" (I.6.3) (Plotinus, 1966). He does so because the physical house "is the inner form," the intelligible form, "divided by the external mass of matter...." Plotinus likewise differentiated the matter from the form; it is the indivisible, incorporeal form, the intelligible, which defines the matter as architecture, in contrast to the diversity of particulars in matter in which the architecture may be consciously perceived. Diverse parts in matter are gathered together and given shape by the Ideal Form for Plotinus, the incorporeal intelligible. Matter in itself is without shape or form, but form "composes that which is to come into being from many parts into a single ordered whole..." (I.6.2). The medium by which the Ideal Form acts is the active intellect, in the terms of Themistius, which carries out the forming principles, and grasps and molds things.

In Plotinus, the soul is to the physical universe as the architect is to the house. The house is created by the soul of the architect as the universe is created by the World Soul; Intellect descends into reason, as material intellect is activated by active intellect and discursive reason is able to understand intelligibles, and the beauty of the Good descends into physical form, from the mind of the architect to the house. The house, like the universe, is "ensouled; it has a soul which does not belong to it....The universe lies in soul which bears it up, and nothing is without a share of soul" (*Enneads* IV.3.9). The house is a part of the architect, of the mind of the architect, but is separated from its source, as its matter is impassible. The architecture of the house is as the letters on the surface of the tablet on which no letters are actually written, as active intellect in unconscious thought; the architecture of the house is an intelligible, and only exists in the mind of the architect or the mind of the viewer. The house is in the architect in the same way that the world is in the soul.

The relation between craft and matter is the same as the relation between productive intellect and potential intellect, as "the latter becomes all things, while the former produces all things" (Themistius, 1996, *De anima* 99), according to Themistius. But productive intellect is not external to potential intellect in the way that craft is external to matter. Matter cannot become craft in the way that potential intellect can become productive intellect, or intellect in *habitus*. As actual intellect is added to potential intellect, a compound is created of form and matter, as well as creativity and matter, which both becomes all things and produces all things. Potential intellect has the capacity to be other than matter, while matter does not. The creativity, the capacity to produce all things in productive intellect, is the *dêmiourgia*, which involves the productive intellect or power to become the objects which it thinks. The thinking of the productive intellect is as the craftsman, the demiurge, with the *virtus* through active intellect to comprehend, structure, and produce thoughts, as the *arkhêgos*, founder of thoughts.

Potential intellect is something (*to tode*), according to Themistius, as matter is something, while actual intellect is "what it is to be something" (*to tôide einai*; Themistius, *De anima* 100), as the sensible object as form in the soul is what it is to be something. In the same way, the thinking subject as potential intellect is "I" (*to egô*), as in the Freudian ego, while the thinking subject as actual intellect is "what it is to be me" (*to emoi einai*). The thinking subject is the "intellect combined from the potential to the actual" – in becoming, in discursive, conscious thought – while "what it is to be me" comes from actual intellect – in producing, in intellection – which involves unconscious thought. The potential thinking subject and the actual thinking subject are distinct. The actual thinking subject is the product of productive intellect, which is made possible by potential intellect, which is made possible by the imagination, which is made possible by perception. Perception, imagination, and potential intellect together can only allow for the potential thinking subject; productive intellect, as distinct from what makes it possible, alone allows for the actual thinking subject. Productive intellect alone is a "form of forms" – an incorporeal intelligible, while perception, imagination and potential intellect are tied to the corporeal and are only substrates, as matter is only a substrate for the form of a sensible object.

The thought of the material intellect, in discursive reason, is subject to time, while the thought of productive intellect, actual intellect given by active intellect, is not, as Themistius explained in *De anima* 101, anticipating the thought of Robert Grosseteste and Immanuel Kant. In Aristotle's *De anima*, "in the individual, potential knowledge is in time prior to actual knowledge" (3.5.430a) (Aristotle, 1964), subject to time, but outside the individual potential intellect, there is no temporal relation between potential and actual intellect. Actual intellect is "mind set free from its present conditions … immortal and eternal," incorporeal. Mind as passive, in its material potentiality, is destructible and subject to time, as in the ephemerality of the *phantasmata*, but mind as active is free from its material conditions; the intelligible is permanent and not subject to temporal duration. Discursive thinking is equivalent to thinking in time; time is not present in the same way in unconscious thought or dreams, as Sigmund Freud would establish in his analysis.

As Plotinus explained perception, "nothing will prevent a perception from being a mental image for that which is going to remember it," in the temporal context of the *memoria* in the *imaginatio* or *phantasia*, "and the memory and the retention of the object from belonging to the image-making power" (*Enneads* IV.3.29) (Plotinus, 1966), in the introduction of active intellect to potential intellect in the terms of Themistius. Thus, for Plotinus, "it is in this that the perception arrives at its conclusion, and what was seen is present in this when the perception is no longer there," the ephemeral *phantasma*. "If then the image of what is absent is already present in this, it is already remembering, even if the presence is only for a short time." The introduction of active intellect to material intellect, in the terms of Themistius, transforms the sensible as subject to time to the intelligible as free from temporal and corporeal particulars, in unconscious thought.

In *Enneads* IV.3.30, "an image accompanies every intellectual act": an atemporal intelligible accompanies an act of discursive reason, in the transformation from potential to productive intellect, in the terms of Themistius. The mechanism by which the mnemic residue of the *phantasma* or picture of thought is incorporated into the conceptual, intellective process, the image-making power, the *dêmiourgia* of active intellect, must be, according to Plotinus, language, the mechanism of discursive reason: "the reception into the image-making power would be of the verbal expression [or more accurately, the *logos endiathetos*] which accompanies the act of intelligence." While the word belongs to discursive thought, it reveals as *logos* what lies hidden within – active intellect, beneath the conceptual processes which can be apprehended by discursive, conscious thought itself in material intellect. "The intellectual act is without parts and has not, so to speak, come out into the open, but remains unobserved within ...." The intellectual act is without parts just as the sensible object in exterior reality is without parts once it has been processed in the imagination as sensible form. The progression from the multiple and fragmented in sensible objects, as given in potential intellect, to the whole and continuous as given in actual intellect, corresponds to the progression from the multiple and fragmented nature of potential intellect itself, subject to temporal and corporeal limitations, to the whole and continuous nature of actual intellect, free from temporal and corporeal limitations.

In Themistius' *De anima*, when "supervening on potential sight and potential colors" (98), light "produces both actual sight and actual colors," in the same way that "actual intellect advances the potential intellect" (99), and "constitutes its potential objects of thought as actual objects," the sensible object as the sensible form. The actual object is the enmattered form, the universal derived from the particular, already constituted by the intelligible form. Before it is illuminated by active intellect, potential intellect is a "store-house of thoughts," with no capacity to distinguish between enmattered forms, make transitions between thoughts, or combine or divide them, all being functions of discursive reason. Potential intellect only "deposits the imprints from perception," the *tupos*, "and imagination through the agency of memory," in the form of the trace or mnemic residue.

A *phantasma* comes to exist as a *tupos* or *aisthêma* in the soul in imagination, involving the faculty of discernment. When the potential intellect is encountered by the active intellect, as material objects are encountered by light, the potential and active intellects become the same, just as a material object becomes the same as the form in which it is perceived. Light functions as the productive intellect, which allows the potential intellect to develop as intellect in *habitus*, as described by Alexander of Aphrodisias. As intellect in *habitus*, material intellect is able to make transitions and to combine and divide thoughts, and to understand the intelligible, which makes discursive reason possible, in its relation to sensible objects.

Potential intelligible thoughts are sense perceptions without the productive intellect, which become mnemic residues and are processed by the *phantasia*; they are illuminated by the active intellect, and are compared to potential colors. *Phantasia* is the primary image-making faculty, and preserves the impressions in sense perception, when it is illuminated by the active intellect, and in turn illuminates the imprints of the sense perceptions as intelligibles, as light illuminates colors. It is through *phantasia* that the *phantasma*, or *eidos*, comes to exist in intellect as a *tupos*, imprint, or *morphê* – form – of the *aisthêma*, the sense impression (Themistius, *De anima* 89). Themistius reminded the reader that the name for imagination, *phantasia*, derives its name from the name for light, *phôs*, as did Alexander of Aphrodisias in his *De anima* 73, referring to Aristotle in the original *De anima* 3.3.429a2–3.

According to Themistius, natural light comes from a single source, and becomes multiple in different perceiving subjects. As the unity of active intellect has no relation to the multiplicity of potential intellect in its corporeal attachment, "the imperishability of the light shared has no more relation to each organ of sight than does the eternity of the productive intellect to each of us..." (Themistius, *De anima* 103) (Themistius, 1996). The active intellect is that which illuminates (*ellampôn*), from an inaccessible and unconscious source, while potential intellect, being both passive and active, contains what is illuminated (*ellampomenoi*) and multiple particulars which illuminate (*ellampontes*), as agents of productive intellect. The unitary light of the sun becomes multiple as it is diffused and reflected in particulars, among both sensible objects and the particulars of discursive reason.

In Plato's *Republic*, the light of the sun is analogous to the Good, the source of the forming principles. The light of the Good is the idea which "gives the objects of knowledge their truth and the knower's mind the power of knowing..." (*Republic* 508) (Plato, 1955). In that the Good is "the source not only of the intelligibility of the objects of knowledge, but also of their being and reality" (509), as active intellect, in the terms of Themistius, sensible objects cannot exist outside of active intellect, or the extent to which potential intellect can be participant of it, except as material substrate without form. While potential intellect can participate in the active intellect, and be affected by it, the former is separate from the latter: potential intellect can only participate in time and particulars, subject to the temporal and corporeal conditions of the soul.

When intellect thinks an object in matter, both intellect and object are distinct, according to Themistius (Themistius, *De anima* 97). But, when intellect thinks an immaterial object, the intelligible, because it has become an intelligible through the illumination of the productive intellect, "what thinks and what is being thought are identical." The same could be said for vision: when the perceiver sees the enmattered object, perception and object are distinct, but when the perceiver sees the intelligible form in the mind's eye, illuminated by the productive intellect as an intelligible, what sees and what is seen are identical, because what is seen is the product of what the perceiver sees unconsciously.

Themistius' philosophy of intellect, in his commentary on Aristotle's *De anima*, contains ideas that can be seen as important predecessors to those of figures such as Grosseteste, Kant, and Freud, in particular in the suggestion and development of what can be called "unconscious thought" as active intellect. The Arabic commentators on Aristotle in this discussion – Alfarabi, Avicenna and Averroes – similarly contributed to the development of an idea of unconscious thought, in anticipation of modern philosophies.

Alfarabi

Abu Nasr Alfarabi (c. 872–951) lived in Baghdad from 901 to 941, and died in Damascus. In the *Risala fi'l-'aql* (25–27), also known as *De intellectu*, or *Letter Concerning the Intellect*, Alfarabi wrote that the light of the sun, or transparency (from Aristotle, *De anima* 2.7.418b9–10), makes the eye, or potential vision, transparent or illuminated itself. When both the eye and the medium of the sensible world are transparent – that is, when they are illuminated and can see the intelligible – then vision is possible. Colors become actually visible, and potential vision becomes actual vision. In the same way, active intellect makes potential intellect transparent, and *nous* makes discursive reason transparent. The transparency of light and color illuminates the intellect in the process of perception, making intelligibles transparent to reason. Alfarabi compared what he called the "agent intellect" to the sun, and the potential intellect to the eye in darkness; it is the agent intellect which illuminates potential intellect and allows it to become active. In the *Risala*: "Just as the sun is that which makes the eye sight in actuality and visible things visible in actuality," as it illuminates, "so likewise the agent intellect is that which makes the intellect which is in potentiality an intellect in actuality insofar as it gives it of that principle," illumination in principle, "and through this very same thing the intelligibles become intelligibles in actuality" (Alfarabi, 1967, pp. 218–19), as unconscious thought becomes conscious thought.

Alfarabi thus distinguished between a potential intelligible and an actual intelligible, and it is the agent intellect which is necessary as an entelechy, like the light of the sun, to make the potential intelligible understandable to the potential or material intellect, as a transparent medium, or mediating device. Darkness is potential transparency, and transparency is defined as illumination by a luminous source, that is, the sun. It is the agent intellect which thinks the archetypes and intelligibles, mathematics and geometry, abstractions of material forms. The divisible and impermanent form in matter, the *eidos* in vision, becomes the eternal and indivisible form in the agent intellect, as the particular becomes the universal.

In Alfarabi's interpretation there are in fact four intellects, or four senses in intellect: potentiality, actuality, acquired, and agent. The potential intellect can be seen as the material intellect, and the agent intellect can be seen as the active intellect. Intellect in actuality is intellect which knows actual intelligibles, and acquired intellect is intellect which knows that it knows actual intelligibles, or self-conscious reason. Intellect in potentiality contains an essence which is prepared to "abstract the quiddities" of existing things, as he describes in the *Risala* (Alfarabi, 1967, p. 215), and to abstract form from matter, or to distinguish between sensible and intelligible. In abstracting the essence of material things, intellect makes "a form for itself": that is, it understands the material thing as a form, and the material thing ceases to exist as matter and comes to exist as form to intellect. The form of the material thing is the intelligible; intellect in its acquired state understands that it understands the thing, not in its matter but in its form, which is not the product of perception but rather the product of intellection. The material thing itself does not define its own existence to intellect as an intelligible, rather it is intellect which defines it as an intelligible, so the material thing does not exist other than as being understood as an intelligible by intellect.

Alfarabi used the analogy of the impression in the piece of wax to describe the difference between the intelligible and the material, as did Alexander of Aphrodisias and Themistius. The essence of matter is that element of matter in which "form comes to be," the potential for matter to be understood by intellect as form, in the same way that the essence of potential intellect is its capacity to understand the form. When an impression is stamped on a piece of wax, the impression takes possession of the matter, and the matter becomes the form in its totality. Even the part of the wax which does not take the impression is defined in relation to the impression. The totality is especially complete if the impression on the wax transforms the wax in three dimensions, in the form of a cube or sphere for example. In that case, there can be no distinction between the quiddity, or essence, of the wax in its material existence and the quiddity of the form of the wax. In the same way, the essence of intellect in potentiality cannot be distinguished from the form of the intelligible in intellect. In both cases, the form takes possession of the material in all dimensions, sinks through it completely, and achieves a complete identity.

In Alfarabi's *Risala*, intelligibles as forms, as abstracted from matter, are actualized intelligibles, as opposed to intelligibles in potentiality, *in re* in matter, corresponding to the states of potential and actual intellect. Actualized intelligibles achieve a separate existence from potential intelligibles, as not subject to place and time, or the corporeal. Actualized intelligibles are intelligibles without categories, as they are not subject to discursive reason in potential intellect, and the categories attached to potential intelligibles are understood differently in relation to actualized intelligibles. In the *Risala*, "if you consider the meaning of place in regard to it," the actualized intelligible, or intelligible in actuality, "either you will not find in it any of the meanings of place at all, or, if you should apply the term 'place' it must be understood by you in regard to it in a different meaning, and this meaning according to a different sense" (Alfarabi, 1967, p. 216).

The ability of intellect to grasp the intelligible is the product of the cooperation of material and agent intellect. The phonetic form of a word in language is received as a sensible, but it is only retained as an ephemeral mnemic residue in *phantasia* or imagination as an intelligible, into which it has been transformed by the agent intellect, combining the potential intellect and the active intellect. Once the word in language has become the intelligible in the *imaginatio*, then discursive reason is able to reinsert it into the present particular of language use, as it is able to see it as illuminated by agent intellect. The dialectic of the sensible and the intelligible, as in Plotinus, constitutes thinking or intellection, constructs meaning, and makes communication possible in conscious thought.

In the *Risala*, the actualized intelligible becomes an object of thought in discursive reason, in actualized intellect; it becomes a concrete form of the abstract. The actualized intelligible is the articulation of the intellectual insight, which can be counted and included in a totality;

as Alfarabi said in the *Risala*, "when [the intelligibles] become intelligibles in actuality, they become, then, one of the things existing in the world, and they are counted, insofar as they are intelligibles, among the totality of existing things" (Alfarabi, 1967, p. 216). The actualized intelligibles lead discursive reason back to the intelligibles themselves, which are their source, while the sensible leads discursive reason back to its source, the intelligible. In the *Risala*, when the actualized intelligible becomes the object of the thought of the actualized intellect, the actualized intelligible and the actualized intellect are identical, as "that which is thought is then nothing but that which is in actuality an intellect" (Alfarabi, 1967, p. 216). The intellect in actuality is only so in relation to the form of the actualized intelligible; the intellect remains potential in relation to other intelligibles which are still potential, in the material, and have not become actual. When intellect becomes actual in relation to all intelligibles, and intellect becomes the actualized intelligibles themselves, then the object of the thought of intellect, the actualized intelligibles, is intellect itself: "when it thinks that existent thing which is an intellect in actuality, it does not think an existing thing outside of itself but it only thinks itself," in unconscious thought, as for Plotinus.

Thus, according to Alfarabi, when intellect has separated the intelligible from the object, the intelligible becomes something other than the object, as identical to intellect. Potential intelligibles are "first thought, according as they were abstracted from their matters in which their existence is and according as they are intelligibles in potentiality," but then "they are thought a second time in such a way that their existence is not that previous existence, but their existence is separate from their matters, according as they are forms which are not in their matters and according as they are intelligibles in actuality" (Alfarabi, 1967, p. 217). The intelligible form is not identical to the sensible form; the sensible form is formed through the intelligible form and exists separate from it as a corporeal form. Intellect cannot be intellect in actuality if it thinks things that are separate from and not identical to itself: "if the intellect thinks itself insofar as it itself is an intellect in actuality, there does not come to it from that which it thinks of itself some existing thing whose existence in respect to itself is different from its existence, namely as an intelligible in actuality." The object of thought in sense perception and conscious reason in potential intellect comes from without – as the sensible form, which is seen to be separate from intellect in corporeal reality; but actualized intellect is able to see that the sensible form is a product of the intelligible form, and the object of thought in actualized intellect is the intelligible, which is itself.

Then, according to Alfarabi, "when the intellect in actuality thinks the intelligibles which are forms in it, insofar as they are intelligibles in actuality, then the intellect of which it was first said that it is the intellect in actuality, becomes now the acquired intellect," the third of the Aristotelian senses, *intellectus adeptus* or *nous epiktetos*. For the acquired or actualized intellect which thinks itself as an intelligible, "the statement 'that which belongs *to us* in actuality as an intellect' and 'that which is *in us* in actuality as an intellect' is the very same statement," in relation to "those forms which are not in matters and which never were in them," according to Alfarabi (Alfarabi, 1967, p. 217). That which we perceive and think is our own intellect, which constitutes the forms which define matter. But intellect as the object of its own thought is inaccessible to conscious reason.

In the hierarchy of intellects of Alfarabi, acquired intellect functions as a template for actualized intellect, which is matter for acquired intellect, while actualized intellect functions as a template for the perception of matter. The intelligible can be conceived as being both material and conceptual, as actualized intellect can be both matter and form. While in active intellect form is separated from matter, in actualized intellect form descends into matter, which is why active intellect is compared to light – which bridges the immaterial and material and makes all things materially visible, and actualized intellect is compared to illumination – the activity of the active intellect. The active or agent intellect "is a separated form which never existed in matter nor ever will exist in it" (Alfarabi, 1967, p. 218), which makes matter possible, as it actualizes intellect.

In the *Risala*, the "relation of the active intellect to the intellect, which is in potentiality, is like the relation of the sun to the eye, which is sight in potentiality, as long as it is in darkness" (Alfarabi, 1967, p. 218) and not illuminated by the intelligibles of the agent intellect. Illumination is the equivalent of transparency, following Aristotle, who defined light as a transparent medium, and transparency is the equivalent of the rarefaction of light. The process of the rarefaction of light in matter is equivalent to the illumination of matter by form, and the sensible form by the intelligible form in intellect. Sight becomes actuality in the presence of light in the same way that potential intellect becomes actual intellect in the presence of agent intellect. Sight becomes actuality "with the coming into being of the forms of visible things in the sight," just as intellect becomes actuality with the coming into being of the forms as objects of intellect. Light becomes transparent in actuality because it is prepared by the light of the sun itself, as the sensible form becomes transparent as it is prepared by the intelligible form. The transparency of the sensible is provided by agent intellect, which allows the sensible to be seen as the intelligible, and allows thought to see itself in actualized intellect. Through the transparency which it provides, agent intellect becomes the principle or template for actualized intelligibles.

For Alfarabi, intellect ascends from the material to the agent intellect as it ascends from the particular to the eternal, from the multiplicity of divisions to the unity and simplicity of that which is indivisible. In the ascent to agent intellect, we ascend "to the things which are more perfect in existence," and we ascend "from that which is best known to us to that which is unknown" (*Risala*, Alfarabi, 1967, p. 219), in the unconscious. The knowledge of things which are most accessible to intellect is the lowest form of knowledge; in order to develop, intellect must come to grasp the knowledge which is least accessible and most unconscious. Intellect must challenge its own limitations. The more difficult something is to comprehend, the higher form of intellect it requires. In the *Risala*, "forms are in the agent intellect indivisible, while in first matter they are divisible." The indivisible forms of agent intellect project a likeness of themselves onto matter, but they are only received in matter as divided and corrupted.

Though the forms of agent intellect are received as divided and corrupted, matter is nevertheless perfected in its reception of the archetypal forms; the sensible form is perfected by the intelligible form, though it can only be an inferior copy. The closer the sensible can come to the intelligible, the more it is perfected, as it is more incorporeal, and is illuminated more clearly in the *imaginatio*. For Alfarabi, the ultimate perfection of intellect, the ultimate incorporeality in the corporeal, is "the ultimate happiness and the afterlife," in which state the becoming of a substance, and substance in intellect, is achieved through a completely external force. For Alfarabi, acquired intellect requires no corporeal subsistence, and intellection is perfected when it is independent of the corruption of sense perception and its own material mechanisms, as for Plotinus. In his advocacy of an ascent to that which is unknown in conscious thought, as in the ascent of Plato or Plotinus to noetic thought, Alfarabi made an important contribution to the development of the concept of unconscious thought.

Avicenna

Avicenna (Ibn Sīnā, c. 980–1037) was born in Afshna, near Bukhara, in Persia. He worked briefly for the Samanid administration, but left Bukhara, and lived in the area of Tehran and Isfahan, where he completed the *Kitab al-Shifā* (*The Book of Remedy*), including the treatise on the soul, *Shifā: De anima*, under the patronage of the Daylamite ruler, 'Ala'-al Dawla, and wrote his most important Persian work, the *Dānish-nāma* (*The Book of Knowledge*), which contains works on logic, metaphysics (*Dānish Nāma-i'alā'ī* [*Ilāhiyyāt*]), physics, and mathematics.

In the *Liber Naturalis* (*al-Tabi'iyyat*) of Avicenna, sensory thought, *nous hylikos*, is illuminated by the active intellect, *intelligentia agens*. Avicenna followed Alexander of Aphrodisias in defining the potential intellect, the *nous pathetikos* or *nous dynamei*, as the material intellect, *intellectus materialis*, in contrast to actual intellect or *nous poietikos*. The material intellect is seen as a passive substratum of ideas and as a capacity for thought, as a pure potency in relation to act, by which intelligibles can be apprehended. Avicenna defined the capacity to apprehend intelligibles in the soul as incorporeal, though it is a capacity of material intellect. In the *Liber Naturalis*, "in man there is some substance that apprehends the intelligible by receiving it"; thus "the substance that is the subject of the intelligibles is not body nor does it in any way have being because of body, it being the power [*virtus*] in the body, or its form" (6.5.2) (Brentano, 1977, p. 6, n. 22). That substance or *virtus* of the soul is eternal, to the extent that the active intellect is able to participate in it.

For Avicenna, the potential knowing of the material intellect is actualized when intelligibles are projected onto it from the purely intellectual and incorporeal, which is the active intellect, as for Alfarabi, which is capable of abstracting intelligible forms. In the *Liber Naturalis*, "the cause for giving intelligible form is nothing but the active intellect, in whose power are the principles of abstract intelligible forms" (6.5.5). In the *Shifā: Ilāhiyyāt* (the *Metaphysica* in *The Book of Knowledge*), Avicenna called the active intellect the giver of forms. Forms emanate from active intellect constantly and eternally, but not as the result of any will on the part of active intellect, that is, unconsciously. As with Alfarabi, forms in active intellect are indivisible and perfect in their incorporeality, but matter is not capable of receiving them as such, because it is not properly prepared for them in its particularities and differentiation. Forms thus emanate as differentiated, in sequential arrangements of terms which are particular to human discourse in discursive or cogitative knowledge. Cogitative knowledge is different from knowledge of principles or intelligibles, which requires the participation of active intellect in actual intellect. Cogitative reason is necessary to ascend from material intellect to actual intellect, involving the stage which is called *intellectus in habitu*, habitual intellect. *Intellectus in habitu* is described as an intellect as a state, *nous kath hexin*, a state of preparedness for intellection, as in the *habitus* of Alexander of Aphrodisias.

Intellectus in habitu is an intellect in act, *intellectus in effectu*, though not in constant act, only when turned towards active intellect. *Intellectus in habitu* operates according to principles or first intelligibles, in the participation of active intellect, when the intelligible is present in it, as reflected, illuminated or emanated by active intellect, in an acquired intellect, as for Alfarabi, an *intellectus accommodatus*, or an intellect acquired from outside human intellect, *accommodatus ab extrinsecus*. The *intellectus in habitu* leads to an actualized intellect, which is able to separate itself from the corporeals of sense perception and the mechanisms of material intellect. In the *Liber Naturalis*, "Thus the rational soul, being in a certain kind of union with the forms, is capable of having present in it free from all admixture the forms that come from the light of the active intellect itself" (6.5.5) (Brentano, 1977, p. 7, n. 28).

First intelligibles lead to second intelligibles, as the illumination of active intellect is more clearly received. In this process, *intellectus in habitu* leads to acquired intellect: intellect which operates according to the reflected forms or intelligibles of active intellect into the corporeal world and material intellect. Cogitative reason prepares the material intellect to receive the emanation of the active intellect, by allowing the actual intellect, *nous poietikos* or unconscious thought, to correspond the sensible with the intelligible. The sensible form is presented by the cogitative faculty, in the retention and assimilation of the phantasm in the *sensus communis*, and this provides the substrate for the participation of active intellect in the soul. The phantasm or sensible form retained in *memoria* provides a source to which the soul can return continually for sustenance in its cogitative activities.

The soul does not need to return to the form, image or *eidos*, though, and the more it develops in *intellectus in habitu*, the less dependent it becomes on corporeal sense perception, the less it needs to return to the image. Once the soul has achieved actual intellect, the sensible forms retained in the *memoria* are only distractions, and they should thus be ignored and excluded from the intellective process (*Shifā: De anima* 223) (Davidson, 1992, pp. 78–125 [104]), because by then the actual intellect is able to understand the a priori intelligible form as the basis for the sensible form, and its operation can become solely dependent on that which comes from outside it: for Alfarabi, the emanation of active intellect. Actual intellect is acquired intellect, because all thought in actual intellect is acquired from the emanation of active intellect.

Acquired intellect represents the perfection of intellectual development, in the fullest participation of active intellect.

In the *Liber Naturalis* (6.5.6), knowledge of intelligible objects necessitates the ability of intellect to recall to mind the forms in *phantasia*, both sensible and intelligible, and thoughts or intentions in *memoria*, the two retentive functions of sense perception. Knowledge of intelligibles also necessitates the ability of *intellectus in habitu* to be joined with active intellect, through emanation or illumination, in order for the intelligible thought, *ipsum intellectum*, to be formed, in the conjoining of the sensible and intelligible. Intelligible thought, though, is not always present to intellect or formed in intellect; it is present eternally in active intellect, but its presence in actual intellect requires the development of intellect in *intellectus in habitu*. Through development in *intellectus in habitu*, the soul is able to conjoin with active intellect when it chooses to do so. When the soul is willing, the intelligible form flows into it from active intellect, in the capacity of actual or actualized intellect, made possible through acquired intellect, *intellectus adeptus* or *intellectus accommodatus* (*nous epiktetos*).

Like Alfarabi, Avicenna compared the relation between active intellect and material intellect to the relation between the sun and the sense of sight. In the *Liber Naturalis*, "for just as the sun is actually seen through itself, and what before was not actually visible through its light, so also the disposition of the [active] intellect is in relation to our souls" (6.5.5) (Brentano, 1977, p. 7, n. 25). Active intellect makes intelligibles visible to the soul, if the soul is turned toward active intellect in actual intellect or acquired intellect, *intellectus accommodatus*. The sun is seen in its own light, while objects perceived in vision are seen by the light of the sun. In the *al-Madina al-Fadila* of Alfarabi, active intellect was compared to the sun, and light imprints the *eidos* in the material intellect. For Avicenna, the material intellect is able to see the form of the thing in the *oculus mentis* by the light of the active intellect, which proceeds or emanates from a first cause and illuminates the form of the thing as the intelligible form, in the illumination or reflection in the soul.

In Avicenna's *Shifā: De anima*, intelligibles are differentiated in the compositive imaginative faculty, as in the *Enneads* IV.3.29 and IV.3.30 of Plotinus. Plotinus was not known to Arab scholars by name, but parts of the *Enneads* were paraphrased in the *Theology of Aristotle*. Active intellect transforms sense perceptions into principles, which are the first intelligible thoughts, as in *Enneads* I.3.5. In Aristotle's *De anima* (3.7.431b2), the human intellect thinks the forms in the images, and the sensible is given by the intelligible, which is formed in the imagination or *phantasia* and is presented to discursive reason in the process of perception. According to Avicenna, in the *Shifā: De anima* (235), also known as the *Metaphysica*, the image or *eidos* is formed in the *sensus communis*, and is then received by the imaginative faculty, the *phantasia*, which combines the images in different configurations, according to the spatial and temporal sequencing of discursive reason in material intellect. Discursive reason then receives an abstraction of the *eidos* from the *phantasia*, a representation of the intelligible form, which corresponds to the sensible form.

In the *De anima*, Aristotle compared the active intellect, the cosmic intellect, to light itself, in relation to the potential or material intellect, what can be taken as *ratio* or discursive reason, as "in a certain fashion, light makes potential colors actual... " (3.5.430a10–25) (Davidson, 1992, p. 19). Aristotle contrasted a productive intellect, the *nous poietikos*, with the potential or passive intellect, the *nous pathetikos*. The active intellect illuminates what is intelligible in the sensible world. The active intellect illuminates the intelligible form, what is intelligible in the *eidos*, in the sensible form as formed by the imagination or *phantasia*, from the imprint in sense perception, which is then given to discursive reason. *Phantasia* is composed of afterimages of sensations, mnemic residues or traces in the *oculus mentis*. According to Aristotle, *phantasia* is not part of intellect; it merely supplies intellect, as a material substratum, with the sensible form, which the intellect illuminates, as light makes potential colors actual, to form the intelligible form in actual intellect. *Phantasia*, though it is not part of intellect, is necessary for the functioning of intellect.

Avicenna, in his *Kitab al-Najat* (*Book of Salvation*, 69), compared the essentially visible sun to the essentially intelligible intellect. In the process of vision, rays of light from the sun conjoin with potentially visible colors, which become actually visible, following Aristotle, and potential vision, which becomes actual vision. In the same way, the active intellect illuminates the *phantasia* to render potential intelligibles or particulars actually intelligible as universals, resulting in abstract concepts. In the *Shifā: De anima* (235–6), the light of active intellect conjoins with sensory thought, discursive reason or *phantasia*, which allows the latter to abstract the *eidos*, to see the sensible form as the intelligible form.

In the *Liber Naturalis* of Avicenna, "The rational faculty, illuminated in us by the light of the active intellect, considers the particulars that are in the imagination," and "in this way they are rendered free from matter and its appendages and are imprinted in the rational soul" (6.5.6) (Brentano, 1977, p. 7, n. 30). As in Themistius, the active intellect is that which illuminates, the *ellampôn*, while potential intellect contains what is illuminated, the *ellampomenoi*, and the multiple particulars which illuminate, the *ellampontes*. The illumination of the particulars frees the particulars from their corporeal dependence, in that the incorporeality of light can participate in them; the illumination allows the particulars to be transposed into universals or intelligibles, as they "do not move by themselves from imagination toward our intellect." The intelligible is not possible without the particular, but it is not the particular which causes the intelligible, nor is it the faculty of human intelligence, which alone cannot exceed its corporeal mechanisms in conscious thought.

Because, for Avicenna, intelligibles cannot actually exist in the human intellect – they are incorporeal and properties of active intellect, Platonic archetypes – only knowledge of intelligibles can exist in human intellect; so, the illumination of active intellect is not of the intelligibles themselves, differing from Aristotle, but of the faculty in the soul to know the intelligibles. The illumination is of the *phantasia*, the mechanism of the soul, and not of the potential intelligibles in *phantasia*. The illumination is not of the intelligible form in the *oculus mentis*, but of the perception of the intelligible form in the *oculus mentis*, as in a mirror reflection: for example, in actual or acquired intellect, as active intellect participates in it through emanation or illumination. The *eidos* does not become an intelligible in its being transported from the compositive imagination, but rather in its being perceived by acquired intellect, which is so disposed because it is in conjunction with active intellect through illumination (*Shifā: De anima* 235–56). It is the *oculus mentis*, rather than the *eidos* itself, which is illuminated – the flashlight, rather than the object which the flashlight makes visible.

In the *Shifā: De anima* (247), Avicenna compared the ability of intellect to achieve acquired intellection through the illumination of active intellect, to the eye which has been made healthy in its vision through treatment so it is able to see clearly. In the *Liber Naturalis* of Avicenna, "learning for the first time is like the healing of an eye, which, having been made healthy, can, when it wants to, apprehend a form by looking upon some individual" (6.5.6) (Brentano, 1977, p. 8, n. 33). The healthy eye, like the healthy soul, is able to perceive the intelligible form in the sensible form, and conscious thought is able to apprehend unconscious thought.

Avicenna also compared the ability of intellect to achieve acquired intellection to a mirror. Intellect can only achieve acquired intellection if it is turned towards active intellect and is able to perceive reflections of intelligibles, as in a mirror. The intelligibles are not actually in intellect in the same way that corporeal forms, or sensible bodies, are not actually in a mirror. Acquired intellect is only capable of receiving the intelligible to the extent of its limitations, as differentiated or sequentially arranged in conscious thought, in the same way that the mirror is only capable of receiving an image according to its corporeal state, adjusted in size and position.

In the *Liber Naturalis* of Avicenna, the soul consists of five internal senses. The *sensus communis* is sensory representation in the common sense, which coordinates the five external senses. The retentive imagination, or *phantasia*, preserves the sensations processed by the *sensus communis*. The sensations preserved in *phantasia* are then processed in a compositive imagination. Memory or *memoria* preserves the perceptions of the *vis aestimativa* as traces or mnemic residues. The *vis aestimativa* or *vis existimationis* is the intuitive faculty which performs sensual judgment (Brentano, 1977, pp. 7–8). The internal senses are also explained in the *Shifā: De anima* (44–45). Both the *phantasia* and *memoria* are seen as a kind of "storehouse" for what is apprehended: *phantasia* stores the forms apprehended by sense perception, while *memoria* stores the *intentiones* connected with the *eidos*, the capacity for discernment of intellect, apprehended by the *vis aestimativa*, as what might be the *logos endiathetos* in the formation of language.

The *intentiones* would correspond to the phonetic form of the word as received in sense perception, which is then retained as a mnemic residue in *phantasia* as the *intentio*, into which it has been transformed by the *vis aestimativa* of the actual intellect. Once the word in language has become the intelligible in the *memoria* as the *intentio*, then intellect is able to reinsert it into the corporeal particulars of language in the mechanics of discursive reason, as it is able to see it as illuminated by active intellect, separated from the corporeal. In the *Liber Naturalis*, "learning is nothing but the attainment of a perfect disposition for uniting oneself with the active intellect until this becomes a cognition that is simple," in the unification of the sensible and intelligible, "and from which emanate ordered forms by virtue of the thought activity of the soul" (6.5.6) (Brentano, 1977, p. 8, n. 33). As the unified cognitions are stored in *memoria* as *intentiones*, they will pass as sensible forms in *phantasia* unless the illumination of active intellect is turned toward them through actualized intellect, *intellectus in habitu*.

In the *Liber Naturalis*, "That which receives is not the same as that which preserves. The storehouse of that which is apprehended by sense is the faculty of imagination," *phantasia*, "while the storehouse for that which apprehends intentions," *thesaurus apprehendentis intentionem*, "is memory" (6.4.1) (Brentano, 1977, p. 8, n. 32). *Phantasia* and *memoria* are not active participants in intellection; the memory traces are present in them only when they are not participating in intellection, when the soul is not conscious of them. Thus the image "is preserved in its preserving faculty whenever the soul averts its attention from it," and "these preserving faculties do not apprehend," rather, "they are a storehouse," and "if the apprehending or judging faculty (*vis aestimativa*) of either the intellect or the soul turns towards it, then they encounter that which is already in possession....." When the *eidos* or *intentio* is not playing a role in actual intellect, it can be found in the *phantasia* or *memoria*, in the inert substratum of potential intellect. "A storehouse is assigned to those *forms* that at certain times are not contemplated by the estimative faculty," the forms in *phantasia*, and "a storehouse is also assigned to those *intentions* that, at certain times, are not considered by the estimative faculty," the *intentiones* in *memoria*.

When a perception is forgotten it is preserved in the *phantasia* or *memoria*, but is inaccessible to conscious thought. The forgetting of a perception is a result of the inability of the soul to be able to receive the illumination of the active intellect, to be able to function according to higher intellectual faculties. The memory of a sensory perception is different from the memory of an intelligible. The intelligible, in that it is indivisible, cannot be present in a corporeal organ, or known through a physical faculty, as it cannot subsist in a divisible substratum – as explained in the *Shifā: De anima* (209). Intelligibles can thus not be retained by an internal sense such as the *phantasia* or *memoria*, and not be present in material intellect. The intelligible is only present in active intellect, as an incorporeal; it is accessible to material intellect, and it can participate in material intellect, but material intellect cannot participate in it. Thus, for Avicenna the intelligible is a Platonic archetype, existing separately from human intellect. The intelligible emanates to the soul and participates in it according to the Plotinian model. The intelligible is able to participate in material intellect by acquired intellect, which allows the soul to overcome the defects and limitations to which it is subject in its connection to corporeality. The intelligible is eternally and consistently accessible to material intellect, but material intellect is not always capable of receiving it, as it is subject to temporal and spatial limitations in the same way that unconscious thought would be accessible to conscious thought.

In the *Liber Naturalis* of Avicenna, active intellect and material intellect are mediated by an intellect which is both active and potential, *intellectus in habitu,* which is a state of preparedness for intellection in the participation of active intellect. It is a precondition for knowledge of both sensibles and intelligibles in material intellect, in the connection between the soul and the corporeal. Once the soul is separated from the corporeal, it no longer requires the preparatory sensory potencies assimilated in the *sensus communis,* and is capable of union with the active intellect, insofar as it can receive the participation of active intellect. "But when the soul is once freed from body and from the accidents of body, it will be capable of union with the active intellect, and in this intellect it shall find intelligible beauty and eternal delight" (*Liber Naturalis* 6.5.6) (Brentano, 1977, p. 7, n. 29).

Material intellect is present in human intellect from birth, according to Avicenna. Material intellect then progresses to the stage of *intellectus in habitu,* then to actualized intellect, in which active intellect can participate. *Intellectus in habitu* is capable of operating according to principles, *principia conoscendi,* while actual intellect is capable of operating according to intelligibles. Both the *principia conoscendi* and the intelligibles come from without, from active intellect; they are not properties inherent to material intellect. The memory of the principle or intelligible is not an actual memory: principles and intelligibles are incorporeal, so a trace of them cannot be retained. A memory of an intelligible is actually the memory of the knowledge of the intelligible, not the intelligible itself, as it is reflected onto the *oculus mentis* in the illumination of the active intellect. Human intellect cannot possess the intelligible or the trace of the intelligible; it can only possess the knowledge or awareness of the intelligible, in its heightened state of functioning as material intellect in *intellectus in habitu* or actualized intellect. Conscious thought can only be aware of the presence of unconscious thought.

Material intellect is not capable of retaining abstractions, concepts, universals or intelligibles. The concept is only present in material intellect while it is being thought or cognized. The *oculus mentis* is not capable of retaining the sensible form: the sensible form can only be retained once it has been associated with the intelligible form, from the *sensus communis, phantasia* and *memoria,* and stored in the *imaginatio,* as a mnemic residue. As seen in *Liber Naturalis* 6.4.1 (Brentano, 1977, p. 8, n. 32): "That which receives is not the same as that which preserves. The storehouse of that which is apprehended by sense is the faculty of imagination, while the storehouse for that which apprehends intentions is memory." That which apprehends intentions, *thesaurus apprehendentis intentionem*, is the agent intellect, in connection with the *vis aestimativa*.

The immediate sensible perception can have no permanence until it has been transformed by the agent intellect into a universal, and processed in incorporeal intellection. The sensible form is then received by the soul and becomes the material of the acquired or obtained cognition, *intellectus adeptus* or *intellectus accommodatus*, and actual cognition is possible. The acquired cognition is the acquired intellect, *nous epiktetos*, but is not the same as the *intellectus in habitu*, which is discursive reason as distinct from agent intellect. In relation to Aristotle's doctrine of passive and active intellect, the active intellect becomes the foundation for intellection, as mediated by the *intellectus in habitu* in combination with the *intellectus adeptus*.

Sense objects, of themselves, are subject to the fluctuating and impermanent collection of unrelated particulars that constitute the material world. The same is true of the sensible form in the *phantasia*, as long as it is connected to the corporeity of the *sensus communis* and the *phantasia* in cogitative reason. As the sensible form is processed as the intelligible form and stored in *imaginatio* as *phantasmata* and in *memoria* as *intentiones*, the mnemic residues can be retained by cogitative reason and *vis aestimativa* to varying degrees – according to the extent of the active intellect's participation; so, the intellect is seen as a kind of palimpsest of traces of forms and thoughts of varying clarity in relation to cognition, conscious thought.

Unconscious thought might be seen as the intelligible in cognition (in the Aristotelian model), connected to sense perception, only accessible to conscious thought or actual intellect to varying degrees; unconscious thought would be seen as thought participating in something outside itself, the archetypal intelligible which is the product of the illumination of active intellect. For Aristotle, as can be seen in the third book of *De anima*, thought participates in something external to itself, the active intellect. In the transcendental idealism of Schelling and Hegel, when thought doubles itself in self-consciousness it becomes aware of the necessity of the existence of something other than itself, or outside itself; and in psychoanalysis, the superego of Freud, the collective unconscious of Jung, or the Other of Lacan constitute elements of intellect in unconscious thought which originate from outside the individual intellect. Full access to intelligibles, illuminated by the active intellect, is only possible for Avicenna when the soul is released from the body in a state of beatitude, when intellection is detached from sense perception; though such detachment is possible to varying degrees in the actualization of intellect, though only at various moments and subject to the temporal and spatial limitations of the human soul and conscious reason. Averroes, the last of the Arabic Peripatetics discussed, saw both active and material intellect as transcendent entities that are only present in soul to the extent that they are in operation there. The active intellect of Averroes can be seen as a form of unconscious thought.

3
The Active Intellect of Averroes

Averroes (1126–98) developed a concept of what can be called "unconscious thought" in the theory of active intellect in the philosophy of intellect, commenting on the *De anima* of Aristotle. Union with the active intellect, the final entelechy, is the highest bliss in life. The suggestion of unconscious thought in Averroes' philosophy of intellect, was pointed out by Franz Brentano. Perhaps this was discussed in a seminar taught by Brentano and attended by Sigmund Freud at the University of Vienna. The active intellect of Averroes can be seen as a form of unconscious thought. This essay will present an interpretation of the philosophy of intellect of Averroes in the *Long Commentary on the De anima*: by examining how Averroes expands on Aristotle's *De anima*; by evaluating the commentaries on Averroes by F. Brentano (1838–1917), P. Merlan (1897–1968), H. A. Davidson and R. C. Taylor; by suggesting precedents for the thought of Averroes in the *Enneads* of Plotinus (204–70); and by suggesting the possible influence of Averroes on the Scholastic and peripatetic philosopher Robert Grosseteste (1168–1253) (Hendrix, 2010).

Averroes (Ibn Rushd) was born in Córdoba and died in Marrakech. He was educated in philosophy, theology, mathematics, medicine, and jurisprudence, and held the office of judge for many years. He was called "Commentator" for his commentaries on Aristotle, which are mostly known through Latin translations. Averroes was "an excessive enthusiast of Aristotle," in the words of Franz Brentano, "concerned to develop the latter's pure doctrine" (Brentano, 1977, p. 11). In his *Long Commentary on the De anima* (*Commentarium magnum in Aristotelis de Anima libros*), Averroes posited three separate intelligences functioning in the *anima rationalis*, or the rational soul: agent or active intellect (*intellectus agens*); material or passible intellect (*intellectus materialis, intellectus passibilis* or *intellectus possibilis*); and, speculative intellect (*intellectus speculativus*),

105

or actualized or acquired intellect (*intellectus adeptus*). In Averroes' *De anima* 3.1.5 (Brentano, 1977, p. 11, n. 55, 3.1.5; Averroes, 1953, p. 406; Averroes, 2009, p. 322), "there are three parts of the intellect in the soul; the first is the receptive intellect, the second, the active intellect, and the third is actual intellection ...": that is, material, agent, and speculative.

This is based on Averroes' interpretation of Aristotle's *De anima* 3.5.430a10–15 (Davidson, 1992, p. 317). While Aristotle located both material and active intellects in the soul, Averroes located only their *functions* in the soul, while the intellects themselves are eternal substances (Brentano, 1977, p. 9). Not wanting to be inconsistent with Aristotle, thought requires both the activity of the active intellect and the receptivity of the material intellect, according to Averroes. The result, though, is that the "first principles of thought" (Davidson, 1992, p. 320) are given without an act of will, that is, unconsciously, but the active intellect can be induced through the active will to illuminate the material intellect and images in the imaginative faculty, the *formae imaginativae* or *phantasmata* in the *imaginatio*. The passible intellect of Aristotle (*De anima* 3.5.430a24) is a "sensory power" (Brentano, 1977, p. 9), and Averroes connects it to both imagination and cognition (*virtus cogitativa*), as Franz Brentano explained in *The Psychology of Aristotle*.

While material intellect is "partly generable and corruptible, partly eternal," corporeal and incorporeal, the active intellect is purely eternal and incorporeal. Active intellect is the final entelechy, or final actualization of potentiality. Material intellect is a possible intellect, a possibility, because it is both corporeal and incorporeal; thus, neither corporeal nor incorporeal, a controversial position taken by Averroes which is difficult to rationalize. Material intellect becomes actualized intellect, or "energized" intellect in the analysis of Philip Merlan in *Monopsychism Mysticism Metaconsciousness*, through the affect of the agent intellect, which illuminates, as a First Cause, the intelligible *species*, the *species apprehensibilis* or *forma imaginativa*, the residue of the *species sensibilis*, the sensation or sensible form, in the *anima rationalis* or soul. The illuminated *species apprehensibilis* or intelligible acts on material intellect until material intellect becomes actualized or energized intellect, at which point intellect is able to act on the intelligible. In the words of Merlan, "material intelligence becomes transformed into what Averroes calls speculative intelligence" (Merlan, 1963, p. 85). The speculative intelligence of Averroes is identical to the productive intelligence of Alexander of Aphrodisias.

When the development of the *intellectus speculativus* is complete, it is perfected through active intellect (Davidson, 1992, p. 332). Averroes did not fully explain how the two intellects can be connected in this way, beyond the mediating role of the imaginative faculty. This problem was explored in detail by Paul Sidney Christ in *The Psychology of the Active Intellect of Averroes*. Averroes failed to reconcile the material (hylic) and active intellects posited by Aristotle. For Plotinus and previous commentators on Aristotle, the explanation was given as the pneumatic, but this was not given in Averroes. Both material and speculative intelligence are seen as being immortal, but the immortality is compromised by the perishability of the *formae imaginativae* in the *imaginatio*, the mechanism by which the material intellect is actualized (Merlan, 1963, p. 86).

The *formae imaginativae*, as the basis of actualized intellect, are both corporeal and incorporeal; they bridge the gap or merge the two in the process of intellection. The *formae imaginativae*, like the sensations of which they are residues, are partially connected to the material or corporeal, and cannot be archetypes from without, but intelligibles within human intellect. The affect of active intellect on material intellect toward actualized intellect is a combination of the illumination and the resulting mechanisms of *intellectus speculativus*. The affect is in the combination of the receptivity of material intellect as a passive substratum of cognitive and intellectual activity, like a blank tablet, and the will or desire on the part of the thinking subject to develop cognitive and intellectual *virtus*.

In his *De anima* (3.7.431b2), Aristotle wrote that the human intellect thinks the forms in images. Aristotle compared the active intellect (*nous*) to light itself, in relation to the potential intellect, what can be taken as *ratio* or discursive reason, as "in a sense light makes potential colours into actual colours" (3.5.430a10–25) (Aristotle, 1952a). Aristotle contrasted the active or productive intellect, *nous poietikos* (although not named as such), with the potential or passive intellect, *nous pathetikos*. The active intellect in unconscious thought illuminates what is intelligible in the sensible world. For Aristotle, *phantasia* or imagination is not part of intellect; it merely supplies intellect with the sensible form, which the intellect illuminates, as light makes potential colors actual, to form the intelligible form in active intellect.

In Aristotle's *De anima* 3.7, human intellect thinks the form or *species*, and processes it conceptually, as an image, which must be imprinted in the imaginative faculty. In 3.4, the sensible object is related to sense perception as the form of the object is related to intellect, the intelligible form, in relation to sensible form as it is imprinted in the imagination through sense perception. The intellect is to what is intelligible as sense perception is to what is perceptible. The intellect is receptive of the form as an intelligible; it must think the form in order to perceive it. An object might be perceived as a sensible form alone, but in that way the object would be singular and individual, not part of a totality. In *De anima* 3.4, although the intellect receives a form as an imprint in sensation and becomes identical in thought with the form, the intellect is not affected or altered in any way by the form or the sense object connected with it.

The active intellect is "a cause which is productive..." (*De anima* 3.5.430a12). According to Aristotle, the intellect is passive in that it becomes all things, and active in that it makes all things. In the *De anima* (3.5.430a14–15), Aristotle distinguished between the quality of mind which is "what it is by virtue of becoming all things," and the quality "which is what it is by virtue of making all things," the making of the actual from the potential. In Aristotle's *De anima*, "in the individual, potential knowledge is in time prior to actual knowledge" (3.5.430a21–22). The active intellect illuminates the intelligible form in the sensible form (this double illumination can also be found in Plotinus), as formed by the imagination or *phantasia*, from the imprint in sense perception (as in Plotinus), which is then given to conscious reason, material intellect. *Phantasia* is composed of afterimages of sensations, mnemic residues or traces in the mind's eye or *oculus mentis*. *Phantasia*, though it is not part of intellect, is necessary for the functioning of intellect.

In Averroes' *De anima* 3.1.5, the existence of intelligibles or first principles in intellect, as they are understood in actualized intellect, "does not simply result from the reception of the object," the sensible form in sense perception in material intellect, "but consists in attention to, or perception of, the represented forms...," the cognition of the forms in actualized intellect wherein they can be understood as intelligibles, which requires both the participation of active intellect and the motivation of the individual for intellectual development. This was also described by Plotinus. The goal of intellectual development, for Averroes, was to achieve union with active intellect – the final entelechy, in unconscious thought, as it were – and through this union the highest bliss in life can be achieved. Such bliss can only be achieved "in the eve of life."

Material intellect, in that it is only a possibility, contains neither actual intellectual cognition nor a faculty for intellectual cognition. Both of these are only possible in actualized intellect, through *intellectus speculativus*, acquired intellect, and the affect of agent intellect. Material intellect contains only the possibility of being united with active intellect; all material intellects are equally potential. While they are all part of "the single transcendent material intellect shared by all human beings" (Taylor, 2005, p. 193), as described by Richard C. Taylor, the power of the material intellect in Averroes' thought should not be overestimated. *Intellectus speculativus* is developed as the *oculus mentis* of the *anima rationalis* develops a vocabulary of images or *phantasmata* stored in the *imaginatio* or *phantasia*. The phantasm is corporeal, and potentially intelligible, as the material intellect has the potential to understand the intelligible. The sensible form can only potentially be an intelligible form if it is predetermined by the intelligible form. In Averroes' *De anima* 3.5.36 (Brentano, 1977, p. 10, n. 49, 3.5.36, Fol. 178b; Averroes, 1953, p. 495; Averroes, 2009, p. 395) "this sort of action," of the active intellect, "which consists in generating intelligibles and actualizing them, exists in us prior to the action of the intellect," prior to the formation of the perceived form in *imaginatio*, in unconscious thought, as it were. The corporeal condition of material intellect acts as a substrate for actualized and agent intellect, the partially and completely incorporeal, only as a blank tablet on which letters are written. The corporeal presence of the letters, the sensible forms in *phantasia*, is predetermined by the writing of the letters, based on the idea of the letter, the intelligible form, which pre-exists the letter itself.

The material intellect alone for Averroes differentiates the human being from other animals, not in its potential for intellect but in its sensory powers, the *intellectus passibilis* of Aristotle. The *intellectus passibilis* is able to distinguish and compare individual sensory representations in the *virtus aestimativa* or *virtus cogitativa*, which provides the material substrate for *intellectus speculativus*. The *virtus aestimativa* or *virtus cogitativa* might also be ascribed to the *sensus communis*, common sense; they are both "perishable body powers" (Taylor, 2005, p. 193). In distinguishing and comparing the *phantasmata* in *imaginatio*, intellect applies shape and form to otherwise nebulous, inchoate images. It also organizes them in totalities, in the most rudimentary processes of abstraction, and defines them in relation to organizational systems, such as geometry and mathematics. This was also described by Plotinus. Averroes suggested that the sensory powers themselves entail an element of intellection, in that the imprint of the sensible form would depend on the formation of the intelligible form.

In Averroes' *De anima* 3.1.7 (Brentano, 1977, p. 10, n. 48, 3.1.7, Fol. 167b; Averroes, 1953, p. 419; Averroes, 2009, p. 334) "the cogitative faculty," *virtus cogitativa*, "belongs to the genus of sensible faculties. But the imaginative and the cogitative and the recollective" faculties, *imaginatio*, *ratio* and *memoria*, "all cooperate in producing the image of the sensible thing," the *species sensibilis*, "so that the separate rational faculty can perceive it," as a reflected image in the *oculus mentis*, "and extract the universal intention," the intelligible, "and finally receive, i.e., comprehend it." In the words of Brentano, "Once they have done this, and once the activity of the active intellect has made the images intelligible in unconscious thought, the material intellect, which stands to all intelligible forms in the relation of potentiality, receives from the images the concepts of sensible things" (Brentano, 1977, p. 10).

The form and shape that intellect imposes on bodies are mechanisms of intellect in sense perception, as in Plotinus. As Averroes explained in the *De anima* 3.1.5 (Brentano, 1977, p. 10, n. 51, 3.1.5, Fol. 163b; Averroes, 1953, p. 400; Averroes, 2009, p. 316), "It is necessary to assign two subjects to these actually existing intelligibles," the intelligible as it exists in the form of the sensory object, "one of which is the subject due to which the intelligibles are true, i.e., forms, which are truthful images," sensible forms; "the other, the subject due to which the intelligibles are only a single one of the entities in the world, and this is the material intellect itself." The intellect of the perceiving subject in sensory perception is as responsible for how the sensible world is perceived as the forms which are assigned to the sensible world.

The *Long Commentary* contains Averroes' fullest account of the relation between active and material intellect (Davidson, 1992, p. 317). The sensible form in the *oculus mentis* exists as a potential intelligible, and the material intellect, which is engaged in the formation of the sensible form, is capable of receiving the intelligible from the active intellect. The active intellect makes what is potentially intelligible, actually intelligible. The material intellect is the passible intellect, *intellectus passibilis*, described by Aristotle in his *De anima* (3.5.430a24), which distinguishes and compares the individual representations of sense experience in the *oculus mentis*. Averroes also called the passible intellect *virtus aestimativa* (a term used by Avicenna), and *virtus cogitativa* (a term used by Robert Grosseteste). The *intellectus passibilis* should be distinguished from the *virtus aestimativa naturalis*, which is judgment by natural instinct, and can be found in all animals.

Averroes, in his *De anima*, compared *intellectus passibilis* to *phantasia* or *imaginatio* (Brentano, 1977, p. 9, n. 39, 3.1.20; Averroes, 1953, p. 452; Averroes, 2009, p. 361), the image-making *virtus* or power of intellect in the formation of the *phatasmata*. Following Aristotle, Averroes divided material intellect into the *sensus communis*, or sense perception, the *phantasia*, the *virtus cogitativa*, and *memoria*, in ascending order from corporeal to spiritual, as the active intellect is increasingly engaged. The material intellect cannot distinguish or apprehend intelligibles on its own. The material, passible intellect, becomes an acquired intellect, through the activities of *phantasia* and *memoria*, and is based on the acquisition of habitual knowledge through exercise, *intellectus in habitu*, as a material *intellectus speculativus*. The passible intellect operates according to its capacity for receptivity, not according to an ability to form concepts or abstractions.

Intellectual knowledge for Averroes must be distinguished from the habitual knowledge of passible intellect. Intellectual knowledge is the product of the merging of the material intellect, which is considered to be incorporeal, despite its dependence on the sensible, and the active intellect, which transforms the sensible form into the intelligible form, stripping it of its corporeal attachment and converting it from a particular to a universal, which makes the potentially intelligible *phantasmata* in the *oculus mentis* intelligible. The *intellectus agens* is the intellect which acts, which moves the material intellect, the intellect which only receives or is affected, as described in *De anima* 3.1.5. The active intellect allows the material intellect to be moved by imagination. The *intellectus passibilis*, as *virtus cogitativa* in combination with *phantasia* and *memoria*, forms the phantasm in order that it can be perceived by the active intellect, and prepares it to receive the active intellect, by which the sensible becomes the intelligible, which can be comprehended as a universal.

In Averroes' *De anima*, the transformation from potentiality to actuality takes place in the speculative intellect, which includes the *intellectus in habitu*, and is distinguished from the agent or productive intellect, *intellectus agens*, unconscious thought, and the material or passible intellect, *intellectus passibilis* (Merlan, 1963, p. 85). The actualizing of the material intellect by the productive intellect is the result of the productive intellect illuminating the residues of sensations existing in the mind, the *formae imaginativae*, or mnemic residues. The *formae* act on the material intellect after they have been illuminated, and material intellect is transformed into speculative intellect, which combines the material and productive intellects, the physical and eternal or archetypal, corporeal and incorporeal.

Averroes described the material intellect as the transparent medium in relation to the active intellect, as light. In the relation between *nous* and discursive reason, the activity of the *intellectus agens* must precede that of the *intellectus materialis*. In the material intellect, individual representations are distinguished, in the *virtus aestimativa naturalis*. The material form is seen as color in relation to the light, resulting from the *intentio* in the imaginative faculty, or *phantasia*. In other words, as Averroes said in his *De anima* (Brentano, 1977, p. 10, n. 50, 3.3.18, Fol. 169b; Averroes, 1953, pp. 438–9; Averroes, 2009, p. 351), "the relation of the intentions in imagination to the material intellect is the same as the relation of the sensible to the senses." The material intellect receives the active intellect in the same way that transparent bodies "receive light and colors at the same time; the light, however, brings forth the colors" (*De anima* 3.5.36) (Brentano, 1977, p. 12, n. 59, 3.5.36, Fol. 179b; Averroes, 1953, p. 499; Averroes, 2009, p. 398). The intelligible form results from the cooperation of the material and active intellects. In the words of Davidson, the active intellect "illuminates both the material intellect and images in the imaginative faculty of the soul" (Davidson, 1992, p. 319): an illumination induced through the exercise of the will.

For Averroes, light is the entelechy (*entelecheia*, actualization or *perfectio*) of the transparent medium, just as the active intellect is the entelechy of material intellect. Averroes followed Alfarabi in his explanation of light, but failed to distinguish between light and the source of light (Davidson, 1992, p. 316). This, nevertheless, resulted in a new interpretation of light as entelechy on the part of Averroes, based on his interpretation of Aristotle. The transparent is not affected by color in any way unless it is illuminated, just as discursive reason is not affected in any way by intelligibles unless it is illuminated and perfected by the active intellect, the higher intellect or *nous*. When the material intellect is perfected by the agent intellect it is joined to it as an *adeptio*, or acquisition, and the combination becomes *intellectus adeptus*, or acquired intellect. Averroes saw the material intellect as a medium rather than an organ, enabling consciousness of intelligible thoughts, through the illumination of the *formae imaginativae* in the *imaginatio* (Davidson, 1992, p. 318). The same function of *phantasia* was described by Plotinus.

Once the combination of the material intellect and the active intellect has formed the *species apprehensibilis* and allowed the *virtus cogitativa* to apprehend the intelligible, the concept and universal are able to play a role in cogitation. As Averroes said in *De anima* 3.3.18, when "the relation of the intentions in imagination to the material intellect is the same as the relation of the sensible to the senses, as Aristotle says, it is necessary to assume another mover which makes them actually move the material intellect, and this simply means that it makes actual thoughts by separating them from matter." The *intellectus adeptus* produces the intelligible form when the *sensus communis*, *virtus cogitativa* and *imaginatio* in the *nous hylikos* establish a foundation in cooperation to provide material for the *intellectus adeptus*, which it then processes in relation to the active intellect. The intelligible form is a hybrid of the universal concept, which is the product of the active intellect, and the sensible form, which is the product of sense perception and *imaginatio*.

The intelligible form unites the *virtus cogitativa* with the active intellect, and sense perception with intellection.

The material intellect, *virtus cogitativa*, in that it is tied to the particulars of sense perception, is a singular entity in each individual and cannot produce meaning or communication, cannot unite the cognitive faculties of each individual. The active intellect, on the other hand – in that it is capable of formulating intelligibles, which are incorporeal and not tied to the materials of individual sense perception – is able to unite particular individuals engaging in cognition, in order to create a shared intellection which produces communication and meaning. This is sometimes referred to as "monopsychism," and is also a basic proposition of structural linguistics in the twentieth century. In *De anima* (Brentano, 1977, p. 10, n. 52, 3.1.5, Fol. 164b; Averroes, 1953, p. 404; Averroes, 2009, p. 320) Averroes says, "And since it has already been shown that the intellect cannot unite with all individuals by multiplying according to their number with respect to that part that is the opposite of intellect qua form," material intellect, "the only thing that remains is that this intellect unites with all of us through the union with us of concepts or intentions present to the mind... ." It is thus a "collective unconscious." While the operation of the *virtus cogitativa* is particular to each individual, the intelligible form, which it receives from the active intellect, is universal and shared by every individual, as it is retained as a permanent archetype in intellection.

When the intelligible is received by the material intellect, it is subject to generation and corruption, multiplicity and accident. The intelligible form, when it is connected to the sensible form in material intellect, is not a permanent mnemic residue as an archetype, but is fluctuating and impermanent in its corporeal manifestation. But the intelligible form does not disappear when its corresponding sensible form does: it merely ceases to participate in the sensible form. As Aristotle said, "Mind does not think intermittently" (*De anima* 430a10–25). In his *De anima*, (Brentano, 1977, p. 11, n. 55, 3.1.5, Fol. 165b; Averroes, 1953, pp. 407–08; Averroes, 2009, p. 323) Averroes adds, "And if intelligibles of this kind are considered, insofar as they have being *simpliciter* and not in respect of some individual," as universals, "then it must truly be said of them that they have eternal being, and that they are not sometimes intelligibles and sometimes not, but that they always exist in the same manner... ." The intelligible form can participate in the sensible form, of its own volition, or the volition of the active intellect, but the sensible form cannot participate in the intelligible form, in its corporeal limitations, in the same way that color – for example, because it is tied to the corporeal body – cannot participate in light, although they are perceived simultaneously and are undifferentiated in perception.

Just because the sensible form is no longer visible in the *oculus mentis* does not mean that the intelligible form that is attached to it ceases to exist. The material intellect, in that it is part incorporeal and eternal, also always has the potential to understand the intelligible, the abstract concept. Whether it does or not depends on the degree of union with active intellect and the degree of development of *virtus*, not on the level of potentiality. Material intellect, discursive or conscious reason, is also always thinking; it is not capable of not thinking (in contrast to Plotinus), which shows the presence of the eternal in it.

The material intellect of every individual is capable of receiving the intelligible form; individual material intellects receive intelligibles from the unconscious active intellect to varying degrees, depending on the extent to which the individual aspires to intelligible knowledge. It is not that the material intellect is not always thinking and does not always have the potential to receive intelligibles; it is just that it is not always united with active intellect. It is through the perfected union between the material intellect and the active intellect that intelligibles are apprehended, and that a beatific state can be achieved by the most complete apprehension of them as possible. Intelligibles come to material intellect naturally as first principles, as in the *proten entelecheian* of Aristotle, the first entelechy, but any further intelligibles derived from the first principles require the volition of the material intellect. In *De anima* (Brentano, 1977, p. 12, n. 60, 3.5.36, Fol. 179b; Averroes, 1953, p. 499; Averroes, 2009, p. 399) all individual material intellects are capable of receiving intelligibles naturally: the active intellect "is combined with us potentially whenever the speculative intelligibles are potentially present within us...."

All individual material intellects are capable of some ability to form concepts and abstract ideas at a basic level, but beyond that intellectual development varies among individuals according to the level of volition (what Grosseteste would call *solertia*). The emphasis on individual will is a key element of Averroes' thought. Intelligibles are apprehended the more completely as knowledge of the material world is greater, according to Averroes, as knowledge of sensible objects depends on knowledge of intelligibles. Complete knowledge of the material world results in complete unity between the material intellect and the active intellect, the final entelechy achieved in the "eve of life."

Such an entelechy is the result of the process of active intellect combining "with us through conjoining the speculative intelligibles," in the union of the sensible and intelligible, in stages of potentiality and actuality. The final entelechy requires actuality, in actualized intellect, *intellectus adeptus*, rather than potentiality, in material intellect: so the great mass of potentiality which defines the substratum of human material intellect must be overcome to a great degree, and takes a long time, an entire life. The reason why material intellect is only united with active intellect at the end of life, and not the beginning, is that "potency is part of us so long as there is in us form that exists only potentially," which could be seen as an infinity. Knowledge and understanding are possible only in actualized intellect, which must no longer be potential intellect. Intellectual knowledge, and philosophy itself, which is eternal, as an intelligible, must be seen as the ultimate goal of human life, and the cause of the most perfect bliss.

Aristotle, in his *De anima*, defined light as a transparent medium. For Averroes, the material intellect receives intelligible thoughts as the transparent medium receives colors through illumination. As light makes colors visible to the eye, so light makes intelligibles understandable to the material intellect, discursive reason, resulting in abstract thoughts and concepts. Averroes saw the material intellect as a medium, as light is in the sensible world, an eternal substance independent of the mechanisms of the senses, as much as the active intellect. In Averroes' *De anima*, intellect must be defined as unmixed, in particular as unmixed with the particulars of sense experience and sense knowledge. Material intellect is not altered in any way by the reception of intellect, because, though it is connected to the body, it is not a body itself; it is more of a blank slate, as for Aristotle in *De anima* 3.4.429b30–430a10, the forms of thought "must be in it just as characters may be said to be on a writing-tablet on which as yet nothing actually stands written..."; material intellect is thus the "place of forms" as described by Aristotle in *De anima* 3.4.429a27–28.

For Averroes, following Aristotle, it is necessary that the material or receiving intellect be unmixed so that it can receive and understand all things. If material intellect were a form itself, then it could not receive a form. Material intellect is activated to the extent to which it is able to understand the forms of things which exist in actuality outside the rational soul, or the potential for thought. The rational soul, *anima rationalis*, considers the forms or *intentiones* which are in the imaginative faculty, and material intellect is activated in its process of abstracting forms from material things and creating first intelligibles, intelligibles in actuality derived from potentials in potentiality; in that way, intellect goes from being passive to being active. When intellect is moved by intelligibles, it is passive, but when intellect comes to move intelligibles, it is active; thus, the *anima rationalis* consists of two distinct powers: the passive and the active. Both powers are unmixed, incorporeal – neither generable nor corruptible.

In Averroes' *De anima* (Brentano, 1977, p. 9, n. 44, 3.5.36, Fol. 165a; Averroes, 1953, p. 406; Averroes, 2009, p. 322) "there are formed in the soul of man two parts of the intellect, one being that which *receives*," and "another being that which *acts*," the former being the material intellect, the latter being the actualized intellect, which "makes it the case that the intentions and concepts existing in the faculty of imagination," as connected to the *phantasmata* in *imaginatio*, which are illuminated by active intellect, "actually move the material intellect, while previously they moved it only potentially....." Further, "those two parts are neither generated nor corruptible" as corporeal, and "the relation of the active to the receptive intellect is just like the relation of form to matter." The sensible impression, or *phantasma*, thus acts on matter in sense perception in material intellect, in the *virtus aestimativa* or *virtus cogitativa*, *dianoia*. Further, in *De anima* 3.5.36 (Brentano, 1977, p. 9, n. 44, 3.5.36, Fol. 178b; Averroes, 1953, p. 495; Averroes, 2009, p. 395), there are "two modes of action" in intellect, "one of which belongs to the genus of *affections*" in material intellect, the other belonging to "the genus of *actions*" in actualized intellect, "whose function it is to abstract the forms and to strip them of matter, which is nothing other than making them into actual intelligibles, while previously they were only potential intelligibles," the sensible form made known as the intelligible form.

For Averroes, the *species* or *eidos* must be transformed in order for it to be received by material intellect, as in the *Liber Naturalis* of Avicenna; it must be differentiated as an intelligible in potentiality as opposed to an intelligible in actuality. Material intellect is not corporeal, in that it is capable of receiving corporeal forms, though it must be connected to the corporeal. As Taylor explains, "it is not possible for the material intellect itself to be a particular or definite individual entity, since the received intelligible would be contracted to the particular nature of its subject, the material intellect" (Taylor, 2005, p. 192). At the same time, material intellect cannot be composed of forms, in that it is capable of receiving sensible forms. Material intellect is thus neither matter nor simple form, form separable from body. It is capable of receiving the sensible form, and it is capable of producing the intelligible form, but it is neither matter nor intelligible itself, but rather an indefinable substrate for both.

Material intellect must be defined as being something in between the corporeal and incorporeal, as the mechanism which can connect the two.

Material intellect cannot be seen to contain anything similar to the *species* or form which it is capable of receiving in *phantasia*, but it can be seen to contain something similar to the genus of the *species* which it receives, and to the predication of the *species* which it receives. In other words, there must be a predisposition of the material intellect – while it is a power separate from the body, and has no material form which allows it to receive the sensible form – which is the a priori existence of the intelligible form in the unconscious; which governs the perception of the sensible form and its transformation into an intelligible form in the process of abstraction and conceptualization in actualized or acquired intellect.

Averroes concluded that material intellect can only be defined as a possibility, as Aristotle said that it has only the nature of the possibility for receiving the intelligible forms, and that before it thinks, it does not exist. The material intelligible form, a seeming contradiction in terms, can only exist if the sensible form is seen as a manifestation of the intelligible form, or the intelligible form is seen as a precondition of the material form, and the material form does not exist outside of its conception based on the intelligible form. The material intelligible form, or universal material form, exists only as a potential concept, which is material intellect, which is potentially all of the concepts of universal material forms, and the material intelligible form exists only as actuality when it is understood by intellect.

Material intellect is capable of receiving universal forms, intelligibles, because of its partial separation from the corporeal, which contains only differentiated forms, the particulars of sense perception, as also explained by Plotinus and Grosseteste. For Averroes, material intellect is not corporeal because it can distinguish between sensible particulars and universal forms; if it were corporeal it would not be able to do so, it would only be able to receive forms as differentiated and particular. As material intelligible forms, or universal material forms, exist in material intellect, they exist as speculative intelligibles which are generable and corruptible, subject to the mechanisms of intellect. This is possible because there must be a cause of the generation of the speculative intelligibles, something which allows material intellect to bridge the corporeal and incorporeal.

Averroes and Plotinus

Though Averroes is not generally considered to be sympathetic to Neoplatonic thinking, there are definite parallels between the philosophies of intellect of Averroes and Plotinus. Both can be considered to be "Idealists" in that intelligible form precedes sensible form in perception, and that the material intellect of Averroes or discursive reason of Plotinus, *nous hylikos* or *pathetikos*, depends in its functioning on the agent intellect of Averroes or Intellect of Plotinus, *nous poietikos*, both of which can be seen as a form of unconscious thinking, not available to material intellect or discursive reason in conscious thought. The formation of the image in the *oculus mentis* is coincident with the formation of a thought, and the sensible form is a transient residue of the permanent intelligible form, as if it is reflected in a mirror and projected on a surface. For both philosophers, material intellect and intellect not connected to sense perception are mediated by a kind of *intellectus in habitu* (*intellectus speculativus*), a practicing intellect which leads the individual to higher forms of understanding. The development of *phantasmata* or imprints of forms in the *oculus mentis* in the imagination or *phantasia* is the product of a dialectical relation between the mechanisms of sense perception in material intellect and an a priori understanding of forms in the intelligible, in unconscious thought, prior to the sensible. In order to be perceived, forms must be constructed, in a structuring of reality. For both Plotinus and Averroes, the *formae imaginativae* or *phantasmata* in the *imaginatio* are the mechanisms by which material intellect or *dianoia* is actualized by agent intellect or *nous*.

In the *Enneads* of Plotinus (I.6.3, 1966), shape is not something which is inherent to objects in sensual reality, but is rather something which is imposed upon objects by human thought, in the nature of geometry and ordering principles. The sensible form given by the material intellect connected to sense perception is already a product of intellection. The shape of the impression of the form of the object in Plotinus is something conceived in unconscious thought, and joined to the material object before it is received as an impression; the shape of the object is part of the a priori vocabulary by which intellect orders the sensual world, and reaffirms the existence of the perceiving subject in the world. For Plotinus, "When sense-perception, then, sees the form in bodies binding and mastering the nature opposed to it, which is shapeless, and shape riding gloriously upon other shapes," fragmented and confused, "it gathers into one that which appears dispersed and brings it back and takes it in, now without parts," in apperception, "to the soul's interior and presents to it that which is within as something in tune with it...." As for Averroes, the form and shape that intellect imposes on bodies are mechanisms of intellect in sense perception.

Sense perception transfers the form of the body or material entity as conceptualized, according to Plotinus, "now without parts" (*Enneads* I.6.3); the perceived form must correspond to the a priori or unconscious preconception of it, the intelligible form. *Dianoia* or discursive reason – actualized material intellect, described as "the reasoning power in soul" in *Enneads* V.3.2 – makes judgments about the sensible form given to it, which is already the product of judgments of the higher intellect, *nous poietikos* – the presence of active intellect in actualized intellect – and organizes them in combinations and divisions, corresponding to the principles of geometry and mathematics. As the *phantasmata* or imprints of forms come to reasoning power from intellect, "as for the things which come to it from Intellect, it observes what one might call their imprints," formed in the imagination by the logos, "and it continues to acquire understanding as if by recognizing the new and recently arrived impressions and fitting them to those which have long been within it," unconsciously, in "recollections of the soul," according to Plotinus, as in an actualized intellect or *intellectus in habitu*. Perception is the product of experience in the interaction of unconscious and conscious thought and the sensible world, the dialectic of the incorporeal and corporeal, the universal and particular.

In *Enneads* V.3.3, if sense perception is to make the details of form explicit, "it is taking to pieces what the image-making power gave it," and if it makes a judgment on the form, "its remark originates in what it knows through sense-perception, but what it says about this it has already from itself...." Discursive reason in material intellect does nothing other than process images of forms which it has already defined itself, through the relation between active intellect and material intellect, Intellect and discursive reason. Without the capacity to understand the intelligible, the intelligible form in relation to the sensible form, material intellect can only be unaware or unconscious of the reality of the sensible world that is perceived, and unaware of the role that it plays in the formation and definition of the sensible world that it perceives as external to itself.

For Plotinus there can be no immediate sense perception of an object, without the mediation of the mirror reflection of the intelligible form of the object in intellect, the *forma imaginativa* of Averroes. In *Enneads* I.1.8, the intelligible form in intellect becomes the sensible form in sense perception, "not of itself and body, but abiding itself and giving images of itself, like a face seen in many mirrors," in the same way that active intellect presents the intelligible to acquired intellect. Acquired intellect is only capable of receiving the intelligible to the extent of its limitations, as differentiated or sequentially arranged, in the same way that the mirror is only capable of receiving an image according to its corporeal state, adjusted in size and position, given by logos.

The discerning of impressions printed upon the intellect by sensation for Plotinus is the function of discursive reason, not immediate sense perception. Since the sensual impressions in perception are copies and derivatives of intelligible forms, perception itself is a copy and derivative of conscious and unconscious thought. Reason in Plotinus is composed of mnemic residues of perceived objects, what Plotinus calls "imprints" in "recollections" (*Enneads* V.3.2). Thoughts are propelled by the desire created by the multiple and fragmented images of perception as reconstructed in reason. In *Enneads* IV.7.6, sense perceptions merge together in reason like lines coming together from the circumference of the circle, from multiplicity to unity, subject to the ruling principles. In reality, sense objects are variable and differentiated in terms of size and location; they are multiple and fragmented, and it is only the unconscious thought of the perceiver in apperception which allows them to be apprehended as whole and congruent. Sense objects themselves cannot be immediately perceived as a congruent whole. Once the diverse and multiple sense objects have been transformed into a whole by apprehension in sense perception, and apperception in unconscious thought, they cannot return to their original state. Apprehension permanently transforms sensual reality in conformance with the principles of reason.

Perception, according to Plotinus, divides, multiplies, and otherwise organizes sensual reality, anticipating Kant; in other words, perception is an intellective process. Perceived objects are divided and organized into parts, which correspond directly to the organizational capacities of reason. The relation of parts and subdivisions to the whole and to infinity is the same in the sense object as it is in reasoning capacity. Geometry and mathematics are mechanisms by which sensual reality is represented by perception to reason, though sense objects do not inherently contain geometrical and mathematical properties, again anticipating Kant.

For Plotinus, discursive reason approaches *nous*, as material intellect approaches active intellect for Averroes, when reason recognizes its recent sense impressions and "gathers into one that which appears dispersed and brings it back and takes it in, now without parts," the mnemic residue or memory trace of previous sense impressions, in a process of reminiscence. In the *Enneads*, while perception grasps the "impressions produced by sensation on the living being" (I.1.7), through the mnemic residue, a perception is "a mental image for that which is going to remember it" (IV.3.29), and the "memory and the retention of the object" belong to the "image-making power" or the imagination or *phantasia*. In the representation in the mnemic residue, the intelligible form is present after the sensible form or perception is gone, as for Averroes. Through memory, "an image accompanies every mental act," as described in *Enneads* IV.3.30. Through the intelligible form the intellectual act is without parts and has not come out into the open, but remains unobserved within, unknown to reason, suggesting the "unconscious" element of thought for which Plotinus is known, and which plays a role in the philosophy of Averroes.

Averroes and Grosseteste

Robert Grosseteste is believed to have known the *Long Commentary* of Averroes, translated into Latin c. 1220, as evidenced in works by Grosseteste such as the *Commentary on the Posterior Analytics* (c. 1230), and the *Hexaëmeron* (*On the Six Days of Creation*, 1237), written shortly before or at the time Grosseteste became Bishop of Lincoln (Hendrix, 2010). In the *Hexaëmeron* (VIII, IV, 7) (Grosseteste, 1996), the sensible form or *species sensibilis* is given by the intelligible form or *species apprehensibilis*, which is formed in the imagination or *phantasia* and is presented to discursive reason in the process of perception. The active intellect illuminates the *species apprehensibilis*, what is intelligible in the *species*, in the *species sensibilis* as formed by the *phantasia* or *imaginatio*, from the imprint in sense perception, which is then given to passive intellect. The *species apprehensibilis* is a similitude of the *species sensibilis*, as a mnemic residue, and is thus a representation of the *species sensibilis*, which is itself a representation of the object to which its form corresponds (*Hexaëmeron* VIII, IV, 9–10). The representation of the representation would be the *Vorstellunsrepräsentanz* of Freud.

In the *Commentary on the Posterior Analytics* of Aristotle (I.14, 235–8) (Grosseteste, 1981), Grosseteste compared (but did not equate) *intelligentia*, divine intellect, to the *intellectus agens*, agent intellect, or *actio intellectus*, active intellect: the intellect that is differentiated from the passive, material intellect in Aristotle's *De anima*. Like Aristotle's *actio intellectus*, Grosseteste's *intelligentia* illuminates the lower functions of intellect, *virtus cogitativa* and *intellectus in habitu*, as described by Averroes in the *Long Commentary*. The mediating factor – suggested by Averroes in the *De anima*, of the *intellectus adeptus* or *speculativus* – between the active and material intellects, was not developed by Grosseteste, as it had been by Averroes.

In the *Commentary on the Posterior Analytics* (II.6, 17–21), universals (*principia*) exist in intellect potentially, or unconsciously, and are activated to actuality; as in Aristotle's *De anima* the potential, material intellect is activated by the *intellectus agens* (what Grosseteste called the *virtus intellectiva*). For Grosseteste, sense knowledge plays a role in the activation of the material intellect. Sense perception is not the cause of knowledge, but rather is the condition by which knowledge is possible (I.18, 133–4). As in Aristotle, Plotinus and Averroes, reason, *virtus cogitativa* or *virtus scitiva*, apprehends the intelligible form as a singular or individual, while the *virtus intellectiva, actio intellectus* or *intellectus agens,* illuminated by *intelligentia*, apprehends the intelligible in its totality, as universal knowledge (I.18, 136, 164–5).

For Grosseteste, the active intellect is identified as the *virtus intellectiva* in combination with the *intelligentia,* divine intellect. Grosseteste followed Averroes as seeing the intelligible form, *species apprehensibilis,* formed by the *virtus intellectiva* in combination with the *intelligentia* (as active intellect). In Grosseteste the *virtus cogitativa* plays less of a role in the formation of the intelligible, given the *irradiatio spiritualis* of the *intelligentia,* reflecting the influence of Neoplatonic illumination theory in the interpretation of the Aristotelian doctrine. In the *Enneads* of Plotinus (V.3.8), "And this light shining in the soul illuminates it; that is, it makes it intelligent; that is, it makes it like itself, the light above." In the *Commentary on the Posterior Analytics*, the *lux spiritualis* (incorporeal light) "floods over intelligible objects (*res intelligibiles*)," and "over the mind's eye (*oculus mentis*)," and "stands to the interior eye (*oculus interior*) and to intelligible objects as the corporeal sun stands to the bodily eye and to visible corporeal objects" (I.17, 39–42) (Marrone, 1983, p. 196), following Aristotle, Plotinus and Averroes.

For Grosseteste, the *lumen spiritualis*, light produced by the *lux spiritualis*, allows the mental sight, the *visus mentalis*, to apprehend the intelligible in the *virtus intellectiva*, as the light of the sun, the *lumen solare*, makes vision possible. The *lumen spiritualis* is the "first visible" in interior sight, *visus interior*, as the colored body is the first thing receptive of the light of the sun, recalling Aristotle and Averroes. The more receptive the intelligible object, the *species apprehensibilis*, is to the *lux spiritualis*, the more visible it is to the *oculus mentis*. The object which is most similar to the light, the least material, is the most receptive of it. The power of the mind, the *acies mentis*, is an unconscious spiritual light, an *irradiatio spiritualis*, which operates in the *virtus intellectiva* to illuminate the *species apprehensibilis*, and the *virtus* is strongest when the object is the least material and conforms most easily to the immaterial *species*.

In the *Republic*, Plato compared the sun to the Good, the *lux spiritualis*, which is present to intellect as the sun is to sense perception, through the *lumen solare*, as for Grosseteste. The sun is the presence of the *lux spiritualis* in the material world, as the *anima mundi* is present in matter. In the *Republic*, "that is what I call the child of the good....The good has begotten it in its own likeness, and it bears the same relation to sight and visible objects in the visible realm," the *species sensibilis*, "that the good bears to intelligence and intelligible objects in the intelligible realm" (508) (Plato, 1955), the *species apprehensibilis*. Human vision operates like the light of the sun, as "the eye's power of sight is a kind of infusion dispensed to it by the sun." The light of the sun allows the eyes to have clearness of vision. The vision of the soul in the *oculus mentis* operates like the vision of the eye; it can only see clearly when it is illuminated by the light of the Good, the *lux spiritualis*, which allows the *intellectus* to be illuminated by the *intelligentia*, in the projection of the archetypes and intelligibles. In the *Republic*, the Good, as the *lumen solare*, is "what gives the objects of knowledge their truth and the knower's mind the power of knowing...."

While in the *Republic* "the sun...not only makes the things we see visible, but causes the processes of generation, growth and nourishment, without itself being such a process" (509), thus "the good therefore may be said to be the source not only of the intelligibility of the objects of knowledge, but also of their being and reality" in the material world; "yet it is not itself that reality, but is beyond it, and superior to it in dignity and power." The Good is only accessible itself to *intelligentia*, in unconscious thought, while its *principia essendi* are accessible to *virtus intellectiva*, which can be reflected in conscious, discursive reason. There are thus two powers in the *Republic*, the visible and the intellectual or intelligible, both governed by the same proportions.

Plotinus, in the *Enneads*, distinguished between "the form of the object perceived by the sense" and "the medium through which the form of its object is perceived" (V.5.7) (Plotinus, 1966): that is, the *lumen solare*, which is perceptible to the eye, distinct from the *species*, and the cause of seeing. The light of the sun is within the eye, as the *lumen spiritualis*, projected in the *oculus mentis*, as a spark from a flame, a *scintilla della divinità*. The light produces the *irradiatio spiritualis*, the spiritual light which is responsible for the *acies mentis*, the power of the mind, which illuminates the *species apprehensibilis* in the *virtus intellectiva*. For Plotinus, the eye "will itself sometimes know a light which is not the external, alien light," the *lumen solare*, "but it momentarily sees before the external light a light of its own, a brighter one," the *lumen spiritualis*, originating from an unknown, unconscious source. The inner light of the eye, the *irradiatio spiritualis*, is the equivalent in Plotinus of the Intellect, the *virtus intellectiva* of Grosseteste. In order to ascend to the *intelligentia* of Grosseteste, or the active intellect of Averroes, intellect must be able to see its *irradiatio spiritualis* in the *oculus mentis*. In the *Enneads* (V.5.7), "Intellect, veiling itself from other things," the pathos and disturbances caused by sense perception, "and drawing itself inward, when it is not looking at anything will see a light, not a distinct light in something different from itself," the *lumen solare*, "but suddenly appearing, alone by itself in independent purity," the *lumen spiritualis* in the *irradiatio spiritualis*, the product of the *lux spiritualis* which illuminates the *virtus intellectiva* in Grosseteste's terms.

Averroes, in the *Long Commentary on the De anima*, displayed a connection to the thought of Plotinus, perhaps as filtered through the *Theology of Aristotle* or the *Fons Vitae* of Avicebron (Solomon Ibn Gabirol; translated by John Avendeath and Domenicus Gundissalinus, Canon of Segovia, c. 1150). The theory of knowledge by illumination, promoted by Averroes, was influenced by Neoplatonism; a similar view can be found in the *Fons Vitae*, the *De anima* of Gundissalinus, and the *De intellectu* of Alexander of Aphrodisias (who was known to have influenced Plotinus). Avicebron described the active intellect as a transcendent and incorporeal, or unconscious, cosmic intellect, illuminating the *anima rationalis*. Averroes suggested a kind of world soul or collective unconscious in which individual souls participate, something also promoted by Plotinus.

Subsequently, Averroes influenced the thinking of Latin Scholastics in the concept of the active intellect as the incorporeal agent leading the potential, material intellect to actuality: a concept also found in Alexander of Aphrodisias and Avicebron. Robert Grosseteste may have also been influenced by the *Theology of Aristotle* or the *Fons Vitae*. According to Roger Bacon, Adam Marsh accepted the incorporeal active intellect as a divine intellect, as did Robert Grosseteste, who distinguished a divine or cosmic intellect, *intelligentia*, from an agent intellect, *virtus intellectiva*, which actualizes a material intellect, *virtus cogitativa* or *virtus scitiva*. This distinction can be found in the writings of Roger Bacon, Albertus Magnus, and John Peckham. These three writers, along with Grosseteste, Adam Marsh, and William of Auvergne, also saw the divine intellect, the *intelligentia*, as illuminating the *anima rationalis*, in the *irradiatio spiritualis* of the *lumen spiritualis*, reflected spiritual light, in the synthesis of Aristotelian and Neoplatonic influences anticipated by Averroes.

Brentano and Merlan characterized Averroes as a mystic. Averroes expounded "eccentric mysticism" according to Brentano (1977, p. 12), and a "neo-Aristotelian counterpart of the *unio mystica*," which can be seen as rationalistic mysticism, involving a "flood of sheer light" and "absolute transparency" in intellect, according to Merlan (1963, pp. 19–20). But, as Davidson pointed out, Averroes rejected the idea propagated by Avicenna that scientific knowledge can be attained through prophecy without following scientific procedures. For Averroes, the three forms of prophecy – dreams, clairvoyance and revelation – are products of active intellect. Revelation and prophecy cannot be compared to reason as forms of scientific knowledge, according to Averroes: a very un-mystical approach for a medieval philosopher. Ascension to active intellect in Averroes should be seen as a higher functioning of human intellect towards a unitary thought, with universal laws governing the physical world, communicated by emanation, rather than as the mystical ecstasy characterized by Merlan. The suggestion of the mystical aspect obscures the importance of Averroes' rationalistic philosophy of intellect, a philosophy which laid foundations for Scholastics to Idealists, to twentieth-century structural linguistics and psychoanalysis.

The dialectic of the material and active intellects, between the individual particulars of sense experience in the *intellectus passibilis* and the universal and unconscious matrix into which they are inserted and actualized, to participate in intellect, played a role in the *Vorstellung* (picture thinking) of Georg Wilhelm Friedrich Hegel in the *Phenomenology of Spirit*, and the concept of *la langue* (the matrix of rules that govern language in synchronic linguistics) in the *Course in General Linguistics* of Ferdinand de Saussure. For example, in the *Phenomenology*, *Vorstellung* is the "synthetic combination of sensuous immediacy and its universality or Thought" (Hegel, 1977, §764). According to Saussure, "synchronic linguistics will be concerned with the logical and psychological relations that bind together coexisting terms and form a system in the collective mind of the speakers ... " (*la langue*) (Saussure, 1966, p. 99). Echoes of Averroes can be heard in both of these concepts, contributing to a theme in classical and medieval philosophy which became the basis for the concept of unconscious thought in the psychoanalysis of the nineteenth and twentieth centuries. Along with the other Peripatetics discussed – Alexander of Aphrodisias, Themistius, Alfarabi, and Avicenna – Averroes contributed to the development of the possibility of unconscious thought in his synthesis of Plato, Aristotle, Neoplatonism and Neoaristotelianism, leading to the project by Robert Grosseteste, and ultimately to Hegel and Kant and psychoanalytic theory.

4
Robert Grosseteste: Imagination and Unconscious Thought

In the conclusion of the classical tradition, the Scholastic philosopher Robert Grosseteste (c. 1175–1253) can be seen as a Peripatetic (he wrote the first commentary on Aristotle in Latin), and his writings are similarly infused with Neoplatonic influence, from sources such as the *Theology of Aristotle*. Grosseteste anticipated the Great Synthesis of Albertus Magnus and Thomas Aquinas by synthesizing the Aristotelian ideas with Catholic theology, producing a unique alternative way of conceiving unconscious thought. He contributed additional insights to the classical concepts of noetic thinking, imagination and perception: concepts that can be interpreted as entailing a form of unconscious thought, and which contribute to conceptions of unconscious thought in modern philosophy and psychoanalysis.

Grosseteste studied law, medicine, and theology at Oxford from 1199 to 1208, and became a teacher at the university. He became familiar with Aristotle, Arabic scientific treatises and peripatetic writings, and Neoplatonism filtered through works such as the *Theology of Aristotle*, *Fons Vitae* or *Liber de Causis*. After 1208 he was appointed Master of the Oxford Schools, *Magister scholarum*, or Chancellor – the first of the university. He became Bishop of Lincoln in 1235. His *Commentary on the Posterior Analytics* (*Commentarius in Libros Analyticorum Posteriorum*) was completed by 1233. The *Commentary* is based on the translation of Aristotle from Greek to Latin made by James of Venice, and Grosseteste relied on a paraphrase by Themistius, translated by Gerard of Cremona. Gerard also translated the *De intellectu* of Alexander of Aphrodisias. Grosseteste remained Bishop of Lincoln until his death in 1253, during which time he translated the complete works of Pseudo-Dionysius.

In early treatises, such as his *Hexaëmeron* and *Commentary on the Posterior Analytics* – written between 1228 and 1235, before he became Bishop of Lincoln – Grosseteste developed a philosophy of intellect, influenced by Greek and Arabic commentaries on Aristotle's *De anima*, which contain Neoplatonic influences (Hendrix, 2010). In Aristotle's *De anima*, Book Three, a productive intellect is distinguished from a potential intellect. In the *De Anima* of Alexander of Aphrodisias, the productive intellect is the active intellect (*nous poietikos*), and the potential intellect is the material intellect (*nous hylikos*). The material intellect is perfected as intellection (*intellectus in habitu*) in discursive reason (*dianoia*), which Grosseteste followed. The *nous poietikos* is taken as a purely spiritual substance, acting on human intellect, as in the *intelligentia* or divine intellect of Grosseteste, and the First Cause in the *Liber de Causis*, and can be seen as a form of unconscious thought. The capacity for receiving the influence of the *nous poietikos* is the material intellect, the *nous hylikos*, through which knowledge is acquired.

In the *Liber Naturalis* (*al-Tabi'iyyat*) of Avicenna (Ibn Sīnā), in the eleventh century, sensory thought is illuminated by the active intellect. Avicenna followed Alexander of Aphrodisias in defining the potential intellect, the *nous pathetikos* or *nous dynamei*, as the material intellect, *intellectus materialis*, in contrast to the *nous poietikos*. The material intellect is seen as a passive substratum of ideas and a capacity for thought, by which intelligibles can be apprehended, corresponding to the *virtus cogitativa* of Grosseteste; although the *virtus cogitativa* of Grosseteste does not have the capacity alone to apprehend the intelligibles. Such a capacity for Grosseteste is found in the *virtus intellectiva*, a higher level of intellection. Like Grosseteste, Avicenna defined the capacity to apprehend intelligibles in the soul as incorporeal, though it is a capacity of material intellect.

For Grosseteste, this is because intelligibles are only known by *virtus cogitativa* as impressions or reflections from the *virtus intellectiva*, and not of themselves. For Avicenna, the potential knowing of the material intellect is actualized when intelligibles are projected onto it from the purely intellectual and incorporeal, which is the active intellect, which is capable of abstracting intelligible forms. Avicenna compared the relation between active intellect and material intellect to the relation between the sun and the sense of sight (*Liber Naturalis* 6.5.5); the sun is seen by its own light, while objects perceived in vision are seen by the light of the sun. In Grosseteste's terms, the material intellect is able to see the form of the thing in the *oculus mentis*, the *species sensibilis* or sensible form, by the light of the active intellect, which proceeds from a first cause and illuminates the form of the thing as the *species apprehensibilis*, the intelligible form, in the *irradiatio spiritualis*, the illumination in the *anima rationalis* or soul, which is unconscious, as in the inner light of Plotinus.

Averroes, in the *Long Commentary on the De anima* (*Sharh kitab al-nafs*) in the twelfth century, was less willing than Avicenna to depart from the doctrine of Aristotle. The active intellect and the material intellect are the only intellects which constitute human intelligence. The sensible form in the *oculus mentis* exists as a potential intelligible, and the material intellect, which is engaged in the formation of the sensible form, is capable of receiving the intelligible from the active intellect. The material intellect is the passible intellect, *intellectis passibilis*, described by Aristotle in *De anima* (3.5.430a24), which distinguishes and compares the individual representations of sense experience in the *oculus mentis*. Averroes also called the passible intellect *virtus aestimativa*, a term used by Avicenna, and *virtus cogitativa*, a term used by Grosseteste.

Averroes compared *intellectus passibilis* to *phantasia* or *imaginatio*, or imagination (*De anima* 3.1.20), the image-making *virtus* or power of intellect in the formation of the *phatasmata* of the sensible form, though Aristotle is understood to distinguish *phantasia* from intellect itself. Following Aristotle, Averroes divided material intellect into the *sensus communis*, or sense perception, the *phantasia*, the *virtus cogitativa*, and *memoria*, in ascending order from corporeal to spiritual, as the active intellect is increasingly engaged. The material intellect cannot distinguish or apprehend intelligibles on its own. The material, passible intellect, is an acquired intellect, through the activities of *phantasia* and *memoria*, and it is based in the acquisition of habitual knowledge through exercise, the gymnastics of discursive reason, *dianoia*, as a material *intellectus in habitu*. The passible intellect operates according to its capacity for receptivity, not according to an ability to form concepts or abstractions.

Intellectual knowledge for Averroes must be distinguished from the habitual knowledge of passible intellect. Intellectual knowledge is the product of the merging of the *intellectus materialis*, which is considered to be incorporeal, despite its dependence on the sensible, a position which Grosseteste did not follow, and the active intellect, *intellectus agens*, which transforms the sensible into the intelligible, stripping it of its corporeal attachment and converting it from a particular to a universal, which makes the potentially intelligible *phantasmata* in the *oculus mentis* intelligible, a process which Grosseteste supported. The *intellectus agens* is the intellect which acts, which moves the material intellect, the intellect that only receives or is affected (*De anima* 3.1.5). The active intellect allows the material intellect to be moved by imagination. The *intellectus passibilis*, in combination with *phantasia* and *memoria*, forms the phantasm in order that it can be perceived by the *intellectus agens*, and prepares it to receive the *intellectus agens*, by which the sensible becomes the intelligible, which can be comprehended as a universal.

Avicenna in the *Liber Naturalis* and Averroes in the *Long Commentary on the De anima*, along with Alfarabi, in the *Risala* or *De intellectu*, influenced the thinking of Latin Scholastics in the concept of the active intellect as the incorporeal agent leading the potential, material intellect to actuality, a concept which can also be found in the *De intellectu* of Alexander of Aphrodisias, and the *Fons Vitae* of Avicebron. Avicebron described the active intellect as a transcendent and incorporeal, cosmic, unconscious intellect, similar to the way it was described in the *Paraphrase of the De anima* of Themistius, illuminating the soul. As Roger Bacon wrote, in the Scholastic tradition, Adam Marsh saw the active intellect as a divine intellect, as influenced by the Greek and Arabic commentators on Aristotle. Robert Grosseteste distinguished the divine intellect, *intelligentia*, from the active intellect, *virtus intellectiva*, which actualizes the material intellect, what Grosseteste called the *virtus scitiva* or *virtus cogitativa*, a scheme that influenced Roger Bacon, Albertus Magnus, and John Peckham. These Scholastics, together with Grosseteste, Adam Marsh, and William of Auvergne, also understood *intelligentia* to illuminate the rational soul, through the *irradiatio spiritualis* caused by the *lumen spiritualis* or reflected spiritual light, in the medieval combination of Aristotelian, Neoplatonic, and Christian influences, synthesizing the developments of classical philosophy.

For Grosseteste the material intellect in the lower part of the soul acts according to the impressions received of intelligibles from the *intelligentia*, as illuminated by the *irradiatio spiritualis*. In the *Commentary on the Posterior Analytics* of Grosseteste, as light emanates from the sun, intelligibles are illuminated in the mind (*oculus interior*). The *intellectus* in mind, *virtus intellectiva* or *nous*, abstracts universal ideas from the particulars of sense to form principles, but *intelligentia* functions without a corporeal agent, and is assisted by divine illumination. The universal is the form or *species*, and is seen as a cause or principle of being. The universal exists *in re* in a particular thing, and causes the thing to be what it is. The universal or *species* also exists *post rem* in *intellectus*, as an abstraction from a particular thing, or intelligible. The *principia essendi* in the thing become the *principia conoscendi* in the mind. In

the *Commentary on the Physics* (*Commentarius in VIII Libros Physicorum*)
of Grosseteste, written around 1230, the *principia essendi* of a thing, its
form or *species*, are the subject of human knowledge at three different
levels. At the first level, they are the subject of ontology and natural
philosophy. At the second level they are the subject of mathematics and
geometry, as the universal is abstracted from the particular in the *principia conoscendi*. At the third level, they are the subject of metaphysics,
as the *principia conoscendi* participate in the *virtus intellectiva* and divine
illumination.

The three levels of human knowledge of the *principia essendi* correspond to the three levels of intellect outlined by Grosseteste in his
sermon *Ecclesia Sancta Celebrat*, as described by James McEvoy in *The
Philosophy of Robert Grosseteste*. *Ratio*, reason, is capable of grasping the
objects of the natural sciences. The *virtutes intellectiva et intellectualis*
are capable of apprehending the first principles of science and intelligibles. *Intelligentia* is the participation of divine illumination in intellect. The source for Grosseteste's classifications seems to be the *De Spiritu
et Anima* of Alcher of Clairvaux, who divided the powers of the soul
into five levels: *sensus*, or sense perception; *imaginatio*, the formation of
the *species* of sense perception, the *species sensibilis* (sensible form), in
the *oculus mentis*, as the mnemic residue; *ratio*, discursive reason, which
reflects the *species apprehensibilis* (intelligible form) like a mirror; *intellectus*, which apprehends the *species apprehensibilis* and intelligibles; and
intelligentia, which apprehends the *species apprehensibilis* without the
species sensibilis in the *oculus mentis*, through the *lux spiritualis* (originary, incorporeal, spiritual light), divine illumination. The five levels,
coupled with the four affections of the soul, form a microcosm of the
nine celestial spheres in the soul, and the soul is seen as a *similitudo
omnium*, a similitude of all of reality, which is capable of apprehending
all of reality. The faculties described by Alcher of Clairvaux can also be
found in the *Epistola ad quemdam familiarem suum de anima* of Isaac de
Stella, and there they were derived from the *De Fato* of Proclus.

In the *Commentary on the Posterior Analytics* of Grosseteste, *intelligentia*
is the supreme faculty of the soul. It is a form of knowing which does
not depend on sense perception or abstraction in reason, or any material form, but rather on direct irradiation of the *lux spiritualis*. In the
Hexaëmeron, *intelligentia* is described as a faculty of contemplation, with
no connection to *phantasia*, imagination, or *ratio*. Following Augustine
in *De Trinitate*, *intelligentia* is divided into *memoria*, *intelligentia*, and
amor, in the contemplation of the Trinity without material phantasm,
species sensibilis, or corporeal instruments, *phantasia* and *ratio*. *Ratio* and

imaginatio, and bodily operations themselves, operate in imitation and the reflection of the *similitudo* of *intelligentia*.

In the *Commentary*, Grosseteste described *intelligentia* as the highest part of the human soul, which is seen as separate from corporeal motions and operations, as in the soul of Aristotle (Grosseteste, 1981, I.14, 228–31: "pars suprema anime humane, que vocatur intellectiva [intelligentia] et que non est actus alicuius corporis neque egens in operatione sui propria instrumento corporeo...."). In his treatise *De statu causarum*, the rational soul, or *anima rationalis*, is described as an incorporeal intelligence mediating corporeal *virtus*, the motion of which in the senses are the *phantasmata*, mnemic residues of sense impressions, of the *imagination* (Baur, 1912, p. 125:20: "anima rationalis non solum unitur corpori humano sicut motor sed etiam sicut intelligens mediante virtute corporea. Intelligit enim non sine phantasmate, quod est actus virtutis sensitivae.") The body is an instrument in relation to the soul, and only influences it indirectly. In Grosseteste's treatise *De intelligentis*, as the higher form of substance, the incorporeal soul can be active in the body, but the body cannot be active in the incorporeal substance (Baur, 1912, p. 118:37: "Licet substantiae incorporeae possint agere in corpora, utpote nobiliora in minus nobilia, non tamen, ut videtur, e converso corpora possunt agere in substantias incorporeas, quia ignobilius non potest agere in id quod nobilius est."). This is also expressed in the *Hexaëmeron* (VII, XIV, 1) and the *Commentary on the Posterior Analytics*. The soul is seen as distinct from the body. In the *Hexaëmeron* the action of the body is compared to that of a mirror that acts by means of reflections, created by the *irradiatio spiritualis*, the illumination provided by the *intelligentia* of the higher soul, which is also reflected in the *virtus intellectiva* and the *virtus cogitativa*, the lower levels of the rational soul and the mechanisms of cognition in which the *intelligentia* participates. Conscious thought acts as a reflection of unconscious thought.

Sense perception is defined as the "power of receiving and grasping sensible likenesses without matter" (*Hexaëmeron* VII, XIV, 1) (Grosseteste, 1996), that is, the senses receive the *species* or *eidos* of the corporeal object and not the object itself, following Aristotle. Sense perception, as a lower part of the *anima rationalis*, is passive or potential in relation to the ability of the *anima rationalis* to know or comprehend concepts, in the *virtus cogitativa*, or intelligibles, in the *virtus intellectiva*. The *anima rationalis* is activated, or becomes more attentive, when the body is acted upon, when the senses are stimulated. Sense perception itself is stimulated when the *anima rationalis* is able to free itself to some degree from the corporality of the body which it inhabits, and to overcome its own passivity. The *anima rationalis*, as the source of the movement of the body, moves the body, pushed against it, and it also pushes against the passivity of the corporeal body. As it encounters more difficulties in its task, it becomes more attentive. The *anima rationalis* is aware of the difficulties caused by its pushing against the body's passivity, and as a result sense perception is "painful or troublesome," and causes turbulence in the *anima rationalis*, as in Plotinus.

The passivity of the body is overcome when "the passion of the body," the *amor* or *affectus mentis*, the *pathos*, caused by the multiple particulars of sense perception and the passivity of the body, "fits with the working of the soul," when the *species* of sense perception is corresponded to the intelligible, the *species sensibilis* is corresponded to the *species apprehensibilis*, resulting from interior illumination, *irradiatio spiritualis*, and the turbulence of the cooperation between *anima rationalis* and body can be overcome, and the illumination of the *oculus mentis* can function adequately so that the *anima rationalis* is at peace in its activation in intellection. The *anima rationalis* is aware of the peace that it can achieve in its overcoming of the passivity of the body, and thus aspires to the higher forms of intellection, *virtus intellectiva*, which necessitates a freedom from corporeal desires or *apatheia* in the higher parts of the *anima rationalis*.

In *De intelligentis*, the incorporeal soul is present in the body in the same way that God is present in the universe; the soul is everything and everywhere in the animated or ensouled body (Baur, 1912, p. 114:24: "Sicut autem Deus simul totus est ubique in universo, ita anima simul tota est ubique in corpore animato."). The *anima rationalis*, or *intellectus*, participates in bodily functions, but the body cannot participate in rational soul. It is present in essence, *per essentiam*, and not substance, and is not present at any particular point, only as a universal, "in corpore sine situ praesens, sine loco ubique tota." The soul can be said to be in mind, the origin of all inchoate and vital corporeal motions, as incorporeal intelligence mediating corporeal *virtus*: "Anima in corde situm habere dicitur, quia illinc inchoat motiones corporales vitales" (Baur, 1912, p. 116:6).

In Grosseteste's *De motu supercaelestium*, the faculty of sense perception is controlled by the *vis apprehensiva* of the *anima rationalis* and its primary goal is only that of self-preservation. Sense perception is assisted by *sensus communis*; *imaginatio*, the formation of the *phantasmata* in the *oculus mentis*; and *memoria*. As such, it allows knowledge to be possible: the *scientia*, knowledge gained by abstraction in reason; and the *intellectus*, the knowledge of first principles or intelligibles. But sense perception is not the cause of knowledge. Sense perception alone cannot apprehend universals, which are the materials of knowledge. In the *Commentary on the Posterior Analytics*, sense perception alone can perceive things only "in loco signato et tempore signato, quare non sentit nisi rem unam signatam" (I.18, 137–8), in a particular signified place and time. It can only perceive a particular, without the context given by *intellectus* and *intelligentia*. As space and time, intelligibles in the *virtus intellectiva*, are the conditions of sense experience, sense experience cannot be the cause of *scientia* (*virtus scitiva*) or *intellectus* (*virtus intellectiva*), although it acts as a mediator or instigator in the intellective process. It is up to the *intellectus* to combine and differentiate the particular qualities of objects as given by sense perception in the *species sensibilis* – size, proportion, shape and color.

Because the *species sensibilis*, the form of the object, in sense perception is connected to material objects, sense perception restricts the incorporeal *virtus* of *intellectus* to a certain extent. In the *Commentary on the Posterior Analytics*, the *intelligentia*, as the highest part of the *anima rationalis*, has complete knowledge of both singulars and universals, because it is illuminated by a radiated light, the *irradiatio spiritualis*, or *lumen spiritualis*, and it is separated from the heavy, clouded body in sense perception, in the same way that the *anima rationalis* is separated from the body. As such, *intelligentia* is separated from the *phantasmata* of corporeal objects in the *imaginatio*, the lower function of *intellectus*, and from the desire or *amor* created in the relation between the *virtus intellectiva* and the *phantasmata*, the *affectus mentis*, the desire created by the multiple and fragmented images of perception as constructed in the *virtus cogitativa* or *virtus scitiva*, conscious thought (Grosseteste, 1981, I.14, 228–35: "pars suprema anime humane que vocatur intellectiva... non esset mole corporis corrupti obnubilata et aggravata, ipsa per irradiationem acceptam a lumine superiori haberet completam scientiam absque sensus adminiculo, sicut habebit cum anima erit exulta a corpore et sicut forte habent aliqui penitus absoluti ab amore et phantasmatibus rerum corporalium."). Sense perception supports the *anima rationalis*, but it is lower and separated from it, and is caused by it rather than being the cause of it.

The body corrupts the purity of the eye of the soul, the *oculus mentis*, making it cloudy and heavy. The *virtus* of the *anima rationalis* tends to be focused on bodily and material things, on the body the motion of which it is the source, and such a focus tends to lull the *virtus* of the higher intelligences, the *virtus intellectiva*, to sleep, restricting the incorporeal *virtus*, and restricting the ability of *intellectus* to engage the *virtus intellectiva* and aspire to or be open to the *intelligentia* (Grosseteste, 1981, I.14, 235–8: "Sed, quia puritas oculi anime per corpus corruptum obnubilata et aggravata est, omnes vires ipsius anime rationalis in homine nato accupate sunt per molem corporis, ne possint agere, et ita quodammodo sopite."). In the same way, conscious thought, in its connection to empirical experience, is restricted in its engagement with unconscious thought. The *virtus scitiva* and *virtus cogitativa* are more weighed down by the corporeal *species sensibilis* in the *phantasmata* of the *imaginatio*, and are limited in their abilities of intellection. Scientific, discursive and dialectical reasoning are limited in their functioning, limited in their capacity of apprehension, *vis apprehensiva*, and limited in their understanding of the functioning of intellect and knowledge in philosophical terms. They are limited in their ability to grasp the creative and generative, unconscious functions of intellect, the role of intellect in human and natural creativity and development; conscious reason is limited in its capacity to apprehend unconscious reason, *virtus intellectiva* or *nous poietikos*.

In Grosseteste's *Commentary on the Celestial Hierarchy* of Pseudo-Dionysius, *intelligentia* functions completely only when the soul is released from the body. The capacity for *intelligentia* in the human being, knowledge of God, is what makes the human being unique among beings on earth. In the *Commentary on the Mystical Theology* of Pseudo-Dionysius, *intelligentia* functions independently of *ratio*, *intellectus*, and *phantasia*, or imagination (McEvoy, 1982, p. 306: "Rursus autem ascendentes dicamus quod neque anima est, ipsa videlicet omnium causa, neque intellectus, id est neque angelus...neque habet fantasiam, id est imaginationem....."). Grosseteste compares *intelligentia* to the *intellectus agens*, agent intellect, and *actio intellectus*, active intellect, the intellects which are differentiated from the passive, material intellect, discursive reason, in the commentators on the *De anima* of Aristotle (McEvoy, 1982, p. 306: "...vel intelligentiam, que est actio intellectus, ut per hanc sit intellectus agens, neque est ratio, neque intelligentia, neque dicitur verbo videlicet rationis, neque intelligentur actione intellectus agentis."). In the *Commentary on the Posterior Analytics*, the origin of the *principia essendi*, or universals, is inaccessible to cognition or knowledge, conscious reason, as they are the product of the *intelligentia*; so, they exist in an inchoate state as potentials, and are drawn out from potential to action, in a possible or material state which is in the beginning passive and not active (Grosseteste, 1981, II.6, 17–21: "Manifestatum est igitur quod neque actu habemus principia ab initio neque penitus ignoramus ea, sed sunt in nobis ab initio potentia et extrahuntur in nobis

de potentia ad actum. Habitus itaque eorum in nobis primo est poten-
tialis et materialis passivus et non actives," because in II.6, 21–3: "si
esset activus, tunc esset honorabilior et melior et certior quam habitus
actualis principiorum, eo quod activum est nobilius eo in quod agit
et nobilius effectu."). This reflects the structure of intellect as suggested
by Aristotle, in the relation between the potential, passive or material,
and agent and active intellects.

The *principia essendi* are brought from potential to active in sense
perception; which again is the foundation for knowledge, the knowledge of universals, *principia conoscendi*, but not the cause: "sed fiunt
in nobis a sensu per reductionem de potentia ad actum, et sensus est
fundamentum eorum quo existente poterit esse cognitio universalium."
This was also described in Grosseteste's *De Libero Arbitrio*. As knowledge
of the thing itself is impossible, scientific knowledge is based on the
universals, the *principia essendi ante rem*, which is elicited through sense
perception, as illuminated by the *irradiatio spiritualis* in the *oculus mentis*.
The *principia essendi* become the material for scientific demonstration,
as science cannot be based on the corruptible and variable knowledge of
singulars and particulars given by sense perception alone.

As human intellect does not have complete access to either the particulars of the sense world or the *principia essendi* that correspond to those
particulars in intellect, as in Plotinus, absolute knowledge and comprehension is impossible, mostly because of the corporeal instrument
to which intellection is attached. The *anima rationalis* does not have
perfect vision in the *oculus mentis* of the *principia essendi*, which are illuminated by the *irradiatio spiritualis* of *intelligentia*, as it is clouded by its
connection to the body. The goal of intellection, of intellectual activity,
is to uncloud the lens of the *oculus mentis* as much as possible, to purify
the *anima rationalis* of its corporeal connections, and to aspire to see
the *principia essendi* as clearly as possible; though ultimately completely
clear vision is not possible. The goal of intellection is to uncloud the
lens of the *oculus mentis* in the *anima rationalis* so that it can receive as
much as possible the *irradiatio spiritualis* which illuminates the intelligibles and allows the mind to have clear understanding.

In the *Commentary on the Posterior Analytics*, it must be accepted that
corporeal things are understood to the extent that they correspond to
the *visus mentalis* – the mental vision of them, the intelligible form: "Res
autem dicuntur certe a comparatione quam habent ad cognitionem sive
ad visum mentalem" (I.17, 38–9). The mental vision of them is made
possible by the *lumen spiritualis* of the *lux spiritualis* in the *irradiatio spiritualis* in the *oculus mentis*, as in the interior light of Plotinus, as the *lumen*

solare of the sun makes corporeal things visible to the corporeal eye: "Dico ergo quod est lux spiritualis, que superfunditur rebus intelligibilibus et oculo mentis, que se habet [sol corporalis] ad oculum interiorem et ad res intelligibiles..." (I.17, 39–42). Intelligibles are more receptive of the *lux spiritualis*, as they are not tied to corporeals, and are thus more visible to the *oculus mentis*: "Res igitur intelligibiles magis receptibiles huius lucis spiritualis magis visibiles sunt oculo interiori, et magis sunt huius lucis receptibiles que nature huius lucis magis assimilantur" (I.17, 42–5).

The goal of intellection, in the purifying and unclouding of the lens of the *oculus mentis*, is to make the mind as sharp and insightful as possible, as it is illuminated as much as possible by the *irradiatio spiritualis* and the illumination in the mind is as close as possible to the *irradiatio spiritualis* itself, in the depth of its penetration, which correlates to the depth of apprehension: "Res itaque huius lucis magis receptibiles ab acie mentis quae similiter est irradiatio spiritualis perfectius penetrantur et haec penetratio certitudo maior." This is also explained in Grosseteste's *Commentary on the Mystical Theology* of Pseudo-Dionysius. The goal of intellection is *sapientia*, knowledge of the intelligibles, which is the most certain kind of knowledge, because it is knowledge *ante rem*, and knowledge illuminated by the *irradiatio spiritualis*. In Grosseteste's treatise *De veritate*, "omnis creata veritas non nisi in lumine veritatis summae conspicitur" (Baur, 1912, p. 137:2). Intellection can, nevertheless, not have knowledge of the origin of intelligibles as they are formulated in *virtus intellectiva*, unconscious thought, as illuminated by the *intelligientia*.

Like the *intellectus agens* of Aristotle, the *intelligentia* of Grosseteste illuminates the lower function of intellect, as described by Alfarabi in the *Risala* (*De intellectu*), or Averroes in the *Long Commentary on the De anima* (*Commentarium magnum in Aristotelis de Anima libros*). The mediating factor suggested by Aristotle in the *De anima* of the *intellectus agens* between the *nous poietikos*, active or productive intellect, and the *nous pathetikos*, potential or passive intellect, was not developed by Grosseteste, as noted by Étienne Gilson, as it had been by Alfarabi and Averroes. In Book Three of *De anima*, Aristotle defined an intellect in which thinking is affected, which is taken to be the *nous pathetikos*, because it is not impassive like the productive intellect. For Grosseteste, as expressed in the sermon *Ecclesia Sancta*, the role of *intelligentia* is to transcend and cancel out, as it were, the powers and function of the lower intellectual faculties, to release itself from those faculties, as the soul is released from the body. It is only then that the *intelligentia* as an *intellectus agens* in turn illuminates the lower faculties of intellect, *ratio*, *phantasia* and *intellectus*, but not as a function of intellect itself, as in the thought of Aristotle.

In the *Commentary on the Posterior Analytics*, which contains Grosseteste's most extended commentary on Aristotle's conception of intellect, *intelligentia* is distinguished from *intellectus*. *Intelligentia* is also distinguished from *scientia*, along with *solertia*, the penetrating power of the *oculus mentis*, a function of *intellectus* as illuminated by *intelligentia*. *Intellectus* is given a higher function and a lower function, suggesting the distinction between the *nous poietikos* and *nous pathetikos* of Aristotle in the *De anima*, the *idea* and *scientia* of Plato in the Divided Line in the *Republic*, and the *nous* or Intellect and discursive reason of Plotinus in the *Enneads*. The higher function of Grosseteste, the *cognitio intellectiva*, is the knowledge of first principles, intelligibles, and the universal idea. In Grosseteste's *Ecclesia Sancta*, the *cognitio intellectiva* is defined as the *virtus intellectualis* or *supersubstantialis*. The lower function of *intellectus* is capable of grasping abstract concepts and the principles of scientific reasoning, the *scientia* and *ratio*, defined in the *Ecclesia Sancta* as *virtus intellectiva*, while still being above the *scientia* or *ratio*, discursive reason, and being illuminated by *intelligentia*. In the *Commentary on the Posterior Analytics*, the *cognitio intellectiva quae est dignitatum*, the highest function of *intellectus*, is able to grasp the *dignitates*, the first principles upon which science and reason are based.

Scientific knowledge is based on premises which must be accepted and cannot be proven, according to Grosseteste. Scientific knowledge and reasoning, the *scientia* or *virtus scitiva*, is a demonstrative knowledge based on dialectic and discursive reasoning, concerning the permanent aspects of the material world, abstracted as concepts. Mathematics and geometry are aspects of the *virtus scitiva*, as are the *principia essendi*, the principles of the essence of things. There are four kinds of universals available to the *virtus scitiva*. The first is the eternal *ratione*, the cause of being and knowledge. The second universal is that found in *intelligentia*, contemplative knowledge of celestial beings that the human intellect, *intellectus*, in *virtus intellectiva* or *virtus scitiva*, is not capable of formulating, but which can be communicated to human intellect. The third and fourth universals are genus and species, abstracted from form or *eidos* in sensible perception. The *species*, the form or image of an object as it is perceived, is eternal in a different way than the principle of the archetype or intelligence because it is connected to the sense object; consequently, sense perception is subject to material decay and confusion but is nevertheless abstracted from it as a permanent principle of knowledge. All levels of *intellectus* involve the abstraction of universal ideas from the particulars of sense experience. Universals do not exist in the material world, only in human intellect; the essence of matter, as the *principia essendi*, must be extracted and abstracted from the confusion of the material world and understood in *intellectus* as the *principia conoscendi*, the principles of knowledge.

Given that, for Grosseteste all knowledge and reason must be based on sense experience, following Aristotle. In the *Commentary on the Posterior Analytics* (Fols. 16–17), sense apprehends singulars, and universals can only be arrived at by intellect through induction from singulars. These universals induced from singulars form the basis of demonstration, which forms the basis of scientific knowledge. The knowledge of *intelligentia* is composed of singulars as well, along with the universals. While human knowledge only knows singulars as corrupted and mixed, in *intelligentia* singulars are pure and differentiated, as abstracted and eternal archetypes. The pure knowledge of singulars in *intelligentia*, as given by illumination, is corrupted by the condition of *intellectus* in relation to sense experience. Reason is awakened by sense experience, and is able to clarify and differentiate bodies and objects as they are given in sense perception. The characteristics of the body, in terms of dimension, form, and color, are understood in reason as participating in universals, and through dialectical and discursive processes the random objects of perception are organized and abstracted in ideas and relations of cause and effect, as derived through sense experience. This recalls Plotinus' theory of apperception, an element of unconscious thought, which also plays an important role in the philosophies of Leibniz and Kant.

Universals (*principia*) exist in intellect potentially, and are activated to actuality; as, in Aristotle's *De anima*, the potential, material intellect, *intellectus passibilis*, is activated by the *intellectus agens* towards the active, cosmic intellect. Sense knowledge plays a role in the activation of the *intellectus passibilis*. In sense knowledge a particular object is apprehended in a particular space and time, not as the object itself but in the signification of the object as *species*, or *eidos*, as imprinted on the faculty of sense perception. The individual *species sensibilis* is determined by its position in space and time, and is apprehended as an individual signified, a sign or *species* rather than the thing itself, while the corresponding *species apprehensibilis* is not determined by a particular space and time, and is apprehended as a collective signified: " … sensus talis est quod ipse est apprehensivus rei alicuius signate et non est simul apprehensivus rei alterius, quia necesse est scire rem signatum in loco signato et tempore signato, quare non sentit nisi rem unam signatam" (*Commentary on the Posterior Analytics*, I.18, 135–8). Sensible experience, as defined by space and time – intelligibles in the *virtus intellectiva*, not the *principia essendi* of the material world – is pre-determined by space and time as a priori *principia*: space and time do not exist outside of thinking, *intellectus*; they are not qualities of the physical world but determine the object as it is perceived individually, according to Grosseteste, in sense experience, anticipating the a priori categories of intuition of Kant, seen as a form of unconscious thought.

Sense perception is thus not the cause of knowledge, but rather is the condition by which knowledge is possible, as Grosseteste explained in the *Commentary on the Posterior Analytics*: "Similiter neque contingit scire sensibilia neque sensus est causa scientie, sed occasio..." (I.18, 133–4). Reason results from sense perception because reason is the apprehension of the thing signified, the *species apprehensibilis* in relation to the *species sensibilis*: "Huius autem ratio est quod sensus talis est quod ipse est apprehensivus rei alicuius signate..." (I.18, 134–6). Reason, the *virtus cogitativa* or *virtus scitiva*, apprehends the signification or *species apprehensibilis* still as a singular or individual – it is connected to material things and determined by space and time. The *virtus intellectiva*, on the other hand, illuminated by the *lumen spiritualis* of *intelligentia*, apprehends the signification in its totality, as universal knowledge: "et non est simul apprehensivus rei alterius..." (I.18, 136), "cum sola demonstrabilia et universalia sciantur..." (I.18, 164–5).

This is because what perceives is not contingent to what is perceived. What is perceived is the *species sensibilis*, not the object itself, as determined in its singularity by the preconditions of space and time, of which the perceiver is aware in *virtus cogitativa* but unaware or unconscious in *virtus intellectiva*, as *intelligentia* is not wholly accessible: "...manifestum est quod non contingit sentire per sensum." In that what is perceived is the *species sensibilis* and not the object itself, sense perception already consists of a process of abstraction. As individual sense perception is determined by space and time, there is no possibility of immediate sense perception, or of an immediate knowledge of objects in the physical world outside of intellection (see Plotinus). Sense perception is a spiritual rather than a physical operation, as Grosseteste said in the treatise *De lineis, angulis et figuris*: "In sensu enim ista virtus recepta facit operationem spiritualem quodammodo et nobiliorem" (Baur, 1912, p. 60:25).

The abstractions made by sense perception are primitive in nature, confused and relative. The *species sensibilis* in perception is corrupted, indeterminate, and in flux, while the *species apprehensibilis* in *intellectus* is integrated and clear, as an archetype or intelligible, as described in

Grosseteste's *Commentary on the Physics* (*Summa Lincolniensis Physicorum*) (Grosseteste, 1963, pp. 4–5: "Racio vero diiudicat integritatem atque veras prosequitur differencias, sed sensus invenit quedam proxima et confusa veritati, accipit vero racio integritatem. Racio...accipit vero a sensu confusam ac veri proximam similitudinem."). Sense perception receives reality as multiple, undifferentiated and incomplete, as in Plotinus, but the sensible object generates the singular image of it which is perceived, the *species sensibilis*. Sensation and intellection thus engage in a dialectical process involving the sense object and the perception of it.

In the *Commentary on the Posterior Analytics*, *species sensibilis* is apprehended without matter, as illuminated by *intellectus*; *species apprehensibilis* creates a likeness in understanding, as in Plotinus' *Enneads* V.3.2, where "reasoning power in soul" (Plotinus, 1966), discursive thought, "makes its judgment," derived from the mental images present to it, the *species apprehensibilis*, "which come from sense-perception," the *species sensibilis*. For Plotinus, discursive reason approaches *nous* when reason recognizes its recent sense impressions and "fitting them to those which have long been within it," the mnemic residues or memory traces of previous sense impressions, in a process of reminiscence. This was also described in Grosseteste's *Hexaëmeron*. The same process was described in the *Theology of Aristotle*, a paraphrase of the *Enneads*. *Ratio* is seen by Grosseteste in the *Commentary on the Posterior Analytics* as a mirror reflecting the *virtus intellectiva*, as in *Enneads* I.1.8 and I.4.10. In *Enneads* I.1.8, the soul "is pictured as being present to bodies since it shines into them....." The *principia conoscendi* in intellect or soul, in Grosseteste's terms, become the *principia essendi* of the thing or living being, as the soul "makes living creatures, not of itself and body, but abiding itself and giving images of itself, like a face seen in many mirrors," as described by Plotinus, a play of mirrors which conceals the unconscious and inaccessible source of the *principia*.

Bodies and things in sense experience, as *principia essendi*, are mirror reflections of the *principia conoscendi* in intellect, as it is projected onto the sensible world through sense experience. Just as in Grosseteste's theory of vision, which requires the combination of the intromission of light as reflected off of sensible objects, and the extramission of light as projected from intellect, so the existence of bodies and objects in the world requires a dialectic of their essential being and their definition as projected onto them by intellect. The sense impression itself of the sensible body or object exists in intellect as a reflection of the *principia conoscendi*. There can be no immediate sense perception of an object, without the mediation of the abstraction of the object in intellect, the formation of the *species* of the object, based on prior perceptions, in the process of intellection. Grosseteste can thus be called an "Idealist" in the same sense as Plato and Plotinus.

In the *Shifā: De anima* of Avicenna, intelligibles are differentiated in the compositive imaginative faculty, as in *Enneads* IV.3.29 and IV.3.30. In the *al-Madina al-Fadila* of Alfarabi, active intellect is compared to the sun, and light imprints species in the material intellect. Active intellect transforms sense perceptions into principles, which are the first intelligible thoughts, as in *Enneads* I.3.5. For Grosseteste, light (*lux*) is the first corporeal form, and the cause of all becoming of natural things. Through *lux*, the mind is able to know the *principia essendi*, the intelligibles, as for Plotinus. As illuminated, the *principia essendi* become the *principia conoscendi*, the principles upon which reason is based. In Grosseteste's *Hexaëmeron*, light is the instrument by which the form or *species* apprehended by the particular sense, the *species sensibilis*, corresponds to the form apprehended in the common sense, *sensus communis*, as *species apprehensibilis*. Imagination, *phanatasia*, is the process of making that correspondence, as it was for Plotinus, and it would be for Kant and Hegel.

In his *Hexaëmeron* (VIII, IV, 7), Grosseteste described imagination (*phantasia*) as a process which combines the sense object, and the imprint of the *species* of the sense object in the senses, in intellection. The union of the *species sensibilis* and the *species apprehensibilis* is the union of the corporeal and incorporeal, and the first step in intellection from the passive intellect of sense perception, weighed down by the corporeal, to the active intellect of the *virtus intellectiva*, freed from the corporeal. The best example of the correspondence between *species sensibilis* and *species apprehensibilis* is color, which is visible in the corporeal object and in the *oculus mentis*. Because in the act of perception the color in the sense object is not distinguished from the color in the *oculus mentis*, the two are united, and the perceiver is united with the sense object in the act of intellection in perception, which is not available to discursive reason or conscious thought.

Through the corporeal experience of sense perception, the knowledge on the part of the *anima rationalis* of the *phantasmata* as mnemic residues in the *imaginatio* of the *oculus mentis* is clouded or forgotten, and the *anima rationalis* is not aware or conscious of the correspondence being made in intellection in the process of perception, and takes the sense perception to be immediate of the sensible object, as the *anima rationalis* is weighed down by its corporeity. In the *Hexaëmeron* (VIII, IV, 12), "Our memory, when it has received and retained a memory form [mnemic residue], is not always actually remembering," as it is in a state of passive intellection, tied to its corporeity. But then "when it passes from not actually remembering to actually remembering": that is, when it has been activated by an agent intellect in the *irradiatio spiritualis*, "it begets and expresses from itself the actual intellection or understanding that is in every way like to itself," in the activity of active intellect, *virtus intellectiva*. Through intellection, and the aspiration of the *anima rationalis* to see clearly the *intelligentia* through the *irradiatio spiritualis* in the *oculus mentis*, in the *virtus intellectiva*, the *anima rationalis* becomes aware of the *species apprehensibilis* in relation to the *species sensibilis* in the process of perception, and it becomes aware of the relation between human intellect and the sensible world. Intellect goes from being a functional intellect, in the gymnastics of discursive reason in the *virtus scitiva* or *virtus cogitativa*, to being a creative and generative, productive intellect in the *virtus intellectiva* or *nous poietikos*.

The *aspectus mentis* is the ability of the mind to grasp ideas through the perception of visual forms, the ability of the *oculus mentis* to "see" the concept, the intelligible connected with the *species apprehensibilis*, which is related to the *species sensibilis*, in that the *species sensibilis* is always already a product of the *species apprehensibilis* in intellection in perception. The mind sees the intelligible in the *irradiatio spiritualis* of the *intelligentia*. Grosseteste explained in his *Hexaëmeron*, "the species begotten in the fantasy [*imaginatio*] of the common sense," the *sensus communis*, "begets of itself a species that is like it in the memory" (VIII, IV, 9), as a trace or mnemic residue, which corresponds to the presently perceived sensible object. Perception appears to be a learned process for Grosseteste, a product of the perceiver learning how to recognize objects and relationships in relation to previously perceived objects and relationships, as it would be for George Berkeley, in order to process them in perception. Then, in the *Hexaëmeron*, "the species that can be apprehended by the reason, intellect or understanding" (VIII, IV, 10), the *species apprehensibilis*, projects its likeness (*similitudo*) in the *virtus intellectiva* in the process of perception, illuminated by the inner light, the *irradiatio spiritualis*, and the mind connects the begotten likeness with the form perceived, the *species sensibilis*. As a result, "effective apprehension" is achieved, through an unconscious process.

In the *Commentary on the Posterior Analytics* (II.6), memory receives the *species* as integrated and synthesized in the *sensus communis*, and it receives the *intentiones* connected with the *species*, as detected by the *vis aestimativa*. *Memoria* involves *imaginatio* or *phantasia*, the retention of the *species sensibilis*, and the *memoria proprie dicta*, the retention of the *intentiones aestimatae*, in the integration of the concept formed in the

virtus intellectiva to produce the *species apprehensibilis*. Reason is stimulated to form concepts by the memory traces, which constitutes experience: "sed in rationabilibus iam contingit ex multis memoriis excitata
ratione fieri experientiam..." (II.6, 35–7). Memory is created from sense
experience, and universals in experience result from memory, but not
as separated from particulars: "Ex sensu igitur fit memoria, ex memoria
multiplicata experimentum, ex experimento universale, quod est praeter
particularia, non tamen separatum a particularibus..." (II.6, 37–9).

The *intellectus* abstracts the universal idea from sense knowledge and
experience, both external and internal; universals do not exist separate
from particulars or sense experience. While universals are connected to
the particulars of sense experience, they transcend them or go beyond
them in a dialectical process in intellect, and they are the source of all
particulars of sense experience as well, as intelligibles in *virtus intellectiva*. The relation between the universal and particular is similar
to the relation between *lux*, the source of light, and *lumen*, generated
light. The universal is in the *irradiatio spiritualis* in the *oculus mentis*, in
the illumination which is the source of the perception and cognition
of particulars as *phantasmata*. The unity of the universal exists in the
multiplicity of particulars as the unity of *lux* exists in propagated light,
as described in the *Commentary on the Posterior Analytics* (Grosseteste,
1981, I.17, 121–2: "universale non est figmentum solum, sed est aliquid
unum in multis..."; and I.17, 114–18: "puto quod unitas universalis in
multis particularibus assimilatur unitati lucis in luce gignente et genita.
Lux enim que est in sole gignit ex sua substantia lucem in aere, nec est
aliquid novum creatum ut sit lux in aere, sed lux solis est multiplicata
et propagata....").

The unity of the singular intelligence, as in the One of Plotinus, exists
in the multiplicity of natural things in the universe. The universal intelligence exists in particulars as the quiddity or essential quality of particulars, through the means of the form discovered by Aristotle; so, the
ubiquity of the universal intelligence is the same as the existence of the
intelligence in a particular place (Grosseteste, 1981, I.17, 125–6, "universalia rerum naturalium sunt minus entia quam singularia intelligen-
tiarum" and I.18, 144–7: "Si autem intelligimus universalia per modum
Aristotelis formas repertas in quidditate particularium, a quibus sunt res
particulares id quod sunt, tunc universale esse ubique nihil aliud est
quam universale esse in quolibet suorum singularium."). The universal
form or *species*, as the *principia essendi*, is *in re* as a particular, and *ante
rem* and *post rem* as a universal. In intellection, the *irradiatio spiritualis*
allows the *intelligentia* to exist as a quiddity or the *principia essendi* in

the particulars of the *principia conoscendi* of sense experience and *virtus scitiva* and *cogitativa*, conscious thought.

Species, and genus, only exist in mind: composed of particulars in *virtus cogitativa* or *scitiva*, and abstracted as universals in *virtus intellectiva*. Universals are potential in reality, but only actual in mind. In apperception, the *species* is composed of particulars, as *res inventa in multitudine*, and is determined by the intelligibles of space and time, which precondition all particulars of sense perception, as described in the *Commentary on the Posterior Analytics* (Grosseteste, 1981, I.18, 138–142: "Universale autem, cum sit res inventa in multitudine, non est possibile sentire, quia quod reperitur in multis non est in tempore aut loco signato, quia si esset in loco et tempore signatis non esset idem inventum in omnibus, universale namque est semper et ubique."), anticipating the thought of Immanuel Kant. The universal is not possible in conscious perception, in sensible reality, because of the multiplicity of particulars. Because the universal is always everywhere – in no particular place or time – that which is perceived in a signified place or time cannot be a universal. At the same time, that which is perceived in multiplicity cannot be a particular signified place or time.

The particulars of the multiplicity of apperception are always already conditions of the universal in intellect, and there is an impossibility of there being at any moment or in any way a particular element in sensible reality that is present in and of itself, as the noumenon in Kantian terms. As in the thought of Plotinus, for Grosseteste *intellectus* has complete access to neither sensible reality not the intelligibles of *intelligentia*, the two spheres of phenomena which form a dialectical process on which *virtus cogitativa* and *virtus intellectiva* are based. The concept itself in *intellectus* is not subject to the change and variability of particulars in sense experience, as seen in the *Commentary on the Posterior Analytics*. The universal in concept is related to the particular in the process of *inductio*, where the universal is derived from the particular, and the process of *abstractio*, through which the *principia essendi* of the particular are apprehended as separate from its singularity. The *principia essendi* are the "unum et idem secundum iudicium suum in multis..." (I.14, 249–250), in the dialectic of the particular and universal, sense object and concept. The *intentio animae* takes the *species apprehensibilis*, as formed from the *species sensibilis* in *intellectus*, and balances it in a process of *iudicium*: the universal is derived from the particular. The *iudicium* of the *intentio animae* is necessary for both *virtus scitiva* and *virtus intellectiva*: science cannot be based on the particulars of sense experience alone.

In the *De anima* (3.7.431b2), Aristotle wrote that the human intellect thinks the forms in images; that the *species sensibilis* is given by the *species apprehensibilis*, in Grosseteste's terms, which is formed in the imagination or *phantasia* and is presented to discursive reason in the process of perception. According to Avicenna, or Ibn Sīnā, in the *Shifā: De anima* (235), also known as the *Metaphyisica*, in the eleventh century, the image or *species* is formed in the *sensus communis*, as for Grosseteste, and is then received by the imaginative faculty, the *phantasia*, which combines the images in different configurations. Discursive reason then receives an "abstraction" of the *species* from the *phantasia*, a representation of the *species apprehensibilis* which corresponds to the *species sensibilis*.

The *species apprehensibilis* of Grosseteste is a *similitudo* of the *species sensibilis*, as a mnemic residue, and is thus a representation of the *species sensibilis*, which is itself a representation of the object to which its form corresponds, as in Freud's *Vorstellungsrepräsentanz*. For Grosseteste in the *Hexaëmeron* (VIII, IX, 11), the *virtus* of the retentive memory must be proportionate to the *virtus intellectiva* in order for the *species apprehensibilis* to be formed. Memory is not always active (VIII, IX, 12), but when it is active it produces a *similitudo* of intellection, as the *ratio*, the lower intellect, or discursive reason (as in the conscious process of memory) mirrors the *virtus intellectiva*, the higher intellect, or *nous* (as in the unconscious process of memory), as Grosseteste described in the *Commentary on the Posterior Analytics*. This theory of vision is very similar to that of Plotinus.

In the *Enneads* of Plotinus, while perception grasps the "impressions produced by sensation on the living being" (I.1.7), which are "already intelligible entities," the *species apprehensibilis*, through the mnemic residue, "nothing will prevent a perception from being a mental image for that which is going to remember it, and the memory and the retention of the object from belonging to the image-making power" (IV.3.29), or the imagination (*phantasia*). In the representation in the mnemic residue, the *species apprehensibilis*, "what was seen is present in this when the perception is no longer there. If then the image of what is absent is already present in this, it is already remembering, even if the presence is only for a short time." Through memory, "an image accompanies every intellectual act," as described in *Enneads* IV.3.30. Through the *species apprehensibilis*, "the intellectual act is without parts and has not, so to speak, come out into the open, but remains unobserved within...," in unconscious thought. The *species apprehensibilis* functions as a kind of hieroglyph, communicating the elements of intellect which cannot be communicated by words, and are not accessible to discursive reason in language or conscious thought.

The function of language, or the extent to which language can function, is as the mirror reflection of the *virtus intellectiva* in *ratio*, discursive reason, in the facilitation of memory, in that, as Plotinus says, the *logos endiathetos* unfolds the content of the intellectual act "and brings it out of the intellectual act into the image-making power, and so shows the intellectual act as if in a mirror, and this is how there is apprehension and persistence and memory of it." The mechanism of perception mediates between the sensible world of objects in nature and the inaccessible intellectual, or *nous*, in a dialectical process between the subject and the world. In the perception of an object, "we look there where it is and direct our gaze where the visible object is situated in a straight line from us..." (IV.6.1). The object which is being perceived is already apprehended by the perceiving subject in relation to the perceiving mechanism, the construction of intellect involving the mnemic residue and the *species apprehensibilis*, through the use of geometry; as vision is understood in relation to geometry and mathematics, the intelligible mechanisms as the underlying structure, as for Grosseteste.

In his *Commentary on the Posterior Analytics*, Grosseteste defined *solertia* – a term from the *Posterior Analytics* of Aristotle, translated into Latin by James of Venice – as the penetrating power of the *oculus mentis*, the mind's eye, which is able to see beyond the surface of an image: a form, pattern, or symbol. If the eye sees color, for example, the *oculus mentis* sees the structure of which the color is an effect, as described in geometrical terms by Grosseteste in his treatise *De Iride*. *Solertia* is the ability to understand, in perception, the archetypal and intelligible forms that define perception itself, and define the process of intellection of the perceiving subject. *Solertia* is the clarity of the vision of the *oculus mentis* of the intelligibles of the *intelligentia* as illuminated by the *irradiatio spiritualis* in the *lumen spiritualis*, and is thus a faculty of *sapientia* in the *virtus intellectiva*, the higher part of the *anima rationalis*.

In the writings of Grosseteste, the active intellect is identified as the *virtus intellectiva* in combination with *intelligentia*. *Virtus intellectiva* is closer to *intellectus actio* than *intellectus agens*, but like *intellectus agens* it is separated from cosmic intellect or *intelligentia*. Grosseteste followed Avicenna and Averroes as seeing the *species apprehensibilis* formed by the *virtus intellectiva* in combination with the *intelligentia*, which corresponds to the combination between the *intellectus agens* and *intellectus actio*, though the terms themselves do not correspond. In Grosseteste the *virtus cogitativa* and the *sensus communis* play less of a role in the formation of the intelligible, given the *irradiatio spiritualis* of the *intelligentia*, reflecting the Neoplatonic influence in the interpretation of the Aristotelian doctrine. The theory of knowledge by illumination promoted by Avicenna and Averroes has its roots in Neoplatonic philosophy, and had a great influence on Grosseteste. A similar view can be found in the *Fons Vitae* of Avicebron, Solomon Ibn Gabirol, and the writings of Domenicus Gundissalinus, translator of the *Fons Vitae* and works by Avicenna.

In the *De anima* of Gundissalinus, showing the influence of the *Fons Vitae* and the *De anima* of Avicenna, human intellect is composed of the *virtus activa*, based on the material intellect, and the *virtus contemplativa*, based on the active intellect, and inspiring the *virtus intellectiva* of Grosseteste. The *virtus contemplativa* would correspond to the *sapientia*, the ability to know the intelligibles of the *intelligentia*, and the *virtus activa* would correspond to the *virtus scitiva* or *virtus cogitativa*, discursive reason. Like Grosseteste, Gundissalinus saw the *anima rationalis* as being limited in its ability to see clearly the intelligibles in the *oculus mentis* because of its attachment to corporeity in sense perception, while at the same time it is the sense perception which can activate the *anima rationalis* from the *virtus activa* to the *virtus contemplativa*, through the formation of the *phantasmata* in the *oculus mentis* in *imaginatio*; though, given this process, full access to the intelligibles, as illuminated by the *irradiatio spiritualis*, is impossible.

In his synthesis of Plato, Aristotle, Neoplatonism and Neoaristotelianism, Grosseteste summarized the classical development of a philosophy of intellect in the peripatetic tradition that included a vital element of thought – unconscious thought, which is inaccessible to conscious reason but is necessary for imagination and advanced forms of intellection. Such a conception would lay the groundwork for later suggestions of unconscious thought in modern philosophy, and theories of unconscious thought in psychoanalysis. Grosseteste's theories predict elements of the philosophies of Kant and Hegel in particular, in turn influencing the thought of Freud and Lacan.

5
Unconscious Thought in the Philosophy of Immanuel Kant

At the beginning of modern philosophy, Gottfried Leibniz and Immanuel Kant laid the groundwork for concepts of unconscious thought in psychoanalytic theory, while mining the tenets of classical and medieval philosophy for their concepts and beginning a modern tradition that is linked to the development of philosophies of intellect throughout Western intellectual history.

Immanuel Kant (1724–1804) is the most significant modern philosopher to develop classical concepts of imagination and intellection, and to lay the groundwork for the concept of unconscious thought in the science of psychoanalysis. In an early treatise, *Attempt to Introduce the Concept of Negative Magnitudes into Philosophy* (*Versuch, den Begriff der negative Grössen in die Weltweisheit einzuführen*, 1763) (Kant, 1992), Kant developed a theory about thoughts that are negated or cancelled, obscured or darkened – all suggesting unconscious thoughts. Thoughts come to be and pass away because certain thoughts are cancelled out by other thoughts with greater force, which oppose them. As some thoughts become clearer, the other thoughts become less clear and more obscured (*Verdunkelt*). Kant's concept is influenced by the *petites perceptions* of Gottfried Wilhelm Leibniz. He invoked Leibniz in reiterating that only a small portion of the representations which occur in the soul, as the result of sense perception, are clear and enduring (Kant, 1992, p. 237; Nicholls and Liebscher, 2010b, p. 10).

Leibniz (1646–1716) conceived of minute perceptions of objects or ideas which have too little intensity to effect conscious thought, affirming the existence of unconscious ideas on a physiological level, the first modern philosopher to do so. The minute perceptions contribute to ordinary perceptions, but they are so small and there are so many of them that they pass unnoticed in the consciousness connected to perception. There are far more minute, unnoticed perceptions than there are conscious perceptions. In the *New Essays on Human Understanding*, Leibniz followed Aristotle in presupposing that the mind is always active, and does "not think intermittently" (Aristotle, *De anima*, 430a10–25) (Aristotle, 1964). According to Leibniz, "in the natural course of things no substance can lack activity...," and "at every moment there is in us an infinity of perceptions, unaccompanied by awareness or reflection..." (Leibniz, 1982, p. 53). We are unaware of the objects or ideas being perceived, of the activity of the perception, and of the affect of the perception on conscious thought. Until they are combined with other perceptions, most perceptions are too minute to be distinguished or distinctive. In Leibniz's *Monadology*, conscious perceptions follow unconscious perceptions, because "one perception can in a natural way come only from another perception, as a motion can in a natural way come only from a motion" (Leibniz, 1898, p. 231, paragraph 23). According to Rosemarie Sponner Sand, "...Freud's German and Austrian contemporaries unanimously credited the fundamental formulation of the concept of unconscious mind to Gottfreid Wilhelm Leibniz" (Sand, 2014, p. xi). By the time of Freud, the minute perceptions of Leibniz were referred to as unconscious mental states, representations or ideas (*Unbewusste Vorstellungen*).

In the *New Essays on Human Understanding*, the minute perceptions are "vivid in the aggregate but confused as to the parts" (Leibniz, 1982, p. 55), suggesting that perception is only clear when it has been organized into a totality, as Plotinus described, and which would be the basis of Kant's theory of perception. In Plotinus, perception is organized into a totality by the activity of Intellect through imagination, the image-making power, and the *logos endiathetos*, the linguistic structure in thought. In Kant, perception is organized into a totality by the categories of a priori intuition acting through the schemata in the imagination, producing what Kant called the "manifold." For Leibniz, the relation of the parts to the aggregate in perception represents the relation of the finite to the infinite, and the relation of the individual subject to the universe. An individual is defined by their unconscious perceptions, the vestiges of which form a palimpsest in the individual's consciousness (in discursive reason). Traces of previous perceptions, of sense objects or of ideas, contribute to a present state of consciousness, which is determined unknowingly by unconscious processes. While there is no consciousness of the previous perceptions, "they could be known by a superior mind," that is, the *nous poietikos*, or the Intellect of Plotinus, the higher form of thinking which involves unconscious thought. The traces of the unconscious perceptions in memory play a role in the becoming conscious of the residues of images, or mnemic residues, in the processes of sense perception, imagination, and intellection, in the formation of the aggregate or manifold out of the individual unconscious perceptions.

Unconscious perceptions are also responsible for the "pre-established harmony between the soul and the body" for Leibniz, the relation between intellect and sense perception, and the unconscious perceptions determine equilibrium in behavior and activity. Conscious thought and action are dependent upon unconscious thought and perception. Unconscious perceptions cause a "disquiet," as in the pathos caused by sense perception for Plotinus, and they also cause desire, in the searching on the part of conscious thought, for that inaccessible element of its existence. All conscious perceptions contain unconscious perceptions; they would not exist without them. Leibniz cited Plotinus in asserting the necessity of unconscious perceptions and ideas which are unclear and indistinct, partly resulting from the obscurity of sense knowledge, partly resulting from the inaccessibility of certain mechanisms of intellection to conscious reason. "Although the mind, as Plotinus rightly says, contains a kind of intelligible world within it," the Intellectual or *nous poietikos*, "very few things in us can be known distinctly, and the remainder are hidden in confusion, in the chaos of our perceptions as it were" (Merlan, 1963, p. 61; Bell, 2005, p. 18). Conscious thought and perception are just the tip of the iceberg of the vast and mysterious mechanisms of the unconscious mind. This popular romantic idea was illustrated in the series of etchings called the *Carceri* by Giambattista Piranesi around 1750. The *Carceri* depicted vast, chaotic, threatening, and sublime torture chambers underneath the city of Rome, below the thin layer of conscious reason represented by the rational order of classical and neoclassical architecture. Underneath, order is broken, contradictory, and seemingly irrational.

Piranesi violated the laws of perspective in construction, suggesting an alternative to perspective construction in the representation of visual and mental reality. In such a construction objects and planes are juxtaposed and layered in transparency and not ordered on lines toward vanishing points, not fixed in relation to a singular horizon line, and not collectively limited to a single viewpoint, as in conscious perception. They are not ordered according to a totality or manifold. These non-perspectival spatial relationships would be described by Sigmund Freud in the construction of dream images from unconscious thoughts in *The Interpretation of Dreams* in 1899. The visual construction of these relationships was described by Erwin Panofsky as "psychophysiological space," or non-perspectival space, in the essay "Perspective as Symbolic Form" in 1927. Dream space would be characterized by the absence of the subject, the absence of the horizon line, and images juxtaposed in intensities, rather than being placed in a mathematical or geometrical construction, all qualities of Piranesi's *Carceri*. Such spatial construction is rooted in unconscious thought.

In the tradition of classical philosophy, intellectual ideas "do not come from the senses," according to Leibniz in *New Essays on Human Understanding* (Leibniz, 1982, p. 81). They are the product of the inner reflection of the mind, dependent upon intelligibles not connected to sense perception. Ideas that come from the senses are confused, as Plato established, in the same way that individual perceptions are confused before they are conceived as contributing to an aggregate, which is a product of intellect not connected to the act of conscious sense perception. Products of the *nous poietikos* are distinct and not contaminated by the lack of clarity of the sensible form, *species sensibilis*, in the *nous hylikos*, thought connected to sense perception. Ideas, products of *nous poietikos* or Intellect, exist without our being conscious of them (as in the *species apprehensibilis*), as Plotinus established. Leibniz described them as "natural tendencies...dispositions and attitudes..." (p. 106). We also have traces of perceptions of which we are not conscious (as in the residues of the *species sensibilis*), but it is possible at any time to become conscious of either sensible or intelligible forms, the traces of which form the palimpsest of conscious experience. We are hindered in our awareness of them, in the inner reflection of the mind, by being distracted by the multiplicity and confusion of individual sense perceptions, exactly as Plotinus described.

We are also unconscious of how individual sense perceptions are received and sometimes altered as they are processed in the mechanisms of intellect and imagination. In the simple act of perception, we are unconscious of the mechanisms of intellect and imagination which determine the particular forms that are directly perceived. In *An Essay Towards a New Theory of Vision* in 1709 (Berkeley, 1963), George Berkeley (1685–1753) asserted that the quality of distance cannot be immediately perceived of itself, but must be a judgment that is learned through an accumulation of sense perceptions in relation to discursive thought, as in the thought of Grosseteste. Judgment, according to Berkeley (or acquired understanding, the product of a higher intellect) is the product of experience rather than immediate sense perception; it therefore necessarily involves memory, the traces of perceptions of sense objects and ideas, the accumulation of which leads to the development of the imagination, the image-making power. In the Fourth Dialogue of his *Alciphron*, Berkeley says "we perceive distance not immediately but by mediation of a sign, which has no likeness to it or necessary connection with it, but only suggests it from repeated experience, as words do things" (§8) (Berkeley, 1963). The sign is an intelligible, a product of *nous poietikos*, intellection not connected to sense perception. The sign unconsciously determines the sense perception, especially for a quality like distance, a product of higher intellection.

The sign is constructed by unconscious thought, and has no necessary relation to the sense perception of the object. As Berkeley explained in the *New Theory of Vision*, we are "exceedingly prone to imagine those things which are perceived only by the mediation of others to be themselves the immediate objects of sight" (§66). When we perceive an object, we are unaware that what we are perceiving is the sensible form of the object, the *eidos*, which has no immediate connection to the object itself, and that the sensible form is formed in relation to the intelligible form, the idea of the form of the object, by the inaccessible *nous* or intuition in unconscious thought. It is the idea of the object, as given by intellect, that is immediately grasped, the intelligible form, rather than the image itself of the object, the sensible form, which is imprinted on memory as a seal or sign. The objects themselves, according to Berkeley, "are not seen, but only suggested and apprehended by means of the proper objects of sight, which alone are seen" (*Alciphron*, §12). The proper object of sight is the seal or sign, the imprint or mnemic residue, the intelligible form, which are constructed in intellect and language, memory and imagination, as for Plotinus. In the *Alciphron*, "it will not seem unaccountable that men should mistake the connection between the proper objects of sight and the things signified by them to be founded in necessary relation or likeness ... " (§11). It is thus "easy to conceive why men who do not think should confound in this language of vision the signs with the things signified," the intelligible form and the sensible form, in conscious thought. Conscious thought and perception are dependent on the mechanisms of unconscious thought and the classical concept of the higher intellect.

In his *Critique of Pure Reason* ("A" version, 1781), Kant says that it is impossible to know an object as a pure sensible object outside its conception as an intelligible in intellect: perception in intellection transcends the experience of the sensible world in perception. The experience of the world is based on the inaccessibility of reason to the world. The coherence and totality of the sensible world are necessary for perception, as perception is a basis for reason, but such totality is impossible in perception itself; it is only given by a priori intuition, unconscious thought. The manifold of the sensible world is inaccessible to conscious reason: "The absolute whole of all appearances – we might thus say – is only an idea; since we can never represent it in image, it remains a problem to which there is no solution" (A328) (Kant, 1968). Reason as a whole is unrepresentable to itself: it requires the inaccessible *nous*, intuition or unconscious thought, in order for it to explain itself to itself. Imprints of sensible objects in perception are "mere representations," as for Plotinus or Berkeley, "which as perceptions can mark out a real object only in so far as the perception connects with all others according to the rules of the unity of experience" (A495), in a manifold.

As for Berkeley, the relation between thought and a perceived sense object is never direct and is always mediated by the unconscious understanding of the object in a totality. "Reason is never in immediate relation to an object, but only to the understanding" (A643), the intellection of the object. The transcendental idea, then, is not just a concept of an object, but a "thoroughgoing unity of such concepts..." (A645). The idea of an object is not possible outside the totality of the unity of objects: the sensible is not possible without the intelligible, and conscious thought, taken as discursive reason, *nous pathetikos*, is not possible without unconscious thought, taken as noetic reason, *nous poietikos*. The object is singular while the idea of it is synthetic, composed of traces of previous sense perceptions and ideas, and judgments made, thus, the idea of the object cannot possibly correspond to the object itself.

Kant's *Anthropology from a Pragmatic Point of View* (*Anthropologie in pragmatischer Hinsicht*, 1798), although a late work, addressed subjects that went back to Kant's lectures at the Albertus University of Königsberg, beginning in 1772 (Faflak, 2008, p. 48). In his *Anthropology* Kant identified unconscious thought with the *petites perceptions* of Leibniz. "Sense perceptions and sensations of which we are not aware but whose existence we can undoubtedly infer, that is, obscure ideas...," Kant said, "constitute an immeasurable field" (Kant, 1978, p. 19). Clear ideas are only a minute portion of all ideas, most of which are obscure, Kant explained in Section 5 of the *Anthropology*, "On the Ideas We Have Without Being Aware of Them." He posited two levels of consciousness. The first is direct or unmediated (*unmittelbar*), full consciousness in perception. The second is indirect or mediated (*mittelbar*), partially unconscious perception involving indirect representations that are dark and obscure (*dunkel*): "we can be indirectly conscious of having an idea, although we are not directly conscious of it" (p. 18). We draw conclusions about what we perceive without being conscious of perceiving every detail. The vast majority of our perceptions are of the details, which we do not consciously perceive, but which contribute to the conclusions and judgments we make in the act of perceiving.

Kant did not develop his theory of obscure ideas or sense perceptions because he saw them as a function of natural processes rather than the product of conscious will: they are the subject of "physiological anthropology," the study of man as created and determined by nature; as opposed to "pragmatic anthropology," the study of man as determined by his free will and choices, what man makes of himself based on his knowledge of the world. While nature operates according to the laws of mechanical causality, Kant preferred to see the human subject in terms of a freedom from mechanical causality, and determined by moral imperatives (Bowie, 1990, pp. 16–17). Moral imperatives, like all judgments, are based on phenomena, which are detached from the noumena, the *principia essendi*, which are the substance of the mechanical causality. The will that determines the action of moral imperative is a product of inner experience or subjectivity, which is inaccessible to discursive reason, as unconscious thought. The human subject is both bound to the laws of mechanical causality in phenomena in sense perception and discursive reason, *nous pathetikos*, and also free from the laws of nature in intellectual cognition and intuition, *nous poietikos*.

Kant did go on to say that we are often victimized by the obscure ideas and sense perceptions, which cloud our conscious perceptions, and our understanding of ourselves as we become an object of obscure ideas. Cognition and perception are defined as a synthesis of the clear and obscure, conscious and unconscious, ideas and perceptions. Cognition consists of the union of an active and a passive capacity, in the activity of combining and separating ideas. The ideas associated with the passive mind, by which the thinking subject is affected, belong to the "sensual cognitive faculty" (Kant, 1978, p. 25), *nous hylikos*, the lower of the two faculties. Sensual cognition is passive in relation to ideas and also to the "inner sense of awareness," the subjective faculty that makes cognition possible through imagination.

Intellectual cognition, the higher faculty, on the other hand, has the "character of spontaneity of apperception," as in *nous poietikos*, which is "the pure consciousness of the act which constitutes thought," entailing pure logical deduction. Apperception, the apprehension of the manifold or totality of perception, which is composed of mostly unconscious sensuous perceptions, entails a consciousness of the process of thought, the inner sense of awareness of the subject. It involves a consciousness of the relation between the noumenal and the phenomenal, and between intellect connected to sense perception and intellect not connected to sense perception. While intellectual cognition entails a consciousness of the cognitive act, it does not entail a consciousness of the source of the intellectual act. Intellectual cognition is the subject of philosophical logic, while sensuous cognition (passive thought) is the subject of psychology, which is "the foundation of inner experience," the subjective condition of the consciousness of cognition, according to Kant.

All empirical or sensuous perception and cognition can only be of phenomena, of objects as they appear, as opposed to noumena, objects as they are in themselves. The receptivity of objects of sense as phenomena requires an a priori intuition independent of the empirical sense perception. As Plotinus and Grosseteste argued, the *species sensibilis*, sensible form, is always already a *species apprehensibilis*, intelligible form. That which is perceived by the senses is predetermined by the intellectual faculty in the intuition of inner experience. The formal character of the receptivity of sense objects in the inner intuition is time, according to Kant. Time is the category of a priori intuition that makes possible inner experience and sense perception in passive intellect, because it is an archetypal or intelligible category, which is not subject to the divisions and multiplicity of discursive reason in passive intellect or the phenomenal objects of the sensual world. As the ordering of time is a function of intellectual cognition and the source of the consciousness of inner experience that makes empirical experience possible, cognition, in the synthesis of the passive and the active, is not conscious of the role of the a priori category of time in sense perception or discursive or passive reason.

Cognition, which is dependent on judgment, requires consciousness and self-consciousness or reflection, in order to arrange a chaotic multitude of ideas and sense perceptions, conscious and unconscious, into a unity or concept, a manifold or totality. All concepts are totalities, formed independently of perceived phenomena and the activities of passive cognition, but dependent upon them as a substrate. Consciousness consists of discursive consciousness, the logical substrate, and intuitive consciousness, the self-reflection of inner experience, which is given by imagination, as the image becomes an object of conscious thought, unfolding through language in discursive reason, as for Plotinus. Discursive consciousness is defined as the "pure apperception of its mental activity" (p. 26), as the mechanisms of apperception are unfolded in discursive reason in the formal structure of consciousness, which contains no manifold or intuition within itself. Inner experience, intuitive consciousness, contains both the intuition that defines it and the manifold that it produces. Intuitive consciousness is closer to the unconscious thought of which it is an immediate product, prior to its unfolding in discursive reason through a priori intuition.

The inner experience that defines the subjectivity of cognition and the consciousness of the subject, like the objects of sensual cognition, can only be seen as phenomenal, as an appearance to itself, because access to the unconscious is impossible. Access to the ground of cognition, a priori intuition, as the source of consciousness and the basis for discursive reason and sense perception, can only be given as a representation of itself in imagination, as in Plotinus. The self of which I am conscious in my cognition and perception can only be the appearance of a self, because all such consciousness is made possible by time, which is an a priori intelligible and not a quality of experience itself. I can stage the possibility of a consciousness of myself and my experience in my discursive reason, but I cannot be conscious of the ground which makes my discursive reason and sense perception possible. I can be conscious of the appearance or phenomenon of my unconscious thought, which is the ground of my inner experience, but I do not have access to the ground of my subjectivity, my experience in cognition, which is unconscious thought. As in the thought of Plotinus, I am caught between the play of two mirrors, providing representations of both the noumena of sense objects and the sources of inner experience, but granting me access to neither.

Thus "through inner experience I always know myself only as I appear to myself" (pp. 26–7). Appearance is the product of empirical intuition and understanding, that is, intellectual cognition, rather than judgment, or discursive cognition. My perception of my inner experience is in the form of the *species apprehensibilis*, an intelligible form, which I have constructed in my imagination, but the source of which I do not have access to. Imagination (*facultas imaginandi*) is the ability to form an image in the mind's eye that is independent of a sensual object or image. Imagination, like cognition, is a synthesis of the passive and the active. The passive imagination is reproductive, "a faculty of the derived representation (*exhibitio derivativa*)" (p. 56), merely reproducing empirical perceptions as they are recalled to mind within the framework of the category of time in a priori intuition. The active imagination is productive, producing an original representation of an object (*exhibitio originaria*) that precedes experience, taking place in intuition rather than empirical cognition. Perception of intelligibles in the imagination (*phantasia*), and perception of the a priori categories of space and time, is a faculty of productive imagination. Passive imagination is connected to empirical cognition, or experience, and is presupposed by it. Active imagination is a function of intellectual cognition, while passive imagination is a function of discursive cognition, exactly as it was for Plotinus.

The Kantian imagination

Kant outlined a theory of the imagination in his *Reflections on Anthropology* (*Reflexionen zur Anthropologie*) of 1776–78, and continued to develop it in the *Critique of Pure Reason* (1781, 1787) and the *Critique of Judgment* (1790). The imagination in the *Critique of Pure Reason* is seen primarily as the higher, productive imagination, and the imagination in the *Critique of Judgment* is seen in relation to aesthetic judgment. As for Plotinus, the imagination mediates between sense perception and intellectual cognition. The primary role of imagination is to transform the categories of a priori intuition into the schemata that organize sense perception and discursive reason. The importance that Kant placed on the imagination is the equivalent of the importance that Plotinus placed on the imagination in classical philosophy. As in Plotinus, there is a higher imagination and a lower imagination, one instrumental in the reception and understanding of intelligibles, and one instrumental in the reception and understanding of sense perceptions. In the various *Reflexionen*, the notes prior to 1781, and in the *Reflexionen zur Anthropologie* in particular, Kant defined a variety of imaginative functions in relation to varying degrees of connection to the sensible world, and varying degrees of productive capabilities. These were summarized very clearly by Rudolf Makkreel in *Imagination and Interpretation in Kant* (1990).

The formative faculty (*Bildungsvermögen*) is the power to organize and give form to intelligibles in intuition, which for Plotinus involved the *logos endiathetos*, the word in language, and the production of a visual representation or reflection in the mind's eye, representing unconscious thought to conscious thought in discursive reason. The lower imagination, operating in relation to sense objects or phenomena, storing and preserving them as the *eidos* or *species sensibilis*, is called the *Bildungskraft* by Kant. The imagination is the storehouse (*Vorrath*) of representations. The *Bildungskraft* is seen to have the power to give form to an intuition or an intelligible, to create a sensible form, *species sensibilis*, from an intelligible form, *species apprehensibilis*, in Scholastic terms. The higher imagination, called imaginative formation or *Einbildung*, operates without any connection to phenomena, or sensible or intelligible form.

It is able to produce rather than just reproduce, and create rather than just recreate. *Einbildung* is a function of *nous poietikos*, while *Bildungskraft* is a function of *nous hylikos*. *Einbildung* forms images through invention (as in the *fingendo* of Alexander Gottlieb Baumgarten) and abstraction (as in the *abstrahendo* of Christian Wolff) (Makkreel, 1990, p. 13).

Rudolf Makkreel summarized eight levels of image formation, six of them involving the mechanisms of imagination. *Bildung* is the general ability to organize and give form to intelligibles in intuition, which is made use of by the mechanisms of imagination. *Urbildung* is the form of intellectual intuition which is put to use by the higher forms of imagination in the higher intellect, *nous poietikos*. The lower imagination is composed of *Abbildung*, *Nachbildung*, and *Vorbildung*. *Abbildung* is direct image formation, the power to depict a sensuous object, or reproduce it as phenomenon. *Abbildung* makes the image of a sensible object visible so that it can be processed by the other levels of imagination within the temporal category of a priori intuition. The image of the *Abbildung* is limited only to the present moment. *Nachbildung* involves the reproduction of images that have already been formulated by the *Abbildung*, thus adding a temporal dimension. The *Vorbildung*, as a function of *Abbildung* and *Nachbildung*, reproduces images from the past and present in anticipation of future images, adding the temporal dimension of the future, and creating a storehouse of images, which becomes the vocabulary for sense experience and discursive reason. The activities of *Abbildung*, *Nachbildung*, and *Vorbildung* are connected to conscious thought and sense perception, the *nous pathetikos*, and contribute to the substance of experience, which is defined by the manifold in the process of apperception, the building of sense experiences of objects and ideas in an architectonic that provides the ground of experience and the self-consciousness of thought. The architectonic is subject to the temporal categories in intuition in the inner experience, and the spatial categories of intuition in sense perception. The activities of *Nachbildung* and *Vorbildung* generate images according to empirical laws of association and are connected to sense objects, but they nevertheless become functions of an active intellect rather than a passive intellect, in that they are governed by the categories of a priori intuition in unconscious thought.

The higher imagination is composed of *Einbildung*, *Ausbildung*, and *Gegenbildung*: the three categories of imagination that are not connected to sense perception or empirical experience, and are thus solely the product of intellectual cognition or the *nous poietikos*, unconscious thought. *Einbildung* is the power to invent images not connected to sense perceptions. It is an activity of the soul rather than material representation, although its invented image (*Erdichtung*) must be derived from the images of sense perception. *Einbildung* "loves to wander in the dark" (Makkreel, 1990, p. 15; Kant, 1902–83, 312; xv, 121), that is, it is an unconscious process. *Einbildung* comes into conscious thought through the formation of the invented image. *Ausbildung* is responsible for the completion of the invented images in unconscious thought or *nous poietikos*, which leads to the final formation of the invented image in *Gegenbildung* as symbolic or analogical, an archetype or intelligible, formed by the schemata from the categories in a priori intuition.

In *Gegenbildung*, the invented, intelligible images become linguistic signifiers, in the same way that the intelligibles of Plotinus are reflected as images formed by the *logos endiathetos*, unspoken language, in discursive reason. The *Gegenbildung* completes the process of the intelligible, the source of which is an active intellect, or intellectual cognition (unconscious thought), becoming a material form in a representation or an image in conscious thought, through the analog (*symbolum*) or sign of the logos. The schemata for the three stages of higher imagination unfold from the temporal categories of a priori intuition. The pure form of archetypal formation in the *Gegenbildung* is the *Urbildung*, which has no connection whatsoever to the material world, but is solely a pure quality of the soul. The *Urbildung* precedes the mechanisms of imagination in cognition, and is produced from a source that is inaccessible to conscious thought.

Kant's *Lectures on Metaphysics* (*Vorlesungen über Metaphysik*) are a set of lectures delivered between 1778 and 1780 and preserved in student notes. In them the functions of the lower imagination are elaborated upon, leading to more developed discussions in the *Critique of Pure Reason*. *Abbildung* creates images which are representations in the present; *Nachbildung* recreates images which are representative of the past; and *Vorbildung* creates images which anticipate future image formation in cognition and sense perception. Each is tied to the mechanisms of sense perception and material images, but also depends on active intellect and intellectual cognition in its formative powers. The manifold, for example, is present even in *Abbildung* as individual perceptions, conscious and unconscious, immediately participate in a totality, in a process of "running through" (*durchläuft*) the manifold. The mind is conscious in sense perception of forming and receiving images which are composites of many points of view, in the process of apperception. The varieties of *petite perceptions* of an object are "gathered together" (*zusammen nimmt*), although sometimes they can be overwhelming, which Kant discussed later in the *Critique of Pure Reason* and the *Critique of Judgment.*

Abbildung combines perceptions from the present, past and future. It thus involves the reproductive processes of *Nachbildung* and the anticipatory processes of *Vorbildung.* The mechanism of imagination connected to each is a form of empirical, discursive reason. Its function is to preserve objects of perception. The functions of the higher imagination, *Einbildung, Ausbildung,* and *Gegenbildung,* have the capacity of "producing images out of themselves (*aus sich selbst*) independently of the reality of objects" (Makkreel, 1990, p. 19; *Lectures on Metaphysics,* XXVIII, 237). They have the ability to absorb the particular perceptions connected to empirical or discursive reason into the manifold or totality of experience, and they have the ability to form images not connected to immediate sense experience, in a higher form of intellection, as in *nous poietikos,* that operates without the consciousness of sense perception. The linguistic signifiers of *Gegenbildung,* or symbolic analogs, manufacture links between sense perception and intellection that are not given by perception or discursive reason alone. While, even at the lowest level of imagination, objects of sense perception are pre-formed rather than directly given, in *Gegenbildung,* images in imagination are formed without any connection to the objects of sense perception.

Critique of Pure Reason

In the first edition of the *Critique of Pure Reason,* or the "A" version (1781), the "transcendental aesthetic" is the "science of all principles of *a priori* sensibility..." (A21) (Kant, 1968). In the transcendental aesthetic, space is defined as an a priori concept that is applied to sense experience, rather than being a quality of sense experience or being derived from sense experience: "Space is a necessary *a priori* representation, which underlies all outer intuitions" (A24). Unconscious thought is understood as being other to conscious thought, but within conscious thought itself, not external to it. Thus an a priori representation, or intuition of sensibility, is taken as a concept. Space does not exist in empirical reality: it only exists as a concept in intellection. At the same time, space can only be a representation, to discursive reason, and not a directly knowable reality. Space is a necessary representation because it is impossible to conceive of the absence of space, thus, all intuition is based on the presence of space in representation. In the second edition of the *Critique of Pure Reason,* or the "B" version (1787), space must therefore be "the condition of the possibility of appearances" (B39), and thus a condition of the possibility of all images formed in imagination. Space must necessarily be an unconscious intuition of sensibility: we are not conscious of the necessity of the a priori concept of space during the process of perception, because space appears to us to be an empirical perception in discursive, conscious reason. The grounds of perception and reason are inaccessible to us in conscious thought.

Space is a manifold, because it cannot be divided. As a consequence, geometry, or the geometrical representation of space, does not exist as an empirical reality, but rather only an a priori concept of intuition that is applied to empirical reality in perception and discursive reason. Therefore all products of geometry in intuitive imagination, in *Gegenbildung* and the higher forms of imagination not connected to sense perception, exist only as conceptual structures applied to empirical reality. An example is architecture: architecture is composed of geometry and mathematics, conceptual structures derived from the a priori intuitions of space and time; architecture only exists as a manifold, as a conceptual structure in higher imagination, and not as an object of perception or an inherent property of empirical reality. All geometrical propositions are "bound up with the consciousness of their necessity" (B41) independent of any judgment derived from experience. Space is the "subjective condition of sensibility" (A26/B42), and the "form of all appearances of outer sense." In that it is the form of all appearances, it is the necessary condition for the *eidos*, and the intelligible form, which is the unconscious basis of consciousness in perception and discursive reason. The forms of appearances, as intelligibles, precede actual perceptions, as established by Plotinus or Robert Grosseteste. Forms of appearances are based on principles, the *principia conoscendi*, that are the categories of a priori intuition unfolded in the imagination to form the underlying basis of sense perception and discursive reason, in the same way that for Plotinus the intelligibles are unfolded in imagination through the *logos endiathetos*, the linguistic signifier of Kant's *Gegenbildung*.

Time is also not an empirical concept derived from any experience, but rather a concept in a priori intuition that is defined by its apodictic necessity, as Kant explained in Section II of the Transcendental Aesthetic. Time is only a representation to conscious reason and sense experience, and is a necessary basis for the existence of the manifold: a manifold cannot be conceived outside of a relation to the successions made possible by the concept of time, along with the concept of space. It is impossible to conceive of any sensible reality outside of time or space. Time, like space, underlies the possibility of all sense experience and conscious reason, without our being conscious of it as a purely a priori intuitive concept with no necessary connection to the perceptions and thoughts of which we are conscious. These concepts would provide an important basis for the division in the psyche of conscious/unconscious thought in the psychoanalytic theory of Freud and Lacan.

As space determines the form of perception, it is the form of outer sense. Time has no relation to the shape or position of the objects of perception, so it is the form of the inner sense, or the relations of representations in cognition. Time has no existence in spatial representation, but we attempt to represent it to ourselves in the form of spatial analogies: the continuous, undivided line representing linear time, or the infinitely recurring circle representing cyclical time. In either case time is represented as a manifold which cannot be interrupted, although it can be divided, unlike space. The division of time is a function of conscious reason operating on the intuition of the inner sense. Regarding space, conscious reason cannot operate on outer sense, or the empirical reality to which it responds. The representation of both space and time to ourselves in conscious thought is the product of an a priori intuition that is not accessible to conscious thought.

Because all sensual phenomena are representations and determinations of the mind, time precedes space in its apodictic necessity as an a priori condition of experience. The condition of the inner appearance, the intelligible form, determines the condition of the outer appearance, the sensible form. All representations, whether empirical or intuitive, are connected to the inner sense. Time in the inner sense is the condition of the possibility of the manifold: all things, all sensible perceptions, are given a relationship in time. In apperception, the combination of perceptions which conform to the a priori manifold, all sense objects are given a place in space and time. The placement of the sense object is determined by a priori relationships of intuition. A sense object that is perceived is understood in a particular spatial relation to other objects, while the perception of the object is understood in relation to the perception and representation of other objects in time. In dreams, objects in the imagination may appear independent of the spatial relations that governed their perception as sense objects, and independent of the temporal relations that governed the perception of them, as analyzed by Freud. Dreams function independently of the manifold of space and time that organizes conscious reason. As Freud would say, dreams have no intention of communicating anything, so they are able to operate outside the framework of the linguistic mechanisms, the linguistic signifier or the *logos endiathetos*, that transform intelligibles into images, establishing the basis of the relation between reason and perception, between the human mind and the world as it is perceived and represented. Dreams must be a function of the higher forms of imagination, the *Einbildung*, *Ausbildung*, and *Gegenbildung*, which operate independently of the relations of empirical perception and conscious reason, the relations dictated by the manifold or a priori categories of space and time.

Time is necessary for a manifold to be understood or represented as a manifold to conscious thought. Time is the basis for the "synthesis of apprehension" (A99) that is connected to the representation of the manifold and the intuition that is the basis of the manifold. The synthesis of apprehension is a priori, prior to empirical experience and representation, and not connected to empirical experience. Thus, it functions in the higher forms of imagination, as in *nous poietikos*, or unconscious thought. The representations of space and time that are given to discursive reason depend on the synthesis of apprehension, as a manifold itself. The manifold, composed of space and time as the categories of a priori intuition, depends on the synthesis of apprehension, which is a synthesis of the inner and outer sense, and of a priori intuition and empirical experience. It is thus a synthesis of the subjective (ideal) and the objective (real), and represents an absolute in Hegelian terms. The absolute, as the manifold and the synthesis of apprehension, is necessary for all thought and experience. Without the categories of a priori intuition, empirical imagination would be unknowable to conscious reason, and would be unable to function in relation to sense perception.

Time, as the a priori category of inner sense or intuition, is the necessary ground of the "synthetic unity of appearances" (A101) in the manifold, and makes possible the reproduction of them in the imagination, and the representation of them to conscious reason. Appearances "are not things in themselves," but rather "the mere play of our representations," as phenomena rather than noumena, based on the determinations of inner sense, and the categories of space and time. The play of the representations of appearances is possible in the higher forms of imagination and *nous poietikos*, thinking and imagining not connected to the empirical experience. Freed from the relations of empirical experience governed by the rules of synthetic apprehension and the categories of the manifold, appearances can be reproduced and reconstructed by imagination in such a way that different realities than empirical reality can be created. Different realities are bound to the categories of space and time in conscious thought, but in unconscious thought and imagination, in dreams for example, realities can be created from the representation of appearance, the *Vorstellungsrepräsentanz* of Freud, outside the unconscious manifold. The transcendental synthesis of imagination, which is a product of the synthesis of apprehension in the manifold, or the absolute, is the condition for the possibility of all experience, which is the condition for the possibility of the reproduction of appearances in imagination.

Thus, the "synthesis of apprehension" in reason is "inseparably bound up with the synthesis of reproduction" (A102) in imagination. The synthesis of apprehension is the transcendental ground of the possibility of all knowledge, both empirical and a priori, while the synthesis of reproduction in imagination is the transcendental ground of all thought. The succession of representations in the reproduction of images in the imagination is made possible by the category of time; without the succession of images, conscious thought would not be possible. Conscious thought is not possible without unconscious thought. The unity of the manifold can only be given as a representation in conscious thought; as an a priori category, time is inaccessible to conscious thought. The unity of time only exists as it is unfolded in conscious thought or discursive reason through the mechanisms of imagination, in the translation of intelligibles to images through language. The products of the categories of space and time, geometry and mathematics, can only function as organizing principles in relation to empirical experience in conscious reason, although as pure concepts they only exist in intuition, as intelligibles. The organizing and the unity of the manifold occur in conscious thought, as "the concept of the number is nothing but the consciousness of this unity of synthesis" (A103), as it is unfolded from unconscious thought in a priori intuition.

Sense perception, imagination, and apperception are sources of knowledge that are both empirical in relation to appearances or representations, and thus also the product of a priori intuition. While appearances are represented empirically in sense perception, and in relation to one another in a manifold in imagination, the association between the appearance and its representation and reproduction in imagination, in the terms of the *Vorstellungsrepräsentanz*, occurs through "empirical consciousness" (A115) in apperception. The a priori intuition of time in the inner sense, the pure synthesis of imagination (higher imagination not connected to empirical experience), and empirical consciousness in apperception, or the mechanisms imparted to conscious reason by the categories of the manifold, are all necessary in order for the perception of a sensible object to take place. The combination constitutes a "unity of knowledge necessary for a possible experience..." (A116). Intuitions have no value unless they can be unfolded in conscious thought.

While conscious thought is not possible without unconscious thought, if the latter was not able to be translated into conscious thought (although the mechanisms of the translation may themselves be unconscious), unconscious thought would have no value. All knowledge depends on the translation of unconscious thought to conscious thought, in representations in the imagination. Representations depend on both the consciousness of discursive reason and the unconscious processes of a priori intuition as *nous poietikos*. The manifold of representations must exist in both conscious and unconscious thought as the "transcendental principle of the unity of all that is manifold in our representations…," in the synthesis of apprehension and according to the categories of a priori intuition. The principle of the synthetic unity in intuition is provided by pure apperception, which must transcend empirical consciousness as a higher form of apperception, corresponding to the higher forms of imagination and not connected to empirical experience.

The transcendental unity of apperception involves an a priori synthesis, and is related to the pure synthesis of the higher imagination. While the productive synthesis of the imagination takes place a priori, the reproductive synthesis of the imagination, in the lower imagination, *Abbildung*, *Nachbildung*, and *Vorbildung*, can only take place in connection to empirical experience. Synthetic transcendental apperception, along with a priori intuition, are functions of a form of thought that is not accessible to conscious thought: they are the *nous poietikos*, or unconscious thought. The a priori combination of the manifold, the transcendental synthesis of imagination, is the basis for all possible knowledge, and all possible empirical experience or sense perception, which it represents a priori to conscious thought.

The relation of the unity of apperception to the synthesis of imagination is defined as understanding. We understand something in sense perception or conscious thought when it corresponds to its a priori idea, as it has been apprehended in imagination. All possible empirical experiences must conform to the "necessary unity of the pure synthesis of imagination" (A119); otherwise, they would not be knowable. The a priori modes of knowledge that contain such unity in the understanding are the categories, the "pure concepts of understanding." Empirical knowledge must include an understanding related to the objects of sense perception; such understanding is given by a priori intuition and imaginative synthesis. It is inaccessible to conscious perception, thus, it is unconscious thought. All appearances and representations must conform to the understanding, as the sensible form must conform to the intelligible form. All experience of perception is made possible by unconscious thinking of objects as phenomena or representations in the unity of the manifold of synthetic apperception in a priori intuition;

objects cannot be known in themselves, nor can they be known as phenomena. Neither the objects nor the thinking of them is accessible to conscious thought, which is caught in a play of mirror reflections, as it were. Appearances have a "necessary relation to the understanding": they would not be possible without it.

Consciousness is necessary for perception, for an appearance to be an object of knowledge, according to Kant. If an appearance were not an object of knowledge, it would have no objective reality and no existence, recalling the Idealism of Berkeley. All appearances contain a manifold a priori, and can only be known in combination, derived from the transcendental synthesis of intuition and higher imagination, in combination with the empirical synthesis of lower imagination. The action of the productive synthesis of the imagination directed at sense perceptions is apprehension. Apprehension invests the form of the image in perception with the manifold of intuition, and in order to do so, it must have previously processed the image in the imagination, recalling again the thought of Berkeley, as in the *Alciphron*, "we perceive distance not immediately but by mediation of a sign, which has no likeness to it or necessary connection with it, but only suggests it from repeated experience, as words do things" (§8) (Berkeley, 1963), and in the *New Theory of Vision*, we are "exceedingly prone to imagine those things which are perceived only by the mediation of others to be themselves the immediate objects of sight" (§66). None of this is possible without the "subjective ground" of the inner sense or category of a priori intuition that is time, which organizes perceptions in relation to past and subsequent perceptions in the empirical faculty of the imagination: *Abbildung*, creating representations in the present; *Nachbildung*, recreating images which represent the past; and *Vorbildung*, creating images which anticipate future images.

The subjective ground of time governs the rules of association between images in perception, imagination, and apprehension. While the subjective ground is the inner sense or intuition, unconscious thought, the objective ground is consciousness in perception and apprehension. The objective ground of consciousness is necessary to unite all appearances in empirical imagination as part of the same and only consciousness. Even if the appearances were ordered in succession by the intuition of time, they would still not need to participate in the same unity. The single consciousness ensures that all appearances conform to the categories, the universal principles that are the basis of knowledge. The unity is found in apperception, and all appearances must conform to the unity of apperception in order to be apprehended. The unity of apperception is the "objective unity of all empirical consciousness in one consciousness" (*Critique of Pure Reason*, A123) (Kant, 1968), which is "the necessary condition of all possible perception." All appearances must have a certain affinity, which is a consequence of the transcendental synthesis in imagination.

The necessary unity of apperception is provided by the transcendental synthesis of the productive imagination, the subjective inner sense, in combination with consciousness in empirical experience and conscious thought, the Cartesian "I think." Transcendental apperception is distinguished from empirical apperception, just as transcendental imagination is distinguished from empirical imagination, because there must be an a priori representation for all empirical representations, in order that empirical representations might exist. As empirical representations are dependent on a priori representations, a priori representations cannot be dependent on any empirical reality outside of apprehension and imagination. Transcendental apperception is the "transcendental unity of self-consciousness" (B132), as all representations are only unified in belonging to one and the same consciousness. The self-consciousness of empirical representations is made possible by the transcendental unity of apperception, which is made possible by the unconscious thought processes, the manifold in intuition. While the unity of apprehension depends on the self-consciousness of the perceiving individual, it also depends on the participation of individual self-consciousness in a universal or self-consciousness, ensuring the universality of the linguistic rules, derived from the principles of the categories, that govern the apprehension of a representation in imagination. Kant was in this way an early structuralist, arguing for the necessity of universal rules of thought and language.

The apperception of the manifold involves a synthesis of representations that is made possible through a consciousness of the synthesis in discursive reason or conscious thought, connected to empirical experience. Empirical consciousness has no necessary relation to the inner sense, or the subjective experience without all individual representations being combined in a synthetic consciousness. Consciousness comes about in the relation between perception and language, specifically in the formation of the intelligible or apprehensible image in imagination, which connects the perceiving subject to what is being perceived, in the representation. I am only conscious of the world around me in my perception of it when I can represent it to myself in apperception and imagination. I am only conscious of the world around me as a representation to myself; my consciousness is my perception of my own representations, in relation to my use of language, which provides the representations. The "analytic unity of apperception" (B133), in empirical, conscious thought, is given by the "synthetic unity of apperception" in the transcendental aesthetic, the principles of a priori sensibility in unconscious thought, which paves the way for the transcendental unity of self-consciousness, and the possibility of knowledge and experience.

The synthesis of the manifold in pure concepts relates them to the unity of apperception, both transcendental and empirical, and is the basis for a priori knowledge, which depends on understanding, and the faculty of representation in imagination. Through the manifold of representations in imagination, in relation to the synthetic unity of apperception, understanding is able to identify the intuition in the inner sense as the basis of experience, as conscious thought might be aware of the presence of unconscious thought. The categories, the forms of the pure concepts, take objective form in the representations in the imagination and are thus connected to the objects of sense perception, as they are themselves representations in the imagination. They are only appearances, "for it is solely of appearances that we can have *a priori* intuition" (B151).

The a priori synthesis of the sensible manifold of intuition, as it is represented to conscious thought, is called the "figurative synthesis" (*synthesis speciosa*), in contrast to the synthesis of the manifold in the categories of intuition in understanding, which is the "intellectual synthesis" (*synthesis intellectualis*). Both forms of synthesis are a priori and transcendental, and necessary for all other a priori knowledge. The figurative synthesis is the transcendental synthesis of the imagination, wherein the imagination represents an intelligible of a sense object in intuition. It is the higher, productive imagination, that is able to represent a sense object without the sense object being present. As for Plotinus, imagination operates midway between intuition (intellection) and sense perception. It connects sensible representations from empirical experience with the synthesis in the categories of a priori intuition, in its transcendental synthesis in the understanding. The intellectual synthesis is a product of understanding alone, without a connection to imagination, or to empirical experience. Figurative synthesis is connected to the lower, reproductive imagination, and the empirical laws of sense perception. Intellectual synthesis is connected to the higher, productive imagination, which does not involve the empirical laws of sense perception, as in the *nous poietikos*, or productive intellect. Figurative synthesis is a rhetorical synthesis, as opposed to a literal synthesis, that is, a synthesis represented in language.

In the thought of Plotinus – in a scheme that seems very similar to the Kantian one and anticipates the concepts of Hegel and Freud – imagination facilitates the translation of sensible objects in perception to intellection. The intellectual act is not possible without an accompanying mental image. The ability to form the image (*eidos*), appearance or representation, in the mind's eye is always accompanied by a "verbal expression" (*Enneads* IV.3.30) (Plotinus, 1966): or, more accurately, the *logos endiathetos*, the word in thought, as Plotinus seems to have intended it. The intelligible image, and thus the sensible image, is not possible without its linguistic expression, and linguistic expression is not possible without the intelligible image. Perception of sensible objects is only possible after the idea of the sensible object is articulated in language in intellection. While the "intellectual act is without parts," according to Plotinus, as in the a priori synthesis of the manifold in intuition, it has not been differentiated in conscious thought through the *logos endiathetos* in imagination, and thus in sense perception, and it "has not, so to speak, come out into the open, but remains unobserved within," as unconscious thought.

But "the verbal expression," or the *logos endiathetos*, "unfolds its content," from intellection or intuition, "and brings it out of the intellectual act into the image-making power," allowing imagination to form the intelligible image that corresponds to the sensible image in memory, as in the thought of Kant. In doing so, the linguistic articulation "shows the intellectual act as if in a mirror," for Plotinus, or a representation, as a mirror reflection might represent a sensible object. But the linguistic articulation in conscious thought does not contain the intellectual act; the intellectual act, like the intellectual synthesis, and the productive imagination, remains separate from sense perception and sensible reality, and discursive reason, wherein can be found the figurative synthesis as the linguistic representation, *logos endiathetos*, of the intelligible, or the transcendental synthesis. The intellectual act, of Plotinus, is inaccessible, as unconscious thought, or the a priori transcendental synthesis of the manifold.

The *logos endiathetos*, as the unarticulated word, can be seen as Plotinus' "silent rational form" (*Enneads* III.8.6) and the "rational principle" which "must not be outside but must be united with the soul of the learner, until it finds that it is its own," like the categories of a priori intuition in the inner sense of Kant. Once the soul, according to Plotinus, has "become akin to and disposed according to the rational principle," the logos, or the schemata of Kant unfolding the categories, it "utters and propounds it," forming the representation of the intelligible idea in relation to the representation of the object of sense perception. The spoken word in language, *logos prophorikos*, is an imitation of the *logos endiathetos* in the same way that the figurative synthesis is an imitation of the intellectual synthesis; and reproductive imagination is an imitation of productive imagination, but connected to empirical experience. According to Plotinus, the *logoi* of discursive reason, conscious thought, "by means of sense-perception – which is a kind of intermediary when dealing with sensible things – do appear to work on the level of sense and think about sense objects" (*Enneads* I.4.10). Conscious thought in discursive reason depends on representations of thought in intellect, or the representations of the categories in imagination. Consciousness "exists and is produced when intellectual activity is reflexive and when that in the life of the soul which is active in thinking is in a way projected back," as the representation formed by the logos, "as happens with a mirror-reflection when there is a smooth, bright, untroubled surface."

In the *Critique of Pure Reason*, the consciousness of self, the thinking subject, is given by the transcendental synthesis of the manifold and the synthetic unity of apperception, but as a reproduction in thought rather than as a pure intuition. Self-consciousness requires the combination of the intuition of the manifold in inner sense, as the *nous poietikos*, and the act of thought, as the *nous hylikos*. It is only possible to know oneself as an appearance to oneself, as the manifold of intuition is unfolded in thought through the logos and the mechanisms of imagination that mediate between intuition and sense perception. Consciousness of self is "very far from being a knowledge of the self" (B158); consciousness of self as knowledge of self is an illusion brought about by the inaccessibility of the categories in intuition to conscious thought, that is, by the inaccessibility of unconscious thought to conscious thought, although unconscious thought is the basis of conscious thought, and the categories are necessary to "constitute the thought of an object in general" through apperception. Kant appears to establish the basis of an understanding of an unconscious thought that would lead to the Freudian conception of the unconscious as the underlying basis of the definition of the self that is generally inaccessible and which must be accessed in order to address problems with the self in terms of psychological functioning.

In order to have knowledge of self it is necessary to have an intuition of the manifold in self that determines thought: in other words, not direct knowledge of the manifold, but only of the possibility, or necessity, of the manifold. It is impossible for conscious thought to have direct knowledge of unconscious thought; unconscious thought can only be inferred, through absences in conscious thought, for example. It is only possible to have direct knowledge of self in conscious thought, in its exercise of the "power of combination" outside the manifold, "subjected to a limiting condition" (B159). The combinative powers of conscious thought are made possible by the category of time in the inner sense, but only insofar as time is unfolded in relations outside pure understanding, and in relation to empirical experience. It is only possible to have self-knowledge in the appearance of self as it is manifested in relation to empirical experience, through a reproductive intuition in imagination that cannot be the pure intuition of understanding, which is inaccessible to the limited mechanisms of sense perception, and inaccessible to conscious thought.

According to Kant, the "schematism of our understanding, in its application to appearances," forms and representations, "is an art concealed in the depths of the human soul, whose real modes of activity nature is hardly ever likely to allow us to discover, and to have open to our gaze" (A141/B181). Productive imagination and intellectual synthesis are processes of unconscious thought, while reproductive imagination and figurative synthesis are processes of conscious thought. In the words of Theodor Lipps, in *Psychological Studies*, "the pure concepts of the understanding (categories) seem to belong to the unconscious ideas, so far as they lie beyond cognition..." (Lipps, 1926, p. 21). The source of cognition is left unexplained, except insofar as unconscious thought is the foundation for conscious thought.

For Kant, the thinking subject is made possible by the synthetic unity of apperception and the representations that are presented by it in the process of thought. The thinking subject is split between the condition of its possibility in the inner sense and its activity in conscious thought; the subject is thus split or self-alienated, having no access to the necessity of its existence in intuition. The thinking subject is unable to think itself as inner sense or the manifold of intuition, the basis of its possibility. The Cartesian self-consciousness is an illusion, and the subject is defined in romantic self-alienation. Knowledge of the self is dark and obscure: it is given by the indirect, mediated (*mittelbar*), partially unconscious perceptions involving indirect representations that are dark and obscure (*dunkel*). In the thought of Plotinus, the thinking subject did not have complete access to itself either, to the mechanisms of Intellect or *nous poietikos*, but there was no concept of self-alienation. Perhaps because science established that the mechanisms of nature were not completely accessible to human intelligence, that man was no longer the measure of all things, the romantic alienation from nature translated into a romantic alienation from self, or whatever is natural in self: the *principia essendi*, the noumena, the inner sense and pure intuition.

Thus, bound by the limitation of succession in time, self-knowledge is only possible in the activity of conscious thought, as in the passive *nous pathetikos*, connected to empirical experience. Self-knowledge is only possible as an other to self that is defined by temporal experience but made possible by the self that is inaccessible to temporal, empirical experience and the thought that is connected to it. The thinking subject within the representation of time, from the category in a priori intuition or the manifold of inner sense, would be the "ego," according to Gilles Deleuze in *Kant's Critical Philosophy*, as opposed to the "I" that is the inaccessible self in the inner sense, what Freud would call the id. The inaccessible "I," in the interiority of unconscious thought, affects and makes possible the cognitive activity of the ego in the exteriority of temporal discursiveness, creating a self-alienated and split subject. In the words of Deleuze, "our interiority constantly divides us from ourselves, splits us in two: a splitting in two which never runs its course, since time has no end....an oscillation which constitutes time" (Deleuze, 1984, p. ix). The human subject is thus caught between the play of mirror reflections, as in the thought of Plotinus, with no access to the interiority of intuition, or exteriority of the objects of sense perception. Further, the subject is defined as split, and in constant oscillation, circling around a void, an inaccessible object of desire created by the function of language that has no access to its source, the *das Ding* of Freud or the *objet a* of Lacan. In the thought of Kant can thus be found the basis of the modern psychoanalytic subject, as described in the writings of Freud and Lacan.

In the *Critique of Pure Reason*, time can only exist in its representation to the conscious ego by the inner sense. Time is represented a priori "through the synthesis of the manifold which sensibility presents in its original receptivity" (A99–100) (Kant, 1968). In the apprehension of the intuition, time is generated or manufactured, in the productive intellect and the productive imagination, in unconscious thought. Time is then the framework of the inner sense in which the faculties of the reproductive imagination can operate, combining the particulars of sense perception into the manifold of subjective experience. In the framework of time, imagination reproduces past representations, and anticipates future representations, in order to incorporate them into present representations, in a temporal succession. The association of the different representations in time is based on a priori principles or the categories of intuition, communicated to the imagination by the schemata, or the logos, as it were.

The schemata, in the words of Rudolf Makkreel, in *Imagination and Interpretation in Kant*, are "a priori products of the imagination that mediate between concepts and empirical appearances" (Makkreel, 1990, p. 1), as the *logos endiathetos* might mediate between the intelligible and the sensible in the thought of Plotinus. The schema has no empirical content, but must be both intellectual and sensible, as the imagination of Plotinus is both intellectual and sensible. The schemata apply the categories to imagination in order to form the groundwork of the subjective empirical experience of the objects of sense perception. Imagination mediates between the categories as universal concepts and sensible intuition, as composed of empirical particulars. The framework for the mediation is time, within which the categories are unfolded as particulars, from the subjective intuition of inner sense to the objective cogitation of conscious thought. The framework of time allows for the temporal associations of representations to be combined in such a way as the manifold can be translated into sense experience. The most important function of the productive, transcendental imagination is to produce the temporal schemata, through representation in language, so that the sensible can be experienced as a manifold in intuition.

There are schemata of both sensible concepts in conscious thought and pure concepts of the understanding in intuition. As the framework for the function of imagination, which is both sensible and intelligible, reproductive and productive, schemata are both sensible and intelligible. The schemata of the pure concepts are independent of any sensible form and thus cannot be translated into an image, while the schemata of the sensible concepts are that through which images are possible in imagination. The schema is not a property of a sensible concept, but is a necessary basis for any sensible concept. The schema is an archetype, the universal concept to which all particular forms must conform, but in relation to which all are imperfect or incomplete realizations. In the *Critique of Pure Reason*, the example is given of the triangle (A141), the schema of which cannot correspond to any image or representation, as it is a construct of geometry and mathematics, manifestations of the categories of space and time, intuitions that are applied to sensible reality a priori, thus preceding any possible formal representation.

Critique of Judgment

In the Introduction to Kant's *Critique of Judgment* (*Kritik der Urteilskraft*, 1790), pleasure is connected with the "apprehension of the form of an object of intuition," and expresses the "conformity of the object to the cognitive faculties brought into play in the reflective judgement..." (VII, 189, 17–24) (Kant, 1952). Pleasure is the result of the reaffirmation of the ego in relation to the sensible world, the reaffirmation of the presence of the subject in the world. The image is the form in the imagination, the intelligible form that is a product of a priori intuition; pleasure is a function of the imagination, not sense perception. All sense perception is dependent on the synthesis of apprehension. Imagination is the active faculty for the synthesis of the manifold, as connected to the understanding. The apprehension that produces pleasure is an apprehension of particular relations of space and time as given by the categories in intuition. Sensations are synthesized in the imagination to create a form or appearance. If the synthesis of sensations corresponds with the pure a priori concepts, then pleasure results, and an object of sense, as the form or appearance in the imagination, is judged to be beautiful. If a sense object does not conform to the organization of reality in sense perception as given by a priori intuition, then it is judged to be ugly. These processes take place in unconscious thought, as do a priori intuition and imagination (in part); aesthetic judgments, like the conformity of what is perceived to the manifold, are not immediately available to conscious thought.

In order for a sense object to be perceived, judged to be beautiful, and give pleasure, it must conform to its intelligible appearance in the imagination, derived from the categories of a priori intuition. Kant sees elements of sense perception such as colors, tones, shadows, etc., to be products of the manifold of sensation, rather than individual sensations. They participate in spatial and temporal sequences, and in a play of sensations that forms the manifold. The spatial and temporal sequences are not present in a sensation itself, in conscious perception, nor are the play of sensations that forms the manifold, but they make the sensation possible. No sense object can be perceived outside a relation to other sense objects. Sensations are brought together in the imagination, and forms in the imagination are a product of the manifold of sensations in imagination, not individual sense objects outside their participation in the manifold. Pleasure and aesthetic judgment are the product of the manifold of sensations, the relations between objects of sense. Works of art and architecture exhibit particular spatial and temporal relationships that organize forms derived from objects of sense that create relationships between each other in the manifold. Works of art, like objects of sense perception, are judged to be beautiful when they reinforce the conformance of objects of sense perception to the organization of the manifold in intuition. In the case of works of abstract art and architecture, they would be judged to be beautiful when they reinforce the organization of the manifold itself as it is given to the imagination through the understanding. Aesthetic sense is a synthesis of the sensible and intelligible, of conscious and unconscious thought. Art is the result of imagination, as a synthesis of the manifold, and the unfolding of the intelligible through the logos in the imagination. All art is metaphysical: a work of art expresses an idea that is not connected to its material presence.

While objects of sense perception participate in a play of sensations that forms the manifold, the cognitive powers connected to them, that produce them as representations, are involved in a "free play of the powers of representation in a given representation for a cognition in general" (§9, 217, 12–13). The free play necessitates a "subjective universal communicability of the mode of representation in a judgement..." (23–4), mechanisms of representation, from the categories to the schemata, from intuition to imagination, that are shared by everyone, in a collective unconscious, as it were. A judgment, including an aesthetic judgment of beauty (*Schönheit*) in nature or in art, constitutes "the mental state present in the free play of imagination and understanding" (26–7), a universally shared mental state from which subjective conditions arise. The harmonious and proportionate relationships in a natural organism, that conform to the expectations of the manifold in relation to space and time, convey a sense of teleology and purpose, that what is perceived in nature contributes to the identity of the subject in self-consciousness. It is not possible to know the organism as noumenon, as thing in itself, as in the *principia essendi*; it is only possible to know it as phenomenon, as it conforms to the manifold. As a result of the free play in the understanding, the purpose associated with the organism as perceived is a subjective purpose as opposed to an objective purpose, because the purpose corresponds with the perception of the organism rather than the organism itself. The pleasure derived from the judgment of an organism in nature as beautiful is the pleasure derived from the subjective experience of nature as constitutive of the thinking subject. The subjective judgment of beauty has no relation to the objective purpose of an organism in nature, its satisfaction of functional requirements outside its correspondence with the harmony of the manifold in intuition.

In §47 of the *Critique of Judgment*, no creative individual "can show how his ideas, so rich at once in fancy and in thought, enter and assemble themselves in his brain, for the good reason that he does not himself know, and so cannot teach others" (§47, 309, 10–13). The process of creation, like the processes of intuition and imagination, is an unconscious one, inaccessible to conscious thought and explanation. The human subject is once again split between the condition of its possibility in the inner sense and its activity in conscious reason; the subject is self-alienated, having no access to the necessity of its existence in intuition or the creative imagination. It is not possible to explain on a conscious level how beautiful works of art are created, or even how beauty is judged, because judgments of beauty are products of unconscious processes. It is not possible to explain on a conscious level how great works of art are created, works of art that say and mean the most to the most people, works of art that have the most resonance.

The splitting and self-alienation of the subject, and the inaccessibility of the subject to itself, is intensified by the romantic concept of the sublime, which is also a product of the discontinuity between the intelligible and the sensible, or between *nous poietikos* and *nous pathetikos*. The sublime, in that it is used to describe that which exceeds conscious thought and perception, and that which exceeds the properties of the manifold in an organism, in a representation of limitlessness, suggests unconscious thought. While the beautiful is limited, in a reasoned association between what is perceived and what is conceived as a manifold, the sublime exceeds that limitation, as something that challenges the reinforcement of the identity of the subject in relation to what is perceived. The sublime "cannot be contained in any sensuous form" (§23, 245, 5–6), and concerns ideas of reason for which no adequate representation is possible. The sublime results in a sensation of displeasure, threatening the accord between intuition and sensible reality and threatening the identity of the subject. The sensation of the sublime causes reason to abandon its reliance on sense perception, and search for higher causes or explanations for phenomena, that are not accessible to that which is possible to know about unconscious thought in conscious thought. The sublime thus suggests the unknowability of unconscious thought in conscious thought, and threatens the security of the Cartesian "I think therefore I am," the illusion of the self-consciousness of reason.

While the judgment of beauty in nature, though derived from intuition, is based on the perception of the object in nature, the sensation of the sublime is based on the failing of reason in apprehension, the failing of the representation in the imagination by apprehension. The sublime invokes the terror of the unknowability of the self to itself. The feeling of the sublime is "a feeling of displeasure, arising from the inadequacy of imagination in the aesthetic estimation of magnitude to attain to its estimation by reason" (§27, 257, 12–15), spatial and temporal magnitude in the a priori categories. While the judgment of beauty confirms the relation between form or appearance and reason, the feeling of the sublime challenges that relation. The sublime, in severing the tie between perception and reason, or the relation of reason to itself, "makes reason confront its own unconscious," in the words of Joel Faflak in *Romantic Psychoanalysis* (Faflak, 2008, p. 47). Reason loses itself in an abyss: "The point of excess for the imagination (towards which it is driven in the apprehension of the intuition) is like an abyss in which it fears to lose itself ... " (*Critique of Judgment*, §27, 258, 6–9) (Kant, 1952). The sublime is a conflict between reason and imagination, in the inadequacy of the understanding.

While the sublime invokes the inadequacy of reason in relation to imagination, it also invokes the limitlessness of the imagination. A judgment of beauty is based on a limitation of imagination, and reason in relation to imagination, while a judgment of the sublime removes that limitation. Conscious thought in discursive reason is given by limitation, while the unconscious is understood to be without limit, an infinite abyss within reason. "As the imagination reaches beyond conscious empiricism toward the purely psychical or unconscious – understood as the 'purely' rational," in the words of Joel Faflak, " – its ability to represent itself and thus to fulfill the Kantian categorical imperative of rational understanding falters" (Faflak, 2008, p. 47). Rational understanding in conscious thought falters at some point because its basis, unconscious thought, is inaccessible, and thus at some point reason cannot be rescued. The abyss of the sublime is the abyss of the unconscious in the romantic self-alienation of the human subject brought about by the dissolution of the teleological in society as a whole and in the perceptual experience of the subject in particular.

The feeling of the sublime appears to "contravene the ends of our power of judgement, to be ill-adapted to our faculty of presentation," and to be "an outrage on the imagination" (*Critique of Judgment*, §23, 245, 29–31). The sublime challenges the basis of judgment as a conceptual act based in conscious thought, and raises the possibility that judgment, and other conceptual acts derived from intuition, may be based on something that is inaccessible to conscious thought, suggesting the presence of unconscious thought. The sublime is "the mere capacity of thinking which evidences a faculty of mind transcending every standard of sense" (§25, 250, 6–8), mind given to itself in pure interiority with no connection to the sensible world, to conscious perception or reason, in the abyss of the excess of the imagination.

The suggestion of the presence of unconscious thought within conscious thought can be found throughout Kant's writings. There are thoughts that can be negated or cancelled, obscured or darkened (*Attempt to Introduce the Concept of Negative Magnitudes into Philosophy*). The whole of all appearances is a problem to which there is no solution (*Critique of Pure Reason*, A328). There exists an indirect or mediated, partially unconscious perception involving indirect representations that are dark and obscure; "we can be indirectly conscious of having an idea, although we are not directly conscious of it" (*Anthropology*, p. 18) (Kant, 1978). *Einbildung*, the power of the imagination to invent images not connected to sense perceptions, "loves to wander in the dark." Consciousness of self is "very far from being a knowledge of the self" (*Critique of Pure Reason*, B158) (Kant, 1968). The "schematism of our understanding," from the categories of intuition, "in its application to appearances, is an art concealed in the depths of the human soul, whose real modes of activity nature is hardly ever likely to allow us to discover, and to have open to our gaze" (A141/B181). No creative individual "can show how his ideas...enter and assemble themselves in his brain, for the good reason that he does not himself know, and so cannot teach others" (*Critique of Judgment*, §47) (Kant, 1952). The feeling of the sublime is "a feeling of displeasure, arising from the inadequacy of imagination in the aesthetic estimation of magnitude to attain to its estimation by reason" (§27).

Kant developed the suggestions of unconscious thought in classical and medieval philosophy, in the Neoplatonic and Peripatetic traditions, and laid the groundwork for the concept of unconscious thought in the psychoanalytic theory of Freud and Lacan. Several other eighteenth- and nineteenth-century philosophers made important contributions to this project as well, though not in as elaborately developed philosophies. Summaries of these contributions are the subject of the next chapter.

6
Unconscious Thought in Eighteenth- and Nineteenth-Century Philosophies

Several other thinkers in the eighteenth and nineteenth centuries contributed to the development of modern concepts of the unconscious and unconscious thought. Their philosophical expositions are not elaborate, so their theories are briefly summarized in this chapter, in chronological order. The thinkers are: Christian Wolff, Alexander Gottlieb Baumgarten, Johann Georg Sulzer, Ernst Platner, Friedrich Wilhelm Joseph von Schelling, Georg Wilhelm Friedrich Hegel, Johann Friedrich Herbart, Carl Gustav Carus, Gustav Fechner, Karl Robert Eduard von Hartmann, and Theodor Lipps. Each of these writers contributed to concepts of unconscious thought in psychoanalytic theory, while basing their concepts in the classical and medieval philosophical traditions, linking the ancient and modern.

Wolff, Baumgarten, Sulzer, Platner

Christian Wolff (1679–1754), in *Rational thoughts on God, the Soul of Man, and also All things in General* (*Vernünfftige Gedancken von Gott, der Welt und der Seele des Menschen, auch allen Dingen Überhaupt*, 1720), defined conscious thought as the representation of external objects of thought and sense perception (§728, 729) (Nicholls and Liebscher, 2010b, p. 8), as in the creation of form in the imagination of Plotinus. Conscious thought is also defined as the ability to differentiate particulars, as in classical discursive reason: *nous pathetikos* as opposed to *nous poietikos*. In conscious thought external particulars are also differentiated from the perceiving subject. The thinking subject becomes conscious of a perceived object only when it is differentiated from other objects in its surroundings, as well as from the self. If we do not differentiate an object from its surroundings, then we are not conscious of it; conscious thought comes about only as a result of the differentiation, which is a product of conscious reason, and which, according to Kant, functions within the framework of a priori categories, or unconscious thought. There are many objects and events that we are capable of perceiving that we do not perceive, for one reason or another. Conscious thought is a function of that which we actually perceive, whether by choice or by chance. Even if something is perceived by chance, it is subject to the will of the perceiver to exercise discursive reason in conscious thought on a particular level.

Conscious thought is thus subject to the freedom of the perceiving subject, in Kantian terms, while unconscious thought is subject to the necessity of nature. Awareness (*Bewusstsein*) is the basis of conscious thought, and there are different levels of awareness, thus different levels of conscious thought. It is possible to infer unconscious thought through conscious thought, because of the different levels of awareness, and it is possible to even conclude that certain ideas in conscious thought may be caused by unconscious thought (Whyte, 1978, p. 102). Wolff distinguished between the clear thoughts of conscious reason and the dark thoughts that are less than conscious, following Leibniz. Wolff was the most important German Enlightenment philosopher linking Leibniz and Kant. He was a pioneer in the subject of psychology in Germany; his most important work was *Empirical Psychology* (*Psychologia empirica*, 1732), along with the *Psychologia rationalis* of 1734.

Alexander Gottlieb Baumgarten (1714–62), in *Metaphysica* (1739), saw dark or obscure perceptions as being the foundation of the soul (Nicholls and Liebscher, 2010b, p. 9), and felt that they needed to be considered further than had been in classical philosophy and metaphysics. In his *Aesthetica* (Part 1, 1750), obscure thoughts and perceptions are connected to the particulars of sensuous cognition (discursive reason) and sense perception, while clear and distinct thought or modes of cognition are connected to higher forms of intellect (as in the *nous poietikos*) in the classical tradition. While the obscure thoughts are the subject of poetry and aesthetics, the clear and distinct thoughts are the subject of philosophy and metaphysics. Baumgarten is credited with initiating the philosophical discipline of aesthetics, by redefining the classical definition of "stimulation of the senses," to apply it to artistic judgment and taste. Baumgarten made important contributions to the development of the philosophy of Christian Wolff.

Johann Georg Sulzer (1720–79), the Swiss professor of mathematics, in his *Brief Definition of All Sciences and Other Parts of Learning* (*Kurzer Begriff aller Wissenschaften Und andern Theile Der Gelehrsamkeit*, 1759), developed the ideas of Wolff and Baumgarten on conscious and unconscious thought. Unconscious ideas underlie conscious ideas, and can be seen as the source of conscious ideas, a cause of how we speak and act in conscious discourse (Bell, 2005, p. 32). Unconscious thought is characterized as dark and unclear ideas, from dark areas of the soul, but the dark ideas can be seen to have considerable effect. Dreams prove the existence of the unconscious. Following Leibniz and Wolff in the *Psychologia empirica*, conscious thought is connected to apperception, the conceptual gathering together of perceptions, but for Sulzer, perception is differentiated from self-awareness. In fact, for Sulzer, conscious thought requires a distinction between the perceiving subject as an embodied being in its consciousness, and the world around it which it perceives (Thiel, 2011, p. 357). Our abstract thoughts and cognitions, the product of higher forms of intellect not connected to sense perception, as in the classical definition, have no connection to the world around us, the world that we perceive and experience in sense perception. Consciousness in perception is dependent upon representation (*Vorstellung*), the representation of the images of perception in the imagination. The *Vorstellung*, although it is connected to the bodily organs and it functions through the senses, following Aristotle, is oriented to the objects of perception and has no relation to the perceiving subject that is receiving the representations.

Representation is thus distinguished from feeling, or sensibility, which is the subjective faculty of the subject in the reception of the representations. Thus, while representation is a bodily function, it is seen in distinction to the perceiving subject in its abstract cogitation. Conscious thought, in that it depends on apperception and representation, is itself a representation; consciousness of oneself is a representation. The most fundamental activity of the mind is the production of representations. Although Kant was critical of Sulzer, many of Sulzer's ideas can be seen to be developed in Kant's discourse. Sulzer's theories on conscious and unconscious thought were continued in his later works on aesthetics, in *Thoughts About the Origin of Sciences and Fine Arts* (*Gedanken über den Ursprung der Wissenschaften und schönen Künste*, 1762), and in his most influential work, *General Theory of the Fine Arts* (*Allgemeine Theorie der schönen Künste*, 1771–74). Extending Baumgarten's theory of aesthetics, the latter work posits that the primary source of pleasure in aesthetic experience is the cognitive condition of the subject; aesthetic pleasure is derived not from the work of art itself, but from the reaffirmation in the work of art of the judgment on the part of the perceiving subject, a key theme in the *Critique of Judgment* of Kant.

Ernst Platner (1744–1818), a follower of Leibniz and professor at the University of Leipzig, in his *Philosophical Aphorisms* (*Philosophische Aphorismen*, Volume I, 1776), is credited with being the first to use the term *Unbewusstsein* (unawareness, or unconsciousness). There are unconscious ideas as well as conscious ideas, and the unconscious mind plays a role even in conscious ideas. Conscious ideas are connected to apperception, the cognitive combining of perceptions, and the awareness of such, as in Wolff and Sulzer, while unconscious ideas are connected to perception itself. Ideas without consciousness are perceptions or dark or obscure images or representations (*dunkle Vorstellungen*); it is possible to perceive without conscious thought, as perception is prior to representation in the imagination (Nicholls and Liebscher, 2010b, p. 9; Whyte, 1978, p. 116). Platner saw conscious and unconscious thought in constant oscillation, as consciousness and unconsciousness (*Bewusstsein und Unbewusstsein*) along with apperceptions and perceptions, waking and sleeping (*Wachen und Schlaf*). This is necessary because the soul must be constantly active, as it has the power to create ideas. Since the soul then must produce ideas during sleep, it is not always conscious of the ideas that it produces.

Schelling

Friedrich Wilhelm Joseph von Schelling (1775–1854) has been called "the first to offer a coherent and systematic theory of the unconscious" (Mills, 2002, p. 45), and "the master architect of the notion of the unconscious" (McGrath, 2012, p. 28), as much of the thought of Sigmund Freud, Carl Jung, and Jacques Lacan can be traced back to Schelling. Schelling saw conscious thought as containing both conscious and unconscious thought: "this simultaneously conscious and nonconscious activity will be exhibited in the subjective, in consciousness itself" (Schelling, 1978, p. 12). In the *System of Transcendental Idealism* (1800), conscious and unconscious thought operate in opposition to each other (p. 210), in an infinite dialectic. Unconscious thought is seen as a product of nature, as in the physiological anthropology of Kant, while conscious thought is seen as a product of freedom, as in the pragmatic anthropology of Kant. The goal is to combine conscious and unconscious thought in intuition, as in the dialectical combination of the ideal (what is thought) and the real in the absolute. The dialectic of the ideal and real is the dialectic of mind and nature, the universal and particular, freedom and necessity. Schelling's conception of unconscious thought is that which is a product of the real, or what is beyond thought, as in the classical tradition. The goal of the absolute, which can best be achieved through artistic expression, is to combine the separate identities of "the conscious and the unconscious in the self" (p. 219), which are "the appearance of freedom [ideal]" and "the intuition of the natural product [real]." Unconscious thought is found in the realm of intuition and the necessity of that which is inaccessible to mind in nature.

"The objective world," the real or noumenal, is "the original, as yet unconscious, poetry of the spirit" (p. 12), which is the basis of all philosophy, and is revealed first in the philosophy of art. The activity of the aesthetic, and every work of art, involves the synthesis of the ideal and real, mind and nature, and conscious and unconscious thought. The infusion of the ideal into the real, of the universal of mind into the particular of an object, the reflection of the "absolutely nonconscious and nonobjective" (p. 13), is only possible through an "aesthetic act of the imagination." As for Kant, the imagination is responsible for the role that unconscious thought plays in conscious thought, and for self-consciousness. While philosophical production is directed toward intellectual intuition, the ideal, artistic production is directed toward the perceived world, the real. The self of the thinking subject, its self-consciousness, is an intellectual intuition, a product of the ideal, that replaces the objective world of the real, as for Kant. Geometry, for example, "would be absolutely unintelligible without spatial intuition ... " (p. 28). Geometry and mathematics are the product of intuition, the ideal, and are not properties of the real. By extension, architecture, as it is composed of geometry and mathematics, is a product of the mind, and not a property of material reality.

While products of freedom or the ideal are brought about consciously, according to Schelling, products of nature are brought about unconsciously. The organic is defined as the making conscious of unconscious activity, as the real is subsumed by the ideal, and objectified in thought. Conscious thought is the product of unconscious thought, the real of the organic in nature. As in classical philosophy, conscious thought is found in discursive reason, but its source, rather than being in intuition, or *nous poietikos*, is found in the organic in nature. Only the work of art can stage the synthesis of the organic and inorganic. The artistic act is the product of the contradiction of conscious and unconscious thought. Such a contradiction is at the core of human identity and self-consciousness, and the work of art facilitates the desire for resolution and synthesis, and self-identity, a desire that is eternally unresolved.

The work of art displays a synthesis of conscious and unconscious thought, which contrast each other in the divided self of the thinking subject. The work of art is able to display what is otherwise inaccessible to conscious thought in self-consciousness, which is intuition, or unconscious thought. As conscious thought and discursive reason are unfolded from the inaccessible core of the organic in nature, and made objective and particular, they are unable to return to unconscious thought themselves; that return can only be represented in the forms of art that are able to display the becoming conscious from the unconscious in the organic. The relation is the same as between *nous poietikos* and *nous pathetikos* in classical philosophy, while here *nous poietikos* or intuition is placed in the inaccessible organic of nature, or the real. Unconscious thought becomes inaccessible, a dark ground of self-consciousness, as opposed to playing an active role in self-consciousness and conscious thought. The source of unconscious thought is an unknowable and obscure but necessary ground of being.

Schelling's conception of unconscious thought recalls the romantic idea associated with the *Carceri* of Piranesi, representing unconscious thought as consisting of unclear and indistinct perceptions and ideas in a realm of chaos and confusion, contradiction and irrationality. For Schelling, the unconscious is an obscure realm that, while playing a productive role in conscious thought, through what are perceived as higher forms of intellection, is also seen in opposition to conscious thought, as something inaccessible to conscious thought, and as something hindering or interfering with conscious thought. This led to the Freudian conception of the unconscious, and the necessity of dream interpretation as an access to unconscious processes. It can be seen that Jacques Lacan would later rescue unconscious thought from its romantic obscurity, and restore its role as an integral and productive component of conscious thought.

In the *System of Transcendental Idealism* of Schelling, "this unchanging identity," unconscious thought in organic nature, "which can never attain to consciousness and merely radiates back from the product, is for the producer precisely what destiny is for the agent, namely a dark unknown force which supplies the element of completedness or objectivity to the piecework of freedom ... " (p. 222). Unconscious thought in the real is the necessary but inaccessible ground for conscious thought in the ideal, creating a dialectic that can only be resolved and synthesized in the aesthetic, or what becomes objective through artistic production. Imagination plays the role of bringing together what Schelling called primordial and productive intuition, a dialectic that can be seen in relation to the *nous poietikos* and *nous pathetikos* of classical philosophy, and the a priori categories and sense perception in the Kantian system. The combinatory role of the imagination provides a single ground of activity for both conscious thought in the ideal and unconscious thought in the real. The opposition between conscious and unconscious thought can never be resolved, but the two can be brought together in imagination. The same can be said of the concept of the imagination in the thought of Plotinus.

In the thought of Plotinus, imagination facilitates the dialectical process of thought. It is suspended between Intellect, the source of thinking, intuition or *nous poietikos* in the ideal, and sense perception, the object of thinking, in *nous hylikos* in the real. For Plotinus, the dialectical process involves a picture-making power in the imagination, an imprint of the sense object in perception combined with an imprint of the idea of the object or intelligible form, including the memory or recollection of past thoughts and perception. The power of the imagination transforms the image, both sensible and intelligible, into the word in language, both the spoken word and the intelligible word. Imagination involves the fitting together of sensible and intelligible images, recollections of both sensible and intelligible images, and sensible and intelligible words in language. It involves the combining of conscious and unconscious thought in the identity of the thinking subject.

In the thought of Kant, consciousness is composed of discursive consciousness, as in *nous pathetikos*, and intuitive consciousness, as in *nous poietikos*, the self-reflection of inner experience, which is given by imagination, as the image becomes an object of conscious thought and is unfolded through language in conscious thought, as the objective real is unfolded from the subjective ideal in the thought of Schelling, through imagination. Intuitive consciousness, for Kant, is an immediate product of unconscious thought, prior to its unfolding in conscious thought through a priori intuition. Access to the ground of cognition, a priori intuition, as the source of consciousness and the basis for conscious thought and sense perception, can only be given as a representation of itself in imagination, as in Plotinus.

According to Kant, the thinking subject can stage the possibility of a consciousness of self and experience in conscious thought, but cannot be conscious of the ground which makes conscious thought and sense perception possible, as for Schelling. The subject can be conscious of the appearance or phenomenon of unconscious thought, which is the ground of inner experience, and forms a dialectical opposition to conscious thought, but the subject does not have access to the ground of subjectivity, experience in cognition, which is unconscious thought. Kant divided the faculties of imagination into passive and active. The passive imagination corresponds to the ability of imagination to reproduce images of perceived forms (the derived representation, *exhibitio derivativa*), as for Plotinus, and the active imagination corresponds to the ability of imagination to create intelligible forms (the original representation, *exhibitio originaria*), as for Plotinus. Then for Schelling, the imagination synthesizes primordial and productive intuition, allowing unconscious thought to participate in conscious thought, in the classical tradition.

Art is, according to Schelling, the only true document of philosophy, because aesthetic intuition is "transcendental intuition become objective" (*System of Transcendental Idealism*, p. 231). Art is able to communicate the element of unconscious thought, and the identity of unconscious thought and conscious thought, which philosophy is unable to "depict in external form." For Schelling, "if aesthetic production proceeds from freedom," that is, conscious thought, "and if it is precisely for freedom that this opposition of conscious and unconscious activities is an absolute one," in the role of unconscious thought in conscious thought, then there can be only one absolute work of art that exists in many versions. Art opens to philosophy "the holy of holies, where burns in eternal and original unity, as if in a single flame," recalling the One of Plotinus, "that which in nature and history is rent asunder...." The original unity is the unity of conscious and unconscious thought, the ideal and real, freedom and necessity, the inorganic and organic, objective and subjective, a unity that has been lost in self-consciousness and language, as played out in history and science. Schelling sought a primordial harmony of the thinking subject, that has been divided, as in the thought of Kant.

For Kant, the thinking subject is made possible by the a priori unity of apperception in intuition and the resulting representations in the imagination. The thinking subject is split between the condition of its subjective possibility in inner sense, intuition or *nous poietikos*, the ideal, and its objective activity in conscious reason, in connection to the real; the subject thus has no access to the necessity of its existence in intuition, to the ground of its existence in unconscious thought. The thinking subject is unable to think itself as the manifold of intuition, the basis of its possibility: it cannot conceive of itself in its own unconscious thought. Knowledge of the self is thus dark and obscure, given only by indirect and mediated unconscious perceptions, and the possibility of access to unconscious thought in the synthesis of conscious and unconscious thought in aesthetic intuition, according to Schelling. Only a work of art can reveal the unity of the subjective and objective, the ideal and the real, conscious and unconscious thought, within intellectual intuition. The work of art is the expression of the philosophical idea, making visible that which is inaccessible to the visible.

For Schelling, the work of art seeks to have the character of an unconscious infinity in the indifference of the universal and particular, freedom and necessity (Hendrix, 2005). The work of art contains that which is other than the product of conscious thought, intention or expectation, that which cannot be explained by reason, by finite understanding. As in mythology, art as a whole is composed of particular works, particular figures, which cannot be explained entirely in relation to the whole, and which contain infinite possibilities within each particular, as they relate to the whole. Like mythology, art functions in symbolic, schematic and allegorical means, but the underlying reason behind the forms is not entirely apparent to conscious thought.

Each individual work of art, as each individual figure in mythology, is a particular which cannot be explained in relation to the universal, all art and all mythology, and yet cannot exist outside its relation to the universal. The opposition and indifference of universal and particular are simultaneously both finite and infinite. The infinite is represented in art through instinct or intuition. It is not the product of a conscious act, but rather the lack of difference between necessity and freedom, the necessity of the artistic act becoming freedom, and the freedom of the artistic act becoming necessity. The work of art displays the infinite in the intellect of the artist, and the limitations of his or her reason; reason in and of itself, as necessity, is maximized and gives way to intuition. The mechanisms of perception on the part of the artist constitute a universal language in a culture, so the indifference of the infinite and finite is communicated through the work of art as it is perceived by the intellect of the observer, which sees its own interior dialectic reflected in the work.

If the art is merely imitative of natural form, it is limited to the conscious activity of the artist, and the mechanisms of his or her reason. The perceiving subject can only be reflected in such a work as itself an imitation of nature, not containing within it the principles of nature as a function of being, but rather as a reflection or a shadow. In such a work, "purpose and rule lie on the surface, and seem so restricted and circumscribed, that the product is no more than a faithful replica of the artist's conscious activity," in sense perception and conscious thought, "and is in every respect an object for reflection only, not for intuition, which loves to sink itself in what it contemplates, and finds no resting place short of the infinite" (*System of Transcendental Idealism*, p. 225).

The infinite tranquility which is achieved by the viewer of the artwork corresponds to the infinite contradiction in the soul of the artist; the work of art is a picture of the dialectical resolution of that contradiction, or of a fragmentation of that indifference (lack of difference). The work of art may also be a picture of the primordial self-alienation itself, between conscious and unconscious reason. The work of art communicates the trauma of internal fracturing, and the ecstasy of internal resolution. The unity of the absolute is equivalent to the chaos and formlessness of the dark night of being in the soul, unconscious thought. The work of art for Schelling is the finite representation of the infinite, the presence of the infinite in the finite, and the infinite division of the finite and infinite. The division between the finite and infinite occurs in freedom. The finite representation of the infinite is beauty; the intuited presence of the infinite within the finite is the sublime. Beauty is the indifference of the infinite and finite, universal and particular.

The beauty of the forms in the work of art is not in the forms themselves, but in the ideas of the forms that the visual images represent; the forms in a painting are beautiful only in that the beauty of the infinite is present. The form is beautiful because the idea that it represents contains the indifference of the finite and infinite as a manifestation of the absolute. In the sublime this indifference is not present, but it is suggested and can be intuited; the beautiful and sublime are thus in opposition in the infinite division of the finite and infinite. Both beauty and the sublime depend on contradiction, the primordial fissure of being, between the real and the ideal. The infinity which is suggested by the sublime is that of the unconscious: beauty contains the indifference of the conscious and unconscious. The intuition of the infinite in the unconscious as differentiation from the conscious and finite is threatening to the finitude of reason, because it suggests that which is alien and inaccessible to it without being reconciled with it.

The stages in the development of the relation between real and ideal in the intellect, between necessity and freedom, the subject of philosophy and the content of art, correspond to the development of the spirit in history toward freedom, which becomes core to Hegel's discourse. Historical development entails the relation between the reason and self-consciousness of a culture, the relation between the functioning mechanisms of the culture in the real and the self-identity of the culture in the ideal. It involves the relation between organization and productivity, the particular and the universal, law and creativity. As art is a presentation of philosophical development in the self-consciousness of the individual subject, so art is a presentation of the historical development in the self-consciousness of a culture, as a catalyst toward freedom in the ideal, and indifference in the absolute. Like self-consciousness itself, art is a dialectic of the universal and particular and functions to symbolize the indifference of the absolute.

As in reason in self-consciousness, art contains the possibility of the ideal, and the dialectic of the real and ideal, unconscious and conscious thought, serves as the productive principle in art, as it does the creative principle in intellect. In order to represent self-consciousness, art must reflect the relation between the real and ideal and the differentiation of them in self-consciousness. Self-consciousness is the basis of transcendental philosophy in that it resolves the contradiction inherent in the relation between the real and the ideal, namely, that the real is only given by the ideal, and the ideal is a product of the real. Unconscious thought can only be given by conscious thought, and conscious thought is a product of unconscious thought. The subject of transcendental philosophy, the philosophy of spirit, is the negotiation between the real and ideal, unconscious and conscious thought, a seemingly self-contradictory state, which is taken to be the basis, and in fact the generating factor, of human consciousness. Philosophy and art entail the production and representation of filters between the real and ideal in their self-contradiction, in both the real and ideal.

The writings of Schelling are filled with mechanisms for the negotiation of the real and ideal: that negotiation being the state of human consciousness in its inner dehiscence and differentiation of the two. Schelling sought to overcome the a priori categories of Kant, the conception of the real as being only given by the ideal, the noumenal as given by the phenomenal. For Schelling the real and ideal are mutually generative: the real (unconscious thought) being that which the ideal (conscious thought) perceives outside of itself; and this schema is based on the definition of consciousness itself as being formed by the relation of the real and ideal, and the self-identity of that relation which necessitates its possibility. The knowledge of consciousness of itself, self-consciousness, depends on the mutual participation of the real and ideal; activity cannot exist without knowledge, and knowledge cannot exist without activity. Art cannot exist without philosophy and philosophy cannot exist without art. All of the particular manifestations of the universal in both the real and the ideal reconfirm the necessity of the coexistence of both, despite their differentiation in consciousness and their self-contradiction, their mutual existence in the absolute and chaos, absolute form and formlessness.

In *Bruno, or On the Natural and the Divine Principle of Things*, in 1802, Schelling described the ability to recognize absolute beauty. The uninitiated will be unable to recognize beauty other than that of the body, while the initiated will be able to recognize the imperfection of the absolute beauty as it is manifest in sensible form, and at the same time will be able to intuit the presence of the absolute. This intuition involves feelings of wonder, terror and fear, as in the sublime (*Bruno* 225). It also involves self-consciousness, and the ability of the soul to distinguish between the inward participation in intuition and the outward participation in the sensible world, and between unconscious and conscious thought.

According to Schelling, sensible beauty does not exist: it is only representative of the presence of absolute beauty in the sensible world, as for Plotinus. The idea of sensible beauty is a product of the identification of the absolute and the productive and procreative functions of nature. Sensible beauty is a product of the identification in the mind between intellectual processes and natural occurrences; "and this identity also clearly explains why beauty shines forth wherever the course of nature permits, though it never itself enters existence" (*Bruno* 225) (Schelling, 1984). Sensible beauty is a product of the projection of the inner self onto the sensible world. Although beauty appears to come into being in the sensible world, this is only an appearance: beauty can only exist if it exists eternally – in unconscious thought, as it were – as the absolute. When something which is beautiful comes into being in the sensible world, it is not its beauty which comes into being but the object itself. The beauty of the object, as for Plotinus, does not exist separately from the perception of the object by the observer. The beauty of the absolute, in the synthesis of conscious and unconscious thought, is mistaken for physical beauty because the manifestation of its qualities, an inferior and deceitful truth, "allies itself with the imperfect, temporal elements of existing forms, with qualities impressed on them from without, rather than with those developed organically from their concepts" (227).

The artist who imitates the beauty of forms in nature is not able to unify the organic and inorganic, the real and ideal, and is thus not able to express being. The beauty of forms in nature should not even be called beauty, but rather a derivative and subordinate to it. Thus art which imitates natural beauty is a derivative and subordinate to real art. As for Plotinus, the artist does not merely imitate natural forms, in the *natura naturata*, but goes back to the principles from which the forms are derived, in the *natura naturans*, in order to reveal the absolute beauty of which the forms are temporary manifestations. The philosopher and the poet must concern themselves with the absolute, and learn to differentiate the sensible and intelligible, conscious and unconscious thought, as the basis of self-consciousness.

The sensible and intelligible worlds must be melded into the absolute. The absolute is always seen as participating in the sensible world, in experience, and the absolute cannot be conceived without the union of the sensible and intelligible, conscious and unconscious thought. For Schelling "the eternal is related to all things through their eternal concepts" (229). The artist allows beauty, existing eternally (pre-existing temporal production) to be revealed or translated into sensible objects. The work of art must exist independently of the artist; that is, the work of art must participate in the universal, in order to reveal absolute beauty. The individual soul of the artist, the particular manifestation of the absolute and universal, must be transcended, in the same way that the particular existence of an object in nature is transcended in the apprehension of the eternal. The individual artistic act becomes a singular manifestation of the *Zeitgeist*, the universal spirit of a people, the correlate to the spirit of the absolute. Only in that way is the work of art beautiful. The beauty of the object of art is identical to the beauty of the soul of the artist, in that both exhibit the participation of the particular in the universal and the real in the ideal. The artist, in order to produce a beautiful work, must be initiated into the mystical vision of eternal beauty, and understand beauty itself, further than the idea of beauty or the physical manifestation of beauty. In creating a beautiful work of art, the artist expresses the beauty within his or her soul, as it is intuited in a mystical vision, and understood in intuition, or unconscious thought. The artist is capable of producing a beautiful work of art insofar as his or her soul is able to participate in the intelligible, and allow the absolute to participate in the particular. Absolute beauty is revealed in the individual soul in the same way that it is revealed in the sensible form, as a particular manifestation of the eternal in time.

Artistic expression requires the dialectic in the soul in artistic production, the intuition of absolute beauty in the mystical vision, and the understanding of the idea of beauty in intuition, as it informs conscious thought or discursive reason. According to Schelling, the dialectic is the dialectic between unconscious and conscious thought in the soul of the artist. In the *Bruno*, the idea exists in the soul of the artist as both an absolute and a concept. Absolute beauty manifests itself as particular in the individual soul, and it is "conceivable that the idea of divine beauty could exist in this way and at the same time exist fully and essentially as well" (230). This is necessary for the individual soul to participate in the universal soul. Absolute beauty exists within the soul of the individual "in an absolute mode, and not as the immediate concept of the individual." The individual soul reveals absolute beauty in the same way as the particular sensible form; in that way, the particular sensible form as well has both a conscious and unconscious being, as it is a function of human perception. The unconscious soul is "possessed by the idea of beauty" just as the sensible form, subdued by the eternal and absolute in its particular manifestation.

The philosopher, unlike the artist, is able to understand conceptually the idea of the absolute in the intellectual, as it plays a role in conscious thought. The artist, though, is able to tap more directly into the force of the absolute and eternal, and allow it to be manifest in the work of art. Rather than understand the concept of eternal beauty, as does the philosopher, the artist is possessed by the absolute, as he or she has more direct access to the unconscious. "The artists most fit to produce beautiful works are often those least in possession of the idea of absolute truth and beauty. They lack the idea precisely because they are possessed by it..." (231). The soul of the artist, rather than understand the idea of absolute beauty through conscious reason, more likely *is* the idea of absolute beauty, or the translation of the idea of absolute beauty into temporal production, as in nature. The artist, unable to attain to the intellectual intuition of the universals, "will necessarily look like one who defiles the mysteries, not their initiate and devotee."

The artist nevertheless utilizes the absolute idea, and would thus appear to understand it, and to understand beauty as the identity of the real and ideal, the noumenal and phenomenal. The soul of the artist appears to be absolute beauty, and to understand absolute beauty, in the same way that sensible form appears to be beautiful. Thus "from the most ancient of times poets were revered as mouthpieces of the gods," as in Orphism. Schelling came to the conclusion that art, no matter how inspired by genius is the artist, can never be absolute beauty, but only the appearance of such, the correlate of the temporal manifestation of absolute beauty in the soul. Philosophy, on the contrary, is capable of recognizing the absolute beauty, because the philosopher is not dependent on the temporal manifestation of the absolute in his or her soul; he or she is able to understand the idea of the absolute, and within the idea he or she is able to view the essence of the absolute.

The work of art, no matter how much it exhibits the presence of the universal and absolute, must always maintain the element of the particular and the individual, no matter how much it is subsumed into and unified with the former. Schelling suggested that the idea of the philosopher is not bound to a concrete particular. He explained, "the principle governing the thought of the man who philosophizes is not the eternal concept insofar as it is immediately related to his individuality, but this same concept considered absolutely and in itself" (232). The unity of the universal and particular is the basis of Schelling's definition of beauty. In this way, though, philosophy is necessarily hermetic, in that it cannot completely account for the essence of the absolute in unconscious thought without the participation of the particular in conscious thought. The absolute in unconscious thought can only be known by a mystical vision. In the *Bruno*, "But the purpose of all the mystery rites is none other than to show men the archetypes of all that they are accustomed to seeing in images."

The archetypes or absolutes that are discovered in the mysteries are that "something unchanging, uniform, and indivisible beyond the things that ceaselessly change and slide from shape to shape" in the appearances of the real, as in the Platonic archetype. The absolute must be known by the soul, according to Schelling, "in some nontemporal way, before birth, as it were," in unconscious thought. The knowledge of the absolute must be by a soul of a prior state, to which it had immediate access, in primordial intuition or anamnesis. The current state of the soul is one which is removed from its originary state, "torn from this state by its union with the body, that is, its transition over to temporal existence" (233), in the dialectic of the ideal and real, conscious and unconscious thought. The composition of the soul includes an unconscious remembrance or anamnesis of a lost origin, and the soul exists in a continual state of being thrown from its origin, of being alienated from itself, other to itself, in the contradiction between conscious and unconscious thought.

The absolute being, accessible through the mystery rites, which open the unconscious, exists in the depths of the soul inaccessible to conscious thought. The remembrance of the lost origin is the remembrance of the mystical vision of the immortal soul: the love of the absolute reality is the love of the self-lack and self-alienation of the soul, the essential soul lost in the sensible world, the inability to unite the ideal and the real. Though beauty is that unification, it is an impossible one, and a sense of beauty must be accompanied by a sense of despair in loss and alienation, the longing for which there is no satisfaction. This, then, is the madness of the philosopher who soars to the heights of essential being with wings, in search of the beatific vision, of the origin which is unknowable, the mystery of existence.

Initiation into the mysteries causes the remembrance of the beatific vision, and the "previously intuited ideas of the true itself, the beautiful, and the good," none of which themselves are present in the sensible world, except as unseen cause. Philosophy is ultimately the teaching of the mysteries of being in unconscious thought, and their paradoxical relation to the intellect. The mysteries, the mystical visions of the immortal soul, are communicated to the human soul by spirits, in the unconscious. The spirits are love, that which compels the soul to discover the mysteries. Love is a spirit between mortal and immortal, between the human and the absolute, and love is the messenger between them. Love is that which binds the universe, and allows it to be whole, as both real and ideal.

Though the philosopher is able to understand the presence of absolute beauty in the sensible world, absolute beauty cannot be completely distinguished from sensible beauty: "it is impossible to say where the realm of exemplars ends and where that of copies begins" (317). Exemplars and copies, the ideal and real, are combined in intellectual intuition. They are both infinite: "actuality within the world of copies is just as infinite as possibility is within the exemplary world." The more sensible beauty partakes of absolute beauty, in nature and in art, the closer the form is to the eternal, the closer the ideal and real, conscious and unconscious thought, are merged, and the more readily the philosopher conceives of the absolute.

The real cannot exist without the ideal, and vice versa. Absolute beauty could not be known without the beauty of the body. Beauty is the synthesis of the dialectic, the combination of the two extremes, which are co-dependent. The task of art is not just to conceive the union of the ideal and real, but then to re-conceive the ideal and real out of that union, to separate them out and differentiate them, to represent eternal beauty and sensible beauty in relation to their union. To do this the artist must represent the finite and infinite, conscious and unconscious thought, and then "we shall grasp how that simple ray of light that shines forth from the absolute and which is the absolute itself appears divided into difference and indifference, into the finite and the infinite" (328), in conscious thought and perception.

The point of the dialectic, as it is represented in art, and pursued in philosophy, in the course of love, love of the absolute, is to identify and differentiate the opposites of ideal and real at every level and in every combination, and to examine the nature of the differentiation, in the same way that multiplicities are resolved into unities in intellect, from *nous pathetikos* to *nous poietikos*, and conscious to unconscious

thought. The union of the ideal and real is the union of the idea of absolute beauty and sensible beauty into beauty itself, and the union of the
unconscious and the conscious mind. Thus, "now when we have scaled
this peak and behold the harmonious light of this wondrous cognition,
we shall realize that this cognition is at the same time that which is real
in the divine essence," in the absolute; "then we shall be granted the
favor of seeing beauty in its brightest splendor and not be blinded by the
sight, and we shall live in the blessed company of the gods." This is the
goal of the philosopher in the consummation of being in the intellect,
in the dialectic of conscious and unconscious thought.

Hegel

In the *Philosophy of Mind* (*Philosophie des Geistes*), Part Three of the
Encyclopaedia of the Philosophical Sciences (*Enzyklopädie der philosophischen
Wissenschaften im Grundrisse,* 1817), Georg Wilhelm Friedrich Hegel
(1770–1831) described unconscious thought as an intelligence which is
a "night-like mine or pit in which is stored a world of infinitely many
images and representations, yet without being in consciousness" (§453)
(Hegel, 1971), inaccessible to conscious thought. "…I do not as yet have
full command over the images slumbering in the mine or pit of my
inwardness, am not as yet able to recall them at will" (§453, Zusatz).
Like Schelling, Hegel placed the unconscious in nature or the real, as a
"germ" from which all qualities come into existence, as in the development of a tree. Intelligence itself is a "subconscious mine," an undifferentiated universal prior to its realization as particulars and separations or
differentiations, much like classical archetypal intelligence, the Intellect
of Plotinus. The origin of the universal as a mental representation must
be found in this subconscious realm, the real of nature, inaccessible to
conscious thought. Following Schelling, the origin of the universal in
thought is in the material reality of nature, as in the material substrate
of Aristotle.

It is through the intuition, following Kant, that the images of unconscious thought are presented to conscious intelligence as objective
representations of universals transformed into particulars. The a priori
intuition is thus a mechanism of unconscious thought, the content of
which is presented to conscious thought in the form of images, as in the
imagination of Plotinus. The objective images presented to conscious
thought in the *Vorstellung*, picture thinking or representation, are not
the content of unconscious thought themselves, but rather a "plastic
shape of an existent intuition of similar content" (§454, Zusatz), that is,

a representation or a copy. The universal unconscious of nature can only be conceived through representations of it as archetypal forms of intuition that can then only be known or cogitated through representations in the particulars of conscious thought. The consciousness of a present plastic, objective form of an intuition then makes us aware that there is an unconscious memory of previous intuitions, as in the schemata of Kant.

The representation or *Vorstellung* is a "'synthesis' of the internal image with the recollected existence," the mnemic residue of the sensible form. The internal image (*Bild*) would be the intelligible image, thus the presentation would be the synthesis of the sensible and intelligible images, formed through language, as in Plotinus. In *Enneads* V.3.3, impressions are received by discursive reason from sense perception, but discursive reason can only respond to them with the help of memory. With that help, discursive reason then performs analytical operations on the impressions from sense perception, "taking to pieces what the image-making power gave it..." (Plotinus, 1966). As the perception of a sensible object entails both the *eidos* of the object and the *eidos* of the intelligible idea of the object, in unconscious thought, "actual seeing is double" (*Enneads* V.5.7). The power (*virtus*) to form the image in the mind's eye is conversely always accompanied by the "verbal expression" (IV.3.30), or more accurately, the *logos endiathetos*, the word in thought, as Plotinus intended it. The intelligible image, and thus the sensible image, is not possible without the linguistic expression of it, and linguistic expression is not possible without the intelligible image. Perception of sensible objects is only possible after the idea of the sensible object is articulated in language in intellection. While the "intellectual act is without parts," as it has not been differentiated in discursive reason, and thus in perception, it "has not, so to speak, come out into the open, but remains unobserved within," as unconscious thought.

As a result of the synthesis of the sensible and intelligible image, according to Hegel, "by this synthesis the internal now has the qualification of being able to be presented before intelligence and to have its existence in it" (*Philosophy of Mind*, §453, Zusatz), as for Plotinus, in conscious thought, through imagination, language and memory. In the presentation in conscious thought, the intelligible forms of unconscious thought, universals or archetypes, are manifest as "singularized and mutually independent powers or faculties" (§451, Zusatz), in discursive reason. The form of the unconscious thought that is produced in the imagination and made available to conscious thought, is a *Vorstellungsrepräsentanz*, a representation of a representation, as for

Freud. Our identity in conscious thought, or our self-consciousness, can only be given as a representation doubled over, far removed from the origin of conscious thought in unconscious thought. Self-consciousness is an illusion; it can only be the representation of differentiated particulars of sense perception and imagination, the shadows on the wall in Plato's Allegory of the Cave, as it were, Plotinus' subject caught in a play of mirror reflections.

Conscious thought, according to Hegel, is dependent upon images in the reproductive imagination, following Kant. The reproductive imagination is an imitation of the productive imagination, connected to the empirical laws of sense perception and the differentiation of particulars. The differentiation of particulars is derived from the universals of space and time, the a priori intuitions in the categories of Kant. Space and time are then not pure concepts for Hegel, but rather qualities of the universal unconscious of nature, the real. The manner in which the universal intuitions become differentiated particulars in conscious thought defines the individuality of the thinking subject. The formation of the image in the reproductive imagination, as it is tied to the particulars of sense perception, is unique in each individual, while the intuition from which the image is formed is a universal in nature. Through recollection, which is the "first form of mental representation" (§455, Zusatz), intelligence, "emerging from its abstract inward being into determinateness," thus "disperses the night-like darkness enveloping the wealth of its images," in the inaccessibility of unconscious thought, "and banishes it by the luminous clarity of a present image" in conscious thought as given by imagination.

There are three stages by which intuition is unfolded as an image in imagination for Hegel. The first is the stage most tied to empirical experience, being the reproductive imagination, by which the image enters into existence. Through connecting and associating the existent image with other existent images, the images are raised to "general ideas or representations." The general ideas or representations are then related to the existent image as a particular, in the third stage, and the representation itself assumes a "pictorial existence." The third stage is the "creative imagination (*Phantasie*)," or productive imagination. The creative imagination produces symbols and signs, mechanisms of the connection between the particular image and the universal idea. The sign connects the present existent image to the unconscious memory of images, and thus to the transition to the universal idea.

In Kant, the reproductive imagination is a passive imagination, creating derived representations and reproducing empirical perceptions in connection with memory within the framework of intuition. The productive imagination is an active imagination, able to produce a representation of an object preceding empirical experience, in intuition. The power to reproduce the form of an a priori intuition in the lower imagination is the *Bildungskraft*. The productive imagination, *Einbildung*, operates without any connection to empirical phenomena, or sensible or intelligible form. There are six levels of image formation in the Kantian scheme, which are summarized in the Hegelian scheme. The reproductive imagination is composed of *Abbildung*, *Nachbildung*, and *Vorbildung*: direct image formation in the present moment, reproduction of images that have already been formulated, and reproduction of images from the past and present in anticipation of future images. The activities of the reproductive imagination are connected to conscious thought and sense perception. While they are governed by the categories of a priori intuition, the activities of the reproductive imagination generate images according to empirical laws of association connected to sense perception.

The productive imagination is composed of *Einbildung*, *Ausbildung*, and *Gegenbildung*, and is not connected to sense perception or empirical experience, thus being a product of unconscious thought. *Einbildung* is the power to invent images not connected to sense perceptions, and comes into conscious thought through the formation of the invented image. *Ausbildung* completes the invented image in unconscious thought, and the invented image is finally formed in *Gegenbildung* as a symbol or a sign, as a representational mechanism, as in Hegel's scheme, connecting the image with the a priori intuition. *Gegenbildung* completes the process of the intuition or intelligible becoming an existent form in a representation in conscious thought as image, through the analogue, symbol or sign, as in the *logos endiathetos* in the imagination in the scheme of Plotinus. The *symbolum* provides the illusion of the self-consciousness of conscious thought, and also the consciousness of the necessity of unconscious thought.

Through the imagination, according to Hegel, the individual is subsumed under the universal, the unconscious of nature, as in the conceptual categories of Kant. The intelligence, unconscious thought, is a "concrete subjectivity" (§456), derived from a "latent content" or "Ideal principle." Latent content is the term used by Freud to describe unconscious dream thoughts before they are transformed into dream images, the manifest content. The Ideal principle recalls the terminology of Plotinus, the intelligible in *nous poietikos* or Intellect, which can be seen as unconscious thought. Such intelligence can only be known by anticipation, as it is represented in the imagination. The creative imagination is that aspect of intelligence, unconscious thought, that is able to associate created images, mnemic images, or images in memory, and existent images, through representation, combining subjective and objective experience, or the ideal and the real, to create conscious thought, and self-consciousness. The creative imagination is seen as "symbolic, allegorical, or poetical imagination," operating through the *symbolum*, or *logos endiathetos* as it were. The allegorical or poetical is figural and tropic, as in the tropic mechanisms of condensation and displacement through which the latent content of dreams is transformed into the manifest content, according to Freud, described by Lacan as metaphor and metonymy. The imagination, which gives us our reality, is not a literal representation, but rather poetic. Reality is constructed by language, and the synthesizing function of the creative imagination. Individual, particular objects of sense perception and reproductive imagination are synthesized into a poetic, tropic totality, as in the manifold of Kant, or the apperception of Plotinus, that necessitates its source in unconscious thought. Poetry itself is seen as a revelation of unconscious thought in conscious discourse.

In the *Phenomenology of Spirit* (1807), seen as a prelude to the *Encyclopaedia of the Philosophical Sciences*, self-conscious mind is united with unconscious thought through the subjective intelligence, or the imagination. The unconscious spirit "rises out of its unreality into actual existence," from the universal to the particular, "out of a state in which it is unknowing and unconscious into the realm of conscious Spirit" (§463) (Hegel, 1977). The unconscious is equated with the unknowing, the universal real of nature, inaccessible to conscious thought, as in Kant and the Neoplatonic and Peripatetic traditions. Unconscious thought is nevertheless seen as the basis of conscious thought. Spirit is differentiated from the appearance of being. Absolute Spirit, the unconscious real of nature, is seen as a void in being, complete formlessness prior to the formation of the image in the imagination. It is "the nightlike void of the supersensible beyond" (§177), inaccessible to conscious thought. Reason becomes aware of itself in abstract thought, given by imagination, and sees itself as other in conscious thought and self-consciousness, in being-for-self, as noted by Karl Robert Eduard von Hartmann (1842–1906) in *Philosophy of the Unconscious* (1868) (Hartmann, 1931, pp. 27–28). The origin of the abstract thought of reason is its being-in-self, in intuition or unconscious thought. In conscious thought, reason becomes alienated from its other, as it becomes aware of its incompatibility with the real, with nature, and with its self-perception of its own absence in nature, in unconscious thought. Reason then attempts to overcome its self-alienation in a dialectical struggle which returns reason to itself, as a tropic representation of the reality that it sees itself a part of.

Hegel described appearance as uniting conscious and unconscious thought (inner being) (Hendrix, 2005). Appearance is a stage of being between understanding (conscious thought) and essence (inner being). As a being-for-self, appearance is a "surface show" (*Phenomenology of Spirit*, §143). As a surface show, appearance is only a "vanishing." Appearance as show or veil is the instrument of reason, in the dialectic of perception for Hegel, in the mediation between unconscious and conscious thought. The surface show as a totality is a form of universal, a product of creative imagination, a reflection of the totality of inner being, or the "inner into self." The operative force of the mediation is appearance, which is part of the movement of the forces of being, in which the object of perception, the "sensuously objective," is the negative of pure being – the unconscious or real of nature, its other. As this occurs in conscious thought, conscious thought is both ground and consequence of perception. As in understanding in perception, it is both the object of perception and the act of perception. The inner being or being-in-self to conscious thought is possessed in its own certainty of self, as intuition or unconscious thought, but the objective being, conscious thought, is outside of itself, fluctuating and unstable, in the flux of the dialectic. The flux is the objective vanishing appearance, the twilight of things in the sensible world.

The supersensible world, unconscious thought, becomes the object of understanding above the sensuous world, in conscious thought: a permanent beyond above the vanishing present, a being-in-self. Inner being is beyond conscious thought and is unknowable by sense knowledge. It is a void around which desire in conscious thought circulates, as in the *das Ding* of Freud and the *object a* of Lacan, a being beyond measurement and the objects of reason. In that supersensible being comes about through appearance, as a mediating factor, appearance itself cannot be said to be of the sensuous world (§147), as it is a representation in conscious thought of intuition or unconscious thought. Perception is not sense-knowledge – it is a product of the dialectic of the particular and universal through conscious and unconscious thought, as for Plotinus. The universal in inner being is an outcome of the flux of appearance (§149). The universal contains within itself a negation and mediation which is the dialectical process from appearance to being-in-self, from the phenomenal to the noumenal. "This difference is expressed in the law," according to Hegel, "which is the stable image of unstable appearance." The supersensible world, unconscious thought, is "an inert realm of laws" beyond the perceived world that only exhibits laws in "incessant change" in conscious thought and perception.

The inert realm of laws "is indeed the truth for the Understanding," but it is not entirely manifest in appearance, but only inconsistently, given the state of flux and particularity, as "with every change of circumstance the law has a different actuality." The world of appearance becomes stable in inner being, as it becomes governed by universal and unchanging laws, concepts in intuition. Through appearance, conscious thought becomes unified with the supersensible world. Conscious thought is able to anticipate beyond appearance, into the ideas or principles which govern it behind the veil of forms. Being-in-self comes about when inner being sees into the inner world, and "this curtain hanging before the inner world is therefore drawn away" (§165). At this point, the dialectical processes of perception and understanding are transcended in unconscious thought, and the inner being becomes unified and identical with the inner world.

It is through self-consciousness that conscious thought attains inner being and transcends the dialectic of appearance and void, particular and universal, toward the absolute, the real of nature. Thus, "it is in self-consciousness, in the Notion of Spirit, that consciousness first finds its turning point," from unconscious to conscious thought, "where it leaves behind it the colorful show of the sensuous here-and-now and the nightlike void of the supersensible beyond, and steps out into the spiritual daylight of the present" (§177). All preliminary forms of conscious thought are abstract manifestations of spirit in intuition, particular manifestations of the universal. Spirit or unconscious thought unfolds in consciousness, as each particular form in conscious thought contains the absolute or unconscious thought. The forms of conscious thought are "only moments or vanishing quantities" (§440), ephemeral representations, as for Plotinus. Conscious thought becomes being-in-self when it "embraces" sense-certainty, perception and understanding, that is, when it becomes self-conscious; the absolute is the unity, or self-identification, of conscious thought and self-consciousness, that leads toward conscious thought. Spirit is conscious thought that becomes aware of itself in self-consciousness, though it becomes clear in the *Philosophy of Mind* that the self-consciousness is an illusion.

The expression of the absolute and the union of subjective and objective, unconscious and conscious thought, in art is the sensible correlate to such expression in religion and philosophy, according to Hegel. Spirit is an artificer capable of producing itself as object on a variety of levels in art. The first form of the artificer in art is the abstract form of under-standing, capable of communicating the presence of the Idea in matter. The abstract form of the understanding is the crystalline geometric form, the pyramid or obelisk, a signifier or *symbolum*, as in the schema of Kant, described by Hegel as "the works of this artificer of rigid form" (*Phenomenology of Spirit*, §691) (Hegel, 1977). The crystalline form oper-ates on the level of an "abstract intelligibleness" but does not contain the absolute in itself, because the abstract form is inorganic, and so does not communicate the intuition in the real as it does not combine universal and particular. In order to communicate the absolute, the work of art must overcome the dialectic of universal and particular, organic and inorganic, unconscious and conscious thought.

In nature, the artificer, the unconscious real, uses organic form to communicate self-consciousness of the absolute as being-for-self. The organic form, which is only a casing or ornament for life forms, subsumes the rectilinear flat shapes corresponding to abstract forms of thought, and "left to itself, proliferates unchecked in particularity, being itself subjugated by the form of thought" (§694). The organic form remains in the realm of the particular, but communicating a quality of the absolute, the conflation of the particular and universal, in the symbol. The organic form is the "shape of individuality" (§695) intro-duced into the aspect of the universal, the abstract form, bringing the absolute nearer to existence, making the form "more in harmony with active self-consciousness."

The form of the artificer of being-for-self in nature is the animal form, which is the self-conscious form of desire outside of the body, in that it is a form of body, but produced by spirit or the unconscious, which is necessarily bodiless. The animal form is thus a *symbolum* of thought in the pure idea, of self-consciousness of spirit. When the animal form is combined with thought itself, the result is the human form. But even the human form in nature does not express spirit as essence or inner being. Although the human form is the form of self-conscious-ness, it cannot speak on its own, cannot communicate thought or idea. Its external shape is only given by perception and remains substance without essence, matter without spirit, though it is the product of the self-consciousness of spirit. In order for nature to express the inner being within the outer shape it must withdraw into its essence, its real, and shed its "living, self-particularizing, self-entangling manifold existence" (§696) of crystalline and organic forms. The inner being first revealed is "still simple darkness, the unmoved, the black, formless stone," the dialectical otherness of light and self-consciousness. The inner being "of multiform existence is still soundless, is not immanently differentiated and is still separated from its outer existence" (§697). The unintelligible form of inner being is the product of the combination of nature and self-consciousness and "the darkness of thought mating with the clarity of utterance," the inexpressible and its form of expression, unconscious and conscious thought. Only such a union can express the absolute in form.

The expression of spirit in form is the doubling of self-consciousness over against itself, the transcendence of matter in relation to consciousness. The outer form retreats inward, and the inner form is self-identical to the intuition. The inner form is the form of self-conscious activity, thought creating itself; "the artificer has given up the synthetic effort to blend the heterogeneous forms of thought and natural objects" (§699). The inner form is "present to its own consciousness" as consciousness itself. The form of spirit is the identity of the changing and the changeless, the outer substance and inner essence of the form, the identity of self-consciousness and being-in-self, which is manifest in the religion of art (*Kunstreligion*) (§748). The form of spirit in art is the externalization of the essence of the absolute, but it is enacted in the material forms of change, of "coming-to-be" (§754) in conscious thought. If the form of the coming-to-be is contained within itself, as an object of conscious thought in perception, then it is a "vanishing object" and aspires to "immediate unity with the universal self-consciousness." If the form of art represents a universality and is also composed of the certainty of conscious thought and perception, then the form of art exists in the world "as existence raised into an ideational representation," in the imagination. Forms of art "constitute the periphery of shapes which stands impatiently expectant around the birthplace of Spirit as it becomes self-consciousness" (§754). At the center of the forms is the pure concept of intuition, "the simplicity of the pure Notion," in which the forms are self-contained.

The Kantian categories of time and space in a priori intuition are "only the imperfect form in which the immediate mode is given a mediated or universal character" in conscious thought; "it is merely dipped superficially in the element of thought, is perceived in it as a sensuous mode, and not made one with the nature of thought itself. It is merely raised into the realm of picture-thinking (*Vorstellung*)," as a representation, "for this is the synthetic combination of sensuous immediacy and its universality or thought" (§764). Form in matter is only a derivative or a copy of the idea of form. In order to participate in the universal, or absolute, form in matter must be perceived, must become a form of picture thinking, thus perception is the medium between the absolute and material, perception in conscious thought.

Reason, as both conscious and unconscious thought in intelligence, according to Hegel, "does not require, as does finite activity, the condition of external materials": it is only in the image of reason, in picture thinking through perception in conscious thought, that form in matter is possible, as *eidos*. Reality given by perception is the realization of reason. Mental images are pre-generated by the process of reasoning, through perception and imagination. It is through perception and picture thinking in imagination, that spirit becomes self-conscious, though perception itself is not the self-consciousness of spirit. Spirit cannot attain self-consciousness in perception because perception entails the separation of being and reason, essence and substance. The content of being, the real in nature, becomes multiple and differentiated in perception: it is subject to time in sequence, and space in measurement and proportion, as with Kant. The essence of being, being-in-self, cannot be known by the level of consciousness as given by perception, but through perception self-consciousness of spirit can be attained, from conscious to unconscious thought.

The *Vorstellung* in the imagination is the middle term between the absolute and existence: the universal and particular, unconscious and conscious thought. The self-consciousness of spirit is its descent into existence. Picture thinking, as the middle term, is the synthetic connection of spirit and existence, the doubling of the self-consciousness of spirit, the "consciousness of passing into otherness" (§767), the self-alienation of conscious thought. Picture thinking is a manifestation of spirit, as is the self-consciousness of the thinking subject. The "dissociation in picture-thinking" of spirit or unconscious thought "consists in its existing in a specific or determinate mode," a particular in the universal diffusion of spirit in existence. In the objectivity of picture thinking, spirit steps forward out of itself toward the absolute, where it is able to "become an actual Self, to reflect itself into itself" (§766) in self-consciousness.

In pure thought or intuition, the absolute is "immediately simple and self-identical, eternal essence" (§769). As an inner essence, the absolute cannot be signification or existent, but pure being-in-self. It is not the substance of picture thinking or of conscious reason, but the negative of conscious thought, "the negativity of thought, or negativity as it is in itself in essence; i.e. simple essence is absolute difference from itself, or its pure othering of itself." Unconscious thought is the othering of conscious thought. In the *Mystical Theology* of Pseudo-Dionysius, "the pre-eminent cause of every object of sensible perception is none of the objects of sensible perception" (136) (Pseudo-Dionysius, 1897), and the absolute is "eminently unknown yet exceedingly luminous, where the pure, absolute and unchanging mysteries of theology are veiled in the dazzling obscurity of the secret silence, outshining all brilliance with the intensity of their darkness" (O'Rourke, 1992, p. 19): in unconscious thought, as it were. The otherness of the absolute is the objective, as given by picture thinking in its differentiation in the reproductive imagination.

For Hegel, the absolute unfolds toward existence in three stages: essence, being-for-self as the other of essence, and being-for-self as self-consciousness in the other (*Phenomenology of Spirit*, §770) (Hegel, 1977). Being-for-self as the other of essence is an externalization, and the self-consciousness of essence itself. Being-for-self as the other of essence is the logos, signification in language, which "when uttered, leaves behind, externalized and emptied, him who uttered it, but which is as immediately heard, and only this hearing of its own self is the existence of the Word," as in the *logos endiathetos* of Plotinus. The externalization of essence as other is the radical otherness from essence or origin which constitutes thought in language, the radical otherness of conscious thought from unconscious thought.

The externalization of essence as other, and the self-consciousness of essence as other, in language, is the *Vorstellung* in imagination, given by reason in signification (through the logos). Essence itself is an other of the absolute, an abstraction in signification and a negation of the universal (§772). Essence is the other of the self-contained and undivided of the absolute in existence, thus the originary self-consciousness in conscious thought. The difference between absolute and essence is resolved in pure intuition, and in pure being, and is not differentiated as in conscious thought or existence. The otherness of the absolute is contained within itself in pure thought and being, though the absolute contains the seed of differentiation and otherness. The absolute, "eternal or abstract spirit" (§774), self-sufficient being, passes into the otherness of existence, when elements of pure being "spontaneously part asunder and also place themselves over against each other" (§773), in differentiation. The creation of the world of otherness is picture thinking, the self-consciousness of spirit that manifests itself in the imagination and perception. Essence is then posited as existence and universals are posited as particulars in conscious thought, in the "dissolution of their simple universality and the parting asunder of them into

206 Unconscious Thought in Philosophy and Psychoanalysis

their own particularity" (§774). Spirit retains its presence in all particularity and is recognized in the particular when the individual self "has consciousness and distinguishes itself as 'other', or as world, from itself," in conscious thought. The individual self must become an other to itself in conscious thought before it can recognize itself as spirit, as the absolute must become other to itself to enter into existence. The self-consciousness of spirit, and the individual self, as other, entails a withdrawal into itself, through self-consciousness. The individual self must become self-alienated, must see its existence as alien to being, in order to become conscious of its participation in spirit.

Herbart

Johann Friedrich Herbart (1776–1841) was educated at the University of Jena, where he was a student of Johann Gottlieb Fichte. He became a professor at the University of Königsberg, assuming the chair previously held by Immanuel Kant. He is mostly known as a pioneer of pedagogy and philosophy of education, which he saw as disciplines of psychology. His best-known works are *Textbook in Psychology* (*Lehrbuch der Psychologie*, 1816), and *Psychology as a science newly founded on experience, metaphysics and mathematics* (*Psychologie als Wissenschaft*, 1824–25). As part of the psychology of education, Herbart developed theories on apperception, representation, and conscious and unconscious thought. Apperception in particular plays a key role in the education process. Apperception, as the cognitive combining of perceptions into totalities, following Wolff, Sulzer, Platner and Kant, is associated with conscious thought. As for Sulzer, ideas are the products of representations (*Vorstellungen*), which Herbart saw as dynamic forces of varying strength and clarity, above or below the threshold of consciousness. Ideas, like perceptions, are both unconscious and conscious. Dark and obscure ideas, like dark and obscure perceptions, are unconscious, while clear and distinct ideas, like clear and distinct perceptions, are conscious. We have many ideas and perceptions of which we are not aware. But as unconscious ideas become stronger and clearer, they may break through a threshold and become conscious ideas; there is a threshold or limen between unconsciousness and consciousness, unconscious thought and conscious thought. In the "law of the threshold" (*Schwellengesetz*), unconscious ideas, though being below the threshold of consciousness, still have the potential to be effective. The clearest and strongest ideas break into conscious thought and apperception. Apperception then may retrieve more unconscious ideas to join the already conscious ideas, and unconscious ideas can join together themselves to break through into conscious thought.

Herbart's *Schwellengesetz* was developed by Gustav Theodor Fechner (1801–87) in his *Elements of Psychophysics* in 1860. In that unconscious ideas are dynamic forces, as sensations and representations, they lose their quality as unconscious ideas when they are understood abstractly in conscious thought. But given that, there is a necessary psychophysical energy that causes unconscious sensations and causes them to emerge into conscious thought. The psychophysical threshold is thus an important basis for the concept of the unconscious (*Elemente der Psychophysik*, 1889, second edition, p. 438 ff.) (Gödde, 2010, p. 273). Herbart's cognition functions much like Kant's imagination, with various levels of combinatory powers, in a similar role integrating the functions of unconscious and conscious thought, representation and apperception.

According to Hartmann, in *Philosophy of the Unconscious*, Herbart saw unconscious ideas as being ideas of which we are not aware, and not able to associate with ourselves or our ego, thus our self-consciousness. Unconscious ideas do not function as representations as conscious ideas do; going back to Plotinus, an unconscious idea is an idea without an image. Unconscious ideas thus have no capacity to signify anything, going back to Hegel. There must be a gradual continuity between unconscious ideas and conscious ideas as they pass through the threshold, a continuity that links the ideas from non-representation to representation and non-signification to signification. In that conscious ideas may retrieve further unconscious ideas, the continuity must be reciprocal, allowing for a continuous dynamic cycle.

If conscious thought is seen as a consequence of underlying unconscious thought processes, then the order of thought can be explained by unconscious causes, and by the interrelation of conscious and unconscious thought in the same system. The recognition of the unified system allows for an understanding of the laws of unconscious thought in a psychology which is a form of natural science. Herbart was a materialist, insofar as he saw unconscious ideas as dynamic forces or sensations, but it is impossible to conceive of a dynamic cycle of continuity between unconscious and conscious ideas on a materialist basis (Hartmann, 1931, p. 33).

Sigmund Freud studied Herbartian psychology in his last year at the Gymnasium, which was mandatory in the Austrian educational system at the time. In 1932, Maria Dorer, in *Historische Grundlagen der Psychoanalyse*, showed that Freud made great use of Herbart's theoretical vocabulary (Sand, 2014, p. 131). Herbart's concept of a "psychic mechanism," or "mechanism of ideas" (*Vorstellungsmechanik*), a dynamic system linking the movement of thoughts to scientific concepts of matter and motion, as explained in his *Textbook in Psychology* and *Psychology as a Science*, is seen as having a direct influence on Freud's concept of the "psychic apparatus." Freud also appropriated Herbart's theory of a unified system of conscious and unconscious thought which can explain the discontinuities in conscious thought. In the essay "The Unconscious," Freud wrote that the existence of the unconscious is necessary because "the data of consciousness have a very large number of gaps in them" (Sand, 2014, p. 137; SE XIV: 166–7), and conscious thoughts are "disconnected and unintelligible" unless they are connected to unconscious thoughts. Herbart's three levels of consciousness – unconscious, conscious, and the threshold of consciousness – became Freud's three "topographic" regions of the mind: unconscious, conscious, and pre-conscious.

Carus and Fechner

Carl Gustav Carus (1789–1869) was a physician and professor in Dresden. He was a friend of Johann Wolfgang von Goethe. He was also a landscape painter and wrote on art theory; he studied under Caspar David Friedrich. With his publication of *Psyche: On the Developmental History of the Soul* (*Psyche: Zur Entwicklungsgeschichte der Seele*) in 1846, he was the first to develop a systematic theory of the unconscious with the unconscious as the focus of a theory of mind. He is thus considered to be "the first proper theorist of the unconscious" (Bell, 2010, p. 156). The first sentence of *Psyche* reads: "The key to an understanding of the nature of the conscious life of the soul lies in the sphere of the unconscious" (Carus, 1970, p. 1). Carus affirmed that conscious thought can only be understood through unconscious thought. He asserted that it is possible to be aware of unconscious thought in conscious thought; it might seem to be impossible, but it is the task of science to discover how unconscious thought can be accessed, and how unconscious thought forms the basis of conscious thought. It is obvious that of the thousands of ideas that are continually created by our minds, we are aware of only a fraction at any given moment. Thus, the majority of our psyche is unknown to us in a present moment, lying in "the night of the unconscious" (*Psyche*, p. 1).

It is necessary to trace the evolution of an idea in order to discover the unconscious components of an idea that to present awareness only exists as a conscious idea; then the psyche will be revealed to be "a great, continuously circling river which is illuminated only in one small area by the light of the sun," that being consciousness. The psyche is seen as a *circuitus spiritualis*, as it were: a continuous reciprocal cycle of conscious and unconscious functions, as in the thought of Johann Friedrich Herbart. The majority of conscious thought "continually sinks into the unconscious" and can only return to consciousness transformed and fragmented, as in the fragmentation and differentiation of discursive reason. The existence of unconscious thought is necessitated by the distinction between conscious thought and the external world; the external world, the subject of sense perception and sense-based reason, as in *nous hylikos*, cannot be the source of conscious thought, although it is its substance, because self-consciousness gives a separation between the thinking subject and the external world, necessitating the existence of unconscious thought. Conscious thoughts are based on images that have been previously formed but that are no longer present to conscious thought, as they have sunk into unconscious thought, and resurface in ways that belie their origin in conscious thought, condensed and displaced as Freud would describe them. Conscious thoughts and the images of the external world in mind are representations of the external world, as in the thought of Herbart, and thus cannot be formed by the external world.

Ideas disappear from conscious thought when they are no longer needed, but they do not disappear from the mind, as they can return to conscious thought. But when they are in unconscious thought they are not static: they continue to develop, on their own and in combination with subsequent thoughts, so that when they return to consciousness they make take a different form. We do not stop thinking while we are sleeping, for example: our thoughts are constantly developing and transforming without our being aware of them, all of which contributes to present consciousness. In order to understand conscious thought, it is necessary to start with conscious thought and trace ideas back into unconscious thought, to discover how present ideas are the products of transformative processes through time that occur outside of conscious thought, and independent of the external world and external stimuli. Carus saw unconscious thought as both organic, in the materialist sense, and spiritual in the transcendentalist sense – both biological and religious. He also considered unconscious thought to be instinctual and the necessary organic real of nature, following Schelling. While unconscious thought is ruled by necessity, as in the physiological anthropology of Kant, conscious thought is ruled by freedom, as in the pragmatic anthropology of Kant. The oscillations between conscious and unconscious thought are seen as a dynamic flux in an organic system. The passage from conscious to unconscious thought can be seen as the highest form of human fulfillment as it is connected to desire and pleasure in its psychophysical function; and it is also connected to the search for fulfillment in language. The lack of awareness on the part of conscious thought of its basis in unconscious thought creates a desire for self-knowledge and fulfillment, which can be achieved in the passage from conscious to unconscious thought. Most conscious thoughts are developed and completed in unconscious thought. Carus linked the oscillation between conscious and unconscious thought to sexual desire, and the source of sexual pleasure and fulfillment (Whyte, 1978, p. 149). The sexual system has both conscious and unconscious components, and it is connected to language and *Vorstellung* or representation. It is not too much of a leap from Carus to the theories of Jacques Lacan that root sexual desire in language.

In an earlier work, *Lectures on Psychology* (*Vorlesungen über Psychologie, gehalten im Winter 1829–30 zu Dresden*), published in 1831, Carus outlined a system of distinctions in the stages of development of unconscious thought, on a biological model (Bell, 2010, pp. 164–70). The development of the psyche is seen as a microcosm of the evolutionary development of a species. The phylogeny, the evolutionary development of the species, is recapitulated by the ontogeny, the biological development of the individual organism. The theory would have an influence on Sigmund Freud in *Totem and Taboo*, in which the development of an infant is compared to the development of social organization in tribal cultures, and on Carl Jung. Roots of the theory can be found in Aristotle, in his biological model of the five stages of the soul in different species in *De anima*. At the bottom, vegetable soul is capable of nutrition and growth. At the second level, soul also has the power of sensation. At the third level, soul has the power of desire. At the fourth level, soul has the power of movement. At the fifth level, soul has the power of intellect. These different levels of soul can be applied to the differentiation of species, and also to the differentiation in the development of a single species. At the lowest level, inorganic matter has no consciousness, while plants have appetition, animals have consciousness, and human beings have intellect. Each stage subsumes the prior stages in the development.

In the *Lectures on Psychology*, the psyche is divided into conscious and unconscious sections. The conscious psyche is further divided into empirical consciousness or consciousness of the world (*Weltbewusstsein*), and self-consciousness (*Selbsbewusstsein*), recalling the division made by Johann Georg Sulzer. The unconscious psyche is further divided into a relative unconscious (*relative Unbewusstes*), similar to the preconscious of Freud, and an absolute unconscious (*absolute Unbewusstes*). The absolute unconscious is further divided into a general absolute unconscious (*allgemeines absolute Unbewusstes*) and a partial absolute unconscious (*partielles absolute Unbewusstes*). The absolute unconscious is the most basic biological aspect of mind and can involve non-sentient activity in the general absolute unconscious, as at the crystalline or embryonic level, or sentient activity in the partial absolute unconscious, as at the level of the appetition of plants. The general absolute unconscious is the basis of organic growth, as in Schelling's organic real. Even at the lowest level, the unconscious psyche in organic growth is in constant activity, or constant flux, "constantly re-forming, always destroying and renewing," as explained in *Psyche: On the Developmental History of the Soul* (p. 24). The sentient activity of the partial absolute conscious is created by the nervous system of the biological organism.

In the *Lectures on Psychology*, mental activity takes place in the relative unconscious. As differentiated from the absolute unconscious, the relative unconscious is connected to conscious thought. It is the repository for conscious ideas that have been forgotten or are below present awareness, as in the preconscious of Freud. All conscious ideas and images at one point return to the relative unconscious, which retains them permanently, unless they return to conscious thought either as is or in an altered form. Conscious thought is always connected to unconscious thought. The same mental functions that are found in conscious thought are found in the relative unconscious, without self-consciousness. Thus an idea may go through the same transformations whether it is processed in conscious thought or thought in the relative unconscious. The relative unconscious is the storehouse (*Vorrath*) of memories, as for Kant the imagination is the storehouse of representations. There must thus be a conscious imagination and an unconscious imagination, as there is conscious memory and unconscious memory. The conscious imagination is the reproductive imagination, as in Kant, and the unconscious imagination is the productive imagination, as in the *nous poietikos*. Perceived images and imagined images, or intelligible images, are stored and reproduced as memories in the imagination, and are subject to transformative processes in the relative unconscious.

Going back to Kant in the *Anthropology from a Pragmatic Point of View* (*Anthropologie in pragmatischer Hinsicht*, 1798), traces of the unconscious perceptions in memory play a role in the becoming conscious of the residues of images: in the processes of sense perception, imagination, and intellection. Imagination is the ability to form an image in the mind's eye that is independent of the sense object, and is a synthesis of the passive and the active. The passive imagination is reproductive, a faculty of the derived representation, reproducing empirical perceptions as they are recalled to mind. The active imagination is productive, producing an original representation of an object, taking place in intuition or unconscious thought rather than in empirical cognition, as in the *nous hylikos*. Passive imagination is connected to empirical cognition or experience. Active, creative imagination is a function of unconscious thought, while passive, reproductive imagination is a function of conscious thought.

For Hegel, in the *Philosophy of Mind* (1817), the reproductive imagination is an imitation of the productive imagination, connected to the empirical laws of sense perception and the differentiation of particulars. The formation of the image in the reproductive imagination, as it is tied to the particulars of sense perception, is unique in each individual in intellection, while the intuition from which the image is formed in unconscious thought is a universal in nature, the biological substratum. The unconscious image becomes a conscious image in three stages, beginning in the reproductive imagination, tied to empirical experience. Through the transformations in unconscious thought, the image becomes an idea or a representation. When the idea or representation is related back to empirical reproductions, intelligible images of the creative imagination are formed, as symbols and signs.

In the Kantian system, the reproductive imagination is the passive imagination, creating derived representations and reproducing empirical perceptions in connection with memory. The productive imagination is the active imagination, able to produce a representation of an object in intuition or unconscious thought. The productive imagination operates without any connection to empirical phenomena, or sensible or intelligible form. The conscious, reproductive imagination consists of image formation in the present moment, reproduction of images in memory, and reproduction of images in anticipation of future images. The unconscious, productive imagination consists of the power to invent images not connected to sense perceptions, coming into conscious thought through the formation of the invented image; the completion of the invented image in unconscious thought; and the formation of the invented image as a symbol or a sign. It is easy to see the relation of the Kantian and Hegelian systems to Carus' structure of the psyche, transformed into a dynamic biological system.

In the *Lectures on Psychology* of Carus, the relative unconscious is also where dreams are produced. Dreams are seen as combinations of biological forces from the absolute unconscious, and traces or residues of images formed in the imagination – both creative and reproductive, intelligible and sensible – that enter into the relative unconscious from conscious thought. The relative unconscious is a buffer or threshold (as in the *Schwellengesetz* or law of the threshold of Johann Friedrich Herbart) between the absolute unconscious and conscious thought, what can be revealed to conscious thought of the unconscious. Ideas flow back and forth between conscious thought and the relative unconscious as dynamic forces, as in the psychophysiological energy of Gustav Theodor Fechner in the *Elements of Psychophysics* in 1860. The psychophysical energy of the nervous system causes unconscious sensations and causes them to emerge into conscious thought.

Conscious thought in the system of Carus is divided between consciousness of world and consciousness of self. Consciousness of world is given by the faculties of sense, connected to the dynamic energy of the nervous system, but is continuously affected by the relative unconscious, just as the empirical functions of the imagination of Kant are continuously affected by the a priori categories of unconscious thought. As always, Carus combined the biological and the transcendental. Consciousness of world cannot be disconnected from consciousness of self, because it depends on "the condition of one's own organization" (*Lectures on Psychology*, 111) (Carus, 1831; Bell, 2010, p. 168), derived from the a priori categories of intuition in unconscious thought, which is also the source of sensations of pleasure and pain, connected to desire. Consciousness of world is also dependent on memory and representations (*Vorstellungen*) in imagination. As Schelling established that consciousness is nature becoming conscious, conscious thought is the result of the becoming conscious of nature in the macrocosm of biological development. The human mind is seen as the ultimate development of nature. Consciousness of world and consciousness of self are both products of nature.

While the unconscious mind is seen as an undifferentiated universal that is shared by all organisms, the thinking subject is differentiated and made a particular in self-consciousness, as conscious thought (discursive reason) involves the differentiation of particulars arising from unconscious thought. In self-consciousness, the thinking subject differentiates itself from the external world and from the other thinking subjects that share its unconscious. As established by Johann Gottlieb Fichte in the *Foundations of Natural Right* in 1796, a necessary condition of self-consciousness is the distinction between the I (as the activity of the self) and the not-I. As conscious thought and the relative unconscious are connected, differentiation and combination, the mechanisms of discursive reason, play a role in the relative unconscious as well. The dream work of Freud could be seen as a relative unconscious, as the dream work contains the mechanisms of condensation and displacement, combination and differentiation, which transform the unconscious dream thoughts into dream images. As the psyche of the thinking subject moves through the levels of consciousness from the absolute unconscious to self-consciousness, it becomes increasingly differentiated and isolated, as well as more complex and fragmented. The simplicity and wholeness of the absolute unconscious are inaccessible to self-consciousness in conscious thought. The subject can only be seen as thrown from its origin, in Hegelian terms, unable to return, self-alienated, and fragmented and dispersed, in Lacanian terms.

Gustav Theodor Fechner's adherence to empirical science and discounting of the metaphysical in the study of unconscious thought, in his *Elements of Psychophysics* (*Elemente der Psychophysik*, 1860, 1889), had an influence on Sigmund Freud. While Fechner developed Herbart's concept of *Schwellengesetz* or law of the threshold between unconscious and conscious thought, he saw Herbart's cycle of continuity between the unconscious and conscious, and their integration in cognition, to be too dependent on metaphysical speculation. Fechner, a professor of physics at the University of Leipzig, is considered to be a pioneer in experimental psychology, and the founder of psychophysics, the study of the relation between physical stimuli and sensations and perceptions. Some of his ideas can generally be traced back to Schelling, but he also rejected the metaphysical basis of Hegel's writings. Freud referred to Fechner in a letter to Wilhelm Fliess in 1898, and later in *The Interpretation of Dreams* of 1899, to his theory that dream processes should be differentiated from conscious thought (Gödde, 2010, p. 272). In *The Interpretation of Dreams*, "Fechner puts forward the idea that the scene of action of dreams is different from that of waking ideational life" (Freud, 1965, p. 574). Freud, following Fechner, found it necessary to ground the study of the unconscious in the new empiricism of the nineteenth century.

Hartmann and Lipps

Karl Robert Eduard von Hartmann (1842–1906), who spent most of his life in Berlin, is known as the "philosopher of the unconscious" because of his most influential work, the *Philosophy of the Unconscious* (*Philosophie des Unbewussten*, 1869, 1890). Hartmann's philosophy of the unconscious begins with Kant, whom he saw as the inventor of the unconscious. Hartmann began *The Philosophy of the Unconscious* by quoting Kant in

the *Anthropology from a Pragmatic Point of View* (*Anthropologie in pragmatischer Hinsicht*, 1798), based on Kant's lectures at the Albertus University
of Königsberg beginning in 1772: "...we may become aware indirectly
that we have an idea, although we be not directly cognizant of the same"
(Hartmann, 1931, p. 1). In Section 5 of the *Anthropology*, "On the Ideas
We Have Without Being Conscious of Them," Kant identified unconscious thought with the *petites perceptions* of Leibniz. Clear ideas are only
a small portion of all ideas, most of which are obscure. Kant posited two
levels of consciousness, direct or unmediated consciousness and indirect
or mediated consciousness involving indirect representations that are
dark and obscure. We draw conclusions about what we perceive without
being conscious of perceiving every detail. The majority of our perceptions are of the details which we do not consciously perceive, but which
contribute to the conclusions and judgments we make.

According to Hartmann, Kant recognized the distinction between the
clear and obscure idea, or conscious thought as opposed to unconscious
thought, but did not recognize the importance of the distinction. For
Hartmann, in distinction to Kant, not every conscious idea is a clear
idea, and not every obscure idea is an unconscious idea. A conscious
idea is only clear when the consciousness is at the level that it can distinguish the idea from other ideas: what Hartmann calls the "consciousness
of the discrimination" in the *Philosophy of the Unconscious* (Hartmann,
1931, p. 21). Before the consciousness has reached that level, the
conscious idea remains relatively obscure. Thus not all obscure ideas are
unconscious. For Hartmann, the distinction is key to Kant's pragmatic
anthropology. What truly distinguishes the unconscious idea from the
conscious idea is the absence of the form of representation, the *repraesentatio* that is the genus of the idea, that is differentiated from the *perceptio*
in the conscious idea.

Going back to Plotinus, in *Enneads* V.3.8, intelligibles exist prior
to bodies, and cannot be thought of in terms of form, until they are
connected to such in imagination, until the *repraesentatio* is connected to
the *perceptio*. Intelligibles themselves are "naturally invisible," according
to Plotinus, invisible even to the soul which possesses them. In the physical world, something is seen when it is illuminated by enough light,
while in the intelligible world, something can only be seen by itself.
Soul itself is an image, a reflection or likeness of Intellect; conscious
thought is an image, a reflection or likeness of unconscious thought,
which has no image. The illumination of a sensible object by light is
a reflection or likeness of the illumination of Intellect by intelligible
light. In *Enneads* V.8.9 and VI.4.7, Plotinus asks the reader to picture the

form of a physical thing in the imagination, and then to subtract the mass, spatial relations and matter, that compose the form, so that the object can be apprehended more clearly, in its conceptual organization not dependent upon its physical appearance to the senses or conscious thought.

Hartmann understood Kant to say that "the pure concepts of the understanding (categories), seem to belong to the unconscious ideas, so far as they lie beyond cognition," as cognition is only possible with the soul "binding up the given manifold of the perceived ideal material into a synthesis" (*Philosophy of the Unconscious*, p. 21). It is in the nature of this synthesis that the concept of the pure understanding can be found. Unconscious thought brings about conscious thought, but this is an "art hidden in the depths of the soul" that Kant did not penetrate, according to Hartmann. Kant left the concept of the a priori forms of intuition unexplained. The intellectual intuition, although it is juxtaposed to the conscious idea, or conscious thought, is never defined as such, as that which is not conscious. All forms of thought other than intellectual intuition are connected to sense perception and discursive reason, that is, conscious thought: the *perceptio*, conscious presentation in perception, feeling, conception, sensuous intuition, and discursive knowledge must all be distinguished from intellectual intuition as conscious thought.

In *The Interpretation of Dreams*, Freud referred to Hartmann: "In discussing the part played by the unconscious in artistic creation, Eduard von Hartmann made a clear statement of the law in accordance with which the association of ideas is governed by unconscious purposive ideas…" (Freud, 1965, p. 567, n. 1 [added 1914]). In the imagination, according to Freud, "every combination of sensuous presentations…requires the help of the unconscious," and "it is the unconscious which makes the appropriate selection of a purpose for the interest" in "the association of ideas in abstract thinking as well as in sensuous imagining and artistic combination," quoting Hartmann in the *Philosophy of the Unconscious*. Freud came to the conclusion that all unconscious ideas are purposive, and that no "influence that we can bring to bear upon our mental processes can ever enable us to think without purposive ideas…" (*The Interpretation of Dreams*, p. 567). Rather than being a cauldron of irrationality, unconscious thought is the seat of the rationality of conscious ideas.

Intellectual intuition must thus be defined as unconscious thought, according to Hartmann. While the "perceived or conscious idea is different from its object" (*Philosophy of the Unconscious*, p. 22) (Hartmann, 1931), in the distinction between the thinking subject and the external world, the non-perceived idea, the intellectual intuition or unconscious thought, is identical with the object of perception, because the object of perception is produced by it, by the categories. Conscious thought is a "derived and dependent human understanding" (p. 23), while intellectual intuition, or unconscious thought, is a "divine understanding" that produces intelligible objects and thereby creates the "world of noumena," like the active intellect of Aristotle. Unconscious thought assists conscious thought by making mental concepts available to it. The higher, intuitive mind implicated by unconscious thought operates without the deductive or discursive method of conscious thought, going back to the classical distinction between *nous poietikos* and *nous pathetikos*. The intuitive mind is "the Pegasus flight of the unconscious," while the discursive mind is "the lame walking on stilts of conscious logic." While Kant never explored how unconscious thought can be explained by the influence of intellectual intuition on the "derived understanding" or conscious thought, according to Hartmann, it was Schelling who first explored such a relation, the relation between unconscious and conscious thought.

Hartmann clearly saw the unconscious as a metaphysical principle, following the influence of Schelling and the metaphysics of Hegel. Hartmann called his system "transcendental realism," involving the induction of what lies beyond experience, by first considering all possible experience. The unconscious is seen as pure potentiality, as the noumenal or thing-in-itself, as in the real of Schelling. The unconscious is the ground of existence, and combines reason with will, following Schopenhauer. It is the will that realizes conscious ideas, from which consciousness arises, in the penetration of intellectual intuition into derived understanding or conscious thought. The redemption of the human condition is a return to the unconscious, or unconscious thought, as the unconscious is seen as the absolute in transcendental idealist terms.

To summarize the theories of Immanuel Kant to which Hartmann ascribes the concept of unconscious thought, the passive imagination is reproductive, only reproducing empirical perceptions as they are recalled to mind within the framework of the category of time in a priori intuition. The active imagination is productive, producing an original representation of an object that precedes experience, taking place in intuition rather than empirical cognition. Perception of intelligibles and the a priori categories of space and time in the imagination, is a faculty of productive imagination, which would be unconscious thought. Passive imagination is connected to empirical cognition, or experience. Active imagination is a function of intellectual cognition, while passive imagination is a function of discursive cognition. The primary role of imagination is to transform the categories of a priori intuition into the schemata that organize sense perception and conscious thought, discursive reason. Appearances can be reproduced and reconstructed by imagination in a way that is different from empirical reality. Empirical realities are bound to the categories of space and time in conscious thought; but, in imagination and unconscious thought, as in dreams, realities can be created from the representations of appearances outside the manifold. The transcendental synthesis of imagination, a product of the synthesis of apprehension in the manifold, is the condition for the possibility of experience, and the condition for the possibility of the reproduction of appearances.

The synthesis of apprehension in reason is "bound up with the synthesis of reproduction" (*Critique of Pure Reason*, A102) (Kant, 1968) in imagination. The synthesis of apprehension is the transcendental ground of the possibility of all knowledge, and the synthesis of reproduction in imagination is the transcendental ground of all thought. The succession of representations in the imagination is made possible by the category of time, without which conscious thought would not be possible. The unity of the manifold can only be given as a representation in conscious thought: as a priori categories, time and space are inaccessible to conscious thought. In the experience of time and space, it is impossible to be conscious of the fact that they are a priori categories rather than properties of empirical experience. While the unconscious nature of the a priori categories is not implicitly stated by Kant, it is sufficiently implied that the concept of the unconscious can be applied to the categories. The unity of time, as empirical experience, only exists as it is unfolded in conscious thought or discursive reason through the mechanisms of the imagination. The products of the categories of space and time, geometry and mathematics, and architecture by extension, only function as organizing principles in relation to empirical experience in discursive reason, although they exist in intuition as pure concepts.

Sense perception, discursive reason, imagination, and apperception are sources of knowledge that are both empirical in relation to appearances or representations, and also the product of a priori intuition. Appearances are represented empirically in sense perception and in relation to one another in a manifold in imagination. The association between the appearance and its representation and reproduction occurs through "empirical consciousness" (A115) in apperception, as opposed to the unconscious. The a priori intuition of time in the inner sense, and the pure synthesis of imagination (higher imagination not connected to empirical experience), which are not functions of empirical consciousness, are necessary for a perception of a sensible object to take place. The source of conscious thought is what is other to conscious thought. Knowledge depends on the translation of what is other to conscious thought to conscious thought. Representations are derived from both the empirical consciousness of discursive reason and the processes of a priori intuition. The transcendental unity of apperception is based on an a priori synthesis, related to the pure synthesis of the higher imagination; it is thus other than conscious. Synthetic transcendental apperception and a priori intuition are functions of a form of thought that is not accessible to consciousness. The a priori combination of the manifold, the transcendental synthesis of imagination, is the basis of knowledge, empirical experience and sense perception, which is given as a representation a priori to conscious thought.

Empirical experience must conform to the "necessary unity of the pure synthesis of imagination" (A119), which is other than conscious thought. The a priori modes of knowledge that contain unity in the understanding are the categories, the "pure concepts of understanding." The understanding of conscious thought in relation to the objects of sense perception is derived from a priori intuition and imaginative synthesis, which is inaccessible to conscious perception. All appearances and representations must conform to the understanding, the categories and the manifold, outside conscious thought. Experience of perception is made possible by the thinking of objects as phenomena or representations in the unity of the manifold of synthetic apperception in a priori intuition; objects cannot be known in themselves, nor can they be known as phenomena. The noumenon, the thing-in-itself, is outside of conscious thought, thus, as Hartmann says, it is the unconscious. Consciousness, according to Kant, is necessary for perception, for an appearance to be an object of knowledge; otherwise it would have no objective reality and no existence. All appearances in conscious thought contain a manifold a priori, and can only be known in combination, created by the transcendental synthesis of higher imagination, in combination with the empirical synthesis of lower imagination. As in Plotinus, the imagination connects intuition with discursive reason. The action of the synthesis of the imagination in relation to sense perception is apprehension. Apprehension invests the form of the image or appearance in perception with the manifold of intuition, which is not possible without the subjective ground of the inner sense or categories of a priori intuition, outside of conscious thought. While the subjective ground is the inner sense or intuition, the objective ground is consciousness in perception and apprehension. The objective ground of consciousness unites all appearances in empirical imagination as one consciousness, a representation of the manifold. A necessary single consciousness insures that all appearances conform to the categories. The unity is found in apperception, and all appearances in sense perception must conform to the unity of apperception in order to be apprehended. That which is inaccessible to conscious thought lays the ground for conscious thought in the perception of the world. The "necessary condition of all possible perception" is the unity of apperception, or the "objective unity of all empirical consciousness in one consciousness" (A123).

The necessary unity of apperception is a product of the transcendental synthesis of the productive imagination in combination with consciousness in empirical experience and conscious reason. Transcendental apperception is combined with empirical apperception, as transcendental imagination is combined with empirical imagination, because empirical, conscious representations can only exist with an a priori representation. Empirical representations are dependent on a priori representations, but conversely a priori representations cannot be dependent on any empirical reality. The world must exist as it is constructed, outside of conscious thought. Transcendental apperception is the transcendental unity of self-consciousness, because all representations are only unified in that they belong to one consciousness. The self-consciousness of empirical representations is made possible by the transcendental unity of apperception and the manifold in intuition. The apperception of the manifold as a representation in conscious thought is based on a synthesis of representations that is brought about by a consciousness of the synthesis in discursive reason, connected to empirical experience. The "analytic unity of apperception" (B133) in conscious thought is made possible by the synthetic unity of apperception in the transcendental aesthetic.

Hartmann's theories have their roots in classical philosophy. The following is a summary of classical concepts that are appropriated in modern concepts of unconscious thought, including Schelling and Hegel. The active intellect, as an intellectual intuition, or "divine understanding," in the words of Hartmann, that produces intelligible objects, was compared to light by Aristotle, in *De anima* 3.5, because light makes potential colors actual. The active intellect, as intuition, leads the material intellect to actuality, or the sensible form to the intelligible form in the manifold. The active intellect would thus lead conscious reason to what is inaccessible to conscious reason. The active intellect is seen as eternal and immutable.

In his commentary on the *De anima* of Aristotle, Alexander of Aphrodisias saw intellect as consisting of both a material and an active element. The active intellect is seen as the cause of the appearance of the material intellect (*De anima*, 88) (Davidson, 1992, p. 21) or its form (85). The material intellect develops through the cause of active intellect, from its ability to apprehend the universal separate forms from matter, in intuition, as it were. The development of material intellect toward active intellect requires the element of self-consciousness in thought. According to Aristotle, the intellect is passive in that it becomes all things, and active in that it makes all things. In the *De intellectu* of Alexander, active intellect is "the cause of the material intellect's separating, imitating and thinking with reference to such a form" (*De intellectu*, 108) (Alexander of Aphrodisias, 1990), the form as object of perception and discursive reason. Active intellect is the cause of the mechanisms of perception and discursive reason on the part of material intellect. The functions of discursive reason are subject to active intellect and the formation of the intelligible. Actualized thought is able to separate the sensible form and intelligible form, as it separates the mechanisms of discursive reason in material intellect from the role of intuition in perception. There must be something in the activity of intellect, for which "what it is to be intellect does not lie in its being thought by us," that is, active intellect, or unconscious thought.

According to Themistius, in his *De anima*, the active intellect perfects the material intellect in the same way that a craft perfects matter in architecture or sculpture. All objects in nature consist of "a matter which is potentially all the particulars included" (*De anima*, 98) (Themistius, 1996), the material substrate or noumena, and "a cause which is productive in the sense that it makes them all," the active intellect. Active intellect imposes intelligible form on the sensible object. Potential or material intellect is something (*to tode*), according to Themistius, as matter is something, while actual intellect is "what it is to be something" (*to tôide einai*, *De anima* 100), as the sensible object as form. The thinking subject as material intellect or conscious thought is "I" (*to egô*), anticipating Freud, while the thinking subject as actual intellect is "what it is to be me" (*to emoi einai*), defined by what is inaccessible to conscious thought. The thought of material intellect in discursive reason is subject to time, while thought given by active intellect is not (*De anima*, 101), just as the categories in the intuition of Kant are not subject to time. In his *De anima*, (3.5.430a) (Aristotle, 1952a), Aristotle surmises that actual intellect (intellect actualized to active intellect) is "mind set free from its present conditions...immortal and eternal," not subject to time, outside of conscious thought. Mind as passive and conscious, in its material potentiality, is destructible and subject to time; but mind as active is free from its material conditions, such as space and time. Conscious thinking is equivalent to thinking in time; time is not present in the same way in unconscious thought or dreams, as developed by Freud.

In the *Risala fi'l-'aql* (*De intellectu*, or *Letter Concerning the Intellect*) of Abu Nasr Alfarabi, form is separated from matter in active intellect. The active intellect "is a separated form which never existed in matter nor ever will exist in it" (Alfarabi, 1967, pp. 218–19), which makes matter possible. The "relation of the active intellect to the intellect which is in potentiality," in conscious thought, "is like the relation of the sun to the eye which is sight in potentiality as long as it is in darkness," not illuminated by the intelligibles of the agent intellect. Intellect ascends from the material to the active as it ascends from the particular to the eternal, from the multiplicity of divisions in discursive reason or conscious thought to the unity and simplicity of that which is indivisible, other than conscious thought. In the ascent to active intellect, we ascend "from that which is best known to us to that which is unknown," from conscious thought to unconscious thought, from forms that are divisible in matter to forms that are "in the agent intellect indivisible...." The indivisible forms of active intellect project a likeness of themselves onto matter and material thought, as representations provided by the categories of intuition, but they are only received in matter and conscious thought as divided and corrupted.

In the *Liber Naturalis* (*al-Tabi'iyyat*) of Avicenna, "the cause for giving intelligible form is nothing but the active intellect, in whose power are the principles of abstract intelligible forms" (6.5.5) (Brentano, 1977, pp. 6–8), the intelligible forms being comparable to the categories of Kant. In the *Shifā: Ilāhiyyāt* of Avicenna, active intellect is the giver of forms. Forms emanate from active intellect constantly and eternally, but not as the result of any will on the part of active intellect, that is, unconsciously. In the classical and medieval tradition, forms are provided by an active intellect without any will on the part of the thinking subject, although the understanding of the forms requires a will to ascend intellectually. Forms in active intellect are indivisible and perfect in their incorporeality, but sensible objects are not capable of receiving them as such, because they are not properly prepared for them in their particularities and differentiation. Forms or intelligibles emanate from active intellect as differentiated, in sequential arrangements of terms which are suitable for conscious thought in discursive or cogitative knowledge. Cogitative knowledge is different from knowledge of intelligibles, which requires the participation of active intellect, something outside conscious thought.

In the *Long Commentary on the De anima* (*Commentarium magnum in Aristotelis de Anima libros*) of Averroes (Ibn Rushd), the active intellect is purely eternal and incorporeal, and it is the final entelechy, or final actualization of potentiality, as the unconscious was described by Hartmann. In the words of Franz Brentano, in *The Psychology of Aristotle: In Particular His Doctrine of the Active Intellect*, "once the activity of the active intellect has made the images intelligible in unconscious thought, the material intellect, which stands to all intelligible forms in the relation of potentiality, receives from the images the concepts of sensible things" (Brentano, 1977, p. 10). Brentano recognized the role of unconscious thought in Averroes' philosophy of intellect. According to Robert Grosseteste, who may have been influenced by Averroes, sensible form is given by intelligible form, through the imagination, and is presented to consciousness in discursive reason in the process of perception. The active intellect illuminates the intelligible form, what is intelligible in the sensible form, as formed by the imagination, from the imprint in sense perception, which is then given to material intellect or conscious thought (*Hexaëmeron*, VIII, IV, 7) (Grosseteste, 1996). The sensible form is a similitude of the intelligible form as a mnemic residue, and is thus a representation of the intelligible form (VIII, IV, 9–10).

In his *Commentary on the Posterior Analytics* of Aristotle (I.14, 235–38) (Grosseteste, 1981), Grosseteste compared *intelligentia*, divine intellect, to *actio intellectus*, active intellect, the intellect which is differentiated from the material intellect in the *De anima* of Aristotle. Like the active intellect of Aristotle, the *intelligentia* of Grosseteste illuminates the lower functions of intellect, discursive reason, as described by Averroes in the *Long Commentary*. In the *Commentary on the Posterior Analytics* (II.6, 17–21) of Grosseteste, universals (*principia*) exist in intellect potentially, or unconsciously, and are activated to actuality by active intellect, as in the *De anima* of Aristotle the material intellect is activated by the agent intellect (what Grosseteste called the *virtus intellectiva*). For Grosseteste, sense knowledge plays a role in the activation of the material intellect. Sense perception is not the cause of knowledge, but rather is the condition by which knowledge is possible (I.18, 133–4). Discursive reason or conscious thought, *virtus cogitativa* or *virtus scitiva*, apprehends the intelligible form as a singular or individual, while the active or agent intellect, illuminated by *intelligentia*, apprehends the intelligible in its totality, as universal knowledge (I.18, 136, 164–5). In Grosseteste's philosophy, the active intellect is identified as the *virtus intellectiva*, in combination with the *intelligentia*. Grosseteste followed Averroes as seeing the intelligible form as formed by the *virtus intellectiva* in combination with the *intelligentia* (as active intellect), in unconscious thought.

In the *Commentary on the Posterior Analytics* (II.6, 17–21), the origin of the universals, or *principia essendi*, is inaccessible to cognition or knowledge, conscious thought, as they are the product of the *intelligentia*: they exist in an inchoate state as potentials, as in unconscious thought, and are drawn out from potential to action, in a possible or material state which is in the beginning passive and not active. The *principia essendi* are brought from potential to active in sense perception, which is the foundation for knowledge of universals, but not the cause. As knowledge of the thing itself is impossible, the thing-in-itself or noumenon, scientific knowledge is based on the universals, the *principia essendi ante rem*, which are elicited through sense perception. The *principia essendi* become the material for scientific demonstration, as science cannot be based on the corruptible and variable knowledge of singulars and particulars given by sense perception alone.

As human intellect does not have complete access to either the particulars of the sense world or the *principia essendi* that correspond to those particulars in intellect – because they lie outside conscious thought and perception – absolute knowledge and comprehension is impossible, mostly because of the corporeal instrument to which intellection is attached in conscious thought. In the *Commentary on the Posterior Analytics* (I.17, 38–45), it must be accepted that corporeal things are understood to the extent that they correspond to the *visus mentalis*, the mental vision of them. This vision is made possible by the *lumen spiritualis* of the *intelligentia* in the *oculus mentis*, in the same way that the *lumen solare* of the sun makes corporeal things visible to the corporeal eye. Intelligibles are more receptive of the *lumen spiritualis*, as they are not tied to corporeals, and are thus more visible to the *oculus mentis*. In the *Hexaëmeron* (VIII, IV, 12) of Grosseteste, "Our memory, when it has received and retained a memory form, is not always actually remembering," not always conscious. But "when it passes from not actually remembering to actually remembering," that is, when it has been activated by an agent intellect in the *lumen spiritualis* and becomes conscious, "it begets and expresses from itself the actual intellection or understanding that is in every way like to itself," as a representation in active intellect. Through intellection, the soul becomes aware of the intelligible in relation to the sensible in the process of perception, and it becomes aware of the relation between itself and the sensible world.

In the *System of Transcendental Idealism* of Schelling, conscious and unconscious thought operate in opposition to each other (Schelling, 1978, p. 210). Unconscious thought is a product of nature, following the physiological anthropology of Kant, while conscious thought is a product of freedom, following the pragmatic anthropology of Kant. Conscious and unconscious thought are combined in intuition, as the ideal and the real are combined in the absolute. The ideal corresponds to mind, the universal and freedom, while the real corresponds to nature, the particular, and necessity. Unconscious thought is a product of the real. In the absolute, the identities of "the conscious and the unconscious in the self" (p. 219), are combined, which are "the appearance of freedom," the ideal, and "the intuition of the natural product," the real. Unconscious thought is found in intuition, and the necessity of that which is inaccessible to mind.

In the *Phenomenology of Spirit* of Hegel, self-conscious mind is united with unconscious thought through the imagination. Unconscious thought "rises out of its unreality into actual existence," from the universal to the particular, through intuition and the imagination, "out of a state in which it is unknowing and unconscious into the realm of conscious Spirit" (§463) (Hegel, 1977). Unconscious thought is found in the unknowing, the universal real of nature. Unconscious thought is the basis of conscious thought, though unconscious thought is not completely accessible to conscious thought. The unconscious is differentiated from the appearance of being. The absolute, the unconscious real of nature, is a void in being, formlessness in the material substrate prior to the formation of the image in the imagination. It is "the night-like void of the supersensible beyond" (§177). Conscious thought is a product of the self-consciousness of reason in abstract thought, given by imagination, and sees itself as an other in self-consciousness, in being-for-self, as noted by Hartmann in *Philosophy of the Unconscious* (Hartmann, 1931, pp. 27–28). The abstract thought of reason originates in its being-in-self, in intuition or unconscious thought. In conscious thought, reason becomes differentiated from its other, as it sees itself as other to the real, to nature, and becomes aware of its own absence in nature, and other to unconscious thought.

Appearance unites conscious and unconscious thought. Appearance is a stage between understanding, or conscious thought, and essence or inner being, being-in-self as unconscious thought. As a being-for-self, appearance is a "surface show" (*Phenomenology of Spirit*, §143) (Hegel, 1977). It is the instrument of reason in the mediation between unconscious and conscious thought. The surface show as a totality is a form of universal, like the manifold of Kant, a product of the imagination and a reflection of the totality of inner being, as much as it can be represented. The object of perception in appearance, the "sensuously objective," is the negative of pure being. The supersensible world, beyond what can be known or perceived in unconscious thought, becomes the object of understanding above the sensuous world, in conscious thought. Supersensible being comes about through representation in appearance, as a mediating factor (§147). As a mediating factor, perception of appearance is a dialectic of the particular and universal in conscious and unconscious thought. The supersensible world, unconscious thought, is "an inert realm of laws" (§149), beyond the perceived world of appearance that only exhibits laws in "incessant change" in conscious thought and perception. The inert realm of laws is not entirely manifest in appearance, but only inconsistently, given the state of flux and particularity of appearance.

Through appearance, the supersensible world is accessible to conscious thought. Conscious thought is able to apprehend that which is beyond appearance, the intelligibles or principles which govern it behind the veil of forms. Unconscious thought is understood when "this curtain hanging before the inner world is therefore drawn away" (§165). Through self-consciousness, conscious thought apprehends unconscious thought, or inner being. Therefore "it is in self-consciousness, in the Notion of Spirit, that consciousness first finds its turning point," in apprehension, "where it leaves behind it the colorful show of the sensuous here-and-now and the nightlike void of the supersensible beyond" (§177), the dialectic of conscious and unconscious thought. All forms of conscious thought are abstract manifestations of spirit: the unconscious, in intuition, particular manifestations of the universal, manifestations of the archetypal in appearance. Spirit or unconscious thought unfolds in consciousness. Each particular form in conscious thought contains the germ or seed of the absolute or unconscious thought. Forms of conscious thought are "moments or vanishing quantities" (§440), ephemeral representations subject to flux and decay.

In the *Philosophy of Mind* of Hegel, unconscious thought is a "nightlike mine or pit in which is stored a world of infinitely many images and representations, yet without being in consciousness" (§453) (Hegel, 1971). The unconscious is found in nature or the real, as a germ or seed from which all qualities come into existence. Intelligence is a "subconscious mine," an undifferentiated universal prior to its realization as separations or differentiations, as discursive reason in relation to the intelligible in *nous poietikos*. The origin of the universal as a mental representation is found in the subconscious realm, the real of nature, inaccessible to conscious thought. It is through intuition that images which originate in unconscious thought are presented to conscious intelligence as objective representations of universals transformed into particulars. A priori intuition is a mechanism of unconscious thought, the content of which is presented to conscious thought in the form of images, through the mediation of language, as in Plotinus. The particular images presented to conscious thought in appearance in the *Vorstellung*, or picture thinking, are not the content of unconscious thought, but are rather a "plastic shape of an existent intuition of similar content" (§454, Zusatz), a representation or a copy. The universal unconscious of nature can only be apprehended through representations of archetypal forms of intuition that can only be known through representations in the particulars of conscious thought. The consciousness of a present objective form of intuition in appearance makes us aware of its unconscious source. Our identity in conscious thought, or our self-consciousness, can only be given as a representation, removed from the origin of conscious thought in unconscious thought. The influence of these philosophical ideas can be seen in Hartmann's metaphysical concept of unconscious thought.

Theodor Lipps (1851–1914) was a professor at the University of Bonn from 1877 to 1890, and a professor at the University of Munich from 1894 to 1914. He was a leading figure in academic psychology and an inspiration to Freud in the empirical science of psychoanalysis. Freud referred to Lipps in his letters to Wilhelm Fliess (Gödde, 2010, pp. 273–74) as an influence on his "metapsychology": the unconscious is the foundation of the mind, all psychic processes are unconscious, all psychic content is a representation, and conscious thought can be explained in physiological terms as a sense organ. In *The Interpretation of Dreams*, Freud cited Lipps as establishing the unconscious as the key issue of psychology (VII, F, "The Unconscious and Consciousness," p. 650), and establishing the study of the unconscious as a science beyond philosophy. Freud began with the thesis of Lipps that all psychical phenomena exist unconsciously. "In Lipps' words," referring to a lecture by Lipps at the Third International Congress for Psychology in Munich in 1896, entitled "The Concept of the Unconscious in Psychology" ("Der Begriff des Unbewussten in der Psychologie"), "the unconscious must be assumed to be the general basis of psychical life" (*The Interpretation of Dreams*, p. 651) (Freud, 1965). Conscious thought is a smaller sphere included within the larger sphere of unconscious thought, according to Freud. Every conscious thought has a preliminary unconscious thought. All mental states are initially unconscious, and some remain unconscious while others rise to conscious thought. The unconscious is "the true psychical reality," which is "as much unknown to us as the reality of the external world," and "as incompletely presented by the data of consciousness," in conscious thought, "as is the external world by the communication of our sense organs." As for Plotinus, human thought has complete access to neither the workings of nature nor the internal workings of the mind.

Freud later distanced himself from Lipps in the differentiation of conscious thought from unconscious thought, a differentiation that must be based in pathological as well as normal thought and behavior. "For what I describe is not the same as the unconscious of the philosophers or even the unconscious of Lipps" (p. 652). The fact that "the whole of what is psychical exists unconsciously" (p. 653) can easily be proven by "the observation of normal waking life." Dreams, neuroses, hysterical symptoms, pathological structures and pathological life must also be considered in understanding the relation between conscious and unconscious thought, and in understanding that there are two kinds of unconscious. There are the unconscious proper, which is "inadmissible to consciousness," and the preconscious, the excitations of which are able to reach consciousness. The excitations must pass through a hierarchy of agencies to reach conscious thought in a spatial or topographical model of the conscious/unconscious system. The preconscious acts as a screen between unconscious and conscious thought, and controls the relation between the two. Freud's concept of the preconscious recalls the concept of the relative unconscious (*relative Unbewusstes*) of Carl Gustav Carus in his *Lectures on Psychology*, in relation to the absolute unconscious (*absolute Unbewusstes*). The screening function of the preconscious recalls the "law of the threshold" (*Schwellengesetz*) of Johann Friedrich Herbart, where there is a threshold or limen between unconscious and conscious thought. For Herbart, unconscious ideas, though inaccessible to conscious thought, still have the potential to be effective, as for Freud.

Freud also cited Lipps' refutation of the "somatic stimulation of dreams" theory, arguing that dreams are not determined by external stimuli on the dreamer while dreaming. Freud argued that external stimuli do not compel a dreamer to dream, and that the unconscious mind in the dream state is capable of receiving and differentiating external stimuli, but has no interest in responding to them (*The Interpretation of Dreams*, p. 257). Freud referred to Lipps' criticism of the theory of somatic stimulation in Lipps' most influential work, *Fundamental Facts of the Inner Life* (*Grundtatsachen des Seelenlebens*), published in Bonn in 1883. Lipps was also well known for his aesthetic theory, in particular his theory of empathy (*Einfühlung*), the act of projecting oneself into the object of a perception.

The adumbrated philosophical concepts of Wolff, Baumgarten, Sulzer, Platner, Schelling, Hegel, Herbart, Carus, Fechner, Hartmann and Lipps, provide an important link between classical and medieval, Neoplatonic and Peripatetic, concepts of unconscious thought, and the Kantian development of those concepts (after Sulzer), toward the psychoanalytic theories of Freud and Lacan. The concepts of the eighteenth and nineteenth centuries are a mix of the philosophical and scientific, metaphysical and empirical, drawing from the classical and medieval traditions, while at the same time exploring new knowledge from empirical observation and laying the groundwork for the theories of psychoanalysis. Anticipations of the thought of Sigmund Freud have been noted throughout this and previous chapters; the following chapter defines the concept of unconscious thought in Freudian psychoanalysis.

7
Unconscious Thought in Freud

This chapter examines the role of unconscious thought in the formation of dream images, and in the distinction between the ego (*das Ich*, the I), and the id (*das Es*, the It). For Sigmund Freud (1856–1939), unconscious thought can be revealed through the analysis of the dream. The thought process in the dream is a *Vorstellungsrepräsentanz*, the *eidos* as a representation in *phantasia*, as in classical philosophy. Freud concluded that unconscious thought is necessary for conscious thought. In the concepts of the ego and the id, the psyche is divided into conscious and unconscious thought. The id as *das Es* (the It) in Freud's original terms suggests an "other" to the "I" (*das Ich*, the ego), as unconscious thought is other to conscious thought. Thus, for Jacques Lacan the unconscious would be "the Other." There is a dynamic transformation of unconscious thoughts to conscious thoughts for Freud, through the word-presentation (*Wortvorstellung*, *logos endiathetos*), as in Plotinus and Hegel, and unconscious dream thoughts are transformed into dream images, the residues of which become the subject of conscious thought, through the imagination (*phantasia*). Unconscious thought is seen by Freud as the basis of the psyche.

Freud's concepts of unconscious thought owe much to his predecessors, as has been seen, and to the classical and medieval philosophical traditions. Despite Freud's disavowals of philosophy and metaphysics as insufficient bases for the science of psychoanalysis, he was well-educated on the subjects, and used them to his advantage. According to William W. Hemecker in *Vor Freud: Philosophiegeschichtliche Voraussetzungen der Psychoanalyse*, Freud attended several philosophy courses taught by Franz Brentano at the University of Vienna between 1874 and 1876: "Ancient and Modern Logic," "The Philosophy of Aristotle," and three seminars on "Selected Philosophical Writings" (Sand, 2014, p. 141, n. 1).

Freud involved the dialectic of the image and the word in his formulation of the perception-consciousness system in *Beyond the Pleasure Principle (Jenseits des Lustprinzips*, 1920), *The Ego and the Id (Das Ich und das Es*, 1923), and *An Outline of Psycho-Analysis (Abriss der Psychoanalyse*, 1940). That which is accessible to conscious thought in the unconscious is the preconscious (*das Vorbewusste*), that which is capable of becoming conscious (*das Bewusste*). That which becomes conscious, from the preconscious, passes a "censorship barrier" (*Zensurschranke*) in what is now referred to as a "topographical" or spatial model (Gödde, 2010, p. 275). What passes to the conscious from the preconscious is not sustained in consciousness, but is rather only temporary and fleeting, as for Hegel. There is no permanent duration of consciousness or conscious thought: it is rather periodic, undulating, and sporadic. The unconscious is revealed diachronically in conscious thought. Conscious thoughts are given to the subject through perception, through images formed in the imagination in relation to language, the logos, recalling the imagination of Plotinus. In *An Outline of Psycho-Analysis*, "the process of something becoming conscious is above all linked with the perceptions which our sense organs receive from the external world" (Freud, 1949, p. 34). In the *Commentary on the Posterior Analytics* of Robert Grosseteste, sense knowledge is instrumental in the activation of the material intellect. Sense perception is the condition by which knowledge is possible.

Freud continued, "there is an added complication through which internal processes in the ego may also acquire the quality of consciousness. This is the work of the function of speech," as in the *logos endiathetos* of Plotinus, "which brings material in the ego into a firm connection with mnemic residues of visual, but more particularly of auditory, perceptions" (pp. 34–35). From the beginning the ego is seen as split: there is an ego given by perception in consciousness, and an ego given by language. In conscious thought the two egos are indistinguishable, as language works in conjunction with perception to actualize consciousness. Consciousness occurs through both thought and perception, and the device which distinguishes the two is called "reality-testing." Such a device in psychoanalysis is intended to distinguish between actual perception and dreams, fantasies and hallucinations, but the distinctions are not always readily apparent.

In *The Ego and the Id*, the ego is defined as the organization of mental processes, and the unconscious is defined as that which is repressed in conscious thought. Conscious thought is attached to the ego. Image formation and language are differentiated in the relationship to conscious thought. Image formation is a product of the unconscious, that part of the unconscious available in the preconscious (*Vorbewusste*), which is brought to conscious thought through perception. The inaccessible unconscious, "cut off from the external world," is dynamically repressed, though there is also a preconscious, that which is accessible to conscious thought in the unconscious, and that which is capable of becoming conscious. The theory of the preconscious can be related to the productive intellect of the Peripatetics, or *intellectus in habitu* or *intellectus speculativus*: the intellect that connects material intellect with active intellect, or conscious and unconscious thought. It can also be related to the *Schwellengesetz* of Herbart.

For Alexander of Aphrodisias, in the commentary on the *De anima* of Aristotle, active intellect is the cause of the material intellect, allowing the material intellect to develop in its ability to apprehend universals in abstraction. While the material intellect is corporeal and perishable, the active intellect is incorporeal. The productive intellect, the third intellect, leads material intellect to active intellect. In Alexander's *De intellectu*, productive intellect operates through material intellect in order to make material or potential intellect actual by "producing a state where thought is possessed" (107) (Alexander of Aphrodisias, 1990). The productive intellect corresponds to what Aristotle described as "the cause or agent which makes all things" (Aristotle, *De anima* 3.5.430a12) (Fotinis, 1979; Aristotle, 1952a). The intellect is passive in that it becomes all things, and active in that it makes all things. For Alexander, productive intellect "is that which is in its own nature an object of thought and is such in actuality ... " (*De intellectu* 107).

In order to be in actuality, thought must have itself as an object of its own activity. The productive intellect is "called from without," and "comes to exist in us from outside," because it is immaterial, and because it is itself an object of thought, as thinking "occurs through the reception of form" in perception. Actualized thought is able to separate the sensible object and the idea of the object as intelligible form, as it separates the mechanisms of discursive reason in material intellect or conscious thought from the role of the intelligible in perception in unconscious thought. Because of this, there must be something at work in thought for which "what it is to be intellect does not lie in its being thought by us," in unconscious thought. The object of perception, the sensible form, becomes an object of thought, the intelligible form, "by the agency of the intellect" (110), productive intellect as an agency of active intellect. The activity of intellect is to "separate and abstract by its own power objects of perception that are such in actuality" from the sensible object which accompanies the object of perception, and to define the object of perception as such. The activity of intellect is caused by productive intellect, which makes potential intellect capable of being active: capable of thinking, capable of understanding forms in perception.

Active intellect, unconscious thought, enables potential intellect to develop and come to completion, without being affected or "coming into existence through something else" (111). When potential intellect is developed and completed, it is capable of independently thinking objects of thought. Productive intellect leads the material intellect to actual intellect as intellect in *habitus*, in the same way that light makes potentially visible colors actually visible. In Alexander's *De anima*, the productive intellect is "the intelligible in act" (107) (Alexander of Aphrodisias, 1979), which produces the "activity of knowing" in material intellect, the self-consciousness on the part of reason. The productive intellect is not the intelligible itself, but actualizes the intelligible, by developing the *habitus* of the material intellect.

In Avicenna's *Liber Naturalis*, active intellect and material intellect are mediated by an intellect, which is both active and potential, *intellectus in habitu*; which is a state of preparedness for intellection in the participation of active intellect. The *intellectus in habitu* can be seen as the preconscious in relation to unconscious and conscious thought. It is a precondition for knowledge of both sensibles and intelligibles in material intellect, conscious thought. Material intellect progresses to the stage of *intellectus in habitu*, then to actualized intellect, in which it can be participated in by active intellect. *Intellectus in habitu* is capable of operating according to principles, *principia conoscendi*, while actual intellect is capable of operating according to intelligibles. Both the *principia conoscendi* and the intelligibles come from without, from active intellect; they are not properties inherent to material intellect. The memory of the principle or intelligible is not an actual memory, as principles and intelligibles are incorporeal, so a trace of them cannot be retained. A memory of an intelligible is actually the memory of the knowledge of the intelligible, not the intelligible itself, as it is reflected onto the *oculus mentis* in the illumination of the active intellect. Human intellect cannot possess the intelligible or the trace of the intelligible; it can only possess the knowledge or awareness of the intelligible, in its heightened state of functioning as material intellect in *intellectus in habitu* or actualized intellect. Conscious thought can only be aware of the presence of unconscious thought, through the agency of the preconscious.

In the *Liber Naturalis*, active intellect, *intelligentia agens*, as unconscious thought, illuminates sensory thought, material intellect or *nous hylikos*. Material intellect is a passive substratum of ideas: a potency in relation to the act of apprehending intelligibles, which is incorporeal. The active intellect is the giver and illuminator of forms; when received by material intellect, forms are particular and differentiated in sequential arrangements in discursive reason. *Intellectus in habitu*, as compared to the preconscious, leads from material intellect to active intellect. While intelligible forms are permanent in active intellect, they are not always accessible to material intellect or conscious thought, and in material intellect they are perishable. Material intellect alone is not capable of retaining concepts and abstractions. Sense perceptions have no permanence until they have been transformed into intelligibles, through higher intellection, involving the influence of the *intellectus in habitu*.

In Avicenna's *Shifā: Ilāhiyyāt*, the active intellect is the giver of forms. Forms emanate from active intellect constantly and eternally, but not as the result of any will on the part of active intellect; thus, unconsciously. Forms in active intellect are indivisible and perfect in their incorporeality, but matter is not capable of receiving them as such, because it is not properly prepared for them in its particularities and differentiation. Forms emanate as differentiated, in sequential arrangements of terms which are particular to discursive reason. Discursive reason or cogitative knowledge, conscious thought, is different from knowledge of principles or intelligibles, which requires the participation of active intellect in actual intellect. Cogitative reason is necessary to ascend from material intellect to actual intellect, involving the stage of *intellectus in habitu*, habitual intellect. *Intellectus in habitu* is a state, *nous kath hexin*, a state of preparedness for intellection, as in the productive intellect of Alexander of Aphrodisias.

Intellectus in habitu is intellect in action, *intellectus in effectu*; though not in constant action, only when turned towards active intellect. *Intellectus in habitu* operates according to first principles or intelligibles, in the participation of active intellect, when the intelligible is present in it, as illuminated by active intellect, in an acquired intellect, or an intellect acquired from outside human intellect, *accommodatus ab extrinsecus*. The *intellectus in habitu* leads to an actualized intellect, which is able to separate itself from the corporeals of sense perception and the mechanisms of material intellect, conscious thought. In the *Liber Naturalis* (6.5.6), knowledge of intelligibles necessitates the ability of *intellectus in habitu* to be joined with active intellect, through illumination, in order for the intelligible thought, *ipsum intellectum*, to be formed, in the combining of the sensible and intelligible. Intelligible thought is not always present to intellect or formed in intellect: it is present eternally in active intellect, unconscious thought, but its presence in actual intellect requires the development of intellect in *intellectus in habitu*. Through development in *intellectus in habitu*, the soul is able to conjoin with active intellect when it chooses to do so. When the soul is willing, the intelligible form flows into it from active intellect, in the capacity of actual or actualized intellect, made possible through acquired intellect, *intellectus adeptus* or *intellectus accommodatus* (*nous epiktetos*).

In his *Long Commentary on the De anima*, Averroes says that there are three separate intelligences functioning in the *anima rationalis* or the rational soul: agent or active intellect (*intellectus agens*); material or passible intellect (*intellectus materialis, intellectus passibilis* or *intellectus possibilis*); and speculative intellect (*intellectus speculativus*), or actualized or acquired intellect (*intellectus adeptus*). Acquired intellect is *intellectus speculativus*, making it possible for material intellect to be united with active intellect, as the preconscious unites conscious and unconscious thought. The *forma imaginativa* in the *oculus mentis* in the imagination is a *species apprehensibilis*, an intelligible form, but it is both corporeal and incorporeal, bridging material and active intellects, through acquired intellect or *intellectus speculativus*.

Intellectus speculativus is developed as the *oculus mentis* of the *anima rationalis* develops a vocabulary of images or *phantasmata* stored in the *imaginatio* or *phantasia*. The phantasm is corporeal, and potentially intelligible, as the material intellect has the potential to understand the intelligible. The sensible form can only potentially be an intelligible form if it is predetermined by the intelligible form. In the *De anima* 3.5.36 of Averroes (Brentano, 1977, p. 10, n. 49, 3.5.36, Fol. 178b), "this sort of action," of the active intellect, "which consists in generating intelligibles and actualizing them, exists in us prior to the action of the intellect," prior to the formation of the perceived form in *imaginatio*: in unconscious thought, as it were. The corporeal condition of material intellect acts as a substrate for actualized and agent intellect, the partially and completely incorporeal, only as a blank tablet on which letters are written. The corporeal presence of the letters, the sensible forms in *phantasia*, is predetermined by the writing of the letters, based on the idea of the letter, the intelligible form, which pre-exists the letter itself. The first principles of thought are given without an act of will, thus unconsciously. Union with active intellect, unconscious thought, is the goal of philosophy and the highest bliss in life, according to Averroes.

The preconscious of Freud can also be related to the *Schwellengesetz* or "law of the threshold" of Johann Friedrich Herbart. In the *Textbook in Psychology*, and *Psychology as a Science Newly Founded on Experience*,

Metaphysics and Mathematics, Herbart described ideas as products of representations, as for Johann Georg Sulzer, which are seen as dynamic forces, both conscious and unconscious. Obscure ideas are unconscious and distinct ideas are conscious. Unconscious ideas may become conscious ideas as they pass a threshold or limen in the law of the threshold. What passes from preconscious to conscious thought is not sustained in consciousness. The ego is defined as the organization of mental processes, and is the ground for conscious thought. The preconscious thought becomes a conscious thought when it is connected with word presentations or language. Herbart also developed theories on apperception. Apperception, as the cognitive combining of perceptions into totalities – following Wolff, Sulzer, Platner and Kant – is associated with conscious thought. As for Sulzer, ideas are the products of representations (*Vorstellungen*), which Herbart saw as dynamic forces of varying strength and clarity, above or below the threshold of consciousness. Ideas, like perceptions, are both unconscious and conscious.

Dark and obscure ideas, like dark and obscure perceptions, are unconscious; while clear and distinct ideas, like clear and distinct perceptions, are conscious. We have many ideas and perceptions of which we are not aware. But as unconscious ideas become stronger and clearer, they may break through a threshold and become conscious ideas; there is a threshold between unconscious thought and conscious thought. In the law of the threshold, unconscious ideas, though being below the threshold of consciousness, still have the potential to be effective. The clearest and strongest ideas break into conscious thought and apperception. Apperception then may retrieve more unconscious ideas to join the already conscious ideas, and unconscious ideas can join together to pass through into conscious thought.

According to Karl Eduard von Hartmann, in *Philosophy of the Unconscious,* Herbart saw unconscious ideas as being ideas of which we are not aware, and not able to associate with ourselves or our ego. Unconscious ideas do not function as representations as conscious ideas do; unconscious ideas thus have no capacity to signify anything. There must be a gradual continuity between unconscious ideas and conscious ideas as they pass through the threshold, a continuity that links the ideas from non-representation to representation and non-signification to signification. In that conscious ideas may retrieve further unconscious ideas, the continuity must be reciprocal, allowing for a continuous dynamic cycle.

In *Lectures on Psychology,* Carl Gustav Carus described the unconscious psyche as divided into the relative unconscious, predicting the preconscious of Freud, and the absolute unconscious. The absolute unconscious is the most basic biological aspect of mind; it is the basis of organic growth, and is in constant activity. Mental activity takes place in the relative unconscious, which is connected to conscious thought. The relative unconscious is the permanent repository for conscious ideas, the storehouse for memories. The relative unconscious is also where dreams are produced. Dreams are combinations of biological forces from the absolute unconscious and residues of images that are formed in the imagination, entering the relative unconscious from conscious thought. The relative unconscious is a threshold, as in the *Schwellengesetz* of Herbart, between the absolute unconscious and conscious thought; it is what can be revealed to conscious thought of the unconscious. Ideas flow back and forth as dynamic forces, as in the psychophysiological energy of Gustav Theodor Fechner in the *Elements of Psychophysics*. The psychophysiological energy of the nervous system causes unconscious sensations and causes them to emerge in conscious thought. In conscious thought, consciousness of world is given by the faculties of sense, in sense perception and sense-based reason, *nous hylikos*, or reason connected to pathos, *nous pathetikos*. The faculties of sense are connected to the dynamic energy of the nervous system, and continuously affected by the relative unconscious.

In the *Lectures on Psychology* of Carus, all conscious ideas and images at one point return to the relative unconscious, which retains them permanently, unless they return to conscious thought either as is or in an altered form. Conscious thought is never not connected to unconscious thought. The same mental functions that are found in conscious thought are found in the relative unconscious. An idea may go through the same transformations whether it is processed in conscious thought or thought in the relative unconscious. There must be a conscious imagination and an unconscious imagination, as there is conscious memory and unconscious memory. The conscious imagination is the reproductive imagination, and the unconscious imagination is the productive imagination. Perceived images and images in the imagination, sensible and intelligible forms, are stored and reproduced as memories in the imagination, as in the mnemic residues of Freud, and are subject to transformative processes in the relative unconscious.

Herbart's *Schwellengesetz* was developed by Gustav Theodor Fechner in his *Elements of Psychophysics*. While Fechner developed Herbart's concept of the law of the threshold between unconscious and conscious thought, he saw Herbart's cycle of continuity between the unconscious and conscious, and their integration in cognition, to be too dependent on metaphysical speculation. Unconscious ideas are dynamic forces as sensations and representations that lose their quality as unconscious ideas when they are understood abstractly in conscious thought, according to Fechner. There is a necessary psychophysical energy that causes unconscious sensations and causes them to emerge into conscious thought. The psychophysical threshold is an important basis for the concept of the unconscious. Fechner's study of unconscious thought had an influence on Freud.

For Freud, the ego in conscious thought is created by discursive reason in language. The ego in language, while it is the externalization of the subject, its being-for-self in Hegelian terms, is that which affects the subject from within language. As the subject develops in language, unconscious thought becomes more and more dominated by the stimuli of language, and the image making becomes indistinguishable from language to conscious thought. This would be played out in the thought of Lacan. Image making is repressed in the unconscious, except as its presence is made known as absence in the gaps in conscious thought.

The goal of psychoanalysis, for Freud, is to fill in those gaps in conscious thought in order to have access to unconscious processes. In *An Outline of Psycho-Analysis*, "we have discovered technical methods of filling up the gaps in the phenomena of our consciousness....In this manner we infer a number of processes which are in themselves 'unknowable' and interpolate them in those that are conscious to us" (Freud, 1949, p. 83). Unconscious thought is inaccessible, and can only be known in absence, in the gaps in conscious thought. According to Jacques Lacan, it was Freud's failure that he did not adequately recognize the gaps, holes and scotomata, in conscious thought, in the perception-consciousness system, as it is given by language. The science of discovering the principles of unconscious thought was the same, for Freud, as any other science: the subject of which "will always remain 'unknowable'," but which is reconstructed through scientific hypothesis. As in psychoanalysis, "the yield brought to life in scientific work from our primary sense perceptions will consist in an insight into connections and dependent relations which are present in the external world," which can be "reliably produced or reflected in the internal world of our thought and a knowledge of which enables us to 'understand' something in the external world, to foresee it and possibly to alter it." There is a disjunction between the whole of conscious thought and what is perceived.

Both conscious and unconscious thought are largely unknowable. For Freud, "the data of conscious self-perception, which alone were at its disposal, have proved in every respect inadequate to fathom the profusion and complexity of the processes of the mind, to reveal their interconnections and so to recognize the determinants of their disturbances" (p. 82). It is impossible to fully understand the mechanisms of our thought and perception through the use of our thought and perception: "in our science as in the others the problem is the same: behind the attributes (qualities) of the object under examination which are presented directly to our perception," behind the image alone, "we have to discover something else which is more independent of the particular receptive capacity of our sense organs and which approximates more closely to what may be supposed to be the real state of affairs." That something else would have to be metaphysical, though Freud renounced the metaphysical as an explanation for unconscious thought. Freud's observation reflects the tradition of the philosophy of intellect and the metaphysical concept of unconscious thought, the realization that conscious thought and perception are the products of inaccessible unconscious processes that allow us to think and perceive the way that we do.

In *The Ego and the Id*, Freud differentiated an unconscious idea or thought from a preconscious idea or thought in that the latter is "brought into connection with word-presentations" (Freud, 1960, p. 12): that is, language. The word presentations are described as residues of memories of auditory perceptions. This led Freud to the conclusion that only a thought which begins as a mnemic residue of a perception can resurface to consciousness from the preconscious, and that any thought arising from within the unconscious must be transformed into an external perception, through the memory trace, in order to become conscious. This is similar to Hegel's conception of picture thinking (*Vorstellung*) in the *Philosophy of Mind* (*Philosophie des Geistes*). The memory trace of the word is as the *logos endiathetos* of Plotinus in the formation of the intelligible form.

For Hegel, the images presented to conscious thought in the *Vorstellung*, picture thinking or representation, are not the content of unconscious thought, but a "plastic shape of an existent intuition of similar content" (*Philosophy of Mind*, §454, Zusatz) (Hegel, 1971), a representation or a copy of an intuition, a *Vorstellungsrepräsentanz* in Freudian terms. The consciousness of an objective form of intuition makes us aware that there is an unconscious memory of previous intuitions. The representation is a synthesis of the internal or intelligible image with the memory of the sensible image, as in the *Enneads* of Plotinus. A presentation is a synthesis of sensible and intelligible images, formed through language, as in Plotinus. In *Enneads* V.3.3, impressions are received by discursive reason from sense perception, with the help of memory. Discursive reason then performs analytical operations on the impressions from sense perception. The perception of a sensible object entails both the *eidos* of the object and the *eidos* of the intelligible idea of the object in unconscious thought (*Enneads* V.5.7). The ability to form the internal image, in Hegelian terms, is always accompanied by the logos (IV.3.30), a *logos endiathetos*, unuttered word in thought. The intelligible image is not possible without the linguistic expression of it, as in the *Vorstellung*. Perception of a sensible object is only possible after the idea of the sensible object is articulated in language in intellection, noetic or unconscious thought, in picture thinking. The intellectual act is not differentiated in discursive reason or perception; instead, it remains unobserved within, as unconscious thought.

For Hegel, when the sensible and intelligible image are synthesized, "the internal now has the qualification of being able to be presented before intelligence and to have its existence in it" (*Philosophy of Mind*, §453, Zusatz), as the image is presented to discursive reason for Plotinus. In the presentation in discursive reason or conscious thought, the intelligible forms of unconscious thought become "singularized and mutually independent powers or faculties" (§451, Zusatz), as the universal becomes the particular, the archetypal becomes the ephemeral. The form of the unconscious thought that is produced in the imagination and presented to conscious thought is a *Vorstellungsrepräsentanz*. Conscious thought is dependent upon images in the reproductive imagination. The reproductive imagination is an imitation of the productive imagination, as discursive reason is an imitation of noetic thought. In the process of recollection, the "first form of mental representation" (§455, Zusatz), intellect, "emerging from its abstract inward being," as noetic or unconscious thought, into "determinateness," as discursive reason or conscious thought, "disperses the night-like darkness enveloping the wealth of its images and banishes it by the luminous clarity of a present image," recalling the incorporeal light of Plotinus.

In Plotinus, imprints or impressions in Intellect are not connected to sense perception and are illuminated by an interior light; in the synthesis of the intelligible and sensible there is a double light shining on a perceived object, informing judgment in discursive reason and the mechanisms of combination and division in apperception, the same mechanisms that Freud attributes to the image-making power of unconscious thought in the formation of dream images from dream thoughts, condensation and displacement. As "actual seeing is double" (*Enneads* V.5.7) (Plotinus 1966) for Plotinus, the eye "has one object of sight which is the form of the object perceived by the sense, and one which is the medium through which the form of its object is perceived...." The medium, the intelligible idea connected to the imprint, precedes the perception of the sensible form, and is the cause of the perception of the sensible form. In normal conscious thought and perception, the form and the medium cannot be separated, and the medium remains in unconscious thought. In the *Commentary on the Posterior Analytics* of Robert Grosseteste, sensible objects are understood insofar as they conform to the *visus mentalis*, the mental image of them, the intelligible form, which is made possible by the *lumen spiritualis* in the *oculus mentis*, as in the intelligible light of Plotinus.

According to Hegel, intuition is unfolded as an image in imagination in three stages. The image enters into existence through the reproductive imagination, tied to empirical experience. The image becomes an idea or representation by association with other images, and then the representation itself takes on a pictorial manifestation. In the creative or productive imagination, the particular image is connected to the universal or intelligible idea through signs and symbols; signs and symbols thus facilitate the synthesis of conscious and unconscious thought. In the thought of Kant, the passive imagination reproduces empirical perceptions as they are recalled to mind temporally in a priori intuition. The active imagination produces an original representation of a sensible object that precedes experience, occurring in intuition rather than in empirical cognition. Perception of intelligibles in the imagination is a faculty of productive imagination, which would be unconscious thought. Passive imagination is connected to empirical cognition. Active imagination is a function of intellectual cognition, noetic thought, while passive imagination is a function of discursive cognition. Imagination transforms the categories of a priori intuition into the schemata that organize sense perception and discursive reason.

Appearances, for Kant, can be reproduced and reconstructed by imagination in a way that is not connected to empirical reality, as for Plotinus. Empirical realities are determined by the categories of space and time as they are manifest in discursive reason or conscious thought, but in imagination and unconscious thought, as in dreams, realities can be created from the representations of appearances outside the manifold that regulates conscious thought. The transcendental synthesis of imagination, from the synthesis of apprehension in the manifold, is the condition for the possibility of empirical experience and cognition, and the condition for the possibility of the reproduction of appearances by imagination. In his commentary on the *De anima* of Aristotle,

Alexander of Aphrodisias saw active intellect as the ground of material intellect. According to Themistius in his *De anima*, the active intellect perfects the material intellect. In the *De intellectu* of Abu Nasr Alfarabi, active intellect makes passive intellect possible. Going from potential to active intellect is going from what is known to what is unknown. In the thought of Avicenna, forms are provided by active intellect without will, unconsciously. Undifferentiated forms become differentiated forms in sequential arrangements, as for Kant and Hegel. In the thought of Averroes, the active intellect is incorporeal, and is the final entelechy or actualization of potentiality, as the modern unconscious is seen to be.

Freud concluded from dream analysis that "what becomes conscious in it," visual thinking, "is as a rule only the concrete subject-matter of thought, and...the relations between the various elements of this subject-matter, which is what specially characterizes thoughts, can not be given visual expression" (*The Ego and the Id*, p. 14) (Freud, 1960). The underlying nebula of thoughts is only given concrete existence in a direct correspondence with a word in language. Freud concluded that "thinking in pictures is, therefore, only a very incomplete form of becoming conscious," because mnemic images, whether in perceptions or dreams, cannot correspond completely to the underlying structures of unconscious thought from which they are derived.

Freud saw language as that which transforms unconscious thought into perception. "The part played by word-presentations now becomes perfectly clear. By their interposition internal thought-processes are made into perceptions" (*The Ego and the Id*, p. 16). There are no internal thought processes prior to perception; perception is the result of the intersection of language and image identification, and the thought processes of the image formation are then retroactively created by the intersection of language and perception. In the hypercathexis of the process of thinking, thoughts are perceived "as if they came from without." Ego is a product of perception.

The distinction between the image and the word, and the preservation of the image through language, is played out in the dream work described by Sigmund Freud in *The Interpretation of Dreams* (*Die Traumdeutung*, 1900), *On Dreams* (*Über dem Traum*, 1901), *Introductory Lectures on Psycho-Analysis* (*Vorlesungen zur Einfuhrung in Die Psychoanalyse*, 1916), and *An Outline of Psycho-Analysis* (1940). The dream is not unconscious thought, although it is seen to reveal the structures of unconscious thought, and only the memory of the dream can be analyzed, rather than the dream itself. The dream is seen as a mnemic residue of perception. The content of the memory of the dream is labeled the manifest content of the dream, and the product of the conceptual analysis of the dream is labeled the latent content, or dream thought, of the dream. The latent content of the dream is not a content of the memory of the dream itself, but something which is ascribed to it by conscious thought. Dream work is the process which transforms the latent content of the dream into the manifest content, the process by which the dream is generated from unconscious thought. The structures of both unconscious thought and conscious thought contain particular linguistic constructions, as both are languages, the relations of which can be found in the relations between images in the manifest content of the dream.

Freud saw a direct relationship between the dream thought, which is unconscious thought, and the dream content (image) as two sides of a piece of paper, and the transcription between the two is governed by a linguistic syntax, a complex system of rules which operates according to a logic which does not always correspond to conscious thought. The mechanisms of representation in the dream, as they are developed between the dream thought and the dream image, are different from conscious mechanisms of representation in the intersection of perception and language, although the mnemic residues of dream thoughts and images are derived from those of external perception, and the linguistic mechanisms of representation in unconscious thought are derived from conscious language. Unconscious mechanisms are seen as a variation of conscious mechanisms not under the control of conscious thought. The ego, conscious thought and perception, is always present in the dream, as the insertion of the perceiving subject into the unconscious mechanisms of language and perception.

Dream thoughts and dream content are, for Freud in *The Interpretation of Dreams*, "two versions of the same subject-matter" presented in two different languages in a transcript "whose characters and syntactic laws it is our business to discover by comparing the original and the translation" (Freud, 1965, pp. 311–12). The meaning of the dream is discerned from the unconscious dream thoughts, in their relation with the dream content. Dream content is seen as a "pictographic script, the characters of which have to be transposed individually into the language of dream thoughts." Relations between dream images depend on relations between dream thoughts in a syntactical matrix. There is no direct relationship between sequences of images in dreams and thought processes in the dream thoughts, which led Freud to a suggest that there is no unconscious thought per se, but only mimetic repetitions and reproductions of thoughts which correspond to mimetic reproductions of images in perception, the mnemic residues of such. Unconscious thought does not operate in a way corresponding to conscious thought; it is rather a primordial form of conscious reason, recalling the thought of Schelling, imitating excitations that are products of linguistic concepts, but whose excitations are not connected to any linguistic concepts of its own.

The mechanism of the transposition from dream thoughts to dream images in the process of dreaming is labeled *imagination*, and the "mental activity which may be described as 'imagination'" is "liberated from the domination of reason and from any moderating control" (p. 116). Dream imagination "makes use of recent waking memories for its building material," in mimesis and repetition, and "it erects them into structures bearing not the remotest resemblance to those of waking life." Dream imagination is "without the power of conceptual speech" and has "no concepts to exercise an attenuating influence," thus being "obliged to paint what it has to say pictorially." The linguistic structure of the dream image is seen as "diffuse, clumsy and awkward"; it is clearly missing the organization of conscious thought, while its forms are mimetic of it. Imagination "reveals itself in dreams as possessing not merely reproductive but productive powers," as in the productive imagination of Kant. Rather than just represent an object, dream imagination produces an "event" resulting from the involvement of the ego of the dreaming subject.

Dreams have "no means at their disposal for representing these logical relations between the dream-thoughts" (p. 347), or for representing logical relations between conscious thoughts, the relations created by syntactical rules. Dream images are compared to the visual arts in their incapacity to incorporate to any significant degree the syntactical structures of language. The desire on the part of the visual arts, in particular architecture, to engage as much as possible the syntactical structures of language, reflects the desire on the part of the arts to interweave image and language as they are interwoven in imagination. Dreams remain primarily a function of image-making, rather than language, in the projection of the ego in a pre-linguistic identification in primordial unconscious thought. Dream thoughts can be as complex as conscious thoughts, the different portions of which stand "in the most manifold logical relations to one another" (pp. 346–47).

As unconscious thoughts are brought into dream work they are fragmented, broken apart, and recombined, in displacement (*Verschiebung*) and condensation (*Verdichtung*). Dream interpretation involves the restoration of the connections between dream thoughts that the dream work has destroyed. There are dreams in which "the most complicated intellectual operations take place," but the dream only reproduces relations between thoughts, and not the substance of the thinking. This is not to say that conscious thought does not play a role in the formation of the dream; but it is not reproduced by the dream thought, although it may be apparent in the dream itself, the manifest content. Dreams vary in terms of how the relations between thoughts are represented, and how thoughts occur chronologically. Logical relations are often represented synchronically, or as "simultaneity in time" (p. 349).

Thinking does not occur in the dreams themselves either, according to Freud. Any thought processes which might be perceived in memories of dreams are only a representation of thought processes which occur in the dream thoughts, which are themselves a representation of conscious thought processes, in a *Vorstellungsrepräsentanz* – a representation of a representation. Dreams are thus "thrice removed from reality," as the visual arts are for Plato: forms which are copies of sensible forms which are copies of intelligible forms. According to Freud, the interpretation of dreams "is part of the material of the dream-thoughts and is not a representation of intellectual work performed during the dream itself." Thus, "what is reproduced by the ostensible thinking in the dream is the subject-matter of the dream-thoughts and not the mutual relations between them, the assertion of which constitutes thinking" (pp. 347–48). Dream images constitute a kind of façade, like the luminous embroidered veil in Plato's *Republic,* hanging between the finite and the infinite: between images which are mnemic residues of perceived images, and thoughts which, if they exist in the unconscious, are themselves mnemic residues of auditory forms.

The memory of the dream image enacts the same dialectic as is found in conscious thought, between what is perceived and what is conceived in imagination. Any thought activity represented in dreams is represented as having already been completed, according to Freud; so, thought activity, whether conscious or unconscious, is crystallized into a structure in the dream, made abstract, and made synchronic. A contradiction in a dream, for example, cannot correspond to a contradiction in a conceptual sequence which is a product of the dream analysis. The logic of the dream is independent of conscious logic. There is an approximation of a conceptual contradiction, though, to the extent that representation in mimesis would allow. Any correspondence between conscious conceptual structures could only be an indirect one. Dreams vary in the clarity of their correspondence with conceptual structures; some seem to correspond fairly clearly, which can be a deception, and others make no sense at all. Dreams appear to contain varying degrees of linguistic structures in relation to images as they are interwoven. Chronological sequences occur in dreams as imitations of chronological sequences in conceptual thought, but they have no logic of their own, and any correspondence with conceptual chronological sequences is an accident.

Diachronic sequences, as they are understood in conscious reason, may as a result be compressed into synchronic events or images; or they may be fragmented, or reversed, in a logic which might correspond to the dream image in relation to the linguistic structure, in the interaction of the ego of the subject and the linguistic structure in which it is participating, but which does not correspond to conscious reason. Because conscious thought is itself a function of language, it is not in control of the structure of the dream. Any logic which can be found in the correspondence between conscious thought and the dream is the logic of the linguistic matrix in which perception participates, what Lacan would call the Symbolic order, and thus the mnemic residues in dreams. Though the conceptual correspondence is arbitrary, the structuring of dream images as described by Freud corresponds fairly closely to linguistic structures. The dream can be seen as a mimesis of language. According to Freud, the rules of collocation in dream images correspond to the rules of collocation in language.

Dream images are distinct from one another in the same way that words are distinct from one another in the syntax of a sentence and the logic behind the combination is usually evident, one that corresponds to the logic behind syntactical structures in language. Dreams appear to obey the grammatical and syntactical structures of language in conscious thought, regardless of whether a sense can be derived from them which corresponds to conscious thought. Dream images operate independently of the dream thoughts that they are attached to, and any signification that they appear to produce is a product of their combinations as systems of differences in syntax. Dreams have no intention of communicating anything, so they produce no actual signification. Such communication would require a recognizable syntactical structure that corresponds to logic in conscious thought, which does not exist in dreams, despite the periodic correspondences and similarities which are reproduced in imitation of logical relations in conscious thought. Dreams are not unconscious thought, but they can reveal the mechanisms of unconscious thought, in relation to conscious thought, mechanisms of representation and presentation, which do not constitute the deviations from conscious thought that the dreams themselves present.

One example of the inability of dreams to correspond to conscious thought, in addition to the lack of distinction between the synchronic and diachronic, is the simultaneity of contraries and contradictions.

Opposite forms are combined into a single form, in condensation, or appear as the same form, or a form might be replaced by its opposite, in displacement, or represented by its opposite. There is no distinction between positive and negative, no sign of a conclusion that can be drawn from conscious thought as given in the syntactical structure of language. The same kind of reversals occur in dream images; the conceptual structure of the order of images has no importance that is discernible by conscious thought. Dreams display the *coincidentia oppositorum*, the coincidence of opposites, as in the Hegelian dialectic of becoming in reason, in the development from the particular to the universal. Representation in dreams, according to Freud, is often facilitated by replacement, as in the *coincidentia oppositorum*, or a condensation. In *The Interpretation of Dreams*, "When a common element between two persons is represented in a dream, it is usually a hint for us to look for another, concealed common element whose representation has been made impossible by the censorship" (p. 357) of the dream. "A displacement in regard to the common element has been made in order, as it were, to facilitate its representation."

The two principal mechanisms of the formation of dream images are displacement and condensation. Displacement is responsible for the fact that dream images do not correspond to conscious thought, and causes the dream to be seen as a distortion of logic, a deceptive façade. Displacement is a primary mechanism of both metaphor and metonymy in tropic language, resulting in a figurative or poetic signification that goes beyond literal function, introducing the presence of unconscious thought in conscious thought, through the gaps in conscious thought. Dream thoughts can be seen as a form of tropic language, combining conscious and unconscious thought. Condensation involves the *coincidentia oppositorum*, the representation of two contrary ideas by the same word or syntax, along with the diachronic combined into the synchronic, and "collective and composite figures." Condensation is the most active mechanism in dream formation, as "in dreams fresh composite forms are being perpetually constructed in an inexhaustible variety" (Freud, 1952, p. 30), as described by Freud in *On Dreams*. In condensation the dream image is over-determined by material in dream thoughts, or in the mnemic residues of visual or auditory perception. A single dream image may be the combination of several pictorial or linguistic forms, which have no apparent relation to each other. Condensation can be seen as a form of displacement, and thus as a mechanism of metaphor and metonymy in tropic language. Condensation and displacement are functions of the dream as a pictorial language.

Though, for Freud, there is a direct correspondence between the dream thought and the dream image, the construction of the dream entails a more complex relationship between thought and image. Through the mechanisms of condensation and displacement, "just as connections lead from each element of the dream to several dream thoughts, so as a rule a single dream thought is represented by more than one dream element..." (p. 32). The connection between the unconscious thought and dream image is not a direct one: "the threads of association do not simply converge from the dream thoughts to the dream content, they cross and interweave with each other many times over in the course of their journey." The displacement which occurs in dreams is responsible for distorting the "psychical intensity" of the thoughts that correspond to the dream images. The psychic intensity is described as the significance or "affective potentiality" (p. 34) of the thought or perceptual trace; the system of differences between the traces is a system of intensities as much as a system of signifiers; some images or words are perceived at a different level of intensity than others, and the variations in intensities are translated in the composition of the dream images. The variations are illegible in relation to any conceptual structure in conscious thought. Thus, "the psychical intensity, significance or affective potentiality of the thoughts is, as we further find, transformed into sensory vividness." The psychical intensity is seen as a *Lebenskraft*, a life force or vital power, as found in the theories of Carl Gustav Carus and Karl Eduard von Hartmann (Gödde, 2010, p. 276). Freud's understanding of unconscious thought was based on a dynamic rather than purely cognitive model.

As a result of the complex network of psychical relationships which produces the dream images, and the mechanisms of condensation and displacement, dreams are composed of "disconnected fragments of visual images, speeches and even bits of unmodified thoughts," which "stand in the most manifold logical relations to one another" (Freud, 1952, p. 40). The network of logical relations, which contributes to the composition of dream images, is too complex to be unraveled in dream analysis. In the process of the dream formation "the logical links which have hitherto held the psychical material together are lost" (p. 41). It is the task of analysis to restore the logical connections which the dream work has destroyed, as dreams are seen as the "royal road to a knowledge of the unconscious activities of the mind" (*The Interpretation of Dreams*, p. 647), a knowledge of unconscious thought on the part of conscious thought. Unconscious thoughts are revealed as images in the manifest content of the dream.

In that the dream is always a product of the thinking subject, or of the ego of the thinking subject, the dream is always necessarily in relation to the subject. Although the dream has no intention of communicating anything, it is a product of the relation of the subject to itself, a product of the insertion of the subject into language, and the intersection of the image and word in the definition of the subject to itself, its self-identity. The dream is a representation of the subject to itself as a construct of language subsuming the image, as in the Other of Lacan. The dream is the identity of the subject, the unconscious thought of the subject, speaking to the subject. The dream "behaves toward the dream content lying before it just as our normal psychical activity behaves in general toward any perceptual content that may be presented to it" (*On Dreams*, p. 49), unconscious thought functioning in the same way as conscious thought. The dream "understands that content on the basis of certain anticipatory ideas, and arranges it, even at the moment of perceiving it, on the presupposition of its being intelligible...." In the anticipation of the dream content by the dream, according to Freud, the dream "runs a risk of falsifying it, and in fact, if it cannot bring it into line with anything familiar, is a prey to the strangest misunderstandings." This is true of conscious thought as well: "we are incapable of seeing a series of unfamiliar signs or of hearing a succession of unknown words, without at once falsifying the perception from considerations of intelligibility, on the basis of something already known to us." This would be a key element of Lacan's theory of communication. Between the "floating kingdoms" of the signifier and the signified, correspondence only takes place in anticipation, what Lacan calls the *point de capiton*.

In the process of revealing both conscious and unconscious thought in the subject, "a dream that resembles a disordered heap of disconnected fragments is just as valuable as one that has been beautifully polished and provided with a surface." In the condensation and displacement in dream work, words and images are taken out of the context in which they are perceived in conscious thought, and they are freely recombined and substituted in the mimetic process. As opposed to conscious thought, the nature of which is to "establish order in material of that kind, to set up relations in it and to make it conform to our expectations of an intelligible whole" (*The Interpretation of Dreams*, p. 537), as in the Kantian manifold, dreams are not subject to such orderings, and produce both chronological and pictorial hybridizations, along with displacements and distortions of what is perceived according to conscious thought and perception. Thus, dreams are perceptions without conscious thought, with the same mechanism or underlying linguistic structure.

For Freud, then, "it is our normal thinking," conscious thinking, "that is the psychical agency which approaches the content of dreams with a demand that it must be intelligible," in the dream analysis, "which subjects it to a first interpretation and which consequently produces a complete misunderstanding of it" (p. 538). The production of dream thoughts must then be seen as external to the dream itself, as that which conscious thought projects onto the dream in the memory of the dream. "However many interesting and puzzling questions the dream-thoughts may involve, such questions have, after all, no special relations to dreams and do not call for treatment among the problem of dreams" (p. 544). The dream thoughts are not only external to the dream, but they have no particular relationship with it. The language of the unconscious thought is external to the unconscious image. Though conscious thought does not provide a direct relationship between dream thought and the dream content, there is a correspondence in dreams between the word and the image, given by the underlying syntactical structure of the dream. The mechanisms of metaphor and metonymy are in operation visually in dreams, in the transformation of mnemic residues of auditory perceptions to visual images, as in the *Vorstellung*, and *logos endiathetos*. Relationships between the mnemic residues of visual images are also transformed into auditory images in dreams, indicating the complexity of the dream that is so difficult to unravel, and the complexity of the relation between conscious and unconscious thought.

The mechanisms of condensation and displacement occur in dream images as they are transformed from the mnemic residues of auditory perceptions, and the images are combined and interwoven with straightforward transformations of linguistic structures, rendering them virtually impossible to translate. A manifest element of the dream might correspond simultaneously to several latent elements, and a latent element might play a role in several manifest elements (p. 318). As a result an attempted translation of a dream can never be literal nor follow a fixed set of rules given by conscious thought. The "precondition of intelligibility," and the precondition of association, must always be present for language to function. The same is not true in dreams. There is no precondition of intelligibility, because nothing is being communicated; and there is no precondition of association between images, because the mnemic residues have been disassociated and taken out of context from the structure in which they were perceived.

The linguistic structure of the dream is distorted from the linguistic structure of conscious thought, which makes understanding the dream in relation to conscious thought even more difficult. The dream thought, the unconscious thought, is unusable in analysis until it has been transformed into the pictographic image in the dream. Dreams, being a mass of composite structures of images, do not always reveal the dream thought. Dreams, for example, "feel themselves at liberty," with no intention of communicating anything, "to represent any element by its wishful contrary" (p. 353); there is thus "no way of deciding at a first glance whether any element that admits of a contrary is present in the dream-thoughts as a positive or as a negative." Dreams therefore often have the quality of "multiple determination" (p. 342) and can be subject to multiple interpretations. A dream might also have the quality of "over-determination" (p. 343), in a variation of psychical intensity, causing a disjunction between the dream thought and the dream image, called a "dream-displacement." Dream displacement and dream condensation contribute to the distortion of the dream image in relation to the dream thought. Dream thoughts that are over-determined or have multiple determinations have greater psychical intensity and are thus more likely to be transformed into dream images in the process of dream work (p. 330). Dream condensation is the product of the combination of logical syntactical relations between dream thoughts in the preconscious and unconscious mnemic residues of visual images (p. 635).

Freud's dream analysis, and psychoanalysis in general, established the importance of the relation between unconscious and conscious thought, and in fact established the primacy of unconscious processes in relation to conscious thought. For Freud, "the most complicated achievements of thought are possible without the assistance of consciousness" (p. 632). There is an unconscious thought, intelligible through dream work, that has similarities with conscious thought. The unconscious is seen by Freud as constituted by repression, as a linguistic mechanism, and by gaps in conscious thought. The structure of the Freudian unconscious is seen to contain the same internal differences and differentiations as does language in conscious thought. Mnemic residues of perception are already traces, presences of absences which are constituted in the dream. If the dream can be compared to a hieroglyph, then the pictographic script of the hieroglyph can only be seen as a trace, a mark which does not correspond to conscious thought, but which suggests the presence of conscious thought, as mnemic residues suggest the presence of auditory and visual perceptions, in memories of dreams. The psyche is thus seen by Freud as a space of writing, but it is a writing which is exterior and posterior to the spoken word, the auditory perception, as the word, the *logos endiathetos*, is exterior to the image. Perception is already an inscription, and there is a gap between what is perceived and what is reconstructed in the mind through the intersection of perception and reason; the gap manifests itself as the dream, revealing unconscious thought. The trace, the pictographic script of the hieroglyph, in both unconscious and conscious thought, is given by the dialectic of the image and the word: or objective and subjective spirit in Hegelian terms, Imaginary and Symbolic in Lacanian terms. It is the absence contained in the identification between the image and the word, especially as it contributes to the definition of the subject, and the role of the ego in language.

The dream is composed of the same network of signifiers in language that defines the subject. The subject finds itself in the layers of images in dreams in which the network of signifiers is played out. The optical model of the dream, in the intersection of the image and word, consists of layers in which unconscious thought is played out, as a reflection of the ego in imagination, in the mnemic residue of perception, the construction of which forms the subject. The layers of unconscious thought are that which is other than given by reason in perception in conscious thought or the ego. The layers of the optical model of the dream through which the matrix of language is filtered, in the form of the subject, are situated between perception and consciousness. The optical model of the dream is located between the mnemic residues of perception which produce the dream on the pictorial level, and the matrix of language that produces the subject in conscious thought. The subject is constituted in the layered apparition of the intersection of the image and the word, which is the locus of the trace.

A distinction between perception and conscious thought is necessary in order for the traces of perception (*Wahrnehmungszeichen*) to become mnemic residues, to pass into memory. The traces must be effaced in perception, in the temporal and particular mechanisms of experience, in conscious reason, and must be constituted simultaneously in the universal concept, in the categories of intuition or unconscious thought. The passage from perception to conscious thought is the passage from the particular to the universal, as in Hegel and the Neoplatonic and Peripatetic traditions, as given by unconscious thought. The passage begins in perception, in the particular of the mnemic residue. Both conscious and unconscious thought are implicated in perception, as in dreams. It is the mnemic residue which differentiates conscious thought from perception, which was the discovery of Freud in the analysis of dreams, and which renders conscious thought as other than the constitution of the subject. The passage from the particular to the universal, from the diachronic to the synchronic, occurs for Freud in the passage from perception to conscious thought, from the image (or *eidos*) to the word (as in the *logos endiathetos*) in imagination (recalling Plotinus), in which is found the constitution of the subject.

The *Wahrnehmungszeichen*, traces of perception, are transformed into a synchronic signification from a diachronic excitation as they become signifiers. The layers between perception and conscious thought are the layers in which the traces of perception enter language as signifiers, and the perceiving ego of the subject is objectified as the linguistic ego, as the Imaginary is objectified as the Symbolic for Lacan. The permeation through the layers entails a dialectical process of fragmentation and dispersal combined with unification and coalescence, as in displacement combined with condensation in dream work, in the interaction between image and word. Such a dialectical interaction is present in tropic language, in metaphor and metonymy. The mechanisms of language reveal the same interstice between perception and conscious thought in which the constitution of the subject is to be found. The definition of the subject between perception and conscious thought, as between the image and the word, is one of discontinuity in the lacunae or gaps which are present in language, revealing unconscious thought.

The image in the dream, the transposition of the mnemic residue of perception, is the *Vorstellungsrepräsentanz* described by Freud, the representation of the representation, or that which would take the place of the representation, according to Lacan, between perception and conscious thought, or unconscious thought and conscious thought, the gap in which the subject is constituted. The mnemic residue of perception disappears when it is inserted into the signifying chain of the dream and is replaced by the *Vorstellungsrepräsentanz*. The *Vorstellungsrepräsentanz* is that which replaces the absent subject (the absence of the knowledge of unconscious thought) in the ego in language, the void around which desire circulates. The *Vorstellungsrepräsentanz* is as the binary signifier in the metaphor, which in the process of condensation and displacement produces signification by substituting the name of one thing for something else, and an idea is formed in the combination of two names (Lacan, 1981, p. 276).

As the *Vorstellungsrepräsentanz* is the binary signifier in the metaphoric process of condensation and displacement in the formation of the dream, as that which takes the place of the representation, it is the supersession (*Urverdrängung*) of the signifier in condensation, between the image and word, which creates the point of attraction (*Anziehung*), through which the unconscious is momentarily revealed, and which creates repression in the *Unterdrückung* of the signifier, which is the

Vorstellungsrepräsentanz. It is that which occurs in the gap between the image and word, or between unconscious and conscious thought, which is repressed, through the *Vorstellungsrepräsentanz*. Signification occurs in the *Vorstellung* (picture thinking), while the representation occurs in perception itself. The thinking subject is unable to identify itself as an image in the context of its own disappearance in language. The ego, the mechanism of conscious thought, is itself an object, which appears in the world of objects – a being-for-self in Hegelian terms. Conscious thought, the self-identity of the subject with its ego, is defined as a tension between the ego that has been divorced from the thinking subject in its experience in language, and the perception on the part of the subject which is external to ego, the primordial object identification in unconscious thought, the Imaginary order of Lacan.

The *Vorstellungsrepräsentanz* is an intelligible, which is self-generating and self-supporting in intellect because it has entered into language. The internal perception of the *Vorstellungsrepräsentanz* in imagination is taken as the archetype of the perception of sensible objects, which is only ephemeral and given by the ego or conscious reason. In dreams, the particular quality of the image is that it does not correspond to the perception of the subject inserted into language, although linguistic structures are seen to compose the dream. The ego – in language, in discursive reason or conscious thought – is present in the dream: in the latent content in the dream, the unconscious dream thought, as revealed by Freud. Furthermore, the ego in perception is present in the dream, as images in the dream are products of the object identification of the thinking subject and there is a transformative process between the latent and manifest content of the dream, as Freud has shown. A difference between the dream and waking perception is that the interaction between the linguistic and perceptual egos, word and image, which constitutes the subject in conscious perception, is missing in the experience of the dream, as it has been transformed through processes such as condensation and displacement.

As the dream image is the *Vorstellungsrepräsentanz*, the representation of the mnemic residue, the connection between the word and image is lost between the *Vorstellungsrepräsentanz* and the mnemic residue, the memory trace. In the dream, the perceiving ego is not subsumed into and repressed by the linguistic ego as it is in conscious perception; the dream represents more of an equal partnership, given the lack of requirement for communication in the dream. Conscious perception is always in reference to the relation with the object identification of the perceiving ego, which is only a fragment or a residue absorbed into language in conscious thought. The dream image is a product of the relation between the thinking subject and language, but the structuring of the relation between the subject and the perceived object in relation to language, the image in relation to the word, as the perception is subsumed into language in conscious thought, is not present in the dream, or unconscious thought.

Images in the dream present themselves differently from images in perception. In *The Interpretation of Dreams*, Freud described dream images as competing in intensity and superimposition (p. 359), and color impressions are given hallucinatory clarity in relation to the mnemic residues (p. 586). As dreams are disconnected fragments of visual images, dream images do not appear in relation to the insertion by the subject of itself into the field; they are independent of the interaction between a representation of the subject and the *Vorstellungsrepräsentanz*, though the object identifications of the subject are present in the dream. The dream is not a product of perception, organized in relation to the subject. Seeing in conscious perception is impossible in the dream. The thinking subject is not able to apprehend itself in the dream in the way that it apprehends itself as conscious thought, in the relation between the image and the word that places the subject as a reference point in constructed perception in language.

In writings in the 1920s, in particular in *Beyond the Pleasure Principle* (1920), "Something about the Unconscious" (*Etwas vom Unbewussten*, 1922), and *The Ego and the Id* (*Das Ich und das Es*, 1923), Freud expanded his concept of the unconscious to include the elements of eros and the death drive, and dynamic relationships between the ego, id and superego (*Ich, Es, Über-Ich*) (Gödde, 2010, p. 278). These new elements constituted a more structural and dynamic, as opposed to topographical or spatial, metapsychology. Both systems are seen as a metapsychology, describing a complex of mobile psychical energy with instruments engaging in cathexes, investments of mental energy, and transfers through a network of representations, recalling the psychophysics of Fechner (Boothby, 2001, p. 4). The words used by Freud, *das Ich* (the I) and *das Es* (the It), as opposed to the Latin words in the English translations, suggest that the id is seen as an "other" to ego, alienated from it, as the id is inaccessible.

The concept of eros provides a link between physical and mental functions, while involving unconscious elements that challenge the control of conscious thought. The id is located in unconscious thought, as inaccessible and difficult to control, the source of libidinal and destructive impulses, with no organization other than the drive to satisfy instinctual needs in relation to the pleasure principle. It is not possible to have direct access to the id, as it is not possible to have direct access to unconscious thought, but only to its appearance in conscious thought, through dreams and symptoms. The ego is seen as a modification of the id in the development of the subject, including the development of certain control over the id on the part of the ego. The ego involves both unconscious and conscious thought. The superego projects the ego into the macrocosm of culture and universal ideas. Thus, the id and superego are forms of the ego in various stages of development, all constituting unconscious thought in the framework of conscious thought.

The Ego and the Id was written to develop theories presented in *Beyond the Pleasure Principle*. The fundamental premise of psychoanalysis is the division of the psychical into conscious and unconscious thought. The essence of the psychical cannot be found in conscious thought, but conscious thought can be seen as a quality of the psychical, a product of unconscious thought. The concept of "being conscious" on the part of the subject is deceptive, dependent on a superficial perception. States of "being conscious" are transitory, in relation to a more permanent condition of unconscious thought. The unconscious itself, as opposed to the latent preconscious or conscious thought, in that it is inaccessible, is described as dynamically repressed. While the unconscious is dynamically repressed, not all of it is necessarily repressed as a part of the ego can be considered to be unconscious. The ego constitutes a "coherent organization of mental processes" (*The Ego and the Id*, p. 8) (Freud, 1960), and is the ground for conscious thought, though part of the ego is unconscious. The ego is "that part of the id which has been modified by the direct influence of the external world" (pp. 18–19), through the medium of the perception-consciousness system. The ego attempts to influence the id with the affects of the external world, and attempts to substitute the reality principle of conscious thought and language for the pleasure principle of unconscious instinct.

In *An Outline of Psycho-Analysis*, the conscious perception of our thoughts or thought process, or self-consciousness, is momentary and transitory. Momentary conscious perceptions become conscious from the latent preconscious, all of which is capable of becoming conscious, but not all thoughts in the preconscious become conscious. Thoughts in the unconscious proper have little chance of becoming conscious, and therefore must be inferred and translated, as in the processes of dream work. The unconscious proper is "cut off from the external world" (Freud, 1949, p. 85), like the id, which is within the unconscious. Unconscious thought for Freud, as it is throughout the history of philosophy, is that which is inaccessible to conscious thought of itself. We have no hope of knowing the "real state of affairs" (p. 82), unconscious thought, because we are limited by the "language of our perceptions," conscious thought, from which it is impossible to free ourselves.

In *The Ego and the Id*, the preconscious thought becomes a conscious thought when it is connected with word presentations or language, as the intelligible is transformed into the image in imagination through the *logos endiathetos*. The word presentation is as the *logos endiathetos* as it is a mnemic residue of auditory perception or uttered speech, *logos prophorikos*. Only a thought that is a mnemic residue of a perception can enter conscious thought from the preconscious. In the *Vorstellung* or picture thinking of Hegel, images are thought by the unconscious prior to conscious perception. The existence of unconscious thought allows perception to be seen as the medium between the subjective and objective, between unconscious thought and language in conscious thought, in the same way that for Freud language itself is a residue of perception and it is that by which unconscious thought becomes conscious thought. The picture thinking of Hegel preserves the disjunction between conscious thought and perception; if there is unconscious thought, then reason in conscious thought "does not require, as does finite activity, the condition of external materials" (*Phenomenology of Spirit*, §764) (Hegel, 1977), as for Freud the unconscious is cut off from reality. Conscious thought is self-generating from unconscious thought and self-supporting; thus, it is only in the image (*Bild*) of conscious thought, which takes objective form in language through perception, that the form (*eidos*) in matter is possible, recalling Plotinus.

In the *Enneads* of Plotinus, "soul's power of sense-perception need not be perception of sense-objects, but rather it must be receptive of the impressions produced by sensation on the living being; these are already intelligible entities" (I.1.7) (Plotinus, 1966). The discerning of impressions printed upon the intellect by sensation is the function of conscious thought, not perception. Since the sensual impressions (mnemic residues) in perception are copies and derivatives of intelligible forms (forms conceived by unconscious thought), perception itself is a copy and derivative of unconscious thought. In *The Ego and the Id*, Freud concluded from dream analysis that picture thinking is an incomplete form of conscious thought, because the mnemic residues of perception cannot precisely correspond to unconscious thoughts, but through language unconscious thoughts are transcribed in some way into images in perceptions.

The coexistence of phonetic and symbolic or pictographic elements in the writing of the dream in dream work is the coexistence of the image and the word, and the coexistence of the mnemic residue of the visual perception, the image in imagination, and the mnemic residue of the auditory perception, as in the *logos endiathetos*. The visual residue is the "thing presentation" (*Sachvorstellung*, or *Dingvorstellung*), and the auditory residue is the "word presentation" (*Wortvorstellung*), as in the *logos endiathetos* of Plotinus, in the formation of the dream image, in a transition from the latent content to the visual image of the dream in a "concern for representability" (*Rücksicht auf Darstellbarkeit*) (Lacan, 1977, p. 160). The coexistence of the *Sachvorstellung* and the *Wortvorstellung* in the *Rücksicht auf Darstellbarkeit*, in the writing of the dream, is a "double inscription" (*Niederschrift*), which involves condensation and displacement. The double inscription also involves the coexistence of conscious images and unconscious or repressed images, which may be revealed in the preconscious, in the memory of the dream. The double inscription reflects the structure of language in the mechanisms of metaphor and metonymy.

The double inscription can also be seen in the dialectic of subjective and objective spirit in the *Phenomenology of Spirit*. As subjective spirit (the ideal, unconscious thought) becomes objective spirit (the real, conscious thought), subjective spirit or unconscious thought comes to be seen as reality, the inner being or being-in-self of the world that "relates itself to itself and is determinate," becoming "being-for-self, and in this determinateness, or in its self-externality, abides within itself ... " (§25). Subjective spirit is implicit in its nature as self-contained (*an sich*): it does not exhibit the qualities of the perceived object in conscious thought, of differentiation in the particular, until the initial doubling of itself as otherness or externality. Subjective spirit becomes objective spirit; but, as objective spirit it is immediately negated. Unconscious thought is negated in conscious thought. Thought becomes self-reflected in the object which is the product of its doubling, as all objects are given to conscious thought in perception through language.

Spirit becomes self-conscious through perception, or picture thinking. Perception consists of moments of thought "appearing as completely independent sides which are externally connected with each other" (§765), differentiated in discursive reason or conscious thought. Perception is the mediator between the ideal and the real, subjective and objective, universal and particular. Perception involves the doubling of the self-consciousness of thought, the "consciousness of passing into otherness" (§767). Absolute spirit is "the negativity of thought, or negativity as it is in itself in essence; i.e. simple essence is absolute difference from itself, or its pure othering of itself" (§769). As the subject enters into language, it is negated in the self-doubling of its conscious thought. For Hegel the division of the subject is synonymous with its formation. It is through the alienation (*Entfremdung*) of thought to itself that the subject discovers itself. In the Hegelian subject, existence (being-for-self) is set against nothingness (being-in-itself), which is not present in existence, or reality as given by language in conscious thought. Being-in-itself, subjective spirit, in unconscious thought, is synthesized into the dialectic of conscious thought, and in that way conscious thought becomes other to itself. Unconscious thought is the absence within conscious thought. The thinking subject is present in conscious thought only as an absence; conscious thought is only given by that which is other to it, unconscious thought, which is an absence. Memory in perception cannot establish presence in language. The presence of the subject is impossible in language, as for Lacan. The subject is objectified in language as that which is in the process of becoming, which is non-being.

Freud translated the self-negation of conscious thought in Hegel as a symptom of unconscious repression. In the essay "Negation" of 1925, the "content of a repressed presentation or thought can thus make its way through to consciousness on the condition that it lets itself be negated," according to Freud (Wilden, 1968, pp. 285–86). "The *Verneinung*," the denial, "is a way to take cognizance of what is repressed; indeed it is already a 'lifting and conserving' of the repression, but not for all that an acceptance of what is repressed." The Freudian unconscious is seen as being present in the Hegelian dialectic, in the form of repression as a symptom of self-negation, which is given by the insertion of the subject in language, in the objectification of conscious thought. The ordering of reality in the ego is possible with the entrance of the subject into language.

An example of this is the *Fort! Da!* Game, described by Freud: the gone/here game enacted by the infant to compensate for the temporary departure of the mother. As Freud explained in *Beyond the Pleasure Principle*, the interpretation of the game "was related to the child's great cultural achievement – the instinctual renunciation (that is, the renunciation of instinctual satisfaction)," in the unconscious id, "which he had made in allowing his mother to go away without protesting. He compensated himself for this, as it were, by himself staging the disappearance and return of the objects within his reach" (Freud, 1961, p. 14). In the game, the ordering of reality in language becomes a substitution for the instinctual displeasure which the infant feels at the departure of its mother, as well as the instinctual joy which the infant feels upon her return, or the anticipation of that joy. The departure of the mother is enacted in anticipation of the return in order to simulate the instinctual feeling in language. As soon as the linguistic game is constructed, the infant becomes a subject of the game, and the linguistic construction replaces the actual relation with the mother. Both the infant and the mother are defined as subjects by the network of relations that connect them and determine them in language, the ordering of reality, the Lacanian Other. Language assumes a primacy over perception. As the subject becomes redefined to itself in language, it loses its definition of itself in relation to itself in perception. The absence of the subject, the absence in language, is perpetually recreated in language, as in the *Fort! Da!* Game, in which is inscribed the trace of presence, the presence of the image of perception, in language.

Despite his desire to replace the philosophical and metaphysical concept of unconscious thought with an empirical and experiential concept of "the unconscious," the metaphysical concept of unconscious thought, developed throughout the history of philosophy, is clearly an important basis for Freudian ideas and plays a role in Freud's theories about imagination, perception, dream images, and the division of the psyche into the ego and the id. Jacques Lacan also insisted that psychoanalysis is not philosophy. According to Lacan, the premise of philosophy is that reason can understand itself (which is clearly not the case in the Neoplatonic and Peripatetic traditions), while the premise of psychoanalysis is that reason cannot understand itself. Nevertheless, there is an unmistakable metaphysical element to Lacan's theories, and important influences from classical and medieval philosophies of unconscious thought, interwoven with the Freudian theories of the unconscious, and structural linguistics.

8
Unconscious Thought in Lacan

This chapter examines the role of unconscious thought in Lacan's linguistic structuring of unconscious processes and in the definitions of the Imaginary and Symbolic orders of the psyche, and the Real. Jacques Lacan (1901–81) is considered to be the most important post-Freudian writer on the science of psychoanalysis, or the science of the letter as Lacan calls it. Lacan's concept of unconscious thought combines an analysis of Freudian dream work with an analysis of the structural linguistics of Ferdinand de Saussure. In this way Lacan was able to make a substantial development of Freudian psychoanalysis. Lacan's concepts also owe much to classical and medieval concepts of unconscious thought, in particular to Plotinus. For Lacan, the unconscious is language, the Other, so unconscious thought can only be conceived with the same linguistic structure as conscious thought. Unconscious thought is present in conscious thought as an absence. The mechanisms of the transition from the unconscious thought to the dream image in Freudian dream work, condensation and displacement, are the linguistic mechanisms of metaphor and metonymy. For Lacan, the Imaginary order of the psyche involves the role of the image or *imago* in imagination and sense perception; the Symbolic order is the matrix of language into which the *imago* is inserted, which is the unconscious. The Real is that which is inaccessible to both the Imaginary and Symbolic, and can be compared to the One of Plotinus, that which is inaccessible to *nous poietikos* and *nous pathetikos*, unconscious and conscious thought.

For Lacan, unconscious and conscious thought are interwoven, along with the Imaginary and Symbolic, in a Borromean knot. Because conscious thought cannot know itself as based in unconscious thought, it cannot know itself. It can only experience *méconnaissance*, misknowing. The resistance to unconscious thought is the same as the resistance of the signifier to the signified in language. The signifier represents the subject, and the subject becomes an absence to itself. Absence and presence oscillate in language, as do unconscious and conscious thought. The absence in conscious thought, the "gaze," is the source of desire, desire for the Other as a substitute for the missing subject or object, the *objet a*, in the impossibility of fulfillment caused by the inaccessibility of unconscious thought.

In the structural linguistics of Ferdinand de Saussure (*Course in General Linguistics*), the signifier is the phonetic sound of the word, as in the *logos prophorikos*, and the signified is the idea to which it corresponds. In *Écrits*, Jacques Lacan placed a bar between the signifier and the signified, the signifier placed over the signified, in the algorithm S/s (Lacan, 1977, p. 158), to suggest the identification between the signifier and the signified defined by Saussure, but at the same time to suggest the inaccessibility of the signifier to the signified, the inaccessibility of language to the ideas that it is purported to communicate. The algorithm is designed to suggest the inaccessibility of conscious thought to unconscious thought. According to Jean-Luc Nancy and Philippe Lacoue-Labarthe in *The Title of the Letter: A Reading of Lacan*, "Lacan introduces a resistance such that the crossing of the bar, the relation of the signifier to the signified, in short, the production of signification itself, will never be self-evident" (Nancy and Lacoue-Labarthe, 1992, p. 36). Lacan denied the possibility of a direct or pre-inscribed relation between the signifier, the phonetic unit, and the signified, the idea, which is the picture thought (as in the *Dingvorstellung* of Freud) or the word presentation (as in the *Wortvorstellung* of Freud or *logos endiathetos* of Plotinus) in imagination.

The signifier can only represent the subject as a signifier in language to another signifier; it represents the insertion of the speaking subject into the network of signifiers that constitute signification in language. The sliding (*glissement*) of the signifier across the bar, where the bar between signifier and signified is not crossed, constitutes an endless system of differences between signifiers alone, and a deferral of "meaning," as in the *différance* of Derrida. Meaning can only be present as absence, as unconscious thought can only be present as absence in conscious thought. The absence of the signified plays the role of the object of desire, the *objet a*, in the signifying chain, the void around which conscious reason circulates, which is the unconscious. The absence of the signified is the absence of the thinking subject itself, which is present in every signifier as it is present in language.

Desire in the signifying chain necessitates the trace of absence. Without the trace of absence, neither the desire nor the process of signification would exist. The desire is found in metonymy in tropic language, where the bar between signifier and signified is not crossed, and signification is constantly deferred. Metaphor, in the operation of substitution and the eliding of the second signified, enacts desire in the substitution of the signified for the signifier, the substitution of the idea for the word. The object of desire in the metonym is the lack of being, the absence in signification. The signifying chain is a mechanism of deferral. Metaphor and metonymy are the principal mechanisms that constitute the matrix of operational rules that determine language and unconscious thought. The elision of the signified in the process of signification is seen as distortion (*Enstellung*) in the translation of unconscious thought into dream images and language. The metaphoric process is a condensation (*Verdichtung*), the metonymic process is a displacement (*Verschiebung*), and the translation of images into language is a process of representation (*Rücksicht auf Darstellbarkeit*), in the terms of Freudian dream work.

The bar between the signified and signifier reifies the presence of the subject in signification, as that absence which is present in every signifier. Language produces the subject, rather than the subject producing language. But the subject is impossible as soon as it enters into language, because the subject is immediately divided between the idea (image, *eidos*) and the word. The subject is only possible in language, and as soon as that possibility is realized in signification, the subject becomes impossible, because of the inaccessibility of the signifier to the signified, the premise of the presence of the subject. As the presence of the absence in the signifier, the subject fades into the signifier; and, as the subject can only be represented by a signifier to another signifier, it cannot be present in the process of signification, the sliding of signifiers above the bar of the signified. "Through the word," then, "already a presence made of absence – absence itself gives itself a name ... " (*Écrits, A Selection*, p. 65) (Lacan, 1977).

As the subject enters language as a negation and is divided by the process of signification, the subject is self-alienated in language, in its participation in the "symbolic order." The subject is self-alienated in the division between the word and the idea, between sensible reality as perceived and the representation of reality in that perception in language. The subject can only participate in language as divided, as being both present and absent, and absent in its presence. The subject is an effect of language; the self-representation of the subject in language or picture thinking is a masking of the impossibility of the presence of the subject, as conscious thought is a masking of the impossibility of the presence of unconscious thought. The subject finds identification in the play of signification in language, caught in the representation of signifier to signifier.

Signification can only occur retroactively in the play of signifiers, at the "anchoring point" (*point de capiton*), which is the point at which the subject inserts itself into language, as an absence. The being of the subject entails a lack of self-knowledge, as it is impossible for conscious thought to know itself or unconscious thought. The division of the subject from itself, between conscious thought and unconscious thought, in its representation in language, is perpetuated by language. The production of signification in the play of signifiers in representation in language is defined by Lacan as *signifiance*, which refers not to significance or signification, but to the operation of signification, which is the *glissement* of the signifier above the bar between signifier and signified; it is a signification which "makes signification possible" (*The Title of the Letter*, p. 62) (Nancy and Lacoue-Labarthe, 1992). The key element of *signifiance* is the transformation of the signified into the signifier.

The signifier initially resists the possibility of signification, and posits the bar between signifier and signified. In the metonym, the bar is maintained between signifier and signified; the signifiers slide along the bar, and the elided signified is present as absence, in the nonsensical aspect of the metonym. In the metaphor, the bar is crossed in the elision of the second signified, in the presence of an absence in relation to the chain of signifiers, which allows the chain of signifiers to create signification. The crossing of the bar is constituted by the substitution of one signifier for another and the elision of the proper signified. It is thus a process of negation, in particular the negation of the subject in language. Substitution in metaphor renders "signification inaccessible to the conscious subject," according to Lacan (*Écrits, A Selection*, p. 166), while metonymy enacts a perpetual desire for that which is elided. "The signifying game between metonymy and metaphor" is "there where I am not, because I cannot situate myself there."

The result is "the radical excentricity of the self to itself with which man is confronted" (p. 171), the excentricity of conscious thought to unconscious thought. The gap (*écart*) which has been identified in signification in language is associated with a gap or tearing in the subject (*s'écarte*), and that which is torn away (*écartelé*) within the subject. Signification is only possible with the presence of absence, which is unconscious thought. Language is the product of a subject that is not present to itself, that is dictated by unconscious processes, while the conscious subject is a product of language. The conscious subject is assured of its presence in language even by its absence.

In the *Of Grammatology* of Jacques Derrida (1930–2004), *différance* is like *glissement*, the system of differences of the signifier that prevents a relation to the signified. Signification in *différance* is described by Derrida as a supplement, filling in for the absence which desire seeks to overcome in presence. All expression, in language and art, is a supplement designed to fill a void, the gap in conscious thought and the inaccessibility of unconscious thought. Representation in writing "claims to be presence and the sign of the thing itself," but the substitute for the sign makes "itself pass for the plenitude of speech whose deficiency and infirmity it nevertheless only *supplements*" (Derrida, 1976, p. 144). It is the task of artistic expression not to conceal its role as supplement, not to conceal the presence of unconscious thought in conscious thought. In order to reveal itself as supplement, the art form must contain both presence and absence, and must contain the resistance of the signifier to the signified, in the disjunction between conscious and unconscious thought. Such is the difference between literal speech and figurative, tropic speech, the absence of the signified, and the presence of unconscious thought as absence. Figurative speech is necessary as the enactment of desire in reason, and it is always supplemental.

The supplement represents both a presence and an absence, the absence that it is designed to replace. The sign in language is a supplement, and it contains both presence and absence, the absence of the thing that it represents in signification. Language as presence denies the possibility of the presence of that which it represents, the object in perception. Figurative language, and figurative forms in art, reintroduce the presence of the elided object in representation as absence, the absence created by the representation. The supplement contains "the power of substitution" that "always has the form of the sign" (p. 147). Language is a supplement as "the regulated substitution of signs for things" (p. 149), but it is impossible to know that which is supplemented, just as it is impossible to know unconscious thought. Supplement is generated by the unconscious desire for which there is no object available. Supplement is "representation in the abyss of presence" (p. 163), desiring the absence of unconscious thought, and "the desire of presence is…born from the abyss…of representation, from the representation of representation," the *Vorstellungsrepräsentanz* of Freud. Presence is the absence of *différance*, according to Derrida (p. 166); *différance* is thus a mechanism of unconscious thought, being other than conscious thought. Being neither presence nor absence, it is structure as supplement "within which one can only shape or shift the play of presence or absence…" (p. 167).

The structure of the relationship between the signifier and another signifier in the signifying chain in the *signifiance* of Lacan is the structure of the subject: thus, "a signifier is that which represents the subject for another signifier" (*Écrits, A Selection*, p. 316). The subject is always present in the signifying chain, but only present as an absence. The presence of the subject is the void of being in the signifying chain; the subject is present as "excentric" to itself in the supplement of representation. In psychoanalysis, "it is the subject who introduces division into the individual..." (p. 80), and it is the goal of psychoanalysis to formulate the structure of the identity of the disjunctive subject. The first principle in psychoanalysis is the identification of the deception of consciousness of the subject in relation to the identity of the individual. The consequence is the revealing of the presence of unconscious thought in conscious thought.

Freud's discovery of unconscious thought as the other in conscious thought "brought within the circle of science the boundary between the object and being that seemed to mark its outer limit" (p. 175): according to Lacan, the absence that constitutes the other in conscious thought. One purpose of this book is to show that unconscious thought has been present as an other in conscious thought throughout the history of Western philosophy. Language is defined by Lacan as a self-enclosed system with gaps or absences within that reveal a connection to what is other to it, unconscious thought. What is exterior to language is not revealed in the function of language, nor in conscious thought. The dialectic of the signified and signifier in the structural linguistics of Saussure occurs in the dialectic of the synchronic and diachronic in Saussure's distinction between language and speaking, *langue* and *parole*. According to Saussure, "synchronic linguistics will be concerned with the logical and psychological relations that bind together coexisting terms and form a system in the collective mind of speakers," or *langue*, while "diachronic linguistics, on the contrary, will study relations that bind together successive terms not perceived by the collective mind but substituted for each other without forming a system," or *parole* (*Course in General Linguistics*, pp. 99–100) (Saussure, 1966).

The structure of language is synchronic, manifest in universal laws, while the diachronic occurs as a result of what is imposed upon language from without, manifest in particular events. Speech is seen as the conscious use (*parole*) of unconsciously determined structures (*langue*). According to Lacan, "if the algorithm S/s with its bar is appropriate, access from one to the other cannot in any case have a signification" (*Écrits, A Selection*, p. 152). Relations between signifiers consist of "reciprocal encroachments and increasing inclusions" as differential elements in a closed system. The relation between signifier and signified is always anticipated and inferred but never actualized, always deferred. The result is the *glissement* of the signifier, as in metaphor and metonymy. The unconscious, which only exists as an absence in conscious discourse, is the axis between the signifier and the signified, or the bar that prevents their connection.

The Imaginary of Lacan, the perceiving ego, the subject identity in image, is prior to the Symbolic, the subject identity in language, in the formation of the psyche. The formation of the Imaginary occurs during what Lacan calls the "mirror stage," when a child between six and eighteen months old is able to identify itself as the image that it is looking at in a mirror. The role of the Imaginary in the psyche, the formation of conscious and unconscious images, involves the intervention of the perceiving subject in the world around it. Image formation involves the role of the ego, the self-perception of the subject, which is determined by the Symbolic, the function of language. Similarly, image formation in the *phantasia* of Plotinus was facilitated by the *logos endiathetos*. The Imaginary of Lacan, the perception of the image, is only given to the subject as interwoven in the Symbolic, in the matrix of language which is the Other, or the Lacanian unconscious. The Imaginary and the Symbolic are always interwoven, in conscious and unconscious thought. The experience of the mirror stage also constitutes a fundamental disjunction between the two, which can never be overcome, and which causes a gap within the subject, as it is constituted by the image and the word. This is the fundamental problem for Lacanian psychoanalysis.

The ego is formed in the Imaginary image of the self in the mirror stage prior to the development of the subject in relation to the Other, which is defined by Lacan as the network of identifications which determine the subject in interpersonal relations. The image of the self formed by the mirror must be reconciled with the image of the self formed in relation to language and other people, which is an impossible reconciliation. Perception is a dialectic of the Imaginary and Symbolic, the image and the conceptual framework in which the image is perceived. The development of the child in the mirror stage is the passage from behavior based on object identification which is not regulated by any kind of conscious logic to the insertion of the subject into the Symbolic order, language, where the object identifications are reconciled with unconscious conceptual structures. The Imaginary ego, the experience and formation of images, is prior to the Symbolic, and thus neither depends on the self-identification of the subject as a body, nor on a conceptual order. The subject is determined by the Imaginary ego – picture thinking or image formation in the imagination, and by the Symbolic – the use of language. According to Lacan in *Seminar I*, "if we must define that moment in which man becomes human, we would say that it is at that instant when, as minimally as you like, he enters into a symbolic relationship" (Jameson, 1988, p. 90). The subject is formed when language is gained, and the subject is defined in the inability of conscious reason to know itself in language, the inability of Hegelian being-for-self, the objectification in language in conscious thought, to access being-in-self, unconscious thought. The Imaginary is absorbed into the constitution of the subject, as the other of conscious thought in language, the lost totality of Hegel. The division of the subject is preserved in language use. The subject is divided when it enters into language in the form of a representative pronoun, as the signifier resists the signified from crossing the bar of signification in language.

The signifier "I," pronoun, becomes representative of or a substitute for the subject, while the subject disappears under the bar. The subject is excluded from the signifying chain at that point that it is represented in it, as the signifier represents the subject for another signifier. The subject is divided in language, and is represented by its own absence, which is the elided signified, which is the presence of the unconscious. The subject is defined by language, which at the same time assures its non-being. The presence of the unconscious as absence in conscious thought is given by language, so the unconscious is constituted by language as well. The distinction between *langue* and *parole* is the distinction between the unconscious and conscious subject, and the structure of its division. Unconscious thought appears through the primary repression of language. As the subject is inserted into language, it is inserted into the Other, which is the shared system of laws that language produces. If the unconscious is structured by language, according to Lacan, then unconscious thought is the discourse of the Other.

The subject is subverted in its subordination to the signifier in language, which is a function of the Other, which is the discourse of unconscious thought. It is unconscious thought, as absence in the signifying chain of language, to which the subject is subverted, the subject as it is known to itself as represented in language. All forms of human expression are unfolded within the framework of the Other, because the Other is established by language. The concept of the Other was inherited by Lacan from the structural anthropology of Claude Lévi-Strauss, who saw society as "an ensemble of symbolic systems, in the first rank of which would be language, marriage-rules, economic relations, art, science, religion" (Lévi-Strauss, 1950, p. xix; Dews, 1987, p. 74), placing importance on interpersonal relations in the definition of the subject in society. The Other assumes predominance over instinct as the Symbolic assumes predominance over the Imaginary, and conscious thought assumes predominance over the unconscious. The Symbolic, though, is ultimately irreducible to human experience. In *Seminar II* of Lacan, language is "constituted in such a way as to found us in the Other, while radically preventing us from understanding him" (Dews, 1987, p. 79), according to Lacan.

The "L-schema" of Lacan is a diagram which represents the quadrature of the subject: the ego, the unconscious subject, the Other, and the other (perceived object). The relation between the subject as ego and the other is an Imaginary relation, a relation of identification in conscious desire, but that relation is determined by the relation between the unconscious subject and the Other, or language. Individual conscious thought is shown to be determined by unconscious thought, and the subject is shown to be a product of language. The desiring relation of the ego to the other is seen as *parole*, or enunciation, individual speech in language, a function of the ego as representative of the subject in language, in the use of the pronoun as signifier. *Parole* is intersected by *langue* in language in the same way that the conscious desire of the subject as ego is intersected by the discourse of the Other in unconscious thought. The ego projects itself onto the other, the perceived object, in desire, and it seeks a reinforcement of itself in a response from the other. Beyond the identification of the projection of the ego as representative of the subject in language, it is impossible to know what the significance of the desire of the ego for the other is for the subject, as it is a product of the unconscious. The ego is an Imaginary ego, but the Imaginary has been subsumed by the Symbolic, by the reformulation of the subject through insertion in the mirror experience and the Symbolic order.

The resistance of the conscious ego to the unconscious is the resistance of the signifier to the signified. It is also impossible for the ego to know what the other is, as the thing-in-itself, because the other is already constituted by the Symbolic. In *Seminar II* of Lacan, the reality of the subject is thus not in the ego, but in the unconscious, and "in the unconscious, excluded from the system of the ego, the subject speaks" (Lacan, 1991, p. 58). The reality of the subject in unconscious thought exceeds the reality of the subject as ego in conscious thought: "If this *I*," speaking subject, "is in fact presented to us as a kind of immediate given in the act of reflection by which consciousness grasps itself as transparent to itself," in self-consciousness, "for all that, nothing indicates that the whole of this reality...would be exhausted by this" (p. 6). Conscious thought cannot know itself. The reality beyond language in conscious thought is given by the absences in language, the gaps and scotomata that reveal unconscious thought.

Language is complicit with both conscious thought and perception in its representation of the subject as ego, in its totality as that which is represented by language. In *Écrits*, "Freud seems suddenly to fail to recognize the existence of everything that the ego neglects, scotomizes, misconstrues in the sensations that make it react to reality" in the perception-consciousness system, "everything that it ignores, exhausts, and binds in the significations that it receives from language..." (*Écrits, A Selection*, p. 22). This is "a surprising *méconnaissance*," misknowing, "on the part of the man who succeeded by the power of his dialectic in forcing back the limits of the unconscious." The *méconnaissance* or misknowing is surprising to Lacan because it is Freud himself who drew attention to those gaps and scotomata, in the form of jokes, puns, neologisms, slips of the tongue, etc.

The diachronic differentiation of signifiers, the *glissement* in the signifying chain in language, the "vector of enunciation," is intersected by the relation between the elided subject in signification, the signified, and the ego ideal, or the identification of the ego with the Other. This relation is predicated by the Other, the network of signifiers in which the subject is able to form an identity. The point at which the elided subject is identified is the point at which the line of the relation between elided subject and ego ideal is intersected by the vector of enunciation, which occurs retroactively in the signifying chain, in anticipation of signification, as the *point de capiton*. "The diachronic function of this anchoring point is to be found in the sentence, even if the sentence completes its signification only with its last term, each term being anticipated in the construction of the others, and, inversely, sealing their meaning by its retroactive effect" (p. 303).

Signification is never present in the signifying chain: it only exists as retroactive anticipation, the point at which the subject inserts itself into the *glissement* of signifiers, which is the point at which the absence of the subject is revealed, unconscious thought in conscious thought. The anchoring point is the *point de capiton*, in the metaphoric chain, the point at which the bar between the signifier and signified is crossed. The vector of the relation between the elided subject and the ego ideal is a Symbolic vector in the L-schema, a vector rooted in the unconscious, in image identification subsumed in language, so the crossing of the bar is along the Imaginary vector. Every act of speech must be supported by a self-conception of the subject in the insertion of the subject into language as ego ideal, in relation to the Other (unconscious thought), but the subject can never be realized, as it is always an expectation, a becoming being in Hegelian terms. "This is a retroversion effect by which the subject becomes at each stage what he was before and announces himself – he will have been – only in the future perfect tense," according to Lacan (p. 306).

This makes it impossible for the subject to recognize itself in language as other than ego ideal, because the subject is in part the elided subject in the *glissement* of signifiers, and only occurs as absence after the fact. "At this point the ambiguity of a failure to recognize that is essential to knowing myself (*un méconnaître essentiel au me connaître*) is introduced." In relation to the other, "in this 'rear view' (*rétrovisée*), all that the subject can be certain of is the anticipated image coming to meet him that he catches of himself in his mirror," the Imaginary vector between the elided subject and the ego ideal, which announces the absence of the subject in language, and the presence of unconscious thought, but bars the subject from its own absence as unconscious thought.

In the absence of the elided subject in language, "he cannot fail to recognize that what he desires," in the vector of enunciation, along which flows the desire of the ego for the other, "presents itself to him as what he does not want, the form assumed by the negation in which the *méconnaissance* of which he himself is unaware is inserted," a "*méconnaissance* by which he transfers the permanence of his desire to an ego that is nevertheless intermittent," as conscious thought, "and, inversely, protects himself from his desire by attributing to it these very intermittences" (pp. 312–13). The vector of enunciation intersects with the vector of the relation between the elided subject and the ego ideal, and the result is that in the *glissement* the elided subject cannot be present except at the one moment of retroactive presence which is connected to the Imaginary, so that otherwise the elided subject can only be represented in the signifier as ego, intermittently in the diachronic process of the signifying chain in conscious thought, and the intermittence itself guarantees the perpetual absence of the elided subject.

As the subject is displaced in relation to itself in language, in its *méconnaissance*, in the dialectic of the other and the Other, of the Imaginary and the Symbolic, the subject is elided as the anchoring point of the signifying chain, the point at which the unconscious reveals itself, which is the point of *méconnaissance*, the point of the misrecognition by the subject of itself. The subject is displaced in relation to both the Imaginary and Symbolic orders. The ego is formed as a necessary replacement for the elided subject in the structure of language. "Thus the founding drama of the ego...is repeated in miniature as the imaginary dimension of every act of enunciation," in the words of Peter Dews in *Logics of Disintegration* (Dews, 1987, p. 99). The subject is divided in language, between unconscious thought and conscious thought, signifier and signified, Symbolic and Imaginary, and the result is "the moment of a 'fading' or eclipse of the subject that is closely bound up with the *Spaltung* or splitting that it suffers from its subordination to the signifier," as described by Lacan (*Écrits, A Selection*, p. 313). The subject cannot be adequately represented by signifiers in language. It is only in the gap between signifiers, the scotoma, that the subject is revealed.

Unconscious thought is found in the gap between signifiers. It is in the gap that the ego is revealed as representation, and the unconscious comes forward. The structure of the subject is one of discontinuity: the subject is never always present in language, in conscious thought, as being, and never always present as non-being. Absence and presence oscillate in the *glissement* of signifiers. Freud did not conceive of this relation between conscious and unconscious thought because he did not have the benefit of structural linguistics, the work of Ferdinand de Saussure and Roman Jakobson, according to Lacan. "'Geneva 1910' and 'Petrograd 1920' suffice to explain why Freud lacked this particular tool" (p. 298). The Lacanian unconscious is predicated on the correspondence between the Freudian unconscious and the concept of the signifier in structural linguistics, a correspondence which corrects a "defect of history" in the progress of the "science of the letter," psychoanalysis. Condensation and displacement in dream work correspond to the effects of metaphor and metonymy in language, "in other words, the signifier's effects of substitution and combination on the respectively synchronic and diachronic dimensions in which they appear in discourse."

The ego ideal, the identification of the ego with the Other, is a product of the mirror stage, and the insertion of the subject into language. The reality of the speaking subject (*je*) is opposed to the Imaginary ego (*moi*). The Imaginary ego is a subjective ego "before it is objectified in the dialectic of identification with the other, and before language restores to it in the universal, its function as subject" (p. 2). The objectification of the subject in language, in the universal, is the Hegelian transition from the subjective to the objective, which is enacted through perception. Perception is differentiated from sense-certainty by Hegel in that perception "takes what is present to it as a universal" (*Phenomenology of Spirit*, §111) (Hegel, 1977). The specular image of the infant in the mirror stage is not taken as a universal, because the infant does not have the use of language, so the image is of the subjective ego, being-in-self, as opposed to the objective ego, being-for-self, as defined by its exteriority, its representation in language. The differentiated particulars given by perception in conscious thought, which are products of the dialectic between the universal and particular, are an "essence-less by-play" (§687) of self-conscious spirit, according to Hegel. The variable forms of appearance in perception are indeterminate and insubstantial adornments of reality, acting as a veil between the finite and the infinite, the sensible and the intelligible. Through language, according to Hegel, spirit descends into externality. The objectified subject as ego in language is the self-confirmation of conscious thought in its negation of its other, unconscious thought.

The Imaginary ideal ego is a form which "situates the agency of the ego, before its social determination, in a fictional direction, which will always remain irreducible for the individual alone," according to Lacan (*Écrits, A Selection*, p. 2). It will "only rejoin the coming-into-being (*le dévenir*) of the subject asymptotically," irregardless of "the success of the dialectical syntheses by which he must resolve as *I* his discordance with his own reality." When the subject is subsumed into language, the Imaginary in unconscious thought becomes inaccessible, except in glimpses, which approach the presence of unconscious thought in language as absence, but cannot accede to it. The image of the infant in the mirror stage is in contrast to prior sense-experience, before it is conceptualized in the Symbolic, which constitutes an organic discord in the infant. The form of the body is fixed in the mirror by the infant in contrast to its inner psychical excitations that are precluded by the structure of language. The excitations are constituted by the images of the Imaginary ego. The Imaginary ego is absorbed into a logic other than that of conscious thought. As Freud showed, traces of the primordial Imaginary ego are present in dream images, while the Symbolic is also present in dreams, as a product of the immersion of the subject in the Other.

The unconscious *imago*, the Imaginary image previous to the intersection with the Symbolic, is present in conscious experience as those "veiled faces it is our privilege to see in outline in our daily experience and in the penumbra of symbolic efficacity" (p. 3), that is, as phantoms, shadows, residues of conscious experience. The mirror image is the "threshold of the visible world," because it preserves a remnant of the unconscious subject to itself in the conscious experience of perception, which organizes the visible world. The subject is transformed into a "totality that I shall call orthopedic" (p. 4) in the mirror image, which assumes the role of the "armor of an alienating identity, which will mark with its rigid structure the subject's entire mental development." The alienating identity is sustained by the formation of the ego as signifier in language; the objectified body image perceived in the mirror stage is the visual equivalent of the ego in language, the formation of which develops from the specular image identification.

Unconscious thought is defined by Lacan as "that part of the concrete discourse, in so far as it is transindividual, that is not at the disposal of the subject in re-establishing the continuity of his conscious discourse" (p. 49). As the subject becomes redefined to itself in relation to the Other, in the Symbolic, it loses its definition of itself in relation to itself in the Imaginary. The absence of the subject in language is perpetually recreated in language, as in the *Fort! Da!* game of the infant for Freud, in which is inscribed the trace of presence, the Imaginary presence, the desire for the other, in the Symbolic, the "world of meaning of a partic-ular language in which the world of things will come to be arranged" (p. 65), as *parole* is arranged in *langue*. "It is the world of words that creates the world of things." In order for an object to be perceived, it must be constructed, in unconscious thought. "Man speaks, then, but it is because the symbol has made him man." Language is defined by the Other, which is the "intersubjectivity of the 'we' that it assumes" (p. 86). The subject enters language in relationship with the other, in order to be recognized by the other. "What constitutes me as subject is my ques-tion. In order to be recognized by the other, I utter what was only in view of what will be." The subject is present in language in anticipation of a response from the other. "I identify myself in language, but only by losing myself in it like an object."

The distinction between the Symbolic, the I (*je*), and the Imaginary, the me (*moi*), is found in the distinction between unconscious and conscious thought. According to Lacan, Freud wrote "*Das Ich und das Es* in order to maintain this fundamental distinction between the true subject of the unconscious and the ego as constituted in its nucleus by a series of alienating identifications" (p. 128). The cycle of alienating identifications, which constitutes the ego in language, is impossible to escape; just as unconscious thought is inaccessible. The principle of objectification that determines the unbreakable cycle is the principle of *méconnaissance*, misrecognition. When the subject speaks, it is always of something which is other to the subject and which is inaccessible to the subject, that is, unconscious thought. The identity of the subject cannot be found within the "infinity of reflection that the mirage of consciousness consists of" (p. 134). Ego identity is an indefinite play of reflections in which the subject is trapped without access to the "supposed progress of interiority" in which the subject sees itself constituted in *méconnaissance*. The subject becomes that which was defined by Georges Bataille in "The Pineal Eye" as enclosed in the "degrading chains of logic" (*Visions of Excess*, p. 80) (Bataille, 1985), or in "closed systems assigned to life by reasonable conceptions" (p. 128), as described in "The Notion of Expenditure." The subject is defined in the struggle with the Symbolic, the inescapable signifying structure of human thought. In such a struggle, being is ungraspable, it is only grasped in error, in *méconnaissance*.

In the constitution of the Symbolic, the Imaginary ego disintegrates, and the Symbolic shields the subject from that disintegration. The ego would have been described by Bataille as a homogeneous representation of perceived reality wherein existence is a "neatly defined itinerary from one practical sign to another" (p. 82), and "acts undertaken with some rational end are only servile responses to a necessity" (p. 231). According to Lacan, "it is thus that the functions of mastery which we incorrectly call the synthesizing functions of the ego," establish "the development that follows from it, namely... the paranoiac principle of human knowledge, according to which its objects are subjected to a law of imaginary reduplication, evoking the homologation of an endless series of notaries..." (*Écrits, A Selection*, p. 138). The Symbolic is predicated on a relation to the Other that is mutually self-sustaining and mutually exclusive of Imaginary identification. The Imaginary self is a homogeneous and functionary self, conscious thought without access to unconscious thought or being-in-self. But "the decisive signification of the alienation that constitutes the *Urbild* of the ego appears in the relation of exclusion that then structures the dual relation of ego to ego." The ego is reaffirmed by the other in its functionalism.

Bataille desired to escape the cycle of functionalism created by the constraints of the ego. In *Eroticism, Death and Sensuality*, there is in nature and man "a movement which always exceeds the bounds, that can never be anything but partially reduced to order. We are generally unable to grasp it" in conscious thought. "Indeed it is by definition that which can never be grasped, but we are conscious of being in its power: the universe that bears us along answers no purpose that reason defines" (Bataille, 1986, p. 40). The movement is of unconscious thought, which exceeds the bounds of conscious thought. In the thought of Lacan, the recognition of the Symbolic order begins when the subject "recognizes and therefore distinguishes his action in each of these two registers," the Symbolic and Imaginary, and unconscious and conscious thought, "if he is to know why he intervenes, at what moment the opportunity presents itself and how to seize it" (*Écrits, A Selection*, p. 140). This is realized in the understanding of the relation between the subject and the other, in distinction from the relation between the subject and the Other. The subject "should be thoroughly imbued with the radical difference between the Other to which his speech must be addressed," in the ego ideal, "and that second other who is the individual that he sees before him, and from whom and by means of whom the first speaks to him in the discourse that he holds before him." Such recognition would enable the subject to accomplish the "annulling of his own resistance when he is the other with a small *o*," and then "he will be able to be he to whom this discourse is addressed."

This is not an easy task, because the relation of the subject to the other is determined by the relation of the subject to the Other, and the Imaginary identification that the subject might have with the other has been subsumed by the Symbolic identification with the Other, which has objectified the Imaginary identification into language. The Other has already played a role in the constitution of the Imaginary order, as seen in the original conflict of the mirror stage. The Other is "the locus in which is constituted the I who speaks to him who hears, that which is said by the one being already the reply ... " (p. 141). The subject in language is objectified in the anticipation of signification, but the Other extends into the subject as it enters into language. The relation between the subject and the other is dictated by the relation between the subject and the Other, insofar as the linguistic mechanisms of repression, displacement and distortion, are operative both in unconscious and conscious thought. The unconscious appears in conscious thought through the primary repression of language, which is also a mechanism of unconscious thought, as shown in the analysis of dreams by Freud. As unconscious thought is the discourse of the Other, the relation between the subject and the other is a relation determined by the Other, as conscious thought is determined by unconscious thought.

Language is the source of *méconnaissance*, in the network of symbols into which the subject is inserted. In its participation in the Other, the ego misrecognizes its own unconscious, as it is conscious thought which constitutes the ego, the Imaginary function. The subject is exterior to the ego, to its own mechanisms of thinking, and does not know what it is. It is impossible for the subject to know itself, given the dichotomy of the Imaginary and Symbolic. The knowledge on the part of the subject of its unconscious thought is replaced by the illusion of consciousness. Language detaches itself from the subject, and objectifies the subject in its detachment. In language, in its objectification, the subject is disconnected, but the ego of the subject retains the unity given by the specular image in the mirror stage. The subject is divided in language, and further divided by the relation between the Other and the other. The ego begins as an Imaginary function, but is then objectified as a Symbolic function in the entrance of the subject into language. The Imaginary reinforces itself in the image of the other, while the Symbolic reinforces itself in the structure of language. The subject in language is a "body in pieces" (*Seminar II*, p. 54) (Lacan, 1991). The fragmented body image of the Symbolic, and the *imago* of the Imaginary, are in contrast to the body image of the ideal ego, a unified body between the Imaginary and Symbolic that is reinforced in the dream. The body of the other appears in the dream to reinforce the unified body image of the ideal ego of the subject, but the unified body is inserted into a fragmented structure which reflects the structure of language, the structure of the Other. The dream is an "imaginary iridescence" (p. 57) of shifting forms, condensations and displacements, which fragment the unified possibility of experience of the ideal ego, as language fragments the Imaginary ego of the subject.

Unconscious thought is "manifested as that which vacillates in a split in the subject," between the Imaginary and the Symbolic, as Lacan described in *The Four Fundamental Concepts of Psycho-Analysis* (Lacan, 1981, p. 28). If unconscious thought is structured like a language, then that structuring is one of discontinuity, vacillation, a "strange temporality" (p. 25). The vacillation in the split of the subject is manifest in metaphor and metonymy in language, in the relation between the signifier and the signified, the subject and the other. The unconscious is a primordial "cut" in thought. The function of the unconscious is in "relation with the function of the concept of the *Unbegriff* – or Begriff [idea] of the original *Un*, namely, the cut" (p. 43), as in the *point de capiton*. The function of the conscious thought of the subject is predicated on the cut or split, which manifests itself in a temporal "pulsation" in language, as the subject is elided and then re-emerges from underneath the bar between the signifier and the signified. Language can only establish the possibility of the presence or absence of the subject temporarily, as for Hegel, thus the temporality of unconscious thought is a pulsative one, in the coming and going of the illusion of consciousness in conscious thought.

The dialectic of the ego and the Other is the dialectic of the ego and the unconscious. The subject can only experience itself in the Other, in the unconscious, as fragmented. The perception-consciousness system is itself fragmented, and unknowable in its entirety to the subject, which is divided in the Symbolic order. As the subject reaffirms its ideal ego in the other, in the Imaginary function of the ego, it has consciousness, but the consciousness is only a representation, the product of the play of reflections given by perception. The consciousness of the subject is only the consciousness of the other. Consciousness becomes self-consciousness as it becomes objectified in the Other, but as such consciousness only sees itself as the consciousness of the other. Consciousness cannot see itself; the subject cannot identify itself in language – it is only present to itself as an absence. The subject cannot see itself from the Imaginary body image of itself, the reflection of the other, because it is separated by the wall of language, because "it is in the space of the Other" that the subject sees itself (p. 144). The place of the Other from which the subject sees itself is also the point from which the subject speaks in language, and it is the place of the unconscious thought that determines the subject in language as a construct of the Other.

Because the image of the unified body can only be perceived in the other, it is only perceived from the outside, exterior to the subject. "Because of this double relation which he has with himself, all the objects of his world are always structured around the wandering shadow of his own ego" (*Seminar II*, p. 166). According to Lacan, the unattainable unity of the subject in the ideal ego is evoked at every moment of perception. The object identification that the subject experiences, and the identification with the other, subsumed in the Symbolic, can never satisfy the subject faced with its own absence and fragmentation in such an ego identification. The subject is separated from the objects of perception, from the world that it perceives, because it cannot find itself there. The object can only be perceived in unity with the subject from without, temporarily, and this causes fragmentation in the subject. Perception can only be sustained "within a zone of nomination" (p. 169): the Imaginary can only be sustained by the Symbolic. The name has no relationship to the "spatial distinctiveness of the object," the Imaginary object identification, but rather to its temporal dimension in perception. The object, while it is "at one instant constituted as a semblance of the human subject, a double of himself" in the Imaginary order, it "nonetheless has a certain permanence of appearance over time," as given by the insertion of the object in perception, and the insertion of the subject in the Symbolic. Perception is not possible without naming, without language.

The self-perception of the subject is one of unsatisfied desire. When the subject sees itself as a unity in the other, in the Imaginary, the world becomes fragmented. When the subject sees the world or the Other as a unity, in the Symbolic, it is the subject that becomes fragmented. Such an oscillation in perception is manifest in the dream. The subject is either in one place, in the Imaginary, or in several places, in the Symbolic. If the subject is in several places in the Symbolic, it is in the form of multiple ego ideals that reinforce the Imaginary. The perceived object, or the other, occurs in the dream as the body of the subject itself in the ideal ego, as a reflection of the subject that is not present. The image in the dream is a simulacrum, a *Vorstellungsrepräsentanz* with no origin. The reflection of the subject also occurs in conscious thought, in every act of perception. In perception, the subject is not aware of that which it perceives as its own reflection, while in the dream it becomes apparent, because the ideal ego is not as present in the dream. As a result, in the dream the subject becomes aware of its exteriority from the world that it perceives, which is reproduced in the mnemic residue, the *Vorstellungsrepräsentanz*, of the dream. The isolation that the subject feels in relation to the world that it perceives is alleviated through the inter-vention of the Symbolic, the system of language, but then the subject becomes "no more than a pawn" (p. 168), objectified in the signifying chain of language, and determined by the Other, which is unconscious thought.

In *The Four Fundamental Concepts of Psycho-Analysis*, "The signifier, producing itself in the field of the Other, makes manifest the subject of its signification. But it functions as a signifier only to reduce the subject in question to being no more than a signifier," in language, "to petrify the subject in the same movement in which it calls the subject to function, to speak, as subject" (Lacan, 1981, p. 207). The result is "the temporal pulsation in which is established that which is the char-acteristic of the departure of the unconscious as such…." Unconscious thought perpetually opens and closes within conscious thought. It is never present as other than an absence, a trace, in the gap between the Imaginary and the Symbolic, in which the subject is "born divided" (p. 199). The subject becomes the network of signifiers in language, and in the layers of images in dreams in which the network of signifiers is played out.

The optical model of the dream, in the intersection of the Imaginary and Symbolic, consists of "a number of layers" that are "the locus where the affair of the subject of the unconscious is played out" (p. 45). The layers of the optical model of the dream through which the matrix of the Symbolic is filtered, in the form of the subject, and through which the inner light (being-in-self) of the primordial ego is refracted, is an "immense display, a special specter, situated between perception and consciousness." The optical model of the dream is located between the mnemic residues of perception which produce the dream on the Imaginary level, and the Symbolic matrix which produces the subject in unconscious thought. The Other is situated in the interval that separates perception and consciousness, and it is there that the subject is constituted, in the apparition of the intersection of the Imaginary and Symbolic.

The separation between perception and consciousness is necessary in order for the *Wahrnehmungszeichen*, the traces of perception, to become mnemic residues, to pass into memory. The traces must be effaced in perception, in the temporal and particular mechanisms of objective experience, and must be constituted simultaneously in the "signifying synchrony" (p. 46) of unconscious thought. The passage from perception to consciousness is the passage from the particular to the universal. In the *Phenomenology of Spirit* of Hegel, perception already "takes what is present to it as a universal" (§111). It is the mnemic residue that differentiates consciousness from perception, which is the discovery of Freud in the analysis of dreams, and which renders consciousness as alienated from the constitution of the subject. The passage from the particular to the universal, from the diachronic to the synchronic, occurs for Freud in the passage from perception to consciousness, from the Imaginary to the Symbolic of Lacan. The *Wahrnehmungszeichen* are transformed into a signifying synchrony in that they become signifiers. The layers between perception and consciousness are the layers in which the traces of perception enter the Symbolic as signifiers, and the Imaginary in the subject is objectified as the Symbolic.

The definition of the subject between perception and consciousness, between the Imaginary and Symbolic, is one of discontinuity in the gaps that are present in language, in "the gap itself that constitutes awakening" (*The Four Fundamental Concepts of Psycho-Analysis*, p. 57). That which passes in the gap between perception and consciousness is like that which passes in the gaps in the *glissement* of the signifying chain in language, which is what Lacan calls the Gaze. "In our relation to things, in so far as this relation is constituted by the way of vision, and ordered in the figures of representation, something slips, passes, is transmitted, from stage to stage, and is always to some degree eluded in it – that is what we call the gaze" (p. 73). The Gaze is the presence of absence in perception, the presence of the absence of the subject in perception, and the point at which the subject is defined in relation to unconscious thought. The relation of the subject to the Other is "entirely produced in a process of gap" (p. 206) in both perception and language, in both the Imaginary and Symbolic, and in particular in the intersection between the two. The subject is fragmented in the relation between the *percipi*, primordial object identification, and language. The gap between the *percipi* and language, between the particular and universal, between the signifier and the signified, between the Imaginary and Symbolic, is defined as desire. Desire is the product of the impossibility of the Imaginary in the Symbolic, or conscious thought in unconscious thought; it is the product of the splitting of the subject between identification with the other and identification in the Other, the splitting in which the unconscious is formed, in the repression of desire as misrecognition, *méconnaissance*, which is the only recourse of the subject. The splitting occurs in the processes of language, in metaphor and metonymy, as the impossible representation of what the subject cannot know as itself. Desire is maintained by language, in the fragmentation of the subject, and in the possibility of unconscious thought.

Rather than represent the subject, language misrepresents the subject and is the source of the subject's *méconnaissance*, in the conflict between Imaginary and Symbolic. Language conditions the relation of the subject to the Other, and blocks the relationships of the subject to the other. Intersubjectivity, the specificity of desire, cannot be articulated in language. Unconscious thought, as the discourse of the Other, is the locus of the inarticulation of desire in relation to the other in language. As the discourse of the Other, unconscious thought is that by which the subject is constituted as object, "the sum of the effects of speech on a subject, at that level where the subject constitutes itself from the effects of the signifier" (p. 126). Unconscious thought is the locus of the splitting of the subject, as it is inaccessible to the subject. Unconscious thought can only be grasped by the subject in *méconnaissance*, in the knowledge of its own division and impossibility. The Symbolic order is an insufficiency in relation to the identity of the subject, and the locus of its non-being. The subject is defined as the gap between its self-definition in language and its self-definition in perception, the gap between the Symbolic and Imaginary, from which desire is generated. The relation between the Symbolic and the Imaginary is one of discontinuity, so the subject can only be divided, and impossible to complete. The impossibility of completion is the source of desire. The incompleteness is inscribed into the subject by unconscious thought.

The subject is always given as other to itself in language, in its relation to the Imaginary other in consciousness. The reflection of the other "becomes visible with the particular configuration we call consciousness, in as much as the imaginary function of the ego comes into play." The subject "gets to see this reflection from the point of view of the other. He is an other for himself. This is what gives you the illusion that consciousness is transparent to itself," but we are not "present, in the reflection; to see the reflection, we are in the consciousness of the other" (*Seminar II*, p. 112) (Lacan, 1991). The identification with the other, in the dialectic of the Imaginary and Symbolic, is a function of misrecognition. The dialectic of the Imaginary and Symbolic is a dialectic of the desire of the Other, the desire instituted in the subject by language, and the desire of the other, which is mistakenly taken to compensate for the lack caused by the desire of the Other.

For the subject in the mirror stage, "the image of his body is the principle of every unity he perceives in objects" (p. 166), in the ideal ego. "Now, he only perceives the unity of this specific image from the outside, and in an anticipated manner," in the same way that the subject is inserted into language, in a particular signifier given by the Other, the signifying chain. "Man's ideal unity, which is never attained as such and escapes him at every moment, is evoked at every moment in this perception," which results in desire. The object in which the subject seeks its unity "is never for him definitively the final object. ... it thus appears in the guise of an object from which man is irremediably separated," which is an object "in which he will never truly be able to find reconciliation, his adhesion to the world, his perfect complementarity on the level of desire."

As a result of this, "it is in the nature of desire to be radically torn." It is impossible for the subject to fulfill itself, to mediate the dialectic between the Imaginary and Symbolic. The attempted mediation, desire, is "maintained by a succession of momentary experiences," which constitute the subject in language, the fleeting and vanishing subject in the signifying chain. Consciousness is sustained in the subject by seeing itself be seen by the other, in the gaze or in the reflection, as the Imaginary is subject to the Symbolic. The gaze of the other, the seeing oneself being seen, is a structuring mechanism of the subject in perception. Seeing oneself being seen is translated into understanding oneself being understood in language, the anticipation of the recognition of the subject by the other in the communicative function in language, the *point de capiton*, which reaffirms the Symbolic order. In the same way that the subject cannot in actuality see itself being seen by the other, because the subject only exists as a signifier in the Other for the other, the subject cannot in actuality understand itself being understood by the other. The mirage of consciousness of the subject in the Imaginary is sustained in the illusion that what the subject says is being understood by the other, in relation to what is said. This is never the case. Language only communicates by misunderstanding, *méconnaissance*.

What the other understands to be communicated is never what is intended, because language can only function as a resistance to the Imaginary relation between the subject and the other: the wall of language intersects object identification in the Imaginary order. Repression in language, the *Unterdrückung* in metaphor and metonymy, is the repression of the subject, and maintains the illusion of consciousness in language, while at the same time preventing the subject from knowing its own unconscious thought, and thus preventing the subject from being able to communicate to the other, which it can only identify in the structure of the Other, to which it does not have access. Repression in language is repression of the Imaginary ideal ego, formed in the mirror stage, which nevertheless continues to be present, and through which the subject seeks itself in the other. It is a function of desire, which cannot be consummated because of the inaccessibility of the Other, unconscious thought, in which the desire is formed.

The intercession of the Imaginary order in the maintenance of the Symbolic in language represses the non-being of the subject to itself and prevents the absence of the subject to itself. It is impossible to separate the Imaginary, the recognition of the subject in the other, from the Symbolic, in the objectivity of conscious thought. The identification of the Imaginary and Symbolic, the illusion of continuity in conscious thought, is the locus of *méconnaissance*. The individual speech act in language, *parole*, interjects the Imaginary order into discourse, disrupting the Symbolic order, the unconscious. *Parole* enacts the impossible desire on the part of the subject in the attempted identification with the other, making communication in language impossible. The relation between the subject and the other is impossible, as the Symbolic introduces discontinuity in the Imaginary, and unconscious thought introduces discontinuity into conscious thought. *Parole* is inserted into the signifying chain to announce the presence of the Imaginary and the possibility of unconscious thought in the disruption of the signifying sequence. *Parole* also enacts the *point de capiton* in the retroactive sliding of the signifier in the anticipation of the subject. *Parole* is in opposition to *langue*, which is the underlying structure of language separate from individual speech acts, which is the structure of the Other, unconscious thought, which appears in the signifying chain at the *point de capiton*.

In *Seminar XX*, *langue* is suggested by "*llanguage*," which is defined as that which in language exceeds conscious thought and discourse, but which incorporates them, according to Lacan. "Llanguage serves purposes that are altogether different from that of communication" (Lacan, 1998, p. 138), the signification of the Symbolic. "If I have said that language is what the unconscious is structured like, that is because language, first of all, doesn't exist," because language "is what we try to know concerning the function of llanguage" as conscious thought is what we try to know concerning the function of unconscious thought. "The unconscious evinces knowledge that, for the most part, escapes the speaking being" (p. 139) in language. What is articulated in the subject is beyond the knowledge of the subject in language, and is that which is given by *llanguage*, and is that which is articulated of *llanguage* in language by unconscious thought. The effects of *llanguage* are not something that the speaking subject is able to enunciate, as in *parole*. The linguistic structure of unconscious thought is only a hypothetical structure. *Llanguage* reveals that language is other than communication. Language, as a complex of signifiers which represent the subject, is a function of *llanguage* in revealing the unconscious of the subject. *Llanguage* is the language of unconscious thought, which is unknowable and inaccessible, but which reveals itself as absence in language, in the communicative shortcomings of language.

The speaking subject is an instrument of language as a function of *llanguage*, a function of unconscious thought, in the discourse of the Other. As a result, "the subject turns out to be – and this is only true for speaking beings – a being whose being is always elsewhere" (p. 142). "The subject is never more than fleeting and vanishing, for it is a subject only by a signifier and to another signifier." Language itself is a continuous misconstruction, as language defines the subject in relation to the Other, or unconscious thought. The subject is an effect of language, an effect of misconstruction. The misconstruction of language is the illusion of consciousness, the self-identity of the subject in conscious thought. Conscious thought, as perpetuated by the Imaginary order, screens the subject from unconscious thought; unconscious thought cannot be revealed in conscious thought, except as an interruption or absence, thus "the less we articulate it, the less we talk, and the more it speaks us," according to Lacan in *Seminar III* (Lacan, 1993, p. 157; Ragland-Sullivan, 1986, p. 197).

Every word in language, every signifier, contains the dialectic of the Symbolic and Imaginary, and the Other and the other. The subject is always present and always not present in the fluctuation of language caused by the interjection of unconscious thought, and each word contains the trace of the previous signifier and the trace of an absence.

The splitting of the subject occurs in every word that is spoken, in the very act of speaking. Language is a metaphor for lack of being, the absence which it replaces as supplement. The mechanisms of language, such as condensation and displacement, as revealed in dream analysis, are the mechanisms of the desire of the Other. In metaphor and metonymy, "the subject has to find the constituting structure of his desire in the same gap opened up by the effect of the signifiers in those who come to represent the Other for him, in so far as his demand is subjected to them" (*Écrits, A Selection*, p. 264) (Lacan, 1977). The Imaginary order of the psyche of the subject identifies itself in the other through the mechanisms of the Symbolic, in the gap created by the signifiers in the discourse that is presented to it. The subject recognizes the same effect of desire in the dream, also a desire of the Other, as the dream reveals the discourse of the Other, unconscious thought. "The desire of the dream is not assumed by the subject who says 'I' in his speech," in the Imaginary order. "Articulated, nevertheless, in the locus of the Other, it is discourse...." The effects of desire on the subject in the dream are given by the linguistic structure of the dream, not the mnemic residues that occur in the dream as the subject of Imaginary ego identification.

The effects of desire are instituted by metaphor and metonymy, in condensation and displacement, in the subject as soon as the subject enters into language in the mirror stage. Language provides substitutions for primordial *percipi* and ego identifications, as in the *Fort! Da!* game described by Freud. In the newly constituted Symbolic order, language forms a link in the subject to pre-linguistic experiences and perceptions, and compensates for the alienation and absence experienced by the subject created by the "wall of language," as both the *imago* of the mirror stage and the word intervene in the direct experience of the primordial ego. The metaphoric constitution of the subject in its early formation in language returns to the subject in conscious thought through metaphor and metonymy as that which is repressed in the Other. The signifying chains occur as secondary repressions referring to the repressed signifying chains in the unconscious, the *Urverdrängung*, as in condensation in the dream. The point of the repression of the signifier is the *point de capiton*, the point at which the repressed is revealed, as unconscious thought in conscious thought. The repressed signifiers are translatable in relation to signifiers in conscious thought.

Imaginary ego identification is supported by inaccessible signifying chains that correspond to the signifying chains in language (Ragland-Sullivan, 1986, p. 247). The signifying chains revealed in the structure of the dream correspond to the signifying chains in conscious thought, and carry with them the same relation between the Symbolic and the Imaginary. A relation is established between conscious thought and the repressed discourse of the unconscious as revealed in the dream and thus the psychoanalyst is able to see how the repressed discourse of the unconscious plays a role in the language of the subject, through the interaction of the Imaginary and Symbolic. Given this correlation, unconscious language, or the discourse of the Other in unconscious thought, cannot be seen to operate according to the same rules or logic of conscious language, notwithstanding the occurrences of linguistic structures which can be observed in dream work, as for Freud. The manifest content of the dream is not unconscious thought, but involves the production of the *Vorstellungsrepräsentanz*, which leads to unconscious thought. Similarly, the organization of mnemic residues in dreams is not the product of conscious thought, though the perception of them is, and any signification which might occur in the organization can be read retroactively in the memory of the dream, as it is read retroactively in the signifying chain in conscious thought.

If language is a metaphor, then the dream is a metaphor, for the supplement to the lack of being, a supplement created by the *Vorstellungsrepräsentanz*, and by the Imaginary ego object identification. As a metaphor, the dream also contains repressed content, in the elided subject that is not accessible to conscious thought, but which is present in the dream in the Imaginary ego identification of the *Vorstellungsrepräsentanz*, as it is present in conscious thought in the elided subject of identification with the other, within the context of the Other. Just as in conscious thought, the metaphoric signification of the dream contains gaps and scotomata that disrupt the language of the dream and reveal the mechanisms of unconscious thought. The dream reveals the *llanguage* that is not accessible to conscious thought, giving a hint of the mechanisms of *llanguage*, as they are filtered into conscious thought, in *parole*. The effect that connects the mechanisms of *llanguage* with the mechanisms of *parole* is desire. Desire is the effect of the elision of the subject in the metaphoric chain and the necessity of the subject to assume an altering identity in language; the desire is the desire of the Other, of unconscious thought. It is the effect of the mirror stage, which causes the infant to substitute for the primordial *percipi* and object identifications, to compensate for the internal division caused by the object identification of the Imaginary ego, and to compensate for the othering that goes along with the formation of the Symbolic order.

The product of desire is the vacillating slope of the signifying chain in speech, the disruptive *parole* of Imaginary ego identification attempting to reconstitute the primordial experience in the illusion of reflection of the other, and the lacunae and scotomata produced by the intercession of the unconscious, which gives a hint of those primordial experiences, through the structure of dreams, which is other than the structure of conscious thought. Desire is found in metaphor and metonymy, in condensation and displacement, as the link between the speaking subject and its identity, which is inaccessible to it. It is manifest in the pulsations of conscious thought, the modulations and transformations of alteration and opposition brought about by perception, as in the "alteration of light and dark" (*Seminar III*, p. 167) (Lacan, 1993). Desire is present in every word, as a companion to the absence which is made present in every word, as trace of the subject which has been elided from its own conscious thought, and which seeks its identity in that conscious thought. The instrument of desire is the signifier, which creates the subject, but creates the subject as divided.

The Lacanian subject desires as soon as it enters into language. Desire is not present in primordial Imaginary experience prior to the mirror stage. Desire is the product of the "murder of the thing" (*Écrits, A Selection*, p. 104) (Lacan, 1977) by the symbol in language, which instigates the lack experienced by the subject. The desire of the subject is thus "the desire of the Other" (p. 264), and it is also the desire of the other, in the dialectic of the Symbolic and Imaginary. This can be seen in the desire of the dream, which is not a conscious desire, not regulated by conscious thought. The dream enacts its own desire, which is the desire of the Other in unconscious thought. In the same way, the conscious subject is the subject of the desire of the Other in language. Consciousness is a construct of desire in the Other.

In that the object of desire is a substitute for the *objet a*, the lack of the subject, the object is external to the desire of the subject. Desire is sustained by the subject and not by the object. The subject is an apparatus of absence in which the *objet a* is constituted. "This apparatus is something lacunary, and it is in the lacuna that the subject establishes the function of a certain object, *qua* lost object" (*The Four Fundamental Concepts of Psycho-Analysis*, p. 185). The object of desire is a substitute for the lacuna in the subject, for the gap in the signifying chain that represents the subject. As desire is the desire of the Other, desire is engendered through the language of the Symbolic. The subject does not want what it desires, but desires what it thinks it needs to desire as a speaking subject, in order to sustain itself in language. Thus "the object of desire, in the usual sense, is either a fantasy that is in reality the support of desire" (p. 186), the reaffirming by the ego of the subject that it is desiring what it needs to desire, "or a lure," the deception of the subject by its ego that the object is what it is supposed to desire. The desire of the subject is divided in metonymy, which re-affirms the subject as that which is represented in language, and at the same time eliminates the subject from that representation. Desire is both reaffirmed and negated by language, because desire is constructed by language, by the discourse of the Other, which is unconscious thought. The subject is only partially existent in the Other, and thus only partially existent in its own desire, which is inaccessible to it, as is unconscious thought. The desire of the Other links the signifiers in a signifying chain, and results in the elimination of the subject.

As soon as the subject speaks, it desires, and as soon as the subject desires it does not know itself, and its *méconnaissance* is sustained by its desire. As soon as a signifier represents the subject to another signifier, the subject is alienated from itself in its desire. "Alienation is linked in an essential way to the function of the dyad of signifiers" (p. 236). As soon as the alienation is accomplished in the singular representation of the subject by a signifier to another signifier, the subject is eliminated from any further signification, which becomes inaccessible to the subject. The subject cannot access that by which it is constituted, unconscious thought. The alienation is accomplished with the binary signifier, as "the signifier is that which represents the subject for the other signifier." The binary signifier is also the mechanism of the *Vorstellungsrepräsentanz* of the dream. The representation which takes the place of the representation is the signifier which takes the place of the signifier, which represents the subject to it. The subject is elided in the dream in the same way, as the *Unterdrückung* of the binary signifier. The subject is thus alienated from its desire in the dream as well, which is a product of the *Vorstellungsrepräsentanz*, as the elision of the subject is the product of the binary signifier in the Symbolic, in which the mechanisms of the unconscious, metaphor and metonymy, determine the subject unknown to itself.

The conceptualization of unconscious thought has evolved greatly throughout the history of philosophy and psychoanalysis, from the metaphysical formulations in Classical, Peripatetic, and Scholastic philosophy, to transcendental formulations in Romantic philosophy, to empirical and behavioral formulations in psychoanalysis. The conceptualization of the subject and subjectivity has evolved as well, through different forms of self-knowledge and self-consciousness, and different ways of understanding human existence and identity, perception, imagination, and intellection. An understanding of unconscious thought contributes to an understanding of what it is to be human, to an understanding of self-consciousness, expression, desire, and communication.

Lacan and Plotinus

In his writings, Jacques Lacan made references to Plotinus, and he devoted part of his *Seminar XX* to a discussion of the concept of the One in the *Parmenides* dialogue of Plato. The concept of the One as developed in Plotinus, as that which is inaccessible to reason, or that which cannot be signified, was taken up by Lacan, and can be compared to the concept of the Real in Lacan, as that which escapes the Symbolic or the domain of language, and the concept of the Gaze, as that which escapes perception in vision. For Lacan, the One is a product of language; it is described as that which is revealed in the gap between signifiers. The One is necessitated by the Other, which is the matrix of signification which defines the subject, which is the unconscious, that which is inaccessible to conscious thought. The One is that which cannot be signified, which constitutes the *objet a* of Lacan, the unattainable object of desire. The Real as the One is the lack in the signifier, inaccessible to it, around which signification is structured.

The Intellect or noetic thought of Plotinus, as a manifestation of the One, can be seen as a precursor to the Lacanian concept of the unconscious, which is structured like a language, but which operates independently of conscious reason and sense perception. The archetypal forms of Intellect, described by Plotinus as "impressions produced by sensation on the living being" (*Enneads* I.1.7.12–14) (Plotinus, 1966), which are "already intelligible entities," can be seen as the *Vorstellungsrepräsentanzen* which Lacan develops from Freud, the mnemic residues of perception suggested by Freud as a representation of a representation, and defined by Lacan as that which takes the place of a representation. The *Vorstellungsrepräsentanz* is self-generating and self-supporting, like Intellect; it is the internal perception which is taken as the intelligible, the archetype or form of the sensible object, as in Intellect. Intellect functions as the Symbolic of Lacan in relation to the Imaginary, which is the primordial object identification of the subject prior to the formation of the ego, what would be described by Plotinus as the immediate grasping of sensible objects. The overcoming of the self-alienating ego in Lacan (a concept developed from Hegel) can be seen to have a precedent in the Intellect of Plotinus, which in *Enneads* V.5.7 "sees by another light the things illuminated by that first nature," the light of the sun; the light of Intellect is "suddenly appearing, alone by itself in independent

purity, so that Intellect is at a loss to know whence it has appeared...."
When the subject is aware that the objects of perception are lit by the
light of Intellect, which comes from the One, then the subject becomes
sight itself (I.6.9). In the Gaze of Lacan, the subject becomes a "stain" in
the field of vision, and recognizes itself as the seen rather than the seer,
grasped by the visual field, as a manifestation of the inaccessible unconscious, the Other, as in *Enneads* V.8.11 the subject "must give himself
up to what is within and become, instead of one who sees, an object of
vision to another who contemplates him shining out with thoughts of
the kind which come from that world," Intellect and the One.

For both Plotinus and Lacan, the perception of forms in matter is determined by reason made conscious. This was maintained by Plotinus, for
whom "soul's power of sense-perception need not be perception of sense-
objects, but rather it must be receptive of the impressions produced by
sensation" (I.1.7), which are already intelligible, and external sensation
is an image of internal sensation. The discerning of impressions printed
upon intellect by sensation is the function of reason in apperception,
not perception, while perception is also a function of reason. Since the
sensual impressions, or mnemic residues in perception are copies and
derivatives of intelligible forms, or forms conceived by unconscious
thought, perception itself is a copy and derivative of reason. For Lacan
perception is still a derivative of reason, but the identity of perception
and the possibility of an unconscious thought would perpetuate the illusion of consciousness and the structuring of reality by reason, which
functions as the Imaginary does in language to repress the unconscious,
like discursive reason in the thought of Plotinus might operate to repress
Intellect, and maintain the self-certainty of the *cogito*. For metaphysical
philosophy, as well as Freudian/Lacanian psychoanalysis, the goal is to
discover the unconscious in an unconscious thought that participates in
conscious thought.

The possibility of unconscious thought, or the Intellect of Plotinus,
is preserved in the structural linguistics of Ferdinand de Saussure, in
the concept of the floating kingdoms of signifiers and signifieds, where
thought is seen as an uncharted nebula independent of language, in the
Course in General Linguistics. Language is seen as giving sound and order
to unconscious thought, as language is pictured in its totality as "a series
of contiguous subdivisions marked off on both the indefinite plane of
jumbled ideas and the equally vague plane of sounds" (Saussure, 1966,
p. 112), which constitute the signifier and the signified, and the intersection of which is described as arbitrary. The "thought-sound" division
of language in structural linguistics suggests the presence of unconscious

thought. Hegel saw perception as picture thinking or *Vorstellung*, which also suggests the possibility of unconscious thought, in that images are thought by the unconscious prior to conscious perception. The possibility of unconscious thought allows perception to be seen as the medium between the subjective and objective, between the unconscious and language, as for Freud language itself is a residue of perception and it is that by which the unconscious thought becomes language, as perhaps the *logos endiathetos* of Plotinus. Hegelian picture-thinking preserves the disjunction between reason and perception: if there is unconscious thought, then reason "does not require, as does finite activity, the condition of external materials," as described in the *Phenomenology of Spirit* (§764) (Hegel, 1977). Reason is seen as self-generating and self-supporting – as in the Intellect of Plotinus, and in the unconscious thought of Freud. Thus, forms in matter are only possible in the image or *Bild* of reason, which takes objective form in language through perception, as in the Platonic *eidos*. As in Plotinus, the perception of forms in matter is determined by thought made conscious for Hegel.

Plotinus has been called a philosopher of the unconscious because, although there was no concept of the unconscious in the third century, what we now call the unconscious was clearly the inspiration for an interior knowledge or thought process that was distinguished from an exterior thought process, as noetic thought was distinguished from discursive reason, *nous poietikos* from *nous pathetikos*. A similar distinction was made by Hegel, in the difference between the universal and particular, subjective spirit and objective spirit. The *coincidentia oppositorum* was seen as the dialectic of becoming in reason, in the development from the particular to the universal, which is pre-existent in it. Dreams display the same *coincidentia oppositorum*, as described by Freud in *The Interpretation of Dreams*, that was seen as a sign of the One in nous, or Plotinus' Intellect. Such a sign can also be found in certain words in archaic languages, according to Freud in the *Introductory Lectures on Psycho-Analysis*; for example, in Latin, the word *altus* can mean both high and deep, and the word *sacer* can mean both sacred and accursed. Archaic languages "betray vagueness in a variety of ways which we would not tolerate in our writing today" (Freud, 1966, p. 285), according to Freud.

The Intellect of Plotinus is the source of the universal, as a manifestation of the One, which is concept in reason, and which creates the dialectic in reason, which is the unfolding of the *coincidentia oppositorum*, the differentiations that constitute logic. Intellect is a higher form of reason than logic, and its attributes correspond to dream images. There was an idea in the writings of Plotinus, to which Lacan referred, that there was a different form of thought operating without connection to sense perception. Intellect was described as existing independently of the sensible world, and relying on a different kind of vision, a vision based on intelligible rather than sensible forms. The archetypal forms of intelligible vision, corresponding to the mnemic residues of perception as described by Freud, were seen to be prior to forms in the sensible world, because they were closer to the intelligible forms, the universals, from which the sensible forms, the particulars, are derived. Perception of the sensible world is seen as being constructed by both conscious and unconscious thought, and as being a deception in relation to the totality of thought (as it is both conscious and unconscious), in the thought of both Plotinus and Lacan.

For Plotinus, as the constructed model of perception interacts with that which is perceived, as objects are reconstructed in mnemic residues, perception does not depend entirely on an external light, but also an internal light, as a mnemic residue itself. In *Enneads* V.5.7, "since Intellect must not see this light as external, we must go back again to the eye; this will itself sometimes know a light which is not the external, alien light," the light of the sun, "but it momentarily sees before the external light a light of its own, a brighter one..." (Plotinus, 1966). Internal vision is the truest vision because it is a more immediate perception of that which is constructed in perception; it is the primordially received image that is prior to perception, as given by language. Intellect, that which is other than conscious reason in mind, or unconscious reason, "veiling itself from other things and drawing itself inward, when it is not looking at anything will see a light, not a distinct light in something different from itself...." The inner light that is perceived is that which is other than given by reason in perception, or the Symbolic of Lacan; it is the primordial *percipi*, or perceived image, of the Imaginary order. Hegel defines the inner light as that which is shapeless and formless, thus that which is given by something other than sense-certainty, perception or consciousness, that which does not correspond to the mnemic residues of perception. In the *Phenomenology* (§686) (Hegel, 1977), light as shapelessness is "the pure, all-embracing and all-pervading essential light of sunrise, which pervades itself in its formless substantiality." The genesis of the Hegelian being-for-self, or *Fürsichsein*, of spirit, objective spirit, or reason, consists of torrents of light, while the return into the being-in-itself, or *Ansichsein*, of spirit from the moments of its existence, the return from conscious to unconscious thought, from the manifestation in particulars as given by perception, consists of "steams of fire destructive of structured form," that which is given by language.

The subject of Lacan becomes the network of signifiers in language, which is the dream. The subject finds itself in the layers of images in dreams in which the network of signifiers is played out, in the manifest content of the dream as described by Freud, the images in the dream that correspond to words in unconscious thought. The optical model of the dream of Lacan, in the intersection of the Imaginary and Symbolic orders, image and word, consists of "a number of layers, permeable to something analogous to light, whose refraction changes from layer to layer," as described in *The Four Fundamental Concepts of Psycho-Analysis* (Lacan, 1981, p. 45). "This is the locus where the affair of the subject of the unconscious is played out." This something analogous to light is as an inner light, as in the inner light of Plotinus, a reflection of the perceived light in reason, in the mnemic residue of perception, the construction of which forms the subject. The primordial object of perception exists outside perception or consciousness, outside of ego and the mechanisms of conscious thought. The ego in psychoanalysis, the mechanism of conscious thought, is itself an object that appears in the world of objects, in its being-for-self.

Consciousness, the self-identity of the subject with its ego, is defined by Lacan as a tension between the ego that has been alienated from the subject in its experience in language, and the perception on the part of the subject which is external to ego, the primordial object identification in the Imaginary order prior to the formation of the subject, which is a "pure *percipi*," seizing or receiving, as described by Lacan in *Seminar II* (Lacan, 1991, p. 177). In primordial object identification, "the subject would be strictly identical to this perception," as the seer becomes the seen, or the seer becomes the light for Plotinus, "if there weren't this ego which…makes it emerge from out of its very perception in a relationship of tension," between the Imaginary and Symbolic orders, conscious and unconscious thought. "Under certain conditions, this imaginary relation itself reaches its own limit, and the ego fades away, dissipates, becomes disorganized, dissolves," in the same way that the Plotinian subject withdraws within itself and recognizes its conscious thought as an object of Intellect, unconscious thought, as a being-for-self in relation to the One, or the Lacanian Real, that which is beyond conscious thought.

The dissolution of the ego in the identity of the perceiver and the perceived is accomplished in the Intellect of Plotinus, but for the opposite reason. In the perception of Plotinus, sensible forms are recognized as manifestations of ideas, and thus participate in the universal, as perception would be a product of ego, and participates in the matrix of language. In Intellect, forms are self-generating and self-supporting, as they would be mnemic residues. As forms in Intellect are self-generated and universal, they are not subject to the mechanisms of ego, of the particulars of perception or conscious reason. The perception which Plotinus calls the intelligible is Lacan's *Vorstellungsrepräsentanz*: that which takes the place of the representation of the mnemic residue in perception, which is self-generating and self-supporting in Intellect, as a reflection in a mirror as it were, a form without matter. The internal perception of the *Vorstellungsrepräsentanz* is taken as the archetype of the perception of sensible objects, which is only ephemeral and given by the ego in its imaginary identification with the other, the objects and forms with which it interacts.

If the subject for Plotinus becomes self-generating and self-supporting like the *Vorstellungsrepräsentanz* which it experiences in its intellect, then the subject becomes that which it perceives in the intelligible, and, in *Enneads* I.6.9, "when you see that you have become this, then you have become sight…." The subject becomes identical not with a primordial perception or *percipi* prior to the formation of the ego, but with a perception that is of the Symbolic order, immersed in language, which detaches itself from the perception based on the formation of the Imaginary order, or self-consciousness based on the perception of form. If the intelligible perception is of the Symbolic order, an archetype constructed by language in unconscious thought, unconscious thought plays a role in the perception, in a way not determined by conscious thought but by the insertion of the subject into language, or logos. The perception is predicated on the intersection of the Imaginary and Symbolic orders, which is manifest in the mnemic residues of the *Vorstellungsrepräsentanz* of Lacan, or the intelligible images that appear in the imagination or *phantasia* as reflected images in a mirror for Plotinus, in the process of intellection.

For Lacan the unconscious is structured like a language. For Plotinus the intelligible perception is revealed by logos, *logos endiathetos*, as if reflected in a mirror. In *Enneads* IV.3.30, "The intellectual act is without parts and has not, so to speak, come out into the open, but remains unobserved within," as unconscious thought, "but the verbal expression [or more accurately, *logos endiathetos*] unfolds its content and brings it out of the intellectual act into the image-making power, and so shows the intellectual act as if in a mirror…." If the subject of Plotinus is able to detach itself from the perception of objects, in both the construct of vision and the mechanisms of unconscious thought that produce the perception, and perceives only the intelligible in Intellect, then the subject will be, "instead of one who sees, an object of vision," exactly like the subject as the stain in the field of vision of Lacan, "to another who contemplates him shining out with thoughts of the kind which come from that world" (V.8.11). When the subject of Plotinus is able to perceive vision in its purity beyond appearance, "when you see that you have become this, then you have become sight..." (I.6.9). The unity of the One as manifest in the subject transcends the image as a mechanism of transferal, and the One, the source of the intelligible and unconscious thought in Intellect, is understood as pure light, beyond sensible form, "true light, not measured by dimensions, or bounded by shape...."

The One of Plotinus is what Lacan defines as the Real, which corresponds to the Gaze, which is that which exceeds perception in vision. The Real is other than the Imaginary or Symbolic of Lacan, other than perception and language, and that which is inaccessible to conscious thought. Like the One of the *Phaedrus*, which Plato describes as the "self-moving, never-leaving self" (245) (Plato, 1973) which "never ceases to move, and is the fountain and beginning of motion to all that moves," the Real is the undifferentiated element upon which all differentiation in conscious thought is predicated. Plotinus' One effects all things, but is inaccessible to them. The One is that which cannot be signified in language, and that which cannot be explained in relation to signification. The One is neither thinking nor being. It is the singular signifier prior to signification, the source of the play of reflections which constitutes existence. The One is inaccessible to signification for Lacan, and inaccessible to the multiple for Plotinus.

The gap between the One and the particulars of discursive or conscious reason is revealed in the gaps in conscious thought itself. For Lacan the One or Real is located in the representation of the subject by a signifier to another signifier in language. The linguistic and mathematical mechanisms of signification in discursive reason reveal the One, as a function of desire in language, the self-perpetuation of the subject to itself, in the gaps between the signifiers, in the traces or indexes of language. In *Seminar XX* of Lacan, "for desire merely leads us to aim at the gap where it can be demonstrated that the One is based only on the essence of the signifier" (Lacan, 1998, p. 5). It is signification that reveals that which cannot be signified, conscious thought that reveals unconscious thought, and it is the desire of the subject that reveals the non-existence of the subject in unconscious thought, outside its own self-perpetuation in language.

The gap between the One and existence is manifest in the *méconnaissance* or misknowing of the subject in psychoanalysis, the inability of the subject to know its own lack in relation to its discourse, the inability of the subject to know its unconscious thought. The One of the *Parmenides* is predicated on such a gap; it is necessitated by that element of conscious thought that is inaccessible to itself. The One of Plato suggests unconscious thought, as Lacan explains, "this requirement of the One, as the *Parmenides* strangely already allowed us to predict, stems from the Other" (*Seminar XX*, p. 10), that is, the matrix of language that is the unconscious. The One as the Gaze in vision of Lacan, as that which exceeds perception, is as the pure light of vision in the One of Plotinus. In *The Four Fundamental Concepts of Psycho-Analysis*, "It is not in the straight line, but in the point of light – the point of irradiation, the play of light, fire, the source from which reflections pour forth" (Lacan, 1981, p. 94) where "the essence of the relation between appearance and being, which the philosopher, conquering the field of vision, so easily masters," lies, that is, in the One.

The philosophical, metaphysical and conceptual idea of unconscious thought, as something that contributes to conscious thought but of which we are not aware in conscious thought, is distinguished from the phenomenal concept of "the unconscious" as derived from empirical or scientific evidence in behavior and experience. The concept of unconscious thought has been developed throughout the history of philosophy, laying the groundwork for the possibility of psychoanalysis, and contributing much to modern psychoanalysis and psychoanalytic theory. One goal of the analysis of unconscious thought in this book is that it might contribute to psychoanalytic theory. The practice and theory of psychoanalysis is currently focusing increasingly on its philosophical roots, suggesting new alternatives for practice. As Jon Mills has recently written, "Psychoanalysis has entered a new phase in its evolution and identity by adopting various philosophical paradigms in theory and in its methods of inquiry" (Mills, 2014, p. 14). Knowledge of the concepts of unconscious thought in philosophy can add a great deal to the understanding and practice of psychoanalysis. I have made many connections between the concepts of unconscious thought in classical, medieval, and modern philosophy, and psychoanalytic theory. I have explained and analyzed the concepts of unconscious thought in philosophy and psychoanalysis as much as possible. The hope is that the analysis will be continued by other scholars in the future and will be developed further.

Bibliography

Works cited

Alexander of Aphrodisias (1990) *De intellectu*, (trans.) F. M. Schroeder, in F. M. Schroeder and R. B. Todd (trans.), *Two Greek Aristotelian Commentators on the Intellect* (Toronto: Pontifical Institute of Mediaeval Studies).

—— (1979) *The De Anima of Alexander of Aphrodisias*, (trans.) A. P. Fotinis (Washington, D. C.: University Press of America).

Alfarabi (1967) *The Letter Concerning the Intellect*, (trans.) A. Hyman, in A. Hyman and J. J. Walsh (eds), *Philosophy in the Middle Ages: The Christian, Islamic, and Jewish Traditions* (New York: Harper and Row).

Aristotle (2001) *On the Soul and On Memory and Recollection*, (trans.) J. Sachs (Santa Fe: Green Lion Press).

—— (1964) *On the Soul (De anima)*, (trans.) W. S. Hett (Cambridge, MA: Harvard University Press, The Loeb Classical Library).

—— (1952b) *Metaphysics (Metaphysica)*, (trans.) W. D. Ross, in *The Works of Aristotle* (Chicago: Encyclopaedia Britannica).

—— (1952a) *On the Soul (De anima)*, (trans.) J. A. Smith, in *The Works of Aristotle* (Chicago: Encyclopaedia Britannica).

Averroes (Ibn Rushd) of Cordoba (2009) *Long Commentary on the* De anima *of Aristotle*, (trans.) R. C. Taylor (New Haven and London: Yale University Press).

—— (1967) *Long Commentary on the De anima*, (trans.) A. Hyman, in A. Hyman and J. J. Walsh (eds), *Philosophy in the Middle Ages: The Christian, Islamic, and Jewish Traditions* (New York: Harper and Row).

—— (1953) *Averrois Cordubensis Commentarium magnum in Aristotelis de Anima libros*, (ed.) F. S. Crawford, in *Corpus Commentarium Averrois in Aristotelem*, Vol. 6 (Venice 1550) (Cambridge, MA: The Medieval Academy of America).

Bataille, G. (1986) *Eroticism, Death and Sensuality*, (trans.) M. Dalwood (San Francisco: City Light Books).

—— (1985) *Visions of Excess, Selected Writings, 1927–1939*, (trans.) A. Stoekl (Minneapolis: University of Minnesota Press).

Baur, L. (1912) *Die philosophischen werke des Robert Grosseteste, Bischofs von Lincoln*, in *Beiträge zur Geschichte der Philosophie und Theologie des Mittelalters*, IX (Münster: Aschendorff).

Bell, M. (2010) "Carl Gustav Carus and the science of the unconscious," in A. Nicholls and M. Liebscher (eds), *Thinking the Unconscious: Nineteenth-Century German Thought* (Cambridge: Cambridge University Press).

—— (2005) *The German Tradition of Psychology in Literature and Thought, 1700–1840* (Cambridge: Cambridge University Press).

Berkeley, G. (1963) *Works on Vision*, (ed.) C. M. Turbayne (New York: The Library of Liberal Arts).

Blumenthal, H. J. (1996) *Aristotle and Neoplatonism in Late Antiquity: Interpretations of the* De anima (Ithaca, NY: Cornell University Press).

—— (1977) "Neoplatonic Interpretations of Aristotle on 'Phantasia'," in *The Review of Metaphysics* 31(2) (Washington, D.C.: Philosophy Education Society).

—— (1971) *Plotinus' Psychology: His Doctrines of the Embodied Soul* (The Hague: Martinus Nijhoff).

Boothby, R. (2001) *Freud as Philosopher: Metapsychology After Lacan* (New York and London: Routledge).

Bowie, A. (1990) *Aesthetics and Subjectivity: From Kant to Nietzsche* (Manchester and New York: Manchester University Press).

Brentano, F. (1977) *The Psychology of Aristotle: In Particular His Doctrine of the Active Intellect* (Berkeley: University of California Press).

Carus, C. G. (1970 [1846]) *Psyche: On the Development of the Soul, Part One: The Unconscious* (New York: Spring Publications).

—— (1831) *Lectures on Psychology* (*Vorlesungen über Psychologie, gehalten im Winter 1829–30 zu Dresden*) (Leipzig: Verlag von Gerhard Fleischer).

Christ, P. S. (1926) *The Psychology of the Active Intellect of Averroes* (Philadelphia: University of Pennsylvania Thesis in Philosophy).

Davidson, H. A. (1992) *Alfarabi, Avicenna, and Averroes, on Intellect* (Oxford: Oxford University Press).

Deleuze, G. (1984 [1963]) *Kant's Critical Philosophy: The Doctrine of the Faculties* (*La Philosophie Critique de Kant*), (trans.) H. Tomlinson and B. Habberjam (Minneapolis: University of Minnesota Press).

Derrida, J. (1976) *Of Grammatology*, (trans.) G. C. Spivak (Baltimore and London: The Johns Hopkins University Press).

Dews, P. (1987) *Logics of Disintegration: Post-Structuralist Thought and the Claims of Critical Theory* (London: Verso).

Dillon, J. (1986) "Plotinus and the Transcendental Imagination," in J. P. Mackey (ed.), *Religious Imagination, presented to John McIntyre* (Edinburgh: Edinburgh University Press).

Dodds, E. R. (1990) *Pagan and Christian in an Age of Anxiety* (Cambridge: Cambridge University Press).

—— (1960) "Tradition and personal achievement in the philosophy of Plotinus," in *Journal of Roman Studies* 50 (Cambridge: Society for the Promotion of Roman Studies).

Endress, G. and Aertsen, J. A. (eds) (1999) *Averroes and the Aristotelian Tradition* (Leiden: Brill).

Faflak, J. (2008) *Romantic Psychoanalysis: The Burden of the Mystery* (Albany: State University of New York Press).

Fotinis, A. P. (1979) "Commentary," in *The De Anima of Alexander of Aphrodisias*, (trans.) A. P. Fotinis (Washington, D. C.: University Press of America).

Freud, S. (1966) *Introductory Lectures on Psycho-Analysis, The Standard Edition*, (trans. and ed.) J. Strachey (New York: W. W. Norton).

—— (1965) *The Interpretation of Dreams, The Standard Edition*, (trans.) J. Strachey (New York: W. W. Norton).

—— (1961) *Beyond the Pleasure Principle, The Standard Edition*, (trans. and ed.) J. Strachey (New York: W. W. Norton).

—— (1960) *The Ego and the Id, The Standard Edition*, (trans.) J. Riviere, (ed.) James Strachey (New York: W. W. Norton).

—— (1952) *On Dreams, The Standard Edition*, (trans. and ed.) J. Strachey (New York: W. W. Norton).

—— (1949) *An Outline of Psycho-Analysis, The Standard Edition*, (trans. and ed.) J. Strachey (New York: W. W. Norton).

Gale, J. (2014) "Did Augustine foreshadow Psychoanalysis?," in J. Gale, M. Robson, and G. Rapsomatioli (eds), *Insanity and Divinity: Studies in Psychosis and Spirituality* (New York: Routledge).

Gödde, G. (2010) "Freud and nineteenth-century philosophical sources on the unconscious," in A. Nicholls and M. Liebscher (eds), *Thinking the Unconscious: Nineteenth-Century German Thought* (Cambridge: Cambridge University Press).

Grosseteste, R. (1996) *On the Six Days of Creation, A Translation of the* Hexaëmeron, (trans.) C. F. J. Martin (British Academy, Oxford University Press).

—— (1981) *Commentarius in Posteriorum Analyticorum Libros*, (ed.) P. Rossi (Florence: Olschki).

—— (1963) *Roberti Grosseteste Commentarius in VIII Libros Physicorum Aristotelis*, (ed.) R. C. Dales (Boulder: University of Colorado Press).

Hartmann, E. von (1931 [1868]) *Philosophy of the Unconscious*, (trans.) W. C. Coupland (London: Routledge & Kegan Paul).

Hegel, G. W. F. (1977 [1807]) *Phenomenology of Spirit*, (trans.) A. V. Miller (Oxford: Oxford University Press).

—— (1971) *Philosophy of Mind, Being Part Three of the Encyclopaedia of the Philosophical Sciences* (1830), (trans.) W. Wallace and A. V. Miller (Oxford: Clarendon Press).

Hendrix, J. S. (2010) *Robert Grosseteste: Philosophy of Intellect and Vision* (Sankt Augustin: Academia Verlag).

—— (2005) *Aesthetics and the Philosophy of Spirit: From Plotinus to Schelling and Hegel* (New York: Peter Lang).

—— (2004) *Platonic Architectonics: Platonic Philosophies and the Visual Arts* (New York: Peter Lang).

Hutchinson, D. M. (2011) "Apprehension of Thought in *Ennead* 4.3.30," in *The International Journal of the Platonic Tradition* 5 (2) (Leiden: Brill).

Hyman, A. and Walsh, J. J. (eds) (1967) *Philosophy in the Middle Ages: The Christian, Islamic, and Jewish Traditions* (New York: Harper and Row).

Jameson, F. (1988) "Imaginary and Symbolic in Lacan," in *The Ideology of Theory, Essays 1971–1986, Volume I: Situations of Theory* (Minneapolis: University of Minnesota Press).

Kant, I. (1992) *Theoretical Philosophy 1755–1770*, (trans. and ed.) D. Walford, in *The Cambridge Edition of the Works of Immanuel Kant* (Cambridge: Cambridge University Press).

—— (1902–83) *Reflexionen zur Anthropologie*, 1766–68, in *Gesammelte Schriften, herausgegeben von der Preussischen Akademie der Wissenschaften zu Berlin* (Berlin: Walter de Gruyter).

—— (1978) *Anthropology From a Pragmatic Point of View*, (trans.) V. L. Dowdell (Carbondale: Southern Illinois University Press).

—— (1968) *Critique of Pure Reason*, (trans.) N. K. Smith (London: MacMillan & Co).

—— (1952) *The Critique of Judgment*, (trans.) J. C. Meredith (Oxford: Clarendon Press).

Lacan, J. (1998) *The Seminar of Jacques Lacan, Book XX, Encore 1972–1973, On Feminine Sexuality: The Limits of Love and Knowledge*, (trans.) B. Fink (New York: W. W. Norton).

—— (1993) *The Seminar of Jacques Lacan, Book III, The Psychoses, 1955–1956*, (trans.) R. Grigg, (ed.) J.-A. Miller (New York: W. W. Norton).

—— (1991) *The Seminar of Jacques Lacan, Book II: The Ego in Freud's Theory and in the Technique of Psychoanalysis 1954–1955*, (trans.) S. Tomaselli, (ed.) J.-A. Miller (New York: W. W. Norton).

—— (1988) *The Seminar of Jacques Lacan, Book I: Freud's Papers on Technique 1953–54*, (trans.) J. Forrester, (ed.) J.-A. Miller (New York: W. W. Norton).

—— (1981) *The Four Fundamental Concepts of Psycho-Analysis*, (trans.) A. Sheridan (New York: W. W. Norton).

—— (1977) *Écrits, a Selection*, (trans.) A. Sheridan (New York: W. W. Norton).

—— (1968) *The Language of the Self: The Function of Language in Psychoanalysis*, (trans.) A. Wilden (Baltimore and London: The Johns Hopkins University Press).

Leibniz, G. W. (1982) *New Essays on Human Understanding*, (trans. and ed.) P. Remnant and J. Bennett (Cambridge: Cambridge University Press).

—— (1898) *The Monadology*, (trans.) R. Latta (Oxford: Oxford University Press).

Lévi-Strauss, C. (1950) "Introduction à l'Oeuvre de Marcel Mauss," in M. Mauss, *Sociologie et Anthropologie* (Paris).

Lipps, T. (1926) *Psychological Studies*, (trans.) H. C. Sanborn (Baltimore: The Williams & Wilkins Company).

Makkreel, R. A. (1990) *Imagination and Interpretation in Kant: The Hermeneutical Import of the* Critique of Judgment (Chicago and London: The University of Chicago Press).

Marrone, S. P. (1983) *William of Auvergne and Robert Grosseteste: New Ideas of Truth in the Early Thirteenth Century* (Princeton: Princeton University Press).

McEvoy, J. (1982) *The Philosophy of Robert Grosseteste* (Oxford: Clarendon Press).

McGrath, S. J. (2012) *The Dark Ground of Spirit: Schelling and the Unconscious* (London and New York: Routledge).

Merlan, P. (1963) *Monopsychism Mysticism Metaconsciousness, Problems of the Soul in the Neoaristotelian and Neoplatonic Tradition* (The Hague: Martinus Nijhoff).

Mills, J. (2014) *Underworlds: Philosophies of the Unconscious from Psychoanalysis to Metaphysics* (London and New York: Routledge).

—— (2002) *The Unconscious Abyss: Hegel's Anticipation of Psychoanalysis* (Albany: State University of New York Press).

Nancy, J.-L. and Lacoue-Labarthe, P. (1992 [1973]) *The Title of the Letter: A Reading of Lacan*, (trans.) F. Raffoul and D. Pettigrew (Albany: State University of New York Press).

Nicholls, A. and Liebscher, M. (eds) (2010a) *Thinking the Unconscious: Nineteenth-Century German Thought* (Cambridge: Cambridge University Press).

—— (2010b) "Introduction: thinking the unconscious," in A. Nicholls and M. Liebscher (eds), *Thinking the Unconscious: Nineteenth-Century German Thought* (Cambridge: Cambridge University Press).

Nyvlt, M. J. (2012) *Aristotle and Plotinus on the Intellect* (Lanham: Lexington Books).

O'Rourke, F. (1992) *Pseudo-Dionysius and the Metaphysics of Aquinas* (New York: E. J. Brill).

Plato (1999) *The Symposium*, (trans.) C. Gill (London: Penguin Books).
—— (1990) *Sophist*, (trans.) W. S. Cobb (Savage, MD: Rowman & Littlefield Publishers).
—— (1982) *Phaedo*, (trans.) H. N. Fowler (Cambridge, MA: Harvard University Press, The Loeb Classical Library).
—— (1973) *Phaedrus*, (trans.) W. Hamilton (London: Penguin Books).
—— (1965) *Timaeus*, (trans.) D. Lee (London: Penguin Books).
—— (1955) *Republic*, (trans.) D. Lee (London: Penguin Books).
Plotinus (1966) *Enneads*, (trans.) A. H. Armstrong (Cambridge, MA: Harvard University Press, The Loeb Classical Library).
Pseudo-Dionysius (1897) *The Works of Dionysius the Areopagite*, (trans.) J. Parker (London: James Parker).
Ragland-Sullivan, E. (1986) *Jacques Lacan and the Philosophy of Psychoanalysis* (Urbana and Chicago: University of Illinois Press).
Rappe, S. (2000) *Reading Neoplatonism: Non-discursive Thinking in the Texts of Plotinus, Proclus, and Damascius* (Cambridge: Cambridge University Press).
Sand, R. S. (2014) *The Unconscious without Freud* (Lanham: Rowman & Littlefield).
Saussure, F. de (1966 [1915]) *Course in General Linguistics*, (trans.) W. Baskin (New York: McGraw-Hill).
Schelling, F. W. J. von (1984) *Bruno, or On the Natural and the Divine Principle of Things, 1802*, (trans.) M. G. Vater (Albany: State University of New York Press).
—— (1978 [1800]) *System of Transcendental Idealism*, (trans.) P. Heath (Charlottesville: University Press of Virginia).
Schroeder, F. M. and Todd, R. B. (trans.) (1990) *Two Greek Aristotelian Commentators on the Intellect* (Toronto: Pontifical Institute of Mediaeval Studies).
Taylor, R. C. (2005) "Averroes: religious dialectic and Aristotelian philosophical thought," in P. Adamson and R. C. Taylor (eds), *The Cambridge Companion to Arabic Philosophy* (Cambridge: Cambridge University Press).
Themistius (1996) *On Aristotle's* On the Soul, (trans.) R. B. Todd (Ithaca: Cornell University Press).
Thiel, U. (2011) *The Early Modern Subject: Self-Consciousness and Personal Identity from Descartes to Hume* (New York: Oxford University Press).
Whyte, L. L. (1978) *The Unconscious Before Freud* (London: Julian Friedmann Publishers / New York: St Martin's Press).
Wilden, A. (1968) "Lacan and the Discourse of the Other," in J. Lacan, *The Language of the Self: The Function of Language in Psychoanalysis*, (trans.) A. Wilden (Baltimore and London: The Johns Hopkins University Press).

Works Consulted

Akhtar, S. and O'Neil, M. K. (eds) (2013) *On Freud's "The Unconscious"* (London: Karnac Books).
Borch-Jacobsen, M. and Shamdasani, S. (eds) (2012) *The Freud Files: An Inquiry into the History of Psychoanalysis* (Cambridge: Cambridge University Press).
Bowie, A. (1993) *Schelling and Modern European Philosophy* (London and New York: Routledge).

Bracher, M. (1993) *Lacan, Discourse, and Social Change: A Psychoanalytic Cultural Criticism* (Ithaca and London: Cornell University Press).

Buchholz, M. B. and Gödde, G. (eds) (2005–06) *Das Unbewusste*, 3 Vols.: Vol. 1: *Macht und Dynamik des Unbewussten: Auseinandersetzungen in Philosophie, Medizin und Psychoanalyse*; Vol. 2: *Das enbewusste in aktuellen Diskursen: Anschlüsse*; Vol. 3: *Das Unbewusste in der Praxis: Erfahrungen verschiedener Professionen* (Giessen: Psychosozial Verlag).

Bundy, M. W. (1927) *The Theory of Imagination in Classical and Medieval Thought* (Urbana: University of Illinois Press).

Clark, M. (1971) *Logic and System: A Study of the Transition from "Vorstellung" to Thought in the Philosophy of Hegel* (The Hague: Martinus Nijhoff).

Cook, D. J. (1973) *Language in the Philosophy of Hegel* (The Hague: Mouton).

Culler, J. (1982) *On Deconstruction: Theory and Criticism after Structuralism* (Ithaca: Cornell University Press).

—— (1975) *Structuralist Poetics: Structuralism, Linguistics, and the Study of Literature* (Ithaca: Cornell University Press).

DeVries, W. A. (1988) *Hegel's Theory of Mental Activity: An Introduction to Theoretical Spirit* (Ithaca and London: Cornell University Press).

Dor, J. (1998) *Introduction to the Reading of Lacan: The Unconscious Structured Like a Language* (New York: The Other Press).

Ellenberger, H. F. (1970) *The Discovery of the Unconscious: The History and Evolution of Dynamic Psychiatry* (New York: Basic Books).

Eyers, T. (2012) *Lacan and the Concept of the 'Real'* (Basingstoke: Palgrave Macmillan).

Ffytche, M. (2012) *The Foundation of the Unconscious: Schelling, Freud and the Birth of the Modern Psyche* (Cambridge: Cambridge University Press).

Fichte, J. G. (1992) *Foundations of Transcendental Philosophy (Wissenschaftslehre) Nova Methodo (1796–99)*, (trans. and ed.) D. Breazeale (Ithaca and London: Cornell University Press).

—— (1988) *Early Philosophical Writings*, (trans. and ed.) D. Breazeale (Ithaca and London: Cornell University Press).

—— (1982) *The Science of Knowledge*, (trans. and ed.) P. Heath and J. Lachs (Cambridge: Cambridge University Press).

Gessert, A. (ed.) (2014) *Introductory Lectures on Lacan* (London: Karnac Books).

Giordanetti, P., Pozzo, R., Sgarbi, M. (eds) (2012) *Kant's Philosophy of the Unconscious* (Berlin: Walter de Gruyter).

Giovanni, G. di and Harris, H. S. (trans.) (1985) *Between Kant and Hegel: Texts in the Development of Post-Kantian Idealism* (Albany: State University of New York Press).

Goudeli, K. (2002) *Challenges to German Idealism: Schelling, Fichte and Kant* (Basingstoke: Palgrave Macmillan).

Hegel, G. W. F. (1993 [1886]) *Introductory Lectures on Aesthetics (The Introduction to Hegel's Philosophy of Fine Art)*, (trans.) B. Bosanquet, (ed.) M. Inwood (London: Penguin Books).

—— (1956) *The Philosophy of History*, (trans.) J. Sibree (New York: Dover Publications).

Heidelberger, M. (2004) *Nature from Within: Gustav Theodor Fechner and His Psychophysical Worldview*, (trans.) C. Klohr (Pittsburgh: University of Pittsburgh Press).

Hendrix, J. S. (2006) *Architecture and Psychoanalysis: Peter Eisenman and Jacques Lacan* (New York: Peter Lang).

Ifergan, P (2014) *Hegel's Discovery of the Philosophy of Spirit: Autonomy, Alienation, and the Ethical Life: The Jena Lectures 1802–1806* (Basingstoke: Palgrave Macmillan).

Jones, E. (1981) *The Life and Work of Sigmund Freud* (New York: Basic Books).

Kelly, W. L. (1991) *Psychology of the Unconscious* (Buffalo: Prometheus Books).

Levy, D. (1996) *Freud Among the Philosophers* (New Haven and London: Yale University Press).

Lloyd, A. C. (1990) *The Anatomy of Neoplatonism* (Oxford: Clarendon Press).

MacIntyre, A. C. (1958) *The Unconscious: A Conceptual Analysis* (London: Routledge & Kegan Paul).

Magnus, K. D. (2001) *Hegel and the Symbolic Mediation of Spirit* (Albany: State University of New York Press).

Makari, G. (2008) *Revolution in Mind: The Creation of Psychoanalysis* (New York: Harper Collins).

Marinelli, L. and Mayer, A. (2003) *Dreaming by the Book: Freud's* The Interpretation of Dreams *and the History of the Psychoanalytic Movement*, (trans.) S. Fairfield (New York: Other Press).

McCumber, J. (1993) *The Company of Words: Hegel, Language, and Systematic Philosophy* (Evanston: Northwestern University Press).

Meissner, W. W. (2000) *Freud and Psychoanalysis* (Notre Dame: University of Notre Dame Press).

Mills, J. (ed.) (2004) *Rereading Freud: Psychoanalysis through Philosophy* (Albany: State University of New York Press).

Norman, J. and Welchman, A. (eds) (2004) *The New Schelling* (London and New York: Continuum).

Northridge, W. L. (1924) *Modern Theories of the Unconscious* (New York: E. P. Dutton & Company).

Pippin, R. B. (1989) *Hegel's Idealism: The Satisfactions of Self-Consciousness* (Cambridge: Cambridge University Press).

Plato (1962) *Meno*, (trans). W. R. M. Lamb (Cambridge, MA: Harvard University Press, The Loeb Classical Library).

Rist, J. M. (1967) *Plotinus: The Road to Reality* (London: Cambridge University Press).

Sandler, J., Holder, A., Dare, C., Dreher, A. U. (eds) (1997) *Freud's Models of the Mind: An Introduction* (Madison, CT: International Universities Press / London: Karnac Books).

Schelling, F. W. J. von (1989 [1859]) *The Philosophy of Art* (*Die Philosophie der Kunst*), (trans.) D. W. Stott (Minneapolis: University of Minnesota Press).

Schulting, D. (2012) *Kant's Deduction and Apperception: Explaining the Categories* (Basingstoke: Palgrave Macmillan).

Shamdasani, S. (2003) *Jung and the Making of Modern Psychology: The Dream of a Science* (Cambridge: Cambridge University Press).

Snow, D. E. (1996) *Schelling and the End of Idealism* (Albany: State University of New York Press).

Soler, C. (2014) *Lacan – The Unconscious Reinvented* (London: Karnac Books).

Sulloway, F. J. (1983) *Freud, Biologist of the Mind: Beyond the Psychoanalytic Legend* (New York: Basic Books).

Uehling, T. E. (1971) *The Notion of Form in Kant's Critique of Aesthetic Judgment* (The Hague/Paris: Mouton).

Vater, M. G. (1976) "Schelling's Neoplatonic System-Notion: '*Ineinsbildung*' and Temporal Unfolding," in *The Significance of Neoplatonism*, (ed.) R. B. Harris (Norfolk: International Society for Neoplatonic Studies).

Vidal, F. (2011) *The Sciences of the Soul: The Early Modern Origins of Psychology*, (trans.) S. Brown (Chicago and London: The University of Chicago Press).

Völmicke, E. (2005) *Das Unbewusste im Deutschen Idealismus* (Würzburg: Königshausen und Neumann).

Weber, S. (2000) *The Legend of Freud* (Stanford: Stanford University Press).

—— (1991) *Return to Freud: Jacques Lacan's dislocation of psychoanalysis*, (trans.) M. Levine (Cambridge: Cambridge University Press).

Williams, R. R. (1992) *Recognition: Fichte and Hegel on the Other* (Albany: State University of New York Press).

Winfield, R. D. (2010) *Hegel and Mind: Rethinking Philosophical Psychology* (Basingstoke: Palgrave Macmillan).

Winter, S. (1999) *Freud and the Institution of Psychoanalytic Knowledge* (Stanford: Stanford University Press).

Wolman, B. B. (1968) *The Unconscious Mind: The Meaning of Freudian Psychology* (Englewood Cliffs, NJ: Prentice-Hall).

Zaretsky, E. (2004) *Secrets of the Soul: A Social and Cultural History of Psychoanalysis* (New York: Alfred A. Knopf).

Index

Lightning Source UK Ltd.
Milton Keynes UK
UKOW06n1202210616

276769UK00005B/39/P